THEORETICAL ANALYSES ON ROMANCE LANGUAGES

AMSTERDAM STUDIES IN THE THEORY AND HISTORY OF LINGUISTIC SCIENCE

General Editor

E. F. KONRAD KOERNER
(University of Ottawa)

Series IV – CURRENT ISSUES IN LINGUISTIC THEORY

Volume 157

José Lema and Esthela Treviño (eds)

Theoretical Analyses on Romance Languages. Selected papers from the 26th Linguistic Symposium on Romance Languages (LSRL XXVI), Mexico City, 28–30 March 1996.

THEORETICAL ANALYSES ON ROMANCE LANGUAGES

SELECTED PAPERS FROM THE 26TH LINGUISTIC SYMPOSIUM ON ROMANCE LANGUAGES (LSRL XXVI), MEXICO CITY, 28–30 MARCH 1996

Edited by

JOSÉ LEMA

ESTHELA TREVIÑO

Universidad Autonoma Metropolitana - I, Mexico City

JOHN BENJAMINS PUBLISHING COMPANY
AMSTERDAM/PHILADELPHIA

The paper used in this publication meets the minimum requirements of American National Standard for Information Sciences — Permanence of Paper for Printed Library Materials, ANSI Z39.48-1984.

Library of Congress Cataloging-in-Publication Data

Linguistic Symposium on Romance Languages (26th : 1996 : Mexico City, Mexico)
Theoretical analyses on Romance languages : selected papers from the 26th Linguistic Symposium on Romance Languages (LSRL XXVI), Mexico City, 28-30 March, 1996 / edited by José Lema and Esthela Treviño.
p. cm. -- (Amsterdam studies in the theory and history of linguistic science. Series IV, Current issues in linguistic theory, ISSN 0304-0763 ; v. 157)
Includes bibliographical references and index.
1. Romance languages--Congresses. I. Lema, José. II. Treviño, Esthela. III. Title. IV. Series.
PC11.L53 1998
440--DC21 98-13797
ISBN 90 272 3662 3 (Eur.) / 1 55619 873 6 (US) (Hb; alk. paper) CIP

John Benjamins Publishing Co. • P.O.Box 75577 • 1070 AN Amsterdam • The Netherlands
John Benjamins North America • P.O.Box 27519 • Philadelphia PA 19118-0519 • USA

PREFACE

This volume offers a selection of works presented at the *XXVI Linguistic Symposium on Romance Languages*, celebrated at *La Casa de la Primera Imprenta de América*, of the Universidad Autónoma Metropolitana-Iztapalapa, (UAM-I), Mexico City. In many respects, the XXVI version of the LSRL was a very important event. Being this the first time to be organized beyond the United States and Canada frontiers, it raised high expectations in the linguistics community, but most fundamentally amongst our mexican colleagues. Indeed, 130 abstracts were received, with topics on phonology, syntax, phonology-morphology, the syntax-semantics interface, language acquisition, and sociolinguistics. Unlike previous LSRL events, a high number of papers in phonology were presented, an area that has remained marginally present in LSRL tradition. Nonetheless, due to a rich set of native existent languages in Mexico, the phonology sessions had a great impact especially amongst the mexican linguists, but also among the general attending participants at the Conference. Papers on first and second language acquisition were also high in number according to usual standards, and we think that this fact contributed significantly to realize among the audience the importance of including in events such as this one, research problems directly dealt with from an acquisition perspective. We must acknowledge the fact that a most successful LSRL Conference brought about an immediate profit for linguistics at the UAM-I. We now know that the field in general, has also benefited greatly as students and scholars from other universities have become increasingly interested in our discipline.

Most of the grammatical phenomena dealt with in the articles in this volume are worked in the light of the *Minimalist Program,* the Distributed Morphology, and the *Optimality Theory* frameworks. These recent theoretical developments have motivated reconsidering known or previously discussed grammatical problems under what are felt as new and promising lines of inquiry. Likewise, these developments have greatly contributed to gaining new insights and better explanations for a wide range of phenomena. It was apparent from the diversity of the papers delivered, that these approaches are opening up new venues to inquiry, as well as exposing novel phenomena, which, no doubt, enrich and widen our knowledge and understanding of language. The analyses undertaken in the articles here collected range over a variety of dialects of Romance languages: Spanish, French, Catalan, Italian, Latin, Aromanian and Portuguese.

We greatly thank the participation of our three main invited speakers: Andrea Calabrese (Harvard University, Latin Morphology), Richard Kayne (City University of New York, French Syntax), and Gemma Rigau (Universitat Autònoma de Barcelona, Catalan Syntax and Semantics), as well as that of the other forty participants who visited Mexico City and the House of the First Printing Press in America. Unfortunately, we were unable to reproduce in this volume the entire conference; some articles have been left out by choice of the authors. The participating reviewers helped us organize a most interesting event, and its outcome, the present book.

We would like to acknowledge, for their unrestricted and encouraging support, the *Rector General* of the Universidad Autónoma Metropolitana, Dr. Julio Rubio Oca; the *Rector* of the UAM-I, Dr. José Luis Gázquez Mateos; the Dean of the *División de Ciencias Sociales y Humanidades*, Mtro. Gregorio Vidal. We must also thank for their technical and moral support, Patricia Reyes, Isabel Almaraz and Blanca Moctezuma. We must credit Javier Torres Oyarzún for his expert and careful technical edition of the present volume; Karen Zagona for her many helpful tips regarding the publication; and Konrad Koerner for his concern in maintaining the present collection. Some of our activities were sponsored by the *Consejo Nacional de Ciencia y Tecnología*, grant No. 400200-5-04545H.

José Lema & Esthela Treviño
UAM-I, Mexico City,
November 1997

CONTENTS

GENITIVES IN AROMANIAN DIALECTS*

ANTONIA ANDROUTSOPOULOU
University of California, Los Angeles

1. *Introduction*

The paper deals primarily with the formation of Genitive in Aromanian dialects spoken in Greece.[1] The dialect of Kruševo, Former Yugoslav Republic of Macedonia, will be also discussed. Aromanian belongs to the Romance languages spoken South of the Danube. According to Ethnologue (1988), it split from Rumanian, Meglenoromanian, and Istro-Rumanian, the other Eastern Romance languages between 500 and 1,000 AD. Aromanian speakers live in Greece, Albania, Bulgaria, and the Former Yugoslav Republic of Macedonia, with the largest concentration of them in Greece, currently circa 50,000 (Ethnologue (1988)). Aromanian dialects in Greece are distinguished in Northern and Southern ones (Katsanis and Dinas (1990)) (the terms North and South not in all cases strictly corresponding to the geographical distribution of the speakers).

I have drawn my data mainly from Katsanis and Dinas (1990), a concise grammar of the Aromanian of Greece, Koltsidas (1978), a description of the Aromanian of Greece, Gołab (1984), a study of the Aromanian of Kruševo, and the texts in Exarhos (1986), Rohlshoven (1989), Padioti (1988) (for the Aromanian of Metsovo) and Gołab (1984) (for the Aromanian of Kruševo). I have also consulted Capidan (1932), a basic work on Aromanian, Caragiu-Mariot, eanu (1968) and Papahagi (1974).

Aromanian dialects exhibit a three way variation in the formation of genitive along the lines in (1):

---

* I wish to thank H. Koopman, and D. Sportiche for discussion, and the audiences of LSRL XXV (University of Washington, Seattle, 1995) and LSRL XXVI (Universidad Autónoma Metropolitana, México DF, 1996) and the Colloquium Graeco-Romanica, (Aristotle University of Thessaloniki, 1996) for comments on the contents of this paper. I am also indebted to M. Español-Echevarría for his very useful written comments. The usual disclaimers apply.

[1] Greek authors, who are also native speakers of the language (Katsanis and Dinas (1990) and Koltsidas (1978)), refer to it as Koutsovlahiki (Koutsovlach).

(1) G_1 G_2 G_3
A N+lu^{i}[2] A+l(u) N Al(u) N+lu^{i}

N is the stem of the noun. In all three cases, genitive is formed with the particle *a* and a suffix, the three types being distinguished on the basis of which element bears the suffix. In G_1, it is the N that bears the suffix, in G_2, the suffix appears on *a*, and in G_3, both *N* and *a* have a suffix. In all cases, the suffix is [+def] and agrees in gender with the noun in the genitive. In (1), *-lu^{i}/l(u)* is the form of the suffix for a masculine, singular, definite noun. *-li/l'i* is the form of the suffix for a feminine, singular, definite noun. Rumanian, on the other hand, exhibits genitives of a similar sort (cf. (2)), involving an invariant formative *a* which bears a suffix agreeing in gender, number and Case with the D heading the DP containing the genitive DP:

(2) *prieten* *al* *regelui*
friend(**masc**) A-def/**masc**/sing king-def/masc/sing
'friend(masc) of the king' (from Cornilescu (1994, p. 17))

I propose a unified analysis of these Aromanian and Rumanian genitive constructions in terms of the structure in (3), where the complement of D is a D/PP projection (cf. Kayne (1993, 1994)) the head of which is occupied by the invariant formative *a* (bearing a suffix or not) of the genitives under consideration. I treat *a* as a preposition:

(3) $[_{DP} [_{D/PP} [_{AgrP} [_{NP}]]]]$

The genitive DP sits at the specifier of the AgrP complement of D/P. In view of Kayne's (1994) recent analysis of relative clauses, (3) is essentially a relative clause structure.

Furthermore, I propose that in the languages discussed here, prepositional genitives (genitives involving the invariant formative *a*) correlate with raising of the noun that θ-marks the genitive (N in (3)) by means of DP -internal XP-movement.

2. *The definite determiner in Aromanian*

In Aromanian, the definite determiner is a suffix on the noun. Thus, in this language, the noun overtly raises to left-adjoin to the definite determiner under D. The language distinguishes three grammatical genders. The forms of the

---

[2] Superscipt *u* and *i* represent reduced, nonsyllabic final /u/ and /i/.

definite determiner in the neuter follow the masculine paradigm in the singular, and the feminine paradigm in the plural. Aromanian nouns are marked for Case only when suffixed with the definite determiner:

(4) a. un^{u} fitšor^{u} — a(nom/acc) boy
a'. a unlu^{i} fitšor^{u} — A a(gen/dat) boy

b. luplu — wolf-the(nom/acc)
b'. a luplu^{i} — A wolf-the(gen/dat)

In Table 1, the forms of the definite determiner in the nominative and accusative are given:

(5) Table 1

SINGULAR		
FEMININE		MASCULINE
-a	Nominative	-lu (and its allomorph -le)
-a	Accusative	-lu, -le
PLURAL		
FEMININE		MASCULINE
-le	Nominative	-l'i (and allomorphs)
-le	Accusative	-l'i

3. *Aromanian genitives*

As already mentioned in the introduction, in Aromanian dialects, definite DP's in the genitive may appear in one of the three types of genitive constructions in (6):[3]

(6)	G_1	G_2	G_3
	A N+lu^i	A+l(u) N	Al(u) N+lu^i

N is the noun in the genitive. That is, in Aromanian definite DP's, genitive formation necessarily involves an invariant formative *a* and a suffix. Due to its obligatory presence in the formation of genitive, I will treat *a* as a Case assigning element, more precisely a Case assigning preposition.[4]

In G_1 genitives, the suffix on the noun N is essentially the genitive form of the definite determiner that corresponds to this noun; it varies with the gender and number of the noun and is *-l'i* for a singular feminine and *-lu^i* for a singular masculine noun respectively; it is *-lor^u* for the plural of both genders. It is clear that the suffix on N in G_1 genitives is the spell-out of the features [+def], [+gen], [α gender] and [α number]:

(7) a.	a cartil'i	b. a luplu^i	c. a cartsîlor^u	d. a fratslor^u
	'of the book'	'of the wolf'	'of the books'	'of the brothers'

In G_2 genitives, the noun is bare and is preceded by what native speakers perceive as a proclitic form of the definite article. The form of this proclitic article, which varies with the gender of the noun in the genitive, is *ali* for the feminine and *alu* for the masculine:

---

[3] The dialects under consideration have strictly prepositional genitives as well, that is genitives involving a preposition other than *a*. Determinerless DP's, or DP's headed by quantifiers not varying with Case are introduced with the preposition *di*:

(i) di-Aminciu (ii) di nište fitsior^i
'of Metsovo' 'of some boys'

Katsanis and Dinas (1990) give the prepositional genitive form in (ii) for definite plural nouns:

(ii) dila lukl'i
of wolfs-the(pl)

Prepositional genitives like (ii) apparently co-exist with the type of genitives described in the text.

[4] In Aromanian, the preposition *a* appears only in genitive constructions and in frozen forms like *acasa* 'at home' (Katsanis Dinas (1990, p. 121)).

(8) a. al preftu b. ali fiată
'of the priest' 'of the daughter' (Katsanis and Dinas (1990, p. 38))

It is noteworthy that this article does not vary with number, that is, it is always morphologically singular. Examples of G_2 genitives in the plural are not attested in the sources. We have, however, examples of G_3 genitives where clearly the suffix on *a* doesn't vary with number (cf. (10)). As stated in the sources (cf. Katsanis and Dinas 1990: 49, fn.18)), the suffix on *a* in G_2 is the same as that in G_3 genitives. Then, the suffix on *a* in G_2 genitives is the spell-out of the features [+def], [+gen][5] and [α gender], crucially not of the feature [α number] that is, it is the spell-out of a subset of the bundle of features the spell-out of which is the definite determiner corresponding to the noun in the genitive. In some dialects of Aromanian, for instance the Aromanian of Kruševo, or that spoken at Numfeo, Greece, G_2 genitives occur only with proper names.

[5] It is not possible to determine conclusively whether or not the suffix of the masculine singular form *alu* in G2 is marked as [+gen]. The forms of the definite determiner for a singular masculine noun in the nominative (/accusative) and genitive (/dative) are *-lu* and *-lu^i* respectively (cf. Table 1 and G_1 in (6) above). That is genitive (/dative) definite singular masculine nouns are distinguished from nominative (/accusative) ones by means of the (reduced) vowel [^{i}] and the presence of the invariant formative of the genitive/dative *a*. So, we can take [^{i}] to be the spell-out of the feature [+gen] on the suffix of N (essentially, on the definite determiner) in the dialects that have G_1 genitives. Gołab (1984), who studies the Aromanian of Kruševo, notes that [^{i}], underlyingly an / i /, only surfaces in word final position before a pause, so in the configuration like that in G_2 in (6) it will never surface. I take this to be the case in the other Aromanian dialects as well, though not clearly stated in the sources, because in the texts and descriptions of the dialects I have not encountered a token of [^{i}] in a sentence medial, word final position. In the case of definite, singular, feminine nouns, on the other hand, the form of the suffix on *a* in G_2 genitives is clearly [+gen], that is the spell out of the features [+def], [+gen] and [α gender]. Recall that for a feminine singular noun the forms of the definite determiner are *-a* for the nominative/accusative and *-l'i* for the genitive/dative, and that the suffix of *a* in G_2 genitives is *-li* (it is unclear to me why the *l* of the suffix *-li* on *a* in G_2 genitives is not palatalized as in the case of the suffix *-l'i* of the noun in G_1 genitives). In his study of the Aromanian of Kruševo, Gołab (1984) notes that the feminine proclitic article *ali* is derived from *ale*. Note that in this dialect the form of the definite determiner for feminine, singular, genitive nouns is either *-le^i* or *-l'i* (the two are apparently in free variation; in the Aromanian dialects spoken in Greece, the form *-le^i* is not found, as Katsanis and Dinas (1990, p. 48) note). *Ale* can be understood as *a* + *le^i*, the vowel denoted with superscript *i* necessarily drops in the environment of a G_2 genitive, as already noted for the masculine counterpart of *ali*. I think that the above is good evidence that the feminine form of the proclitic article, *ali*, is marked as [+gen], and that, in the absence of evidence to the contrary, we can conclude that the same is true for the masculine *alu*.

G_3 genitives are described in the sources as a combination of the other two genitive types, G_1 and G_2. In G_3 genitives, a suffix appears both on the invariant formative of the genitive *a* and on the noun N:

(9) a. al γumarlu^{i} b. ali galinil'i
'of the donkey' 'of the hen'

In G_3 genitives, the suffix on the noun N is the same as that on N in G_1 genitives. Similarly, the suffix on *a* is the same as that on *a* in G_2 genitives. This suffix does not vary with number, that is, it is morphologically singular:

(10) G_3
al fitšorlor
'of the boys' (from Exarhos (1986, p. 81))

That is, in G_3 genitives, the suffix on N is the spell-out of the features [+def], [+gen], [α gender] and [α number], while the suffix on *a* is the spell-out of the features [+def], [+gen], [α gender]. In other words, in G_3 genitives, the suffix on *a* is the spell-out of a subset of the features of which the suffix on N is the spell-out, or else, the suffix on *a* is a partial copy of the suffix on N. For instance, in the example in (10) the suffix on *a* is *-l* (< *-lu^{i}*) that is [[+def], [+masc], [+gen]], while the suffix on the noun is *-lor* (<*-lor^{u}*) is [[+def], [+masc], [+gen], [+plural]].

As mentioned, the suffix on *a* is the same in both G_2 and G_3 genitives. Then, as in the case of G_3 genitives, we can view the suffix on *a* in G_2 genitives as a partial copy of the definite determiner corresponding to the genitive noun.[6]

Summing up, in G_1, as well as G_3 genitives, the suffix on N is the spell-out of the features [+def], [+gen] [α gender], [α number], essentially the D corresponding to the noun in the genitive. On the other hand, in G_2, as it is the case in G_3 genitives, the suffix on *a* is a spell-out of the features [+def], [+gen], [α gender], essentially a partial copy of the D corresponding to the genitive noun. My analysis of Aromanian genitives will make crucial use of this fact.

---

[6] Being the case that the suffix on *a* in G2 and G3 genitives, is morphologically singular, in the plural, there is a mismatch between its number and the number of the genitive noun (cf. (10)). We conclude that *al(u)* or *ali* (cf. (9), (10)) are unspecified for number. Then the suffix in question cannot be possibly viewed as the actual definite determiner corresponding to the genitive noun.

4. ***Proposal***

As noted in the previous section, the three types of genitives found in Aromanian definite DP's (cf. (6)) are characterized by the Case assigning preposition *a*. Furthermore, a suffix appears either on the noun N, or on the preposition *a*, or on both. The suffix on *a* is a partial copy of the feature content of the suffix that appears on N. In (11), the three types of genitive are exemplified for the feminine singular noun fiată 'girl':

(11) a. G_1 b. G_2 c. G_3

casa a fiatil'i casa ali fiată casa ali fiatil'i

'the house of the girl'

In (11), the suffix *-l'i* on the noun fiată *'girl' (fiatil'i* < fiată + *-l'i*) is [+def], [+gen], [+fem], [+sing], while the suffix on *a* is [+def], [+gen], [+fem]. Recall that in the general case, the suffix on the noun is [+def], [+gen], [α gender], [α number], while the suffix on *a* is [+def], [+gen], [α gender]. To capture this set of facts, I propose a line of analysis according to which all the three dialectal variants illustrated in (11) share the same basic structure involving *a* and the bundle of features [+def], [+gen], [+fem], [+sing] spelled-out in G_1 and G_3 genitives as the suffix *-l'i* on the noun fiată. This bundle of features in which the gender and number specification is that of the noun in the genitive, fiată *in our example, is generated in the D_0 position dominating the NP headed by* fiată, while *a* occupies the specifier position of this DP. I return to this last point in the following:

(12)

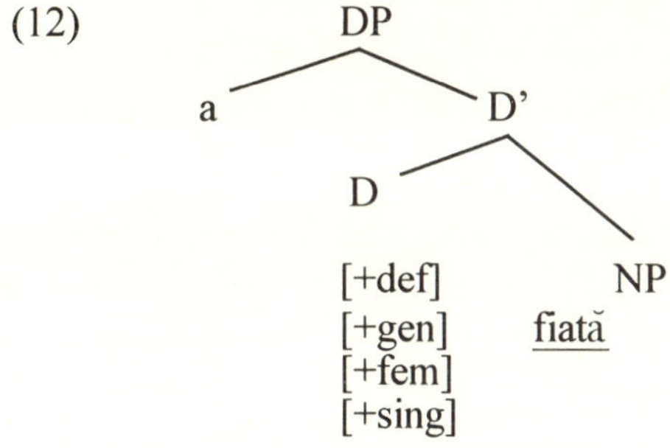

I will follow (Kayne (1993, 1994), Longobardi (1996) among others) in assuming that the DP in (12), being a genitive argument, occupies the specifier position of a designated projection, an AgrP part of the extended projection of the noun casă. *Furthermore, I would like to claim that the DP headed by* -*a*, the definite determiner which corresponds to the noun casă, *takes as complement a D/PP projection (cf. Kayne (1993, 1994)):*

(13)

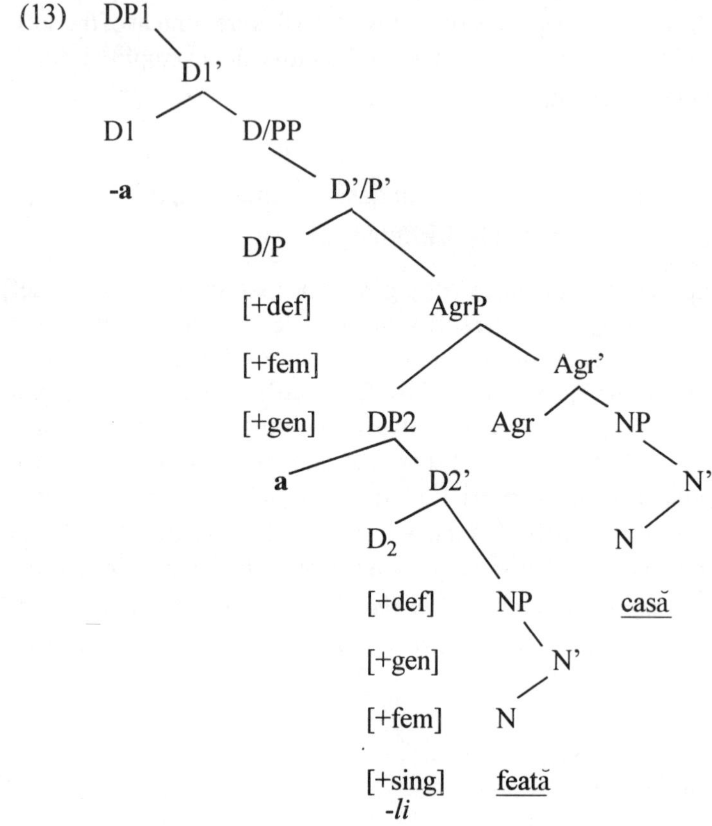

This D/P head, which initially contains only categorial features, to be identified, must contain φ-features also. For this reason, φ-features move from the D head of DP2, to the immediately higher D/P head. The spell-out of the bundle of features under D/P is the suffix on *a* in G_2 and G_3 genitives, -*li* in our example in (11). The morphological make-up of this suffix gives us evidence about which of the features under D_2 move to D/P. As already noted, the suffix on *a* does not have a plural form. In other words, taking the singular form to be the default one, it is not specified for number. Then, we can conclude that [α number] cannot move from D_2 to D/P. On the other hand, movement of [α def], [α Case], [α gen] is unproblematic.

The three way dialectal variation in (11) is derived from the structure in (13) as follows: We have (11a), a G_1 genitive, when the features under D_2 are spelled-out. A G_2 genitive, (11b), obtains when the features under D/P are spelled-out. Finally, (11c), a G_3 genitive, is derived when both feature bundles, those under D2 and those under D/P are spelled-out. In all three cases, the preposition *a* moves from its base position at Spec, DP2 to left-adjoin to the morpheme under D/P, in our case *-li*, the spell-out of the features [+def], [+gen], [+fem], due to the affixal property of this morpheme. Alternatively, one might propose that *a* is base-generated under D/P, and that the bundle of features that move from D_2 to D/P right-adjoin to it. Either of the two technical implementations of the formation of *ali* is possible, the former being preferable under a strict interpretation of Kayne's (1994) LCA, and also in view of the fact that *a* is a genitive assigning preposition and that the [+gen] feature is checked and erased in the sense of Chomsky (1995) under D_2. Finally, within DP2, the noun feată raises to D_2 to check its gender, number and Case features against those of D_2 and left-adjoins to the bundle of features under D2.

In the state of affairs in (13), the N casă which appears adjoined to the left of D *-a*, the resultant form being casă, *house-the, 'the house', cannot raise as a head to its spell-out position crossing the D/P head, because of the Head Movement Constraint.*[7] Then, it must raise as XP, minimally NP to the specifier of D/PP. Subsequently, from this position of the NP, its head N moves to left-adjoin to *-a* (cf. also Kayne (1994), p. 88).

The structure in (13) is essentially a relative clause structure in view of Kayne's (1994) analysis of relative clauses. Kayne (1994) proposes that the structure of a sentence like (14a) is as in (14b):

(14) a. the house that the girl has

b. $[_{DP}$ the $[_{CP}$ [house]$_i$ that $[_{IP}$ the girl has t_i]]]

where *house* has raised to Spec, CP from its thematic position. Note the parallel between the structure in (14b) and that of an Aromanian DP like (11b) repeated here as (15a). Under my proposal (15a) has the structure in (15b):

---

[7] From a minimalist point of view head raising is ruled out because adjunction of casă to D/P is a vacuous movement, since it doesn't lead to the cheking of any feature on D/P.

(15) a. casa ali fiată b. [$_{DP}$ [casă]$_j$-a [$_{D/PP}$ [t$_j$]$_i$ali [$_{AgrP}$ fiată t$_i$]]]

The feature movement proposed in this section captures the intuition, quite pervasive in the literature on genitive assignment (cf. Grosu (1988), Ritter (1988), Cornilescu (1994), Longobardi (1996)) that the D head corresponding to the noun that θ-marks the genitive, plays a crucial role in the assignment of genitive and that there is an interaction between features of the D head of the genitive DP and features of the D head of the DP corresponding to the noun that θ-marks the genitive. It is a well-known fact that in Hebrew or Arabic construct state (cf. Ritter (1988), (1991), Fassi Fehri (1993)) genitives, the specification for definiteness of the genitive DP determines the specification for definiteness of the DP that contains the genitive:

(16) *beyt ha-mora*
house the-teacher
'the teacher's house' (from Ritter (1988, p. 915))

Furthermore, in construct state genitives, the noun heading the construction must be determinerless:

(17) *(*ha)-beyt ha-mora*
the-house the-teacher

I wish to end this section noting a parallelism between English and Aromanian genitives. I believe that English genitives such as that exemplified in (18a) are structurally similar to Aromanian genitives of the G_2 type. Kayne (1993, 1994) assigns to (18a) the structure in (18b). That is, he analyzes *'s* as an Agr head. Thus, (18a) involves a preposition, *of*, and an Agr head. On the other hand, G_2 Aromanian genitives involve a preposition *a* and a head D/P agreeing with the noun in the genitive.

(18) a. a house of John's

b. [$_{DP}$ [$_{QP}$ a house]$_i$ [$_D$ of] [$_{AgrP}$ John [$_{Agr}$'s] t$_i$]]

As noted in Kayne (1993, p. 5, and 26 fn. 9), *'s*, which he takes to be "substantially the same as the morpheme *-s* found on verbs" is incompatible with plural possessors marked with *-s*, but not with those not marked with *-s*:

(19) a. those children's mother

b. *those kids's mother

In a parallel fashion, the suffix on *a* in Aromanian G_2 genitives is morphologically singular. In both cases, the singular morpheme under discussion, *'s* in English, the suffix on *a* in Aromanian, is not semantically incompatible with a plural genitive DP (cf. (10) and (19a)). The difference between Aromanian and English is that in English the genitive DP may not be overtly marked for plural (cf. (19b)), while this is not the case in Aromanian (cf. (10)). Perhaps, this difference is due to the different position occupied by *'s* and *-lu* respectively. Under Kayne's proposal, *'s* in (18a) and (19a) occupies the head of an AgrP projection complement of *D* (cf. (18b) and (20) respectively):

(20) $[_{DP}$ D $[_{AgrP}$ [those children] $[_{Agr}$'s] $[_{NP}$ mother]]]

whereas under my proposal for Aromanian, *-l* in (10) occupies the head of a D/PP projection intervening between DP and AgrP (cf. (13)).

A similar account can be given for the contrast between the ungrammatical (21a) and the structurally similar but crucially not identical, under my view, grammatical Aromanian example in (21b):

(21) a. *the house of John's b. *casa alu Yanni*

'John's house'

Following Kayne's (1993, 1994) analysis of possessive constructions, in an example like (21a), *of* would occupy the D position *of* occupies in (18b). Under the assumption that *the* is necessarily of category D, and that no other D position is available lower than the D occupied by *of* in (18b), the ungrammaticality of (21a) is accounted for: *the* and *of* compete for the same position. On the other hand, in Aromanian the D/P head between D and Agr is available to host *a* and consequently in (21b) the preposition *a* and the definite determiner *-a*, which is a suffix on *casa*, do not compete for the same position.

5. *Proper names and genitive assignment*

In some varieties of Aromanian, the G_2 type of genitive is found only with proper names and kinship nouns like tată 'father', mamă 'mother', etc. (cf. for instance, Katsanis and Dinas (1990, p. 39)). This is shown in (22) with an example from the Aromanian of Kruševo, a dialect in which common names exhibit G_1 genitives:

(22) a. al^u $Mocan^u$ b. a bărbatlu^i
'Mocan's' 'the man's

Longobardi (1994) argues that proper names, as well as other categories of nouns such as kinship terms, raise overtly to D via *substitution*. This structural distinction is meant to capture a characteristic property of proper names, namely, that individual denotation is achieved via *direct reference*, instead of being achieved through an *operator-kind* (article-common noun) configuration.[8] The particular behavior of proper names and kinship nouns in the Aromanian dialects having G_1 genitives with common nouns illustrated in (22) can be accounted for combining Longobardi's N-to-D movement of proper names with the movement of features from the D head of the genitive DP to the head of D/PP argued for in section 4 (cf. (13)). According to the view presented in section 4, G_1 genitives involve covert movement of the Case and gender features from the D head of the genitive DP to the D/P head above AgrP. These features move in order to *identify* a D/P head obviously empty in the dialects with G_1 genitives.[9] Moreover, following Longobardi's ideas, proper names move into D via substitution. I would like to propose that the D head of genitive DP's involving proper names does not contain the Φ-features necessary for the identification of the D/P above AgrP, probably as a result of the substitution type of movement involved in the N-to-D raising of proper names. As a consequence, the set of features leading to D/P identification cannot have its source in the D of the genitive DP, and *a fortiriori* anywhere else. Thus, the failure to identify the D/P head through covert feature movement forces the merging of an overt determiner into D/P in the Aromanian dialects under consideration, as illustrated in (22).[10] This seems a quite natural way of treating the particular behavior of proper names and kinship nouns

[8] Furthermore, according to Longobardi (1994) N-to-D raising in proper names involves checking of a +R(suggesting 'referential') feature in D.

[9] It is not completely clear what *identification* should mean in a minimalist framework such as the one in Chomsky (1995). I would like to incorporate the intuitive idea of identification, at least at PF (i.e. *PF-identification*), as a by-product of the morphological properties of the elements to be identified. For instance, in Aromanian, D heads always carry Case and gender specifications. It seems plausible to think of D heads in Aromanian as items that obligatorily must contain these features. Thus, what I have called PF-identification is just a requirement that all D heads have to meet in order to be readable at the PF interface. Furthermore, I would like to claim that PF-identification may induce attraction of the relevant features, as in the case under consideration (cf. (12), (13)).

[10] On the other hand, Merge is not possible when the movement of the relevant features is available (i.e. with genitive common nouns). This is expected if we think of Merge as a less economical operation than Move (cf. Chomsky (1995)).

in dialects with G_1 genitives of common nouns, and can be seen as providing evidence in favor of an interaction between genitive D heads and D/P heads along the lines developed in this paper.

Let me now turn to Rumanian, a language related to Aromanian, which exhibits genitive constructions similar to the genitives of Aromanian. My aim is to propose an analysis of these Rumanian genitive constructions as minimally different as possible from that of Aromanian genitives.

6. *Aromanian vs. Rumanian*

Rumanian has genitives similar to those found in Aromanian, that is genitives formed with an invariant formative *a* bearing a suffix (AL -genitives henceforth). In Rumanian, both the noun and *a* have a suffix. The suffix on the noun is the genitive form of the definite determiner that agrees with that noun in gender and number. The suffix on *a* is a spell-out of the gender, number and Case features not of the noun in the genitive, as it is the case in Aromanian, but of the noun the extended projection of which is the DP which contains the noun in the genitive. For instance, in (23a), (23b) the suffix on *a* agrees in gender and number with *prieten*, 'friend, masc' *prietena* 'friend, fem' respectively, and *regelui* has suffixed the masculine, singular form of the definite determiner:

(23) a. *prieten* *al* *regelui*
friend(**masc**) A-def/**masc**/sing king-def/masc/sing
'friend(masc) of the king'

b. *prietena* *a* *regelui*
friend(**fem**) A-def/**fem**/sing king-def/masc/sing/gen
'friend(fem) of the king' (from Cornilescu (1994, p. 17))

In contrast to Aromanian, AL-genitives in Rumanian (cf. Dobrovie-Sorin (1987), Grosu (1988), Cornilescu (1994)) appear under specific conditions. When it is structurally possible for the genitive DP to be right adjacent to a form of the definite determiner (which in Rumanian also surfaces as a suffix of the noun) an AL-genitive is not allowed:

(24) a. **prietenul al regelui*
friend-the AL king-the(gen)

b. *prietenul regelui*
friend-the king-the(gen)
'the friend of the king'

This has led Grosu (1988) to propose that genitive Case in Rumanian is assigned under adjacency and by a single element of category D, which is morphologically realized as a form of the enclitic definite article of the language. Cornilescu (1994) assigns to (24b) the structure in (26a) and relates the obligatory presence of *a* in sentences like (25), where the DP contains an adjective besides the genitive DP:

(25) *portretul frumos *(al) regelui*
portret-the beautiful AL king-the(gen)
'the beautiful portrait of the king'

to an intervention effect induced by the adjective *frumos*. In the structure in (26b), the presence of *frumos* disallows raising to Spec, NumP of the genitive DP *regelui*. This results to the lack of adjacency between *regelui* and the determiner *-ul*:

(26) a.

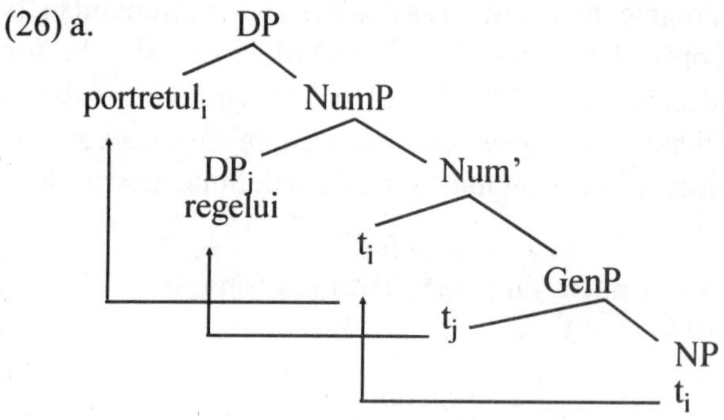

b.

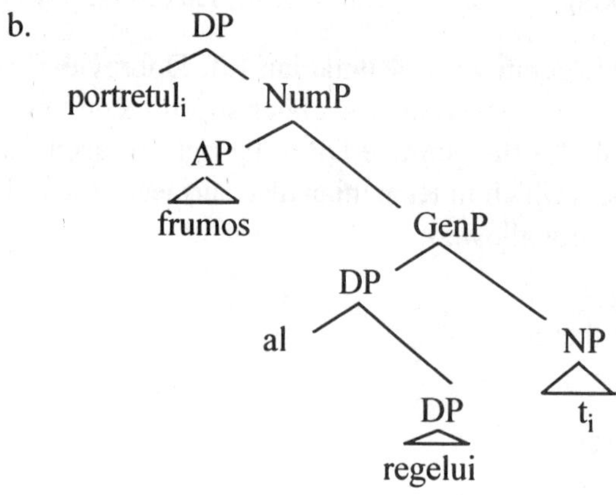

AL surfaces as a result of a last resort strategy to assign genitive Case to the DP *regelui* in the specifier of GenP. In the following section, I will argue that this theoretical account cannot be extended to Aromanian and I will propose an account of Rumanian AL-genitives in terms of the structure in (13), which I proposed for Aromanian. I think that the idea that adjectives block the movement of genitive DP's to the projection complement of D is problematic in view of English examples like that in (27):

(27) John's big book

where following Kayne's (1993, 1994) analysis of possessive constructions, *John* reaches the specifier of the AgrP complement of D in spite of the intervening adjective *big*. Also, in Hebrew construct state genitives, the noun raises overtly to D and the genitive DP must be right adjacent to it, crucially higher than the adjectives (Ritter 1991):

(28) *beyt ha-mora ha-yafe*
house the-teacher the-pretty
'the teacher's pretty house'

7. *XP-movement vs. N-to-D raising*

One main feature distinguishing genitive DP's in Aromanian and Rumanian is that in the former, genitive DP's are always construed with a preposition, *a* in the kinds of genitive discussed in this paper. Thus, (29a), corresponding to the Rumanian DP in (29b) (cf. also (24b)) is unacceptable in Aromanian

(29) a. **casa fiat,il'i*
house-the girl-the(gen)
'the house of the girl'

b. *portretul regelui*
portrait-the king-the(gen)
'the portrait of the king' (from Grosu (1988, p. 933))

Consequently, the surfacing of *a* cannot be attributed, as in the case of Rumanian (cf. previous section), to the failure of adjacency between the genitive assigning D and the genitive DP.

It has been repeatedly noted in the literature, especially with respect to languages with construct state genitive constructions, such as Hebrew, Arabic, Somali (Lecarme (1989)) or Rumanian[11] that the possibility of prepositionless genitive assignment is related to N- to -D raising (N- to -D raising is a syntactic process extensively documented in the literature, cf. Ritter (1991), Cinque (1993), Bernstein (1993), Longobardi (1994), among others). Thus, Longobardi (1996, p. 24) proposes the generalization in (30):

(30) If a common noun raises to D a prepositionless genitive occurs

The author recognizes that in view of languages like Rumanian, a language with overt N- to -D raising of common nouns which has both prepositionless and prepositional genitives,[12] prepositionless genitive assignment is possible but not obligatory when N raises overtly to D.

On the other hand, as already noted, in Aromanian, apparently another language with overt N- to -D raising of common nouns, genitive Case assignment necessarily involves the prepositional element *a*, prepositionless genitives being excluded. In my account of Aromanian genitives in the previous section, I proposed that left adjunction of the noun to the enclitic definite determiner of the language is not the result of head raising of the noun to D. Rather, (cf. (13)) the noun raises as an XP, minimally an NP, to the specifier of the projection complement of D, and only the last step of the movement of the noun is head movement.

I want to propose that the assignment of prepositional or prepositionless genitives in languages like Aromanian or Rumanian, correlates with each one of two kinds of movement available to the noun within the DP. Head raising of the noun correlates with prepositionless genitive. Raising of the noun as part of an XP, minimally an NP, correlates with prepositional genitives.

In Androutsopoulou (1994, 1995, 1996), I argue for an account of constructions involving adjectival determiners in Greek or Albanian (cf. for instance, (31a) and (31b) respectively) in terms of movement of an extended projection of the noun to the specifier of a higher projection complement of D, hosting

---

[11] If DP's like (I) (cf. (29b)):

(i) portretul regelui

involve construct state syntax, as claimed in (see Longobardi (1996:25) fn. 41).

[12] Like Grosu (1988) I take the various forms of *a* + suffix in Rumanian to be prepositional elements.

D features. The head of this projection is occupied by the adjectival determiner, that preceding the adjective in (31a) and (31b):

(31) a. *to vivlio to kalo*
the book the good
'the good book'

b. *djali i mirë*
boy-the the good
'the good boy'

Español-Echevarría (1995) and (1996) argues for a similar kind of movement in his analysis of Spanish examples like (32a) and (32b) respectively:

(32) a. *Juan es guapo de cara*
John is nice of face
'John has a nice face'

b. *el imbécil de Juan*
the stupid of John
'that stupid of John'

This XP movement is to be understood as a possible operation, subcase of the checking of the nominal feature in D_0. Thus, together with overt or covert movement of a nominal feature from N to D (i.e. N-to-D raising as it has been documented in the literature) we have to admit the possibility of pied-piping of some DP- internal constituent by the above nominal feature, as shown in the structures in (33a) and (33b):

(33) a.

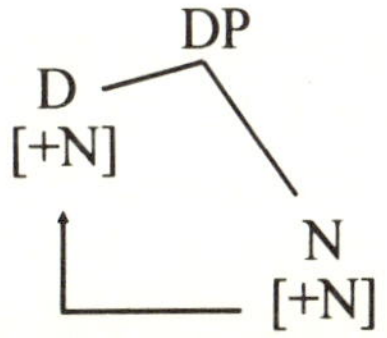

DP
D [+N]
N [+N]

b.

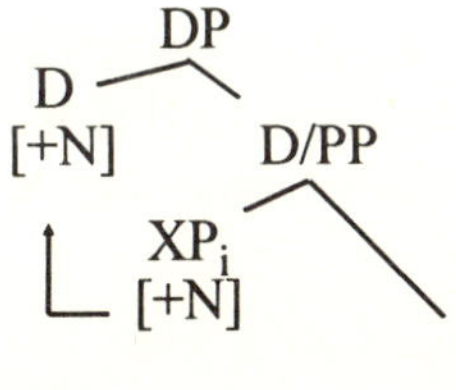

DP
D [+N]
D/PP
XP_i [+N]
t_i

My claim here is that the strategy in (33b) is found not only in Greek or Albanian, but also in Aromanian and Rumanian and that it correlates, at least in the latter two languages with prepositional genitive Case assignment.[13]
In the previous section I proposed the structure in (34b) for the DP in (34a):

---

13 The correlation seems to be valid in Albanian also. Albanian genitives are similar to the G1 genitives of Aromanian. They involve an invariant formative *i* which precedes the noun and a suffix marked for genitive on the noun. Greek genitives seem to involve only genitive morphology and no prepositional element. I have not yet studied Greek genitives, but at this point I expect that they will be shown to involve a null prepositional D/P head.

(34) a. casa ali fiată

b. $[_{DP}$ [casă]$_j$-a $[_{D/PP}$ $[_{NP}$ $t_j]_i$ $[_{D/P}$ ali] $[_{AgrP}$ $[_{DP}$ fiată] ... t_i]]]

I take the existence of overt N-to-D raising in Rumanian sentences like (29b), repeated here as (35), to be uncontroversial:

(35) a. *portretul regelui* b. $[_{DP}$ $[_D$*portretul*$]_i$ $[_{AgrP}$ $[_{DP}$ *regelui*] ... t_i]]
portrait-the king-the(gen)
'the portrait of the king'

I would like to claim, however, that Rumanian AL-genitives have a structure minimally different from that of Aromanian AL-genitives. For instance, (25) repeated here as (36a), has the structure in (36b):

(36) a. *portretul frumos *(al) regelui*
portrait-the beautiful AL king-the(gen)
'the beautiful portrait of the king'

b. $[_{DP}$ [*portret*]$_j$-ul $[_{D/PP}$$[_{XP}$ t_j *frumos*$]_i$ $[_{D/P}$ *al*] $[_{AgrP}$ $[_{DP}$ *regelui*] ... t_i]]]

I think that the availability of structures like that in (34b) in Aromanian DP's containing a genitive (which can be viewed as an adnominal modifier), that is the availability of AL-genitives, is not surprising in view of the existence of adjectival determiners in this language. As shown in (37), adjectivally modified DP's in Aromanian may involve more than one determiner (up to one per modifier):

(37) *omlu bunlu*
man-the good-the
'the good man'

As mentioned above, I have argued in previous work that DP-internal raising of an extended projection of the noun to the specifier of a higher projection, complement of D, hosting D features, is a well-attested overt syntactic operation in languages with adjectival determiners. Here I establish a relation between such syntactic operation and prepositional genitives. Aromanian has adjectival determiners. Thus, it is not surprising that it also has prepositional genitives.

The relationship I establish here between D-nodes and NP-modifiers should be understood as a consequence of NP-modification (by an adjectival phrase or an adnominal genitive) involving a reduced relative clause configuration (cf. Smith (1969), Kayne (1994), Chomsky (1995)). That is, each NP-modification licenses a D-head that may surface in certain languages (multiple determiner languages).

8. *Conclusion*

In this paper I have provided a set of syntactic operations that allows us to formulate the following generalization with respect to raising-to-D movement and genitive Case assignment in Aromanian and Rumanian:

(38) a. prepositionless genitive occurs iff N-to-D raising takes place, and

b. prepositional (*a*-) genitive occurs when the noun raising to D pied-pipes a larger projection containing the noun

Aromanian genitives which apparently involve overt N-to-D raising, but obligatorily require the preposition *a* (lack of prepositionless genitives) are problematic for (38a). (38b) allows for an account of Aromanian genitives and also for a unified account of Aromanian genitives and Rumanian genitives requiring the presence of *a*.

REFERENCES

Androutsopoulou, Antonia. 1994. "The Distribution of the Definite Determiner and the Syntax of Greek DP's". *Proceedings of Chicago Linguistics Society* 30.16-29. Chicago: Chicago Linguistics Society.

———. 1995. "The Licensing of Adjectival Modification". *Proceedings of WCCFL* 14.17-31 Standford: CSLI Publications.

———. 1996. "Adjectival Determiners in Albanian and Greek". Paper presented at the *Worshop on the Syntax of Balkan Languages, GLOW* 96, Athens.

Bernstein, Judith. 1993. *Topics in the Syntax of Nominal Structure Across Romance*. Ph.D. dissertation, City University of New York.

Caragiou-Marioeanou, Matilde. 1968. "Fonomorfologie Aromâna". *Studiu de Dialectologie Structurala.* Bucharest: Editura Academiei Republicii Socialiste Românie.

Capidan, Theodor. 1932. *Aromânii, Dialectul Aromân, Studiu Linguistic.* Bucharest: Monitorul Oficial i Imprimeriile Statului, Imprimeria Nationala.

Chomsky, Noam. 1994. "Bare Phrase Structure". *MIT Occasional Papers in Linguistics* 5. Cambridge Mass: MIT.

———. 1995. *The Minimalist Program*. Cambridge, Mass: MIT Press.

Cinque, Guglielmo. 1993. "On the Evidence of Partial N-movement in Romance DP". Ms., University of Venice.

Cornilescu, Alexadra. 1994. "Rumanian Genitive Constructions". *Advances in Rumanian Linguistics* ed. by Guglielmo Cinque & Giuliana Giusti, 1-54. Amsterdam: John Benjamins.

Dobrovie-Sorin Carmen. 1987. "A propos de la structure du groupe nominal en Roumain". *Rivista di Gramatica Generativa* 12.123-152.

Español-Echevarría, Manuel. To appear. "Inalienable Possession in Copulative Contexts and DP Structure". *Lingua Special Volume on Have/Be and the Syntax of Possession* ed. by M. den Dikken.

Español-Echevarría, Manuel. 1996. "Definiteness Patterns in *A/N of N* Constructions and DP-Internal XP Movement". Student Conference in Linguistics 8. Department of Philosophy, MIT.

Fassi-Fehri, Abdelkader. 1993. *Issues in the Structure of Arabic Clauses and Words*. Dordrecht: Kluwer.

Exarhos, George. 1986. *Vlahoi, Mnemeia zoes kai logou enos politismou pou hanetai.* Athens: Epikairoteta.

Grosu, Alexander. 1988. "On the Distribution of Genitive Phrases in Romanian". *Linguistics* 26.931-949.

Golab, Zbigniew. 1984. *The Arumanian Dialect of Kruševo in SR Macedonia SFR Yugoslavia.* Skopje: Macedonian Academy of Sciences and Arts, Section of Linguistics and Literary Science.

Katsanes, Nikos & Kostas Dinas. 1990. *Grammatike tes Koines Koutsovlahikes.* Thessaloniki: Arheio Koutsovlachikon Leleton.

Kayne, Richard. 1993. "Toward a Modular Theory of Auxiliary Selection". *Studia Linguistica* 47.3-31.

———. 1994. *The Antisymmetry of Syntax*. Cambridge Mass: MIT Press.

Koltsidas, Antones. 1978. *Grammatike kai lexiko tes Koutsovlahikes glossa.* Thessaloniki: Ekdhotikos Oikos Afon Kyriakidhe.

Lecarme, Jacqueline. 1989. "Genitive Constructions, Noun Complement Structures and Syntactic Parameters in Somali". Paper presented at the *11th International Symposium on Cushitic and Omotic Languages*, Turin.

Longobardi, Giuseppe. 1994. "Reference and Proper Names: A Theory of N-movement in Syntax and Logical Form". *Linguistic Inquiry* 25.609-665.

———. 1996. "The Syntax of N-raising: a Minimalist Theory". Ms., Università di Venezia.

Papahagi, Tache. 1974. *Dictionarul dialectului aromân, general i etimologic.* Bucharest: Editura Academiei Republicii Populare Romine.

Padioti, Giorgi. 1988. *Cantiti Armâneti di-Aminciu.* Athens: Gerou Editions.

Ritter, Elizabeth. 1988. "A Head-Movement Approach to Construct-State Noun Phrases". *Linguistics* 26.909-929.

———. 1991. "Two Functional Categories in Noun Phrases: Evidence from Modern Hebrew". *Syntax and Semantics* 26, ed. by Susan Rothstein, 37-62. San Diego: Academic Press.

Rohlshoven, Jürgen. 1989. *Eine Selbstlernende Generativ-Phonologische Grammatik. Linguistische Arbeiten* 218. Tübingen: Niemeyer.

Smith, Carlota. 1969. "Determiners and Relative Clauses in a Generative Grammar of English". *Modern Studies in English* ed. by. David A. Reidel & Sanford A. Schane, 247-263. Englewood Cliffs, N.J.: Prentice Hall.

ON OPTIONALITY IN THE MINIMALIST PROGRAM AND OLD FRENCH WORD ORDER*

DEBORAH ARTEAGA
University of Nevada, Las Vegas

0. *Introduction*

Within the Minimalist Program of Chomsky (1989, 1993, 1994, 1995), movement is motivated by universal principles; parametric differences among languages are assumed to be largely attributable to the relative strength of D- or V- features.[1]

For example, consider the contrast between French and English in (1) - (2) (Marantz 1995:372):

(1) *Elmer lave souvent son chat*
Elmer washes-3sg often his cat

'Elmer often washes his cat.'

(2) Elmer often washes his cat.

(Marantz 1995:372)

According to Chomsky (1993:30), the strong V-features of AGR in French force overt movement of the main verb to T before Spell-Out, as in (1); in English, on the other hand, the V-features of AGR are weak, thereby blocking raising of the main verb out of the VP before Spell-Out, as in (2). Strong D-features of T in turn force raising of the subject to [SPEC, [AGR T]] in both French and English. Note further that in both languages, movement of the

---

* I would like to thank Julia Herschensohn, Heles Contreras, and Karen Zagona for helpful comments and suggestions on a draft of this paper. Any remaining errors, are, of course, my responsibility.

[1] In early Minimalist writings, Chomsky (1989, 1993, 1994) refers to these features as N-features. In more recent work, (Chomsky 1995:233), he employs the term D-features and leaves as an open question possibly differences between N-features and D-features. In this paper, I follow the terminology in Chomsky (1995).

direct object is covert, due to weak D-features of AGR, giving these languages their characteristic SVO word order.[2]

This paper will argue that although such an analysis captures the relevant generalizations for Modern French and Modern English, it must be modified to allow optionality of movement for languages like Old French, which evince more flexible word order.

We begin by a brief overview of Old French word order in Section 1; we then consider how the Minimalist Program can account for this word order in Section 2.0, pursuing an idea proposed by Marantz 1995 in his analysis of Japanese word order, showing that it allows the necessary derivations of the various Old French word orders under consideration here. We conclude by briefly considering the issue of language change.

1. *Old French word order*

Word order in Old French was considerably more flexible than that of its modern counterpart. One characteristic of Old French in main clauses was its V2 word order (see Adams 1987a, Arteaga 1994, Roberts 1993, Vance 1988, among others), as illustrated in (3) - (4), in which the verb occupies the second position:[3]

(3) *Li* *baron* ***regardent*** *les* *letres*
the-m-pl-nom barons-m-pl-nom look-at-3pl the-f-pl-obl letters-f-pl-obl
'The barons look at the letters.'
(Queste 5.22)

(4) *Dont* ***dist*** *li* *dus* *au*
therefore said-3sg the-m-sg-nom duke-m-sg-nom to-the-m-sg-obl
chevalier
knight-m-sg-obl
'Therefore the duke said to the knight.'
(Ch. 217)
(Foulet 1980 §451)

---

2 More recently, Chomsky (1995:352) has suggested that AGR in fact does not exist, a somewhat controversial claim. For the purposes of this paper, we continue to posit the existence of AGR.

3 The abbreviations I will use in this work are as follows: *1sg* (first person singular); *2sg* (second person singular); *3sg* (third person singular); *1pl* (first person plural); *2pl* (second person plural); *3pl* (third person plural). In addition, as Old French had a two-case declension system, I indicate the case on nouns by the abbreviations *nom* (nominative case) and *obl* (for oblique case), with the designations *sg* for singular and *pl* for plural. I indicate gender by *m* for masculine and *f* for feminine. Finally, where I have culled Old French examples cited by other authors, the translation is mine, unless otherwise noted.

In addition to V2 word order, the position of two other elements in a sentence is relevant to our discussion, namely that of subject DPs and object DPs. We first begin with the position of the subject in Old French.

1.1 *Position of the subject DP in Old French*

Provided that V2 word order was maintained, the subject could be preverbal, as in (3), or postverbal, as in (4).[4] But what these examples do not show, is that the postverbal subject could follow an untensed verb form or an adverb. Consider (5) - (7) below:

(5) *Car a ceste Queste ne doit refuser* ***nus***
for to this-f-sg-obl quest-f-sg-obl neg should-3sg to-refuse no-m-sg-nom

preudoms *ne por mort ne por vie*
man-m-sg-nom neither for death-f-sg-obl nor for life-f-sg-obl

'For no man must refuse this quest, either for life or death.'
(Queste 61)
(Vance 1988:76)

(6) *Iluec arrivet sainement* ***la nacele***
there arrives-3sg safely the-f-sg-nom ship-f-sg-nom

'The ship arrives safely there.'
(La vie de St. Alexis 82)

(7) *Cele nuit furent servié*
that-f-sg-obl night-f-sg-obl were-3pl served-m-pl-nom

et ariesié ***li compaignon***
and satisfied-m-pl-nom the-m-pl-nom companions-m-pl-nom

'That night the companions were served and satisfied.'
(La Queste 27)
(Vance 1988:67)

That the word order illustrated in (5) - (7) above is optional can be illustrated by examples like (8) below, in which the subject precedes the infinitive *susfrir* 'to suffer' (cf. (5) above):

---

[4] This is an oversimplification, as other word orders (OVS, VOS, SOV) are found in Old French; see Arteaga (1993) for discussion.

(8) *Pur sun* *seignur* *deit* ***hom*** *susfrir*
for his-m-sg-obl lord-m-sg-obl must-3sg man-m-sg-nom to-suffer

granz *mals*
great-m-pl-obl hardships-m-pl-obl

'For one's lord one must suffer great hardships.'
(Roland 1117)
(Jensen 1990:296)

The word orders illustrated in (5) - (8) above have led many scholars (*inter alia* Vance 1988, 1989, Roberts 1993) to argue that raising of the subject DP out of the VP was optional in Old French.[5]

Similarly, variation was also possible when the subject was preverbal. In an example like (3), assuming that main clauses were CPs in Old French, as in other V2 languages, the subject is in the SPEC of CP. But another possibility exists in Old French, as illustrated by examples like (9):

(9) *De mon* *nom,* *fet* *il,*
of my-m-sg-obl name-m-sg-obl does-3sg he-m-sg-nom

ne peuz ***tu*** *mie savoir.*
neg can-2sg you-m-sg-nom never to-know

'You can never know my name, said he.'
(La Queste 29)
(Vance 1988:80)

In (9), assuming that the negative adverb *mie, 'never'* occupies a position within NegP, the subject *tu*, 'you' a non clitic in Old French, must be in the SPEC of Agr_s.

To summarize, as illustrated by the examples (5) - (9), the subject DP in Old French could occupy the SPEC of CP, the SPEC of $Agr_{s,}$ or remain within the VP. We next turn to the position of the object in Old French.

1.2 *Position of the object DP in Old French*

As is the case in other V2 languages, object raising was possible in Old French. Consider (10) below, in which the object, *grant enor*, 'great honor' has raised:

---

5 Given such optionality, in an example like (4) it is impossible to determine whether the subject occupies the SPEC of VP or has raised to the SPEC of Agr_s.

(10) ***Grant*** ***enor*** *me porterent tuit*
great-m-sg-obl honor-m-sg-obl to-me brought-3pl all-m-pl-nom

'They all showed great honor to me.'

(Yvain 570)
(Jensen 1990:756)

In this way, (10) contrasts with (11) below, where the object ***sa povrete***, remains *in situ*:

(11) *Iluec deduit liedement* ***sa povrete***
there lived-3sg joyfully his-f-sg-obl poverty-f-sg-obl

'There he joyfully lived his poverty.'

(St. Alexis 261)

As the examples (10) - (11) illustrate, object raising was optional in Old French. The question arises as to whether object raising, when it occurred, was obligatorily to the SPEC of CP or could be to some intermediate position. Consider next the example in (12):

(12) *Son compaignon donna*
his-m-sg-obl companion-m-sg-obl gave-3sg e

un hannap *lieement*
a-m-sg-obl drinking glass-m-sg-obl joyfully

'He joyfully gave his companion a drinking glass.'

(Herslund 1980:10)
(Dits C 233)

The example in (12), in which the object DP has scrambled over the adverb *lieement* contrasts with the example in (11), in which the object DP follows the adverb. Note that it is not the direct object *un hannap*, but rather the indirect object *son companion*, that occupies the SPEC of CP in (12).

It would therefore appear that object raising in Old French could be to an intermediate position, which we will assume is to the SPEC of Agr_0, providing that another Xmax occupied the word initial position, thereby maintaining V2 word order. Similar conclusions can be reached by examining past participle agreement in Old French. One striking difference between past participle agreement in Old French and Modern French, is that the older language allowed optional agreement between the past participle and a postverbal DP, as illustrated by the examples in (13) - (14):

(13) *L'* *empere* *ad* ***prise*** *sa*
the-m-sg-nom emperor-m-sg-nom has-3sg taken-f-sg his-f-sg-obl

herberge
camp-f-sg-obl

'The emperor has set up camp.'
(Roland 2488)
(Jensen 1990:336)

(14) *Li* *reis* *se* *drecet,*
the-m-sg-nom king-m-sg-nom himself gets-up-3sg

si *ad* ***rendut*** *ses* *armes*
and has-3sg removed-m-sg his-f-pl-obl armor-f-pl-obl

'The king gets up and has removed his armor.'
(Roland 2849)
(Jensen 1990:336)

In (13), there is agreement between the past participle *prise* taken and the postverbal noun *sa herberge* 'his camp,' but such agreement is lacking in (14) between the past participle *rendut* 'removed' and the postverbal noun *ses armes* 'his armor.'

In this section, we have seen that both subject raising and object raising out of the VP were optional in Old French. We next consider how the word orders illustrated in (3) - (14) might be accounted for within the Minimalist Program.

2. *Optionality in the Minimalist Program and Old French word order*

Within the Minimalist Program, movement does not occur unless it is specifically motivated by universal principles, and where it is motivated, it must occur. While this is unproblematic for many languages with seemingly fixed word orders, it is less clear how such a theory can account for word orders found in languages like Old French, where, as we have seen, many surface orders are found. For a possible solution, we next turn to a proposal by Marantz 1995.

2.1 *Marantz 1995' analysis of Japanese word order*

Word order in Japanese is relatively free, as illustrated by the examples from Nemoto (1995: 257-273) given below in (15)- (16):

(15) *Taroo-ga hon- o kaita (koto)*
Taro- nom book-acc wrote
'Taro wrote a book.'

(16) *hon -o Taroo-ga kaita (koto)*
book-acc Taro -nom wrote
(=14)
(Nemoto 1995:258)

The word orders in (15) - (16) above have been viewed by many scholars as instances of scrambling (e.g., Saito 1985, Hoji 1985, Nemoto 1995). Marantz notes that the existence of scrambling in languages like Japanese, as well as free word order in other languages, is problematic for a Minimalist Program in which all movement is forced and no movement is optional. He suggests that the problem might be resolved in a framework in which features may be optionally strong or weak in some languages. He briefly considers the case of Japanese, offering the tentative proposal that in Japanese, all D-features of T and AGR are potentially weak, so that DPs may remain *in situ* prior to Spell-Out.[6] He further suggests that movement of some of the constituents out of VP could be motivated if some of these D-features could be optionally strong. For example, he argues, if D features of V are optionally strong and all other features are weak, the object will raise to the SPEC of Agr_o, thus appearing to have scrambled over the subject.[7]

In Marantz' approach, the optionality involved would be found in the lexical items themselves, which would have either strong or weak features. In our view, Marantz' proposal of features that may be optionally strong or weak in a given language provides the Minimalist Framework with the means of accounting for Old French word order, as we shall see in the next section.[8]

---

[6] Marantz (1995) actually uses the term N-features; see fn 1 above.

[7] Chomsky (1994:31) also suggests the possibility of optionally strong/weak features in a given language, as in the case of Arabic; however, he equates this optionality with differences in inflectional richness, which cannot be maintained for Old French, whose case system and verbal inflection were equally rich regardless of word order.

[8] Although an in-depth review of Marantz' analysis of Japanese word order is beyond the scope

2.2 *Optionality and Old French word order*

Old French does not possess the variety of word orders available to Japanese, in part because it is a language with V2 constraints. In the classical analysis of V2 languages (see den Besten 1983, Travis 1986, Adams 1987a, Roberts 1993, Rizzi 1990), which we will adopt here, the verb fronts from V to I to C, or recast in current terminology, through Agr_0, to T, to Agr_s to C; an XP occupies the SPEC of CP.

As we have seen, in Old French, the subject DP often occupied the SPEC of CP, as in (3) above; alternatively, however, the subject could occupy the SPEC of Agr_sP, as in (9). As both cases involve fronting of the subject DP out of VP, it would appear that in Old French, like Modern French, D-features of T were strong.

However, examples (5) - (8), above, in which the subject DP follows a non-tensed verb form or adverb, strongly suggest that the subject DP has not moved from the VP; such cases would argue for weak D-features of T in Old French. In order to reconcile these seemingly disparate possibilities, we will propose that D-features of T were optionally strong/weak in Old French, as proposed by Marantz for Japanese.

A similar alternation is found in Old French with respect to the object DP. As illustrated by examples like (10) - (13), Old French is a language with optional object raising. That is to say that optionally, the object DP will overtly raise out of the VP, first to Agr_0, to check its case. In examples like (12) and (13), we have argued, the object DP raises no further.

To motivate such a movement, we would like to propose that the D-features of AGR may be weak or strong in Old French. If they are strong, in a given derivation, the object will front overtly to the SPEC of Agr_0 before Spell-Out.[9] If D-features of AGR are weak, the object will remain in the VP, fronting covertly at LF, as in (11).[10]

---

of the current work, it is perhaps worth noting that other recent studies claim that the subject in Japanese must front obligatorily to the SPEC of Agr_s, as in English (see Ueda 1990, Tada 1992, and Nemoto 1995). If that is indeed the case, then D-features of T in that language must be strong, not potentially weak, as proposed by Marantz.

[9] Due to space limitations, this paper does not discuss the obligatory fronting of the Xmax from the SPEC of AGR_0 to the SPEC of CP or the fronting of the verb to C°; these issues are in fact part of a larger issue, namely how to account for V2 word order within the Minimalist Program. See Arteaga (1996) for further discussion.

[10] Alternatively, following Chomsky's (1995:351) claim that AGR is only present when it is strong, one could say that Agr_0 is optionally present in Old French.

Our analysis differs in one important way from the strong/weak distinction proposed by Marantz, in that we are assuming, following Chomsky 1995, that the strong/weak distinction is not found in the lexical items themselves, but rather should be limited to the functional categories, as in (17) (Chomsky 1995:232):

(17) If F is strong, then F is a feature of a nonsubstantive category and F is checked by a categorial feature.

In Chomsky's analysis, nouns and verbs do not have strong features, which always call for a certain category in the checking domain of the functional category. For Chomsky, checking off these strong features constitutes the only reason for violations of Procrastinate.[11] The operation Move F allows movement of a feature both to check a feature of the target or its own feature.[12]

Our proposal provides a way to account for certain issues of language change relating to French word order, which we briefly consider in the next section.

3. *Optionality and language change*

As illustrated by the examples (3) - (14) above, it is clear that with respect to word order, three major changes have occurred in the history of French, namely the loss of V2 word order, the loss of overt object raising, and the obligatory nature of subject raising. This paper will consider the latter two changes.[13]

The analysis presented here views language change as a change in the relative strength of features. From Old French to Middle French, in the two cases under consideration here, the change was from strong features to weak features, following a period in which features could be optionally strong or weak. For example, we have claimed that D-features of AGR were optionally strong or weak in Old French and weak in Modern French, which makes object rais-

[11] Although such a formulation would seem to run counter to early formulations of the principle Greed, which only allowed movement of an element to check its own morphological features and not those of another element or category, Chomsky (1995:266) redefines Move α as Move F (feature), "F is unchecked and enters into a checking relation."

[12] Cf. Wilder and Cavar's (1994:60) principle of "early altruism."

[13] For an account of the loss of V2 word order in French within the Minimalist Program, see Arteaga (1996).

ing optionally available to Old French but not Modern French. In the second case, that of subject raising, the change was from optionally weak/strong D features of T in Old French, to strong in Modern French. This evolution raises an interesting point, which we leave to further research, namely whether a period of optionally strong/weak features is a requisite for this type of language change.

4. *Conclusion*

This paper has considered various Old French word orders which illustrate the optional nature of subject and object raising in that language. We have argued that this variety provides further support for Marantz' (1995) proposal of V and D-features that may be optionally strong or weak in a given language. We have further argued that according to our proposal, language change should be viewed as a change in the relative strength of features.

REFERENCES

Adams, Marianne. 1987a. "From Old French to the Theory of Pro-drop". *Natural Language and Linguistic Theory* 5.1-32.

———. 1987b. *Old French, Null Subjects, and Verb Second Phenomena*. Ph.D. dissertation, UCLA.

Arteaga, Deborah. 1993. "Syntax and Mood Choice in French". *Language Quarterly* 31.1-21.

———. 1994. "Impersonal Constructions in Old French". *Issues and Theory in Romance Linguistics*, ed. by Michael Mazzola, 141-156. Washington, D.C: Georgetown University Press.

———. 1996. "Sobre la construcción de complemento objeto doble en el francés antiguo". *Revista de filología francesa* 9.25-47.

———. 1996. "On V2 Word Order in Old French and Feature Strength". Ms., University of Nevada, Las Vegas.

Besten, Hans den. 1983. "On the Interaction of Root Transformations and Lexical Deletion Rules". *On the Formal Syntax of the Westgermania*, ed. by W. Abraham, 47-133. Amsterdam: Benjamins.

Brunot, Ferdinand. 1966. *Histoire de la langue française des origines à nos jours* 12 vols. Paris: Librairie Armand Colin.

Chomsky, Noam. 1982. *Some Concepts and Consequences of the Theory of Government and Binding*. Cambridge, Mass.: MIT Press.

———. 1989. "Some Notes on Economy of Derivation and Representation". *MIT Working Papers in Linguistics* 10.43-74.

———. 1993. "A Minimalist Program for Linguistic Theory". *The View from Building 20* ed. by Kenneth Hale & Samuel J. Keyser, 1-25. Cambridge, Mass.: MIT Press.

———. 1994. "Bare Phrase Structure". *Government and Binding Theory and the Minimalist Program* ed. by Gert Webelhuth, 383-439. Cambridge, Mass.: Blackwell.

———. 1995. *The Minimalist Program*. Cambridge, Mass: MIT Press.

Einhorn, E. 1974. *Old French: A Concise Handbook*. Cambridge: Cambridge University Press.

Foulet, Lucien. 1982. *Petite syntaxe de l'ancien français*. Paris: Librairie Honoré Champion.

Herschensohn, Julia. 1996. *Case Suspension and Binary Complement Structure in French*. Amsterdam: Benjamins.

Herslund, Michael. 1980. "Problèmes de l'ancien français. Compléments datifs et génitifs". *Revue Romane*, Numéro spécial, 21.

Hoji, H. 1985. *Logical Form Constraints and Configurational Structures in Japanese*. Ph.D. dissertation, University of Washington.

Jensen, Frede. 1990. *Old French and Comparative Gallo-Romance Syntax*. Tubingen: Max Niemeyer Verlag.

Marantz, Alex. 1995. "The Minimalist Program". *Government and Binding Theory and the Minimalist Program*, ed. by Gert Webelhuth, 349-382. Cambridge, Mass.: Blackwell.

Marchello-Nizia, Christiane. 1979. *Histoire de la langue française aux XIVe et XVe siècles*. Paris: Bordas.

Nemoto, Naoko. 1995. "Scrambling in Japanese, Agr-OP, and Economy of Derivation". *Lingua* 97.257-273.

Nyrop, K. 1930-1935. *Grammaire Historique de la langue française*, 6 vols. Copenhagen: Gyldendalske Boghandel.

Rizzi, Luigi. 1990. "Speculations on Verb Second". *Grammar in Progress*, ed. by Joan Mascaro & Marina Nespor, 375-386. Dordrecht: Foris.

Roberts, Ian. 1993. *Verbs and Diachronic Syntax: A Comparative History of English and French*. Norwell: Kluwer Academic Press.

Saito, Mamoru. 1985. *Some Asymmetries in Japanese and their Theoretical Implications*. Ph.D. dissertation, MIT.

Schaffer, Robyn. 1994. "Negation and Verb Second in Breton". *Natural Language and Linguistic Theory* 13.135-172.

Togeby, Knud. 1974. *Précis historique de grammaire française*. Odense: Akademisk Forlag.

Tomaselli, A. 1989. *La sintassi del verbo finito nelle lingue germaniche*. Ph.D. dissertation, Università di Pavia.

Travis, Lisa. 1984. *Parameters and Effects of Word Order Variation*. Ph.D. dissertation, MIT.
Vance, Barbara. 1988. *Null Subjects and Syntactic Change in French*. Ph.D. dissertation, Cornell University.
———. 1989. "The Evolution of Pro-drop in Medieval French". *Studies in Romance Linguistics*, ed. by K. Kirschner and J. de Cesaris, 479-494. Amsterdam: John Benjamins
La vie de Saint Alexis: Poème du XIe siècle. Paris: Champion, Paris, Gaston, ed., 1980.
Wilder, Chris & Damir Cavar. 1994. "Word Order Variation, Verb Movement, and Economy Principles". *Studia Linguistica* 48.46-86.

INTERACTIONS BETWEEN PRAGMATIC AND SYNTACTIC KNOWLEDGE IN THE FIRST LANGUAGE ACQUISITION OF SPANISH NULL AND OVERT PRONOMINALS

JENNIFER AUSTIN, MARÍA BLUME, DAVID PARKINSON,
ZELMIRA NÚÑEZ DEL PRADO, BARBARA LUST
Cornell University

Introduction

In recent papers, we have argued that there is no developmental stage at which children acquiring either Spanish or English show a syntactic deficit in their knowledge of grammar determining the distribution of null subjects (Austin, Blume, Lust, Núñez del Prado, Parkinson, and Proman 1995a, 1995b). This proposal contrasts with that of others in the field, such as Radford (1990), Rizzi (1994), Hyams (1994), and Hyams & Wexler (1993), who have proposed that various elements of the adult syntax are missing or underspecified in children's early grammars. We have argued that, with respect to null subjects, children acquiring *pro* drop and non *pro* drop languages exhibit early and surprisingly adultlike syntactic knowledge. However, we have argued that in the acquisition of *pro* drop and non *pro* drop languages, there is development in pragmatic knowledge. This pragmatic knowledge affects the distribution of null subjects in both languages.

In this paper, we will present results from our study of Spanish first language acquisition, based on new analyses of young children's natural speech. In our analyses, we further investigate Spanish speaking children's syntactic competence with regard to null subjects, as well as their competence in this area of grammar. We compare the distribution of null subjects with the distribution of null auxiliaries in Spanish speaking children's grammar and we argue that they are governed by similar constraints, and show similarities in their development.

Method

The children's natural speech samples analyzed for this study were chosen at random from the Cornell Language Acquisition Lab's Natural Speech Corpus, the only selection criterion being that they fell within the desired MLU range. The Spanish speech samples coded and analyzed are summarized in Table 1. There are a total of 13 samples from 10 subjects, ranging in age from 1 year 2 months to 3 years 4 months, and in MLU from 1.29 to 4.77.

Table 1
Subject information

Initials	MLU	# of PPDCs*	Subject type: Null	Subject type: Pronoun[1]	Subject type: NP	Data gathered where: by whom
JP2	1.29	6	6 (100.00%)	0	0	Ithaca: MB
MP1	1.31	2	2 (100.00%)	0	0	Peru: MB
JP1	1.73	3	2 (100.00%)	0	0	Ithaca: JA
MP2	2.00	5	3 (60.00%)	1 (20.00%)	1 (20.00%)	Peru: MB
GR	2.16	4	4 (100.00%)	0	0	Puerto Rico: ZNP
JP3	2.97	28	23 (82.14%)	5 (17.86%)	0	Peru: MB
EH	3.66	243	187 (76.95%)	40 (16.46%)	16 (6.58%)	Peru: MB
MA	3.76	103	79 (76.70%)	17 (16.50%)	7 (6.80%)	Puerto Rico: ZNP
SC	3.84	99	80 (80.81%)	9 (9.09%)	10 (10.10%)	Spain: JA
AB	4.10	12	5 (41.67%)	6 (50.00%)	1 (8.33%)	Spain: JA
FB	4.26	51	38 (74.51%)	9 (17.65%)	4 (7.84%)	Peru: MB
AL	4.61	52	38 (73.08%)	10 (19.23%)	4 (7.69%)	Spain: JA
NR	4.77	31	21 (67.74%)	2 (6.45%)	8 (25.81%)	Puerto Rico: ZNP

This MLU range includes children from the very onset of word combination to a point beyond which complex sentence productivity begins. However, as we will see, Spanish-speaking children appear to be relatively precocious in comparison to English-speaking children of a comparable age.

We first analyzed all of the 2395 utterances in the 13 natural speech samples in order to extract those utterances which were what we labeled "potential *pro* drop clauses" (PPDCs). The resulting number of these is shown on Table 1. This category was defined to include all declarative clauses with explicit verbs. Thus, a complex utterance could have more than one clause in which a small *pro* subject would be appropriate. We excluded all imperatives, questions, and sentences with an implicit copula or implicit verb. Examples of each category are given in the Appendix.

[1] The category pronoun includes both personal and demonstratives.

General results

In our Spanish speaking subjects, we found early competence in a variety of syntactic structures. In Table 1 in the Appendix, we give examples of types of syntactic competence demonstrated by our subjects, including use of the subjunctive mood, relative clauses, VP ellipsis, impersonal *se*, and arbitrary plural subjects.

In this paper, we compared the overall occurrence of null and lexical pronominal subjects in PPDCs, and we found that null subjects appear at the earliest MLU stage, and remain productive across development. We found that in Spanish, the lexical pronominal subject appears to be a marked option at all MLUs, with only one occurrence of an overt pronominal among the five children at the low end of the MLU range (as compared with 17 null pronouns in these subjects). First we looked at Spanish speaking children's syntactic knowledge regarding null subjects. Specifically we asked (1) How do early Spanish speaking children show knowledge of the licensing requirements of small *pro*?, (2) Is there a correlation between correct verbal inflection and the presence of null subjects?

Given the claim made by Rizzi (1986), among others, that verbal morphology plays a role in licensing null subjects, we wanted to examine its co-occurrence with null subjects in our samples. Thus we coded all utterances in which null subjects appeared, looking specifically at the verbal morphology. We reported these results in our Penn State paper (Austin et al. 1995b), where we showed that Spanish speaking children master the verbal inflection system of their language early and well. This finding contrasts with that which we obtained for the English speaking children in our earlier study. In English, there was little consistent use of verbal morphology except for the child with the highest MLU studied (3.68). (1) shows some Spanish examples of the critical cases we measured here, namely, null or overt subjects with or without verbal inflectional tense and agreement (TA) morphology.

(1) a. Overt subject +tense/agr morphology:
Estoy haciendo yo. 'I am doing *e*.' (AL; MLU 4.33)
b. Overt subject -tense/agr morphology:
No examples in Spanish
c. Null subject +tense/agr morphology:
pro *es grande*. 'It is big.' (JP1; MLU 1.74)
d. Null subject -tense/agr morphology:
Ahí... e volando... toma. 'Over there, flying...here.' (NR; MLU 4.00)

We found no cases in Spanish of a verbal stem with no morphology whatsoever.[2] With regard to the presence or absence of verbal TA morphology with null subjects, the main finding was that every time the TA morphology was missing, the entire auxiliary was also missing, as in (8) below. Examples of this kind account for 10.29% of *PPDUs* across all subjects (excluding cases of PRO subjects with infinitival verbs).

Comparison of contexts in which null and lexical pronominals occur

In previous acquisition studies, most researchers have not examined the discourse context in which null subjects occur. However, in *pro*-drop, context plays a crucial role in identifying the referent of the null subject and in determining the acceptability of its occurrence. We separated out the third person subjects from the first and second person ones. Our reason for doing this was our assumption that first and second person subjects would always have a pragmatic antecedent in the form of the speaker or hearer. We selected third person (singular or plural) pronominals for context analysis (excluding expletives and PRO).

A *pragmatic antecedent* was any non-linguistic entity in the environment; for example the subject, the data collector and any other participants, something in the room, or in a picture book, whether or not referred to by name, as in (2a). A *linguistic antecedent* was one which was explicitly identified in the discourse, as in (3a, b).

(2) a. Adult: *¿Con qué te las limpias tú?* (EH; 3.66)
'What do you clean them with?'
Child: *Papito, le hizo un hueco.*
(child is referring to the data collector)
'Daddy, (she) made a hole in it'

(3) a. Adult: *¿Un mosquito?* (NR; 4.77)
'A mosquito?'
Child: *¡Ay!, me picó*
'Ay! (It) bit me'
b. Adult: *¿Por qué está llorando tu hermanita, ah?* (MA; 3.76)
'Why is your little sister crying?'
Child: *Po'que se cayó.*
'Because (she) fell down'

---

[2] We did not expect to find any cases of a bare verbal stem in Spanish without any verbal morphology whatsoever, but we hypothesized that we might find infinitives in tensed clause contexts.

We found a total of 234 3rd person null subjects vs. 39 3rd person overt pronoun subjects.[3] The overt pronoun subjects comprise 12% of the total of third person subjects (including NPs), and the null subjects comprise 72%. As shown in Figure 1, we found that nearly all the third person pronoun subjects, both null and overt, had either a pragmatic or a linguistic antecedent.

Percentage of 3rd person null and overt pronoun subjects having no antecedent

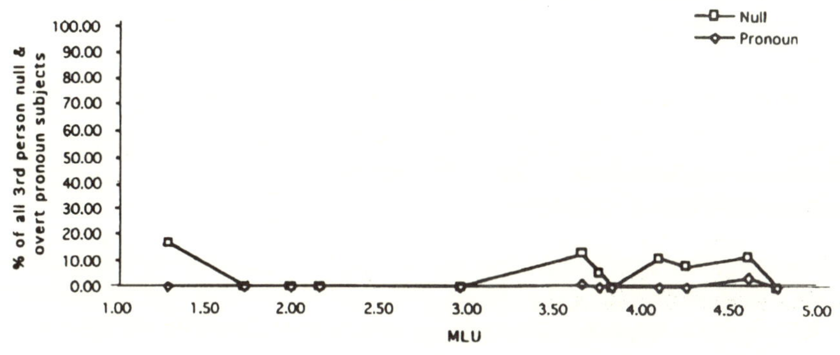

Figure 1

After MLU 3.5, there was a slight increase in the number of null subject without a pragmatic or linguistic antecedent, but the overwhelming majority still had one type or antecedent or the other. These results suggest that the Spanish-speaking child knows that both forms of pronominals need identification. Before, we had shown that syntactic competence for licensing null pronominal subjects is present from the earliest MLUs tested. Now we have shown that children also have the general pragmatic competence necessary for identifying pronominal null or overt subjects.

---

[3] The overt pronouns include personal pronouns and demonstratives.

Development in the interaction between syntax and pragmatics

Up to this point, we may have given the impression that Spanish speaking children do not show any development in their grammar.[4] In our next analyses, we identify two areas where there does appear to be development. These are both areas where the child must integrate knowledge of discourse factors with syntactic knowledge. The first area in which we found development was in auxiliary omission. The examples in (4) show some null auxiliaries that are questionable. In Spanish, we never found examples of a child omitting an auxiliary yet including an overt subject, which we found in child English. However, the Spanish speaking child sometimes omits the auxiliary (and loses the verbal morphology) when she answers a question in present indicative with the present progressive form, as shown in (4a-e). The problem is that these examples contain a mismatch between the tense and agreement features of the adult's question and those of the child's response.

(4) a. Adult: *¿Y qué hacen?* (AL; MLU 4.61)
'And what do they do?'
Child ??*Jugando a cuentos.*
'Playing (with) stories'
b. Adult: *¿Qué hace?* (SC; MLU 3.84)
'What does it do?'
Child: ??*Comiendo las hierbas.*
'Eating grass'
c. Adult: *¿Qué hacen ahí?* (SC; MLU 3.84)
'What do they do there?'
Child: ??*Comiendo.*
'Eating'
d. Adult: *¿Y qué haces allí adentro?* (EH; MLU 3.66)
'What do you do in there?'
Child: ??*Buscando mis cosas, pero no están.*
'Looking for my things, but (they) are not (here)'
e. Adult: *¿Qué hace el gato?* (MA; MLU 3.76)
'What does the cat do?'
Child: ??*Comiendo comida.*
'Eating food'

---

[4] In fact, although not directly related to this paper, we noted that Spanish speaking children have difficulty with some syntactic structures such as flip verbs (like *gustar*), tense, aspect, and mood, and our youngest subjects occasionally omitted copula *ser*. Examples are shown in Table 2 of the Appendix.

f. Adult: *¿Qué estás haciendo?* (GR; MLU 2.16)
'What are you doing?'
Child: ??*Jugar*.
'To play'

The present tense is semantically ambiguous in Spanish. It can be interpreted either as having a habitual aspect or a present progressive one. Thus, a question such as (5a) could be answered either with a present progressive, *están durmiendo* —as the child does— or with a present indicative form, *duermen*. The fact that the child answers with a present progressive form suggests that she understands this ambiguity. It could be argued that children use the present progressive to answer these questions because they don't know how to use present indicative, but as shown in (6), children in our study correctly and consistently use present indicative. The null auxiliary would be correct if s/he were answering a present progressive question, i.e. a question with an overt auxiliary, as shown in the examples in (5).

(5) a. Adult: *¿Y qué hacen?* (SC; MLU 3.84)
'And what do they do?'
Child: *Están también dumiendo*.
'(They) are also sleeping'
b Adult: *Y tu amatxu, ¿dónde está?* (AL; MLU 4.61)
'And your mommy, where is (she)?'
Child: *Tabajando*.
'Working'
c. Adult: *Tú estás leyendo, y él, ¿qué está haciendo?* (EH; MLU 3.66)
'You are reading, and him, what is he doing'
Child: Pintando.
'Painting'

(6) Adult: *¿Qué le hace ella?* (EH MLU 3.66)
'What does she do to it'
Child: *Le hace "wooo"!*
'(She) does "wooo" to it'
(could also be "le está haciendo «wooo»!" '(she) is doing "wooo" to it')

Thus, the context of the preceding utterance is the crucial factor which is needed to license a null auxiliary in the response. In answering the type of question like (5a), Spanish speaking children need to be aware of three factors: first, that the tense/aspect features of the question and answer have to match; second, that the auxiliary can be null or overt; and third, that if there is a null auxiliary, then it has to have a linguistic antecedent. As we showed, our subjects appeared to know that null subjects had to be licensed and identified either by a pragmatic or linguistic antecedent. However, they seemed to extend the identification requirements for null subjects to null auxiliaries and thus had trouble realizing that a null auxiliary must have a linguistic antecedent, rather than a pragmatic one.

This distinction between linguistic and pragmatic antecedents is similar to Hankamer and Sag's (1976) claim that certain syntactic elements in discourse must have a linguistic antecedent while others merely require a pragmatic antecedent. The alternation between present progressive and habitual aspect in Spanish is independent of the occurrence of null subjects. It is also independent of the child's syntactic knowledge, since these examples are potentially syntactically well-formed given an appropriate context (for example, if the response in (4c) were given to the question *¿Qué están haciendo?*). If it were the case that examples such as (4a-e) reflected a simple confusion between habitual and progressive aspect, we might expect to find examples in which the child responds to a progressive question with a present indicative form. We never found such examples in the data.

Dialectal variation

It seems that there is dialectal variation as to the acceptability of responses such as (4). We did a brief preliminary survey of the acceptability of these responses among adult native-speakers of Spanish. These adults were from Spain, Peru and Puerto Rico, and thus were speakers of the same dialects as the children we studied. We didn't get consistent acceptability judgments for these question-answer pairs either between speakers of each dialect or within dialects. This finding is preliminary and we need to compare it with results from analyses of adult natural speech and experimental data. Nevertheless, the data we have right now suggests two possibilities, as given in (7):

(7)A. The child use of a null auxiliary response is consistent with that of the adult speakers of his/her dialect.

There is such variability in the adult use of null vs. lexical responses even within a given dialect that the child doesn't have a clear model to follow.

B. The child use of a null auxiliary response is not consistent with that of the adult speakers of his/her dialect. This possibility could be attributed to the following reasons:

i. The child has a deficit in the knowledge of the pragmatic factors that govern the distribution of the null auxiliary responses.
ii. This distribution interacts with other factors, such as constituent length or choice of verb rather than purely syntactic or pragmatic factors. In this case the child is developing his/her knowledge of the idiosyncratic factors beyond the syntax of the utterance that permit the null auxiliary responses.

In any case, this knowledge is pragmatic as well as syntactic and it is language-specific. It cannot be fully pre-programmed by Universal Grammar and thus must be learned by the child.

Pronoun overuse

Another area where we found development was in the use of overt pronoun subjects. Like the distribution of null auxiliaries, we have suggested above that the use of overt pronoun subjects involves language specific knowledge which integrates syntax and pragmatics.

In these analyses, we first separated out the null and overt pronouns by person and number features, as given in the bar graph in Figure 2:

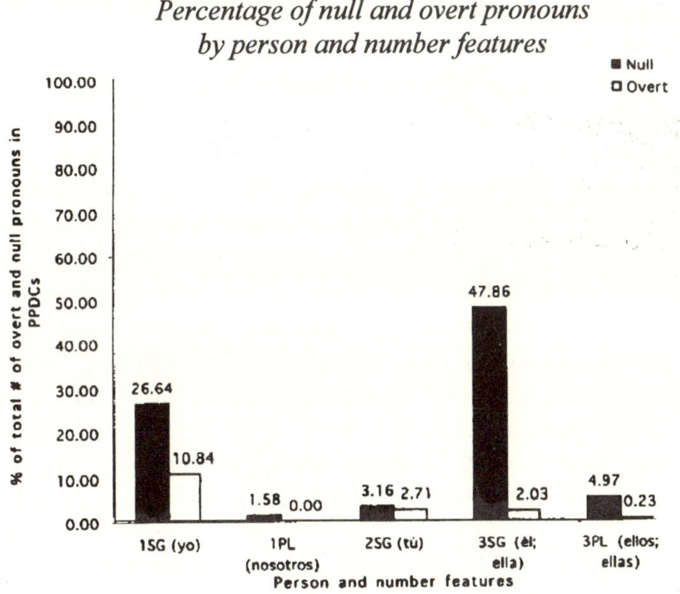

Figure 2

Our results show that children produce a greater proportion of the first person singular overt pronoun *yo* than of any other overt pronoun. The finding that 69% of the children's overt pronouns were occurrences of the first person singular *yo* was surprising, since first person singular always has a pragmatic antecedent which should license a null subject pronoun. It is not clear to us whether this result reflects development in the use of pronouns, or that the excessive use of the first person singular overt pronoun is due to extralinguistic factors, such as the child's egocentric discourse style. Larson and Luján (1992) propose that overt pronouns in adult Spanish are only used for emphasis or contrast; under this analysis, our Spanish speaking subjects do not seem to have acquired this language specific constraint on the distribution of overt pronouns. This suggests that the use of overt pronouns is an area where development takes place, even though children's knowledge of the licensing and identification of null pronouns is present from early on.

Conclusion

In conclusion, our previous results in which we found little evidence for development in the knowledge of the syntax of *pro*-drop led us to initiate a more refined analysis of the precise environments in which null subjects occur in child Spanish. When we did, we found examples where children seem to make errors in integrating pragmatic and syntactic factors. This led us to look at the inter-sentential context of utterances, or what Hankamer and Sag call "the syntax of discourse", rather than examining utterances in isolation.

We have argued that Spanish-speaking children know the syntactic requirements of small pro subjects. That is, they know that null pronoun subjects require both licensing and identification. Licensing requirements are fulfilled by verbal tense/AGR marking, which Spanish-speaking children master from the beginning of speech production. Here our results provide a remarkable contrast with our earlier findings for English: whereas the English-speaking child quite commonly omits tense and agreement features, the Spanish-speaking child does so only rarely, even at the lowest MLUs. They also recognize the need for an antecedent to identify null and overt pronominal subjects, and they know that a pragmatic antecedent fulfills this requirement as well as a linguistic one.

Our results provide subtle evidence of development in the first language acquisition of Spanish. We localized this development in the integration of syntax and pragmatics. We identified contexts where the children produced null auxiliaries which were not licensed by the discourse because they did not match the features of the verbal antecedent in the previous utterance. Although children at these MLUs demonstrate a good deal of knowledge about aspects of syntactic well-formedness related to *pro*-drop, they still have to acquire the language-specific knowledge of how and when to use null subjects and null auxiliaries together in discourse. Children acquiring Spanish seem to believe that only a pragmatic antecedent is required to identify a null auxiliary, when in fact what is needed is a linguistic antecedent. Boser (1995) found similar evidence in children acquiring German, who use verb initial utterances with dropped topicalized phrases that have pragmatic antecedents. In adult German, the topicalized phrase can only be omitted when it has a linguistic antecedent and Boser's work shows that this is an area where children have to integrate language-specific constraints on the distribution of null elements with knowledge of syntax. We argue that there is a parallel case in the area of *pro*-drop in child Spanish. The Spanish speaking child shows early knowledge of syntax (i.e., the licensing and identification of null pronouns) in tandem with a longer process of integrating this syntactic knowledge with language-specific pragmatics, in order to construct and interpret the larger structures of discourse.

The primary result of the research reported here is a change in focus from the way in which null subjects have been investigated previously. If we had limited ourselves to looking at the purely syntactic aspects of the use of *pro*-drop in our subjects, we would have seen very little development, since their syntactic knowledge is so good from the beginning. Only by looking at the wider discourse context have we found where development is taking place; that is, in language specific interactions between syntax and pragmatics which must be learned.

REFERENCES

Austin, Jennifer, María Blume, Barbara Lust, Zelmira Núñez del Prado, David Parkinson, & Reyna Proman. 1996. "Current challenges to the Parameter-setting Paradigm: The *pro*-drop parameter". *Proceedings of GALA* 95, ed. by Charlotte Koster and Frank Wijnen, 87-96. Groningen: Centre for Language and Cognition, Groningen.

Austin, Jennifer, María Blume, Barbara Lust, Zelmira Núñez del Prado, David Parkinson, & Reyna Proman. 1995b. "The Status of Pro-drop in the Initial State: Results from New Analyses of Spanish/English Contrasts". To appear in *Proceedings of the Penn State Conference on the Acquisition of Spanish as a First or Second Language*, ed. by Ana Teresa Pérez-Leroux & William Glass.

Bloom, Paul. 1990. "Subjectless Sentences in Child Language". *Linguistic Inquiry* 21.491-504.

———. 1993. "Grammatical Continuity in Language Development: The Case of Subjectless Sentences" *Linguistic Inquiry* 24.721-734.

Boser, Katharina. 1995. "Verb Initial Utterances in Early Child German: A Study of the Interaction of Grammar and Pragmatics. *Proceedings of the 27th Stanford Child Language Forum*, ed. Eve V. Clark. Stanford, Cal: CSLI.

Brown, Roger. 1973. *A First Language: The Early Stages.* Cambridge, Mass.: Harvard University Press.

Gerken, LouAnn. 1991. "The Metrical Basis for Children's Subjectless Sentences". *Journal of Memory and Language* 30.1-21.

Grinstead, John. 1995. "The Emergence of Nominative Case Assignment in Child Catalan and Spanish". *Proceedings of the 19th Annual Boston University Conference on Language Development*, Vol. 1, ed. by Dawn MacLaughlin and Susan McEwen, 216-227. Somerville, Mass.: Cascadilla Press.

Hankamer, Jorge & Ivan Sag. 1976. "Deep and Surface Anaphora". *Linguistic Inquiry* 390-428.

Hyams, Nina. 1986. *Language Acquisition and the Theory of Parameters.* Dordrecht: Reidel.

———. 1994. "The Underspecification of Functional Categories in Early Grammar". Ms., UCLA.

———, & Kenneth Wexler. 1993. "On the Grammatical Basis of Null Subjects in Child Language". *Linguistic Inquiry* 24.421-459.

Jaeggli, Osvaldo, & Nina Hyams. 1987. "Morphological Uniformity and the Setting of the Null Subject Parameter". *Proceedings of the North Eastern Linguistics Society* 18.238-253. GLSA, University of Massachusetts.

Kapur, Shyam. 1994. "Some Applications of Formal Learning Theory Results to Natural Language Acquisition". In Lust, Hermon, & Kornfilt, 491-508.

Larson, Richard & Marta Luján. 1992. "Focused pronouns". Ms.

Lust, Barbara, Yu-Chin Chien, Chi-Pang Chiang, & Julie Eisele. 1996. "Chinese Pronominals in Universal Grammar: A Study of Linear Precedence and Command in Chinese and English Children's First Language Acquisition. *Journal of East Asian Linguistics* 5.1-47.

———, Gabriella Hermon, & Jaklin Kornfilt, eds. 1994. *Syntactic Theory and First Language Acquisition: Cross-Linguistic Perspectives, Vol. 2: Binding, Dependencies, and Learnability.* Hillsdale, New Jersey: Lawrence Erlbaum Associates.

Mazuka, Reiko. 1995. "Can a Grammatical Parameter Be Set Before the First Word?" *Signal to Syntax* ed. by J. Morgan & K. Demuth. Hillsdale, N.J.: Lawrence Erlbaum Associates.

———, Barbara Lust, Tatsuko Wayakama, & Wendy Snyder. 1995. "Null Subject Grammar and Phrase Structure in Early Syntax Acquisition: A Cross-linguistic Study of Japanese and English". *Recherches Linguistiques de Vincennes.*

Montalbetti, Mario. 1984. *After Binding: On the Interpretation of Pronouns.* Ph.D. dissertation, MIT.

Núñez del Prado, Zelmira, Claire Foley, Reyna Pıoman, & Barbara Lust. 1994. "Subordinate CP and Pro-drop: Evidence for Degree-n Learnability from an Experimental Study of Spanish and English". *Proceedings of the North Eastern Linguistics Society* 24, ed. by Mercè Gonzàlez, 443-460. GLSA, University of Massachusetts.

Pierce, Amy. 1994. "On the Differing Status of Subject Pronouns in French and English Child Language. In Lust, Hermon, & Kornfilt, eds., 319-334.

Radford, Andrew. 1990. *Syntactic Theory and the Acquisition of English Syntax.* Oxford: Basil Blackwell.

Rizzi, Luigi. 1986. "Null Objects in Italian and the Theory of *pro*". *Linguistic Inquiry* 17.501-557.

———. 1994. "Early Null Subjects and Root Null Subjects". In Lust, Hermon, & Kornfilt, 249-272.

Sano, Tetsuya, & Nina Hyams. 1994. "Agreement, Finiteness, and the Development of Null Arguments". *Proceedings of the North Eastern Linguistics Society* 24, ed. by Mercè Gonzàlez. GLSA, University of Massachusetts.

Valian, Virginia. 1991. "Syntactic Subjects in the Early Speech of American and Italian Children. *Cognition* 40.21-81.

———, James Hoeffner & Stephanie Aubry. 1996. "Young Children's Imitation of Sentence Subjects: Evidence of Processing Limitations". *Developmental Psychology* 32(1).153-164.

APPENDIX

Examples of PPDC utterances:

(1) **I. Subject types in potential pro-drop clauses:**

a. *Null subject:*

Adult: *¿Qué está haciendo el perrito?*
'What is the doggie doing?'
Child: pro *está en su casa.*
'(He) is at home.' (AL; MLU 4.61)

b. *Pronoun subject:*

Adult: *Yo creo que el gatito se escondió.*
'I think that the kitty hid.'
Child: *¡Párate! Pa' que tú lo vea.'*
'Stand up! So that you can see him.' (MA; MLU 3.76)

c. *NP subject:*

Adult *¿Qué pasa en el patio?*
'What happens in the patio?'
Child: *Ahí, y eto, me picó un moquito.*
'There, and this, a mosquito bit me.' (NR; MLU 4.77)

II. Verb types excluded from potential pro-drop clauses:

a. *Implicit copula:*

Adult: *¡Ala! ¡Cuántas cosas!*
'Wow! So many things.'
Child: *Mira un nene, esto un palo.*
'Look, a little boy, this a stick.' (AB; MLU 4.10)

b. *Implicit verb:*

Adult: *Muy bien. Y yo digo: el perro va al parque.*
'Very good. And I say: the dog goes to the park.'
Child: *Al paque el perro.*
'To the park the dog.' (AB; MLU 4.10)

III. Verb types included in potential pro-drop clauses:

a. *Explicit verb:*

Adult: *¿Es una tarta?*
'Is (it) a cake?'
Child: *Mira, y esto es la múkika (música).*
'Look, and this is the music.' (AB; MLU 4.10)

b. *Implicit auxiliary:*

Adult: *¿Qué hace?*
'What is (he) doing?'
Child: *Comiendo la hierbas.*
'Eating grass.' (SC; MLU 3.84)

Table 1

Some syntactic proficiencies

Subject	MLU	Age	Construction and Examples
			VP Ellipsis:
EH	3.66	2;11	*"Puedo tocar pero tú no"* '(I) can touch but you can't'
FB	4.26	3;04	*"Po'que está que no piende (prende) y con la fila (pila) tampoco"* 'Because (it) won't start and not even with the battery'
			Relative Clauses:
SC	3.84	2;03	*"Gachito (gatito) que está bailando con este patito"* 'Little cat that is dancing with this little duck'
NR	4.77	2;10	*"El que se salió"* 'The one that fell out'
			***Se* Impersonal:**
MA	3.76	2;06	*"Este no se toca"* 'This one can't be touched'
EH	3.66	2;11	*"Se maneja"* 'It is driven/ one drives it'

Table 1(Continuation)

Subject	MLU	Age	Construction and Examples
			Arbitrary Plural Subject:
AL	4.61	2;06	*"Están llamando a la puerta, ¿eh?"* '(They) are knocking at the door'
EH	3.66	2;11	*"Mira, a éste le sacaron los gordos"* 'Look, (they) took out the stuffing from it' (a doll)
			Subjunctive:
MA	3.76	2;06	*"Cuando yo tenga tos año', yo voy pa' l'e'cuela"* 'When I am two, I'll go to school'
EH	3.66	2;11	*"Papá, yo quiero que me lleves al circo para que vea payasos"* 'Dad, I want (you) to take me to the circus so that (I) can see clowns'

Table 2
Some syntactic difficulties

Subject	MLU	Age	Construction and Examples
			Flip verbs:
AB	4.10	2;03	**Eto te has caído* (There is also a *se* missing) 'This to you (you) have fallen' ('This has fallen on you')
SC	3.84	2;03	* *Me gusta los gatitos* 'To me pleases cats' ('I like cats')
AL	4.61	2;06	* *¿Te gustas pan?* 'To you (you) please bread?' ('Do you like bread?')
			Subjunctive:
AL	4.61	2;06	* *Pa' que hace puiii* (last word unclear) 'So that it does puiii'
EH	3.66	2;11	**Para que yo duerme acá* 'So that I sleep here'

Table 2 (Continuation)

Subject	MLU	Age	Construction and Examples
			Infinitives:
SC	3.84	2;03	**No puedo cogí la luna* '(I) can't (I) caught the moon'
MA	3.76	2;06	**A compra chique* (chicle) 'To buy (3sg., present) gum'
			Wrong person agreement:
JP3	2.97	2;00	* *Se fues a dormir* (should be *fueron*) '(They) go (3sg, past, plural) to sleep'
			Null copula:
SC	3.84	2;03	**Esto no bueno* 'This no good'
AB	4.10	2;03	**Esto un palo* 'This a stick'
GR	2.16	2;03	* *¿ Qué eto?* 'What this?'
MA	3.76	2;06	**¿Eso agua?* 'That water?'
			Null auxiliary:
AL	4.61	2;06	**¿Qué encontrao?* 'What found?'
			Null main verb:
AB	4.10	2;03	Adult: *El perro va al parque.* 'The dog goes to the park' Child: **Al paque el perro.* 'To the park the dog'
			Wrong aspect:
FB	4.26	3;04	Adult: *¿No era noche?* 'Wasn't (imperfect) (it) night' Child: * *De noche fue* '(It) was (preterite) night'

THE MYTH OF EQUIVALENCE
WHERE TWO LIGHTS DO NOT MAKE A LONG[1]

BARBARA E. BULLOCK
Penn State University

0. *Introduction*

Under current analyses of stress systems, trochaic rhythm is characterized by a rather rigid binarism where the primary constituents of a foot are equal (Hayes 1985, 1995, Hyman 1977, Prince 1990). In quantity-sensitive (QS) languages, this translates into a moraic trochee where the foot is either bisyllabic or monosyllabic as in (1), a formalization of the 'principle of equivalence' from classical metrics whereby two short/light syllables are equivalent to one long/heavy syllable.

(1) Moraic Trochee: (QS): Feet are (LL) or (H)

(* .) or (*)
$(\sigma\sigma_\mu\sigma_\mu)$ $(\sigma_{\mu\mu})$

In quantity insensitive (QI) languages the foot must be the binary syllabic trochee in (2).

(2) Syllabic Trochee: (QI): Weight is irrelevant.

(*.)
$(\sigma\sigma)$

Briefly, trochees are distinguished by the evenness of the primary components of their feet, either morae or syllables. Left-dominant quantity sensitive feet of the traditional sort $(\sigma_{\mu\mu}\sigma_\mu)$ = (HL) which are not symmetrical and

[1] I would like to thank the participants of the LSRL for their helpful comments on this paper and particularly for their reassurance that this subtitle appropriately and literally reflects the arguments of this article despite its *ludique* nature. I express a special debt to Andrea Calabrese, Randall Gess, Haike Jacobs, Richard Kayne, Mario Saltarelli and Caroline Wiltshire whose insightful comments have led to improvements in this analysis.

which exceed a moraic binarity are considered to be less optimal than the foot typology in (1) and in some accounts, they are excluded (Kager 1993).

In this paper, I argue against the strictly binary or even view of the foot based on data from two languages which I assume to manifest trochaic feet, Italian and French. I propose that both languages allow uneven trochees generally in their prosodic systems. Italian, a QS language, displays uneven feet that are binary (in that they are bisyllabic) but which exceed a bimoraic maximum. That is, feet in Italian are generally (HL). French, often considered to be the prototypical QI language (Halle and Vergnaud 1987), only permits a binary foot under special conditions, specifically when a full syllable is followed by a syllable containing the reduced schwa.[2] The sole French binary foot is, then, crucially uneven. These proposals, combined with the assumption that French and Italian are trochaic languages give us the typology in (3) which I take as the point of departure for the present analysis.

(3)
- Assumed: French and Italian are trochaic (cf. Selkirk 1978, Montreuil 1993, Jacobs 1994, Bullock 1995 on French; Sluyters 1990, Bullock 1991, Repetti 1991, Prieto 1994 on Italian)
- Binary Feet: Italian = [HL]; French = [σ x] where x = schwa

The foot structures in (3) depart from current metrical and prosodic theory in a crucial way by reintroducing the uneven foot into the inventory of trochees. However, in support of the notion that languages have an overall tendency to move toward optimizing prosodic structure, it will be demonstrated that both languages tend to eliminate the uneven foot within certain prosodic environments and, specifically, within their prosodic morphology. Following McCarthy and Prince (1994), I argue that what emerges from the prosodic phonology and morphology of French and Italian is a minimal Prosodic Word (PrWd) that is predicated of the syllable rather than of a binary foot. The implication of this analysis, as summarized in (4b), is that while French is moving toward eliminating the foot altogether from the Prosodic Hierarchy shown in (4a), Italian has a strict adherence of the hierarchy such that no level can

[2] My analysis of the foot in French follows that of Selkirk (1978) who was the first to propose a role for the foot in this language. I share with her the notion that the foot has a restricted role in the prosody of the language; a detailed analysis of the French foot is contained within Bullock (1995a).

be skipped; thus, morae must be directly parsed into a syllable which is, in turn, parsed into a foot.

(4)

a. Prosodic Hierarchy (Selkirk 1986, Nespor and Vogel 1986):

$$\text{PrWd} > \text{Foot } \varphi > \text{Syllable } \sigma > \text{Mora } \mu$$

b. Restructuring of the Uneven Foot and its Resultant Prosodic Word

	Uneven Foot (φ)		Emergent (σ)	Implication (PrWd)
Italian:	(HL)	⇒	(H)	Parse $^{\mu}/\sigma$: $\varphi = \sigma_{\mu\mu}$
				*Parse$^{\mu}/\varphi$: $\varphi \neq \mu\mu$
French:	(σ x)	⇒	(σ)	Eliminate φ

This paper proceeds as follows. In section 1, I introduce the basic theory assumed in this paper, Optimality Theory, and apply it to an analysis of the role of the uneven foot in Standard and Southern Standard French. In section 2, I draw a parallel between the QI uneven foot in French and the QS uneven foot in Italian and demonstrate that, regardless of the parameter of quantity sensitivity, each language manifests both uneven and unary feet. In section 3, I discuss the emergence of the unary foot in the prosodic morphology of these languages and argue that various truncation processes in these languages conspire to eliminate the uneven foot type in word formation and that the unary foot which surfaces in the prosodic morphology is equivalent to the minimal PrWd in both Italian and French.

1. *The uneven foot in French*

In the theory assumed here, Optimality Theory (OT), a set of constraints which regulate metrical structure and prosodic structure, along with alignment constraints that regulate the correspondence of constituent edges, are universally present in every language. One essential characteristic of this theory is that no constraint is completely unavailable or inactive in a language (Prince and Smolensky 1993, McCarthy and Prince 1993). A constraint that may be generally submerged in a grammar because it is dominated by higher ranked constraints may emerge when those constraints are no longer present in a particular input (McCarthy and Prince 1994).

The universal constraint on Foot Binarity that requires feet to contain either two syllables or two morae appears to play very little role is a language like French where stress arguably forms a demarcative function, falling regularly on the final syllable of a word, as demonstrated in (5).[3]

(5) Stress in Standard French

a. underived forms:	universi'té 'university', mai'son 'house', Thaï'lande 'Thailand'
b. suffixed forms:	universi'taire, maison'nette, Thaïlan'dais
c. verbal forms:	don'nez 'you (pl.) give', donnez-moi-'z-en 'give me some'

Notice that in (5c), final stress falls even on a normally unstressable pronoun if it is in enclitic position.

A problematic aspect to a simple statement of French stress concerns the phonological status of schwa, particularly a word final schwa. Some researchers assume that it is present in the input since within some varieties of French and under some circumstances in Standard French, it may surface, as in the items in (6) and cause penultimate stress (cf. Dell 1976: 237ff.).

(6) Surface word final schwa

a. compounds:	porte̲-plume 'pen-holder', garde̲-fou 'guard-rail'
b. external sandhi:	texte̲ discursif 'discursive text', enorme̲ cyclone 'enormous tornado'

Others have argued that schwa is not underlyingly present but inserted in the output form to break up consonant clusters since, in some cases, it may surface where it is not orthographically present, as in (7).

(7) Final schwa insertion

ours(e) blanc 'white bear', film(e) tchèque 'Czech film'

For the purposes of this paper, I will assume that schwa, the only reduced vowel in French, is not a phoneme rather it is a possible phonetic realization of an empty nucleus position. Within an OT framework, empty structure is

---

[3] I take a conservative stance with regard to stress in French in this paper by claiming that the word final syllable is prominent; this prominence is most noticeably marked by an increase in duration relative to nonfinal syllables.

avoided as it automatically presents a violation of the faithfulness of a candidate output with respect to the structure of the input. In OT, every syllable position must be filled by phonetic material, a contraint formalized as FILL (Prince and Smolensky 1993:25).

The facts of French stress can now be derived as follows. A stressable syllable cannot be formed over an empty nucleus, either in Standard French or southern varieties of French, presumably since phonetic material must be present in order to attract stress. Thus, in cases of a word final, orthographic schwa, there are two possible candidate outputs to consider, one in which the final empty nucleus is present although not stressable and another in which it is simply absent. If present, the empty nucleus must be cliticized to the material to its left; this is the uneven foot. Stress is computed to fall on the rightmost Foot (C) in French, either the uneven trochaic foot, or a fully specified syllable. Relevant candidate outputs illustrating these two scenarios with respect to the constraints necessary to determine optimal prosodic structure are given in (8) where parentheses indicate foot boundaries, a period equals a syllable boundary and empty structure is symbolized by a box.

(8) Relevant Constraints

	Edgemost	Fill	No Coda	Foot Binarity
maiso(net)	√	√	*	*
maiso(ne.t□)	√	*	√	√

In (8), stress falls on the edgemost foot in both cases and is thus satisfied. No Coda, a universal constraint against syllable codas, and Foot Binarity derive the same results and thus cannot be ranked with respect to one another over these forms. Thus, Fill is the tie breaking constraint over these output forms and it turns out to be the dominant constraint in Standard French. In Midi French, however, NoCoda and Foot Binarity (again unranked) hold over Fill giving us the rankings in (9).

(9) Constraint rankings in French

Standard French:	Fill >> NoCoda/Foot Binarity
Midi French:	NoCoda/Foot Bin >> Fill

The same results obtain word internally in Standard French. That is, the faithfulness constraint, Fill, dominates most syllabic and metric constraints as demonstrated in (10a) where the wellformed output is checked in the tableau.

(10) Word Internal Schwa 'Deletion' (input *échelon*)

	Fill	NoCoda/Ft. Binarity
e(ch□.lon)	*!	
√(ech)(lon) [eʃlč)]		*

However, not all prosodic constraints are dominated by the prohibition against Fill; the form in (11) shows that the schwa does surface when a more serious violation of syllabic conditions prevail such as the prohibition against coda clusters, formalized as COMPLEX.

(11) Word Internal Schwa in Output (forgeron 'blacksmith' [fɔʀʒəʀč)]

	Complex\coda	Fill	No Coda	Ft. Bin
(forg)(ron)	*!		**	*
√(for.g□.)(ron)			*	**

The form in (11) is instructive in that it shows the conditions under which a binary foot surfaces in French, some of the same conditions shown for the forms in (6) and (7) above. That is, in order to avoid a violation of the Complex constraint, the epenthetic form is preferred to one with no Fill violation. It also demonstrates that Foot Binarity and No Coda are not necessarily intrinsically linked since multiple violations of No Coda may be accrued without a violation of Foot Binarity.

Complex codas are admitted word finally in French. This cannot be accounted for by assuming that morphological to prosodic alignment demands that the right edge of a Lexical Word (LxWd) aligns with the right edge of the final segment as formalized in (12).

(12) Word final alignment

Align (LxWd, R, Segment R)

Example: port] $|_{\text{LxWord}}$

The alignment constraint, active only at the domain edge, outranks the prohibition on complex codas in French, allowing words to end in a consonant cluster.

This discussion of French has shown that a binary, uneven foot can and does surface in French but only as a bi-product of a convergence of prosodic and faithfulness constraints. However, violations of Foot Binarity are common in the language, demonstrating that it is generally a low ranked constraint and that the language tends to eliminate binary, unbalanced feet in favor of a single, well formed syllable.

2. *The uneven foot in Italian*

An extension of the uneven foot analysis into Standard Italian involves factoring in constraints on syllabic quantity since Italian manifests lengthening properties that are characteristic of QS languages. In central Standard Italian, vowels are lengthened in stressed open syllables while vowels in closed syllables remain short as shown by the comparisons in (13).

(13) Open Syllable lengthening

a.	bara 'tomb'	[bá:ra]	-vs-	barra 'spacebar'	[bár:a]
b.	cosa 'thing'	[kɔ́:sa]		Corso 'Corsican'	[kɔ́rso]
c.	matemàtica	[matemá:tica][4]		mantica 'mantic'	[mántika]

The current standard interpretation of syllabic constraints in Italian is that sonorant consonants and geminates are mapped to moras in the syllable coda; their presence then satisfies the quantitative bimoraic minimum for a stressed syllable (Saltarelli 1970, 1983, Itô 1986, Bullock 1991a, 1991b).[5] In the absence of a parseable coda consonant, vowels must lengthen to fulfill the weight requirements of the stressed syllable.

It is important to point out at this juncture that a bimoraic minimum is enforced within a single syllable constituent. That is, two light syllables are not equivalent to a single heavy in Italian. Thus, forms like those in the rightmost column of (14) do not occur as output forms in central standard Italian.

---

[4] Andrea Calabrese (pc) has indicated that he does not lengthen vowels in stressed antepenultimate position but Sluyters (1990:81,fn.10) points out that 'absence of vowel length in proparoxytones is not the general rule'. This absence of vowel length is not particularly troublesome for the present analysis since the varieties of Italian without lengthened penults may accept (LL) feet along with (HL) since penults do seem to be generally lengthened.

[5] Saltarelli (1995a, 1995b) proposes that Italian stress may be computed without respect to syllable weight. By using a three syllable window approach to stress, similar to that of Burzio and DiFabio (1994), Saltarelli argues that Italian is anti-trochaic, manifesting dactylic feet. I agree with Saltarelli that Italian primary stress is not computable on the basis of syllable weight. I maintain, however, that the lengthening properties of Italian are predictable from stress not vice-versa and that such properties indicate a role, albeit restricted, for quantity in the language.

(14)

(HL)	(HL)	(LL)
[fá:to] 'fate'	[fát:o] 'did', past.part	*[fa.to]
[pó:sa] 'intermission'	[pós:a] 'can' 3rd.sg	*[po.sa]

I assume that Italian enforces a Weight to Stress Principle (WSP) which entails that 'heavy syllables are analyzed as prominent' in a foot (Prince and Smolensky 1993:53).

Combining the constraints WSP and Foot Binarity derives the most common stress pattern in Italian, penultimate stress, as demonstrated in (15) where vowel length is indicated by the presence of an empty mora which, in the general case, is filled by segmental material from the preceding vowel by a separate Fill (mora) constraint (not shown).

(15) Penultimate Stress

	WSP	FtBin.
(bá.ra)	*!	
(bá[$]_{\mu}$)ra		*!
√(bá[$]_{\mu.}$.ra)		

The most optimal parse in (15) is the one which accrues no violation of these constraints. Thus, penultimate words surface with a HL trochaic parse.

A second pattern of weight to stress emerges in words of 3 syllables or more that contain a closed syllable in penultimate position. Aside from two single non-proper lexical items, *mándorla* 'almond' and *pólizza* 'insurance policy' which have atonic but heavy penultimate syllables, stress invariably falls on a closed penult. An interesting exposition of the behavior of these types of words is given in Sluyters (1990:80) who shows that borrowed place names typically shift stress to a heavy penultimate, as shown in (16).

(16) Heavy Penultimates (Sluyters 1990:80) surface as (HL)

[am(búrgo)]	<	Hámburg
[stok(kárdo)]	<	Stúttgart
[gro(níŋga)]	<	Gróningen

There are less than a dozen lexical items in Italian in which a heavy penultimate is skipped in favor of antepenultimate stress and all but those mentioned above are proper nouns. This type of information reinforces the notion that Italian is a QS trochaic language.

Special focus is warranted in the case of final stress in Italian. This is the most unusual position for stress placement in the language and, further, stressed open syllables surface with short vowels in violation of WSP. Examples of lexical items with final stress are shown in (17).

(17) Final Stress in Italian

Monosyllables:	blù 'blue', giá 'already', á 'to', té 'tea', sé 'if' note: à (preposition) ~ a (aux.verb)
Polysyllables:	carità 'charity', colibrì 'hummingbird', caffè 'coffee'

Assuming that a foot is formed over the final stressed syllable, these forms automatically earn a violation of the constraints on binarity. Given that word final position is the only position in which stressed vowels fail to lengthen entails that the purely prosodic constraints must be outranked by an alignment constraint identical to that in French ((12) above, repeated below as (18)).

(18) Alignment Constraint

Align (LxWd, R, Segment R)

The constraint tableau in (19) shows how alignment operates over the two possible output forms for the input form, the stressed monosyllable *se* 'if'.

(19) Alignment beats Prosody

	Align R (LxWd,Segment)	Prosody: WSP
$\surd[(\text{se})]_{\text{LxWord}}$		*
$[(\text{s}[\text{e}]_{\mu}[\ ]_{\mu})_{\varphi}]_{\text{LxWord}}$	*!	

In the less optimal output form, the LxWord fails to align to the final segment and aligns instead to the empty mora which is interpreted in phonetic form as a lengthened vowel.

A well-documented phenomenon in the variety of Italian under discussion here is the fact that within certain syntactic environments, the words of the form given in (17) provoke gemination of the following onset consonant (Nespor and Vogel 1986, Bullock 1991a, 1991b, Repetti 1991).This is known as Raddoppiamento Sintattico (RS); examples are illustrated in (20).

(20) Raddoppiamento Sintattico

tè freddo	=	tè[**ff**]reddo	'cold tea'
a Perugia	=	a[**pp**]erugia	'to Perugia'
virtù cardinali	=	virtù[**kk**]ardinali	'cardinal virtues'

The syntactic conditioning of RS is discussed in depth in Nespor and Vogel (1986) and is described as a junctural rule operative between prosodic words within a larger phonological phrase domain. Of interest to us here is that the alignment of the lexical word to the final segment in Italian does not correspond necessarily with the edge of the PrWord. In a phonological phrase domain, the PrWord aligns with the final in Italian, not with the final segment as shown in (21).

(21) Prosodic Word alignment in RS varieties of Italian

a. Align (PrWord R, φ R)

b. NonCorrespondence of LxWord/PrWd

$[(s[e] \mid_{LxWord} [\ ]_{\mu})_{\varphi}]_{PrWord}$

RS can now be seen as a satisfaction of the WSP constraint when a major morphological boundary (LxWord) intervenes to prevent a vowel from lengthening. That is, the second word in an RS domain aligns not to the edge of the previous Lexical Word but to the edge of the Prosodic Word, creating a larger prosodic domain in which the WSP is satisfied in the output. In this case, Fill is satisfied by the segmental material of the onset consonant since it is the only available adjacent segment within the prosodic domain. Thus, an implication of this analysis is that in Italian the LxWord cannot always correspond to the PrWord which is itself a violation of the universal constraint proposed in McCarthy and Prince (1994): LxWd = PrWd.

In RS, then, the alignment constraint and the WSP are still dominant constraints. What is demoted is the requirement that empty moras be satisfied by adjacent vowels, the Fill (mora) constraint. Thus, WSP must be satisfied while Fill (mora), in the sense here that an empty mora must be filled by a vowel, can be violated by providing consonantal rather than vocalic features to the unsatisfied constituent of the stressed foot.

(22) Alignment of Prosodic Words in Phrase Domain

a. Satisfaction of WSP in a larger domain
   Align(LxWd R, Segment R) / WSP >> Fill mora

b. LxWord = [se] = (L)
   PrWord = $[s[e]_{\mu}[\ ]_{\mu}]$ = (H)

c. Implication: LxWord does not equal a PrWord in these cases

Again we see, as in (22b), that the bimoraic syllable plays a central role in the phonology of Italian by fulfilling the requirement that a wellformed φ must be heavy in the language.

To sum up this discussion of Italian, we find that both the uneven trochee (HL) and the unary foot (H) feature in optimal output forms within the language. This parallels the case of French where the uneven trochee (σ x) surfaces in specific unavoidable environments whereas in other environments, it is restructured into a single syllabic constituent.

3. *Emergent prosodic structures*

The implication of these analyses is problematic for theories of metrical structure, like that of Hayes (1995), that banish uneven feet from the universal inventory of possible foot types. While OT admits violations of constraints on the binary, even structure of trochaic feet, the theory nonetheless maintains that the inventory proposed by Hayes encodes the unmarked type of feet. Thus, with respect to the foot constituent of Classical Latin that was binary at the moraic level and with respect to a contempory binary view of foot constituency, I am arguing that French and Italian are marked in that they display uneven trochaic feet.

The markedness of this foot type in these Romance languages could be eliminated in both languages by a 'readjustment' of the prosodic constituents. For instance, in order to reestablish a trochaic foot based on evenness of constituents, Italian could lighten the heavy left syllable, as it arguably does in certain varieties (cf. Prieto 1994:93 on Pragelato), and French could phonemicize the ill-formed right branch of its trochaic foot as a rounded front mid vowel (cf. Bullock 1995a for details). Alternatively, both languages could rectify the uneven trochee by eliminating the material that follows the head of the foot thereby establishing well-formedness at the syllabic level only.

(23) Options for Eliminating the Uneven Foot

a. Weight/Quality adjustments
Italian: [HL] $\Rightarrow$ [LL]
French: $[\sigma\ x] \Rightarrow [\sigma\ \sigma]$ where the weak branch is phonemicized

b. Weak Branch Elimination
Italian: [HL] $\Rightarrow$ [H]
French: $[\sigma\ x] \Rightarrow [\sigma]$

The (23a) forms would restore the evenness of trochaic timing in accordance with Hayes' Iambic/Trochaic Law. The (23b) forms eliminate the binary foot altogether and, thus, disrupt trochaic evenness.

Facts from the prosodic morphology of these languages indicate that both languages tend toward (23b), the elimination of the binary foot in favor of a single syllable. The monosyllable in both languages functions as the minimal PrWord. This acts to delineate optimal ouputs in word formation. It is a single syllable that emerges in place of a binary foot in many word formation process in French and Italian, combined with a function, MAX, that Maximizes the faithful parse of the input in the truncated form much as it maximizes the phonological material parsed in reduplicants in many languages as shown by Mc Carthy and Prince (1994).

Let us first consider truncation in French. Scullen's (1993) dissertation contains a fairly exhaustive corpus of such forms. The sheer number of truncated forms which end in a final closed syllable in French led her to propose that the PwWord in French is defined by a quantity sensitive iambic foot (LH). Some sample forms from Scullen's corpus, some with parasitic suffixes, are shown below (24).

(24) French Truncations: slang

Abridged forms:

a. cap	<	capable	'able'
b. estom	<	estomac	'stomach'
c. pédé	<	péderaste	'homosexual', pej.
d. costo	<	costume + o	'dress'
e. appart	<	appartement	'apartment'

Word Games

f. louf	<	loufoque	fou + (l) oque	'crazy'
g. ken	<	kéni	(for)niquer	'to fornicate'
h. teb	<	tebi	bite	'penis'
i. enleuk	<	enlécu	enculer	'to commit sodomy'

Truncated Nicknames

j. jean-ber	<	bernard
k. dom	<	dominique
l. nat	<	nathalie
m. clo	<	claude

Truncated forms are simply those which deleted one or more syllables from a given form. The output form is unpredictable but seems to be regulated by exactly the same conditions that hold over word final syllables in French as discussed earlier. The PrWd in French is simply required to be a syllable.

The fact that many such forms end in a final consonant that is detached from an onset in the input form is a function of MAX which tends to make the output as faithful as possible to the prosodic content of the input in French word play. Verlan in forms (24g-i), a reversed syllable language game, is telling in this respect since it is the consonants that bears the functional load of carrying prosodic material from the input into the output form since the vowels are reduced. For example, a monosyllablic input such as *boules* 'balls' simply reverses the syllables to form *le.bou* and further truncates the verlan form to *leb.*

(25) boules > lebou > leb [lœb] 'balls' PrWd = [σ]

The only requirement is that the prosodic word equal a syllable. Here we assume with Leftkowitz (1991) that the final schwa is included in the input to the word game; thus, all monosyllables are input as binary uneven feet. In the output, however, uneven feet fail to surface in favor of wellformed syllables everywhere in truncated forms and languages games.

Italian truncations and reduplications involve more stringent constraints than do French since there is a bimoraic requirement for a prominent syllable thereby excluding any coda content that does not possess the sonority properties required to be parsed to a moraic position. In Italian, then, the function MAX is coupled with a constraint of coda sonority which I will propose as a parse constraint (26).

(26) Italian Coda Constraint

Parse son/μ

(26) is a familiar language specific coda condition that entails that only sonorants may occupy the second mora of a syllable (Itô 1986). Geminate consonants escape such a condition because they are prespecified as moraic.

Examples of Italian truncations and reduplications are given in (27).

(27) Italian Truncations and Reduplications

a. Truncations

cammino	> cammin	'path/walk'
pane	> pan	'bread'
grande	> gran	'big'
bene	> ben	'good'
hanno fatto	> han fatto	'(they) did do'
volere bene	> voler bene	'to love well'
vuole nuotare	> vuol nuotare	'(he/she) wants to swim'

b. Reduplications

benbene	(bene 'good')	'completely'
belbello	(bello 'pretty')	'slowly'
manmano	(mano 'hand')	'bit by bit'
orora	(ora 'now')	'just' -recent past
pianpiano	(piano 'softly')	'successively'

Not surprisingly, both truncated and reduplicated forms are accomplished by eliminating the posttonic vowel. That the coda consonant in the truncated morpheme is mapped to a mora is supported by the fact that the stressed vowels in such configurations no longer surface as long as shown in (28).

(28) No Vowel Length in Truncated Forms

camm[i:]no ⇒ camm[i]n

Furthermore, truncation and truncated reduplication only occur when it is a sonorant that follows the stressed vowel as shown by comparing the ungrammaticality of forms in (29) with the wellformedness of the items those in (27a and b).

(29) ebbe fatto ≠ *eb fatto (3 p. sg. preterite)
allegro allegro ≠ *allegallegro (allegro 'fast')

These types of data from Italian demonstrate that in prosodic morphology, the constraint on Foot Binarity, which is observed generally in the language, is low ranked in the prosodic morphology. In truncations and reduplications, MAX and WSP outrank Foot Binarity completely which entails that within the prosodic morphology, a single heavy syllable is better than an uneven foot (30). This falls out from the definition of the Prosodic Word in Italian.

(30) Prosodic Morphology : [H] >> [HL] : PrWd = [H]

The PrWd is the minimum prosodic output required of reduplicated and truncated forms. Since moras may be filled either by long vowels or by sonorants in Italian, the constraint MAX must dominate WSP. Examples of the constraint interactions are given for truncations in (31a) and for reduplicants in (31b).

(31) Interactions of Parse Constraints in Italian

a) Truncation: input pane

	MAX	WSP	Ft. Bin.
√(pan)<e>			*
(pa)<e>	*!	*	*
(pa:)<ne>	*!		*

b) Reduplication

	MAX	WSP	Ft. Bin
(pia):<no>pia.no	*!		*
(pia)<no>pia.no	*!	*	*
√(pian)<o>pia.no			*

The constraint on foot binarity is shown in (31a) and (b) to demonstrate that it is low ranked and consistently violated. A reduplicated or truncated morpheme is optimal if it satisfies the parse constraints MAX and WSP.

However, the Italian coda condition prevails over MAX if the only available consonant to be parsed into the coda is an obstruent as shown in (32).

(32) Failure of Form to be Truncated

	Parse son/μ	MAX	WSP	Ft. Bin.
(eb)<be> fatto	*!		*	*
√(eb.be) fatto				
(ebb)<e> fatto	*!			*

Although geminates are prespecified to be moraic, the conditions that allow for truncation are more specific allowing only sonorants to be mapped to syllable codas. The first candidate fails to fulfill the moraic requirement which is irrelevant since it has already incurred a fatal violation of the sonorant parse. The same situation holds for the final candidate; it may satisfy the moraic criterion but it does so at the expense of a higher ranked constraint. The optimal parse is the one in which no truncation occurs at all.

The upshot of the analysis of word formation processes in Italian is that the binary foot is systematically restructured in favor of a wellformed heavy syllable constituent.

4. *Conclusion*

This paper has argued that while an uneven trochaic foot surfaces generally in Italian and French, many processes in these languages conspire to eliminate that type of foot. In no case, however, do they do so by trying to restore trochaic evenness. Rather, both Italian and French take a single unary syllable to be equivalent to a binary, uneven foot. French schwa deletion, along with shortened and argotic forms, show that Standard French often prefers to close a syllable by a consonant rather than permit a schwa, and by extension an uneven foot, in the output. In Italian, a series of final vowel deletions display a parallel behavior to that of French; that is, Italian permits a sonorant coda, eliminates a posttonic vowel and consequently shortens the foot.

The implication of this paper for metrical theory is that a trochaic foot based on evenness may, in principle, be an optimal prosodic constituent but in the Romance languages examined here, such a foot cannot be found. Foot based conditions on prosodic size and wellformedness that may have once held in Classical Latin have been yielded over to syllable based conditions. In sum, the syllable has replaced the foot in the prosodic hierarchy for the purposes of determining the Prosodic Word in both the QS and the QI systems of Italian and French.

REFERENCES

Bullock, Barbara E. 1991. *The Mora and the Syllable as Prosodic Licensers in the Lexicon*. Ph.D. dissertation, University of Delaware.

———. 1995a. "Morphological Alignment and Prosodic Constraints in French". *Lingua* 96.95-117.

———. "The Uneven Trochee in French". To appear in *Rivista di Linguistica*. 7 (2).

Burzio, Luigi & Elvira DiFabio. 1994. "Accentual Stability". *Issues and Theory in Romance Linguistics*, ed. by Michael Mazzola, 19-34. Georgetown: Georgetown University Press,

Halle, Morris & Jean-Roger Vergnaud. 1990. *An Essay on stress*. Cambridge, Mass.: MIT Press.

Jacobs, Haike. 1994. "Catalexis and Stress in Romance". *Issues and Theory in Romance Linguistics* ed. by Michael Mazzola, 49-66. Georgetown: Georgetown University Press,

Lefkowitz, Nathalie. 1991. *Talking Backwards, Looking Forwards: The French Language Game Verlan*. Tubingen: Gunter Narr Verlag.

Kager, Rene. 1993. "Alternatives to the Iambic Trochaic Law". *Natural Language and Linguistic Theory* 2.381-432.

Hayes, Bruce. 1985. "Iambic and Trochaic Rhythm in Stress Rules. *Proceedings of Berkeley Linguistic Society* 11. 97-110 ed. by M. Niepokuj, M. VanClay, V. Nikiforidou, and D. Jeder. Berkeley: Berkeley Linguistic Society.

———. 1995. *Metrical Stress Theory: Principles and Case Studies*. Chicago: University of Chicago Press.

Hyman, Larry. 1977. "On the Nature of Linguistic Stress". *Studies in Stress and Accent* ed. by Larry Hyman, SCOPIL, 4. Los Angeles: University of Southern California.

Itö, Junko. 1986. *Syllable Theory in Prosodic Phonology*. Ph.D. dissertation, University of Massachusetts, Amherst. New York: Garland Press, 1988.

McCarthy John J. & Alan Prince. 1986. "Prosodic Morphology". Ms., University of Massachusetts, Amherst and Rutgers University.

———.1993. "Prosodic Morphology 1: Constraint Interaction and Satisfaction". Ms., University of Massachusetts and Rutgers University.

———. 1994. "The Emergence of the Unmarked: Optimality in Prosodic Morphology". *Proceedings of NELS* 24.333-379. GLSA, University of Massachusetts.

———. 1995. "Prosodic Morphology". *The Handbook of Phonological Theory* ed. by John A. Goldsmith, 318-366. Cambridge, Mass.: Basil Blackwell.

Montreuil, Jean Pierre. 1993. "Prosody, Morphology, and Foot Formation in Modern French". Paper presented at the *Linguistic Symposium on Romance Languages*. Northern Illinois University.

Nespor, Marina and Irene Vogel. 1986. *Prosodic Phonology*. Dordrecht: Foris.
Prieto, Pilar. 1994. "Historical Vowel Lengthening in Romance: The Role of Sonority and Foot Structure. *Issues and Theory in Romance Linguistics* ed. by Michael Mazzola, 87-108. Georgetown: Georgetown University Press.
Prince, Alan. 1990. "Quantitative Consequences of Rhythmic Organization". *Parasession on the Syllable in Phonetics and Phonology* ed. by M. Ziolkowski, M. Noske, and K. Deaton, 355-398. Chicago: Chicago Linguistic Society.
Prince, Alan & Paul Smolensky. 1993. "Optimality Theory: Constraint Interaction in Generative Grammar". Ms., Rutgers University and University of Colorado, Boulder.
Repetti, Lori. 1989. *The Bimoraic Norm of Tonic Syllables in Italo-Romance*. Ph.D dissertation, UCLA.
———. 1991. "A Moraic Analysis of Raddoppiamento Fonosintattico. *Rivista di Linguistica* 3.307-330.
Saltarelli, Mario. 1970. *A Phonology of Italian in a Generative Grammar*. Mouton: The Hague.
———. 1983. "The Mora Unit in Italian Phonology". *Folia Linguistica* XVII.7-24.
———. 1995a. "Sulla cardinalitá del parametro metrico nell'evoluzione prosodica delle lingue neolatine". *XXI Congresso Internazionale di Linguistica e Filologia Romanza*. Palermo, 18/24 September.
———. 1995b. "From Latin Meter to Romance Rhythm". *International Conference on Historical Linguistics XII*. Manchester, England. August 1995.
Scullen, Mary Ellen. 1993. *The Prosodic Morphology of French*. Ph.D. dissertation, Indiana University.
Selkirk, Elizabeth O. 1978. "The French Foot: On the Status of 'Mute' e". *Studies in French Linguistics* 1.141:150.
———. 1984. *Phonology and Syntax: The Relation Between Sound and Structure*. Cambridge Mass.: MIT Press.
Sluyters, Willebrod. 1990. "Length and Stress Revisited: A Metrical Account of Diphthongization, Vowel Lengthening, Consonant Gemination and Word Final Vowel Epenthesis in Modern Italian". *Probus* 2.71-101.
Vogel, Irene & Sergio Scalise. 1982. "Secondary Stress in Italian". *Lingua* 58.231-242.

SOME REMARKS ON THE LATIN CASE SYSTEM AND ITS DEVELOPMENT IN ROMANCE[1]

ANDREA CALABRESE
Harvard University

0. *Introduction*

One of the most striking aspects of the development of Romance from Latin is the major reduction in the Case system. The first goal of this paper is to account for this reduction. As we will see, different Case systems are found at the different stages of the history of Romance, in particular we have the two Case systems of Gallo-Romance and Rumanian. The second goal of this paper is to account for these Case systems. The final goal is to explain why the plural morphemes in languages such as French, Spanish and Portuguese seem to be etymologically based on the Latin accusative, whereas the plural morphemes of a language like Italian seem to be etymologically based on the Latin nominative, as shown in (1):

(1)	Italian (and Rumanian)		Latin		Western Romance	
	case	←	N. case		casas	'house'
			A. casas	↗		
	campi	←	N. campi		campos	'field'
			A. campos	↗		

My analysis in this paper will be based on two main ideas:

1) First, I will hypothesize that the elements of a Case paradigm are part of an abstract system of contrasts similar to those characterizing phonological inventories. Thus along the lines of Jakobson (1936) and Hjelmslev (1935) we

---

[1] This paper greatly benefited from comments and suggestions by Erich Groat, Morris Halle, Jim Harris, Craig Melchert, Lisi Oliver, Steve Peter, Bert Vaux, Calvert Watkins. Responsibility for errors remains, as usual, with the author.

can say that Cases are bundles of distinctive features. The feature system I propose is discussed in Section 2.1.

Along the lines of my 1995 analysis of phonological inventories, I propose that the combinations of features that can appear as Case forms in the morphology of a language are governed by constraints, which I call Case restrictions here. These Case restrictions are part of the morphological component of the grammar. An active Case restriction disallows combination of features from appearing in the terminal nodes provided by the syntax. Thus, as we will see below, the Case restriction in (2) disallows the appearance of the instrumental in Latin:

(2) *[+source, +association]

Each Case is characteristically identified by a Case restriction. These Case restrictions may be active or inactive in a language. If a Case restriction is active in a language, the relevant Case is not present overtly. If it is inactive, the relevant Case is present. The set of Case restrictions in (27) will account for the structure of the different Case systems.

A change in a Case system is implemented by the activation of a Case restriction. This Case restriction will eliminate the relevant Case by adjusting the Case feature bundles in the terminal nodes provided by the syntax. As shown in diagram (32), this occurs in the morphosyntactic component which manipulates the Case configurations provided by the syntax —where all types of Case distinctions are present— and produces the surface Case distinctions characterizing the given languages.

2) Secondly, I will propose that the morphological structure for a Latin Case marked NP is that in (3) which represents the fact that the Case suffix is not only the exponent of Case distinctions, but also of number ones. The structure in (3) will be obtained by assuming that there is an autonomous morphological component where the KP provided by the syntax is manipulated by the operations of merger and fusion:

(3)

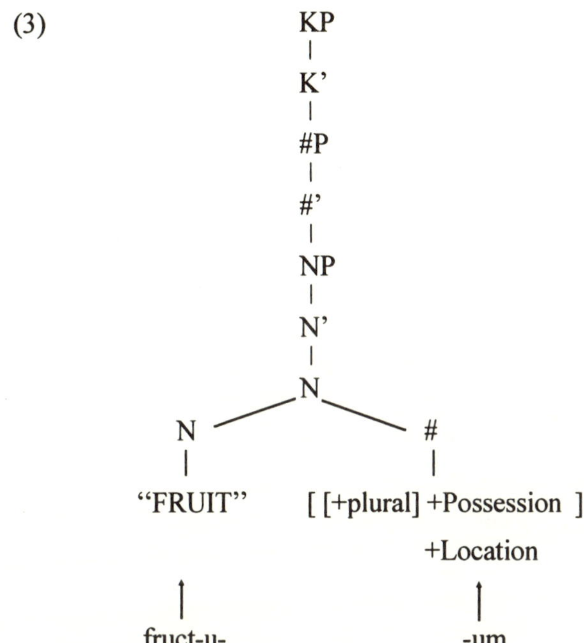

My paper is organized as follows. In Section 1 I will account for how Case is realized as a morphological suffix in Latin. That is, I will deal with the issue of how the morphological component manipulates the syntactic structures provided by the syntax and produces (3). Section 2 deals with other theoretical issues: in Section 2.1, a system of Case features is introduced and the notion of Case syncretism is discussed. Section 2.2 addresses the issue of what features are assigned to lexical items. Section 3 deals with the Latin Case system. In Section 4, I describe the development of this system in the Romance languages. Finally in Section 5, this development is accounted for by using the theoretical machinery introduced in the earlier sections.

1. *Case as a morphological suffix*

Following Bittner and Hale (1996), I assume that Case is a functional head. Thus a Case-marked nominal is a Kase Phrase, as shown in (4) where the Head of KP consists of a bundle of features. For reasons of simplicity throughout the paper I will simplify the syntactic representations by not including the Determiner Phrase projection. No major theoretical consequence hinges upon this choice:

(4)

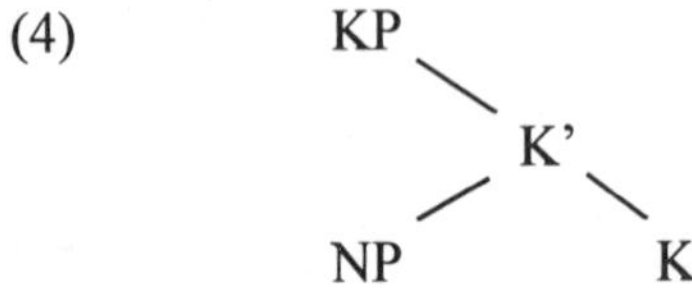

If Case is a syntactic head, then it is expected that it will exhibit canonical headlike behavior. This behavior is transparent when Case is realized as an adposition. Thus, in a head-final language such as Miskitu, overt K, a particle, is final in a Case-marked nominal, as expected (Example from Bittner and Hale (1996)):

MISKITU (Misumalpan: Nicaragua)

(5)	Waitna	ba	sula	ba	ra	kaik-an
	[man	the]	[deer	the	ACC]	see-PST.3

And also according to expectation, the same particle is initial in Case-marked nominals in a head initial language such as Khasi (Example from Bittner and Hale (1996)):

KHASI (Mon-Khmer: Assam. India)

(6)	ka	la	yo''ii	ya	'u	khlaa
	she	PST	see	[ACC	the	tiger]

Let us consider the morphological realization of Case in Latin. What is peculiar about what we traditionally call Case in opposition to what we call a postposition is that it is morphologically realized as a suffix of the adjacent NP. Insofar as it is a morphological suffix, a Case will display a number of variants determined by the nature of the word or the stem to which it is attached. Another correlated property of Case that needs to be explained is that a Case suffix is not restricted to the phrase final position as the postpositions in (5) but is also found on the head noun and on all of its dependents. If we assume Distributed Morphology, we can account for these properties of Case.

Distributed Morphology (Halle (1993, 1994), Halle and Marantz (1993, 1994), Harris (1994), Noyer (1995)) assumes that there is an autonomous morphological component shown in (7) where the structures provided by the syntax can be modified by the set of well motivated operations listed in (8) and formally represented in (9) (see Halle (1996, Halle and Marantz (1993) for more on these operations).

(7)

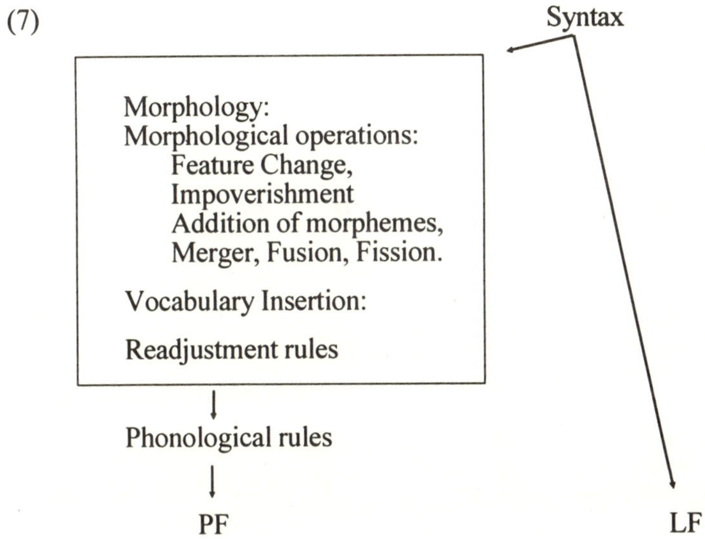

(8) a. Feature Change is an innovation with respect to the other operations proposed by Halle and Marantz (1993).
By Feature Change, a feature in a feature bundle associated with a terminal node is replaced by its opposite value. Thus the lexical item characterized by the disallowed configuration can no longer be inserted. Instead, the lexical item characterized by the configuration which is the output of delinking is inserted.
b. Impoverishment, which deletes a feature in a feature bundle associated with a terminal node (see note 15 for more discussion of this operation.)
c. Addition of morphological constituents that are not directly motivated by the syntax.
d. Merger, which is a special case of head-to-head movement and has the effect of rebracketing adjacent constituents in the terminal string.
e. Fusion of two adjacent terminal nodes dominated by given higher node into a single terminal node.

f. Fission, splitting of a given terminal node into a sequence of two separate terminal nodes.

(9) a. Feature Change

bF→-bF/[__, aG]

b. Impoverishment

bF→∅/[__, aG]

c. Morpheme Addition

∅→ y [x] ___

d. Adjunction/Merger (an instance of head-to head movement):

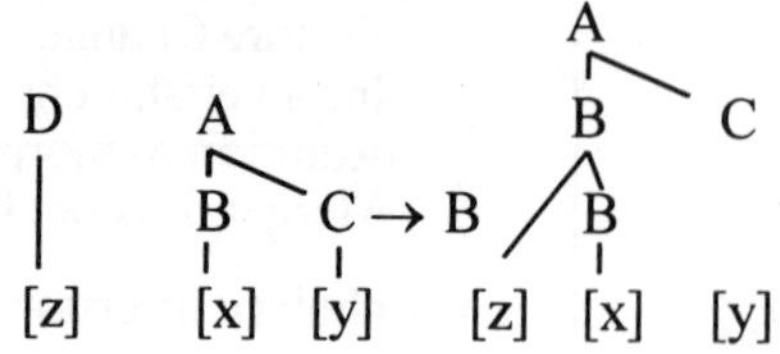

e. Fusion

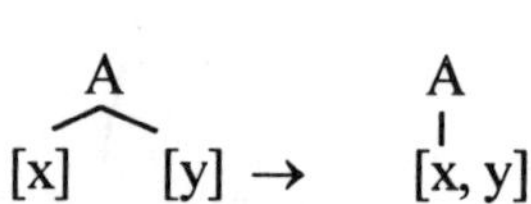

f. Fission

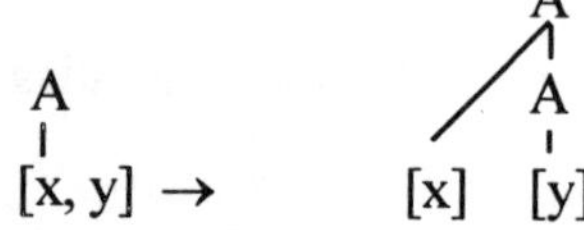

These operations account for the mismatches between the organization of the morphological pieces and the structures provided by the syntax. After the application of the morphological operations in (9) vocabulary insertion, which is governed by the Subset principle defined in (10), fills in the terminal nodes of the modified syntactic structures.

(10) The Subset Principle (Halle and Marantz (1994):

If two vocabulary items of category X in (a) compete for insertion at a node of category X in (b), the competition is won by Vocabulary Item A because it contains a larger subset of the features in the node X than does Vocabulary Item B.

a. Category X

Vocabulary Item A: [F1, F2] → P_A
Vocabulary Item B: [F1] → P_B

b. X — F1, F2, F3

Before considering the morphological realization of Case in Latin, let us consider a language like Turkish where Case is realized as a suffix which follows the number suffix, as shown in (11):

(11) elma -lar -ɨ 'the apples-ACC'
'apple-PL-ACC'

The Case suffix in (11) is integral part of the nominal head from the morphological and phonological point of view, as the fact that it undergoes vowel harmony shows. The Case suffix is part of the word containing the nominal head. Assuming the existence of a Number Phrase (#P), I propose that in the syntax the extended projection of the NP in (11) will look like (12):

(12)

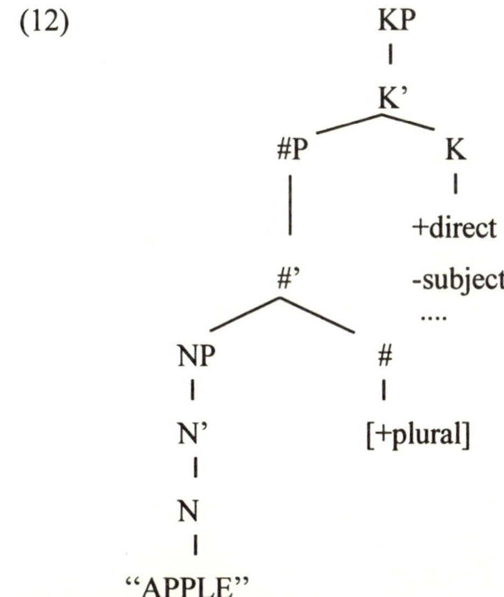

According to the structure in (12) the Case head should be realized as an independent postpositional particle. We have to account for why it is a suffix and thus an integral part of the word including the NP head.

In Distributed Morphology, the operation by which a syntactic head is realized as an affix to another head is merger. Merger is formally represented in (9d). Merger joins terminal nodes under a category node of a head but mantains two terminal nodes under this head. Thus Vocabulary Insertion places two separate lexical items under the derived head, one for each of the merged terminal nodes. Therefore Merger forms a new word from the heads of independent phrases; but these heads remain separate morphemes within the newly derived word. The morphological properties of Case in Turkish can then be accounted for by recursive application of merger between the head of KP, the Number Phrase head and the head noun. First the merger between the head of KP and the adjacent head of #P will create the morphological structure in (13). In (13) merger joins the head of KP with the head of #P under a #P head node. If we stopped at this point, Kase would be realized as a suffix of the head of #P:

```
(13)              KP
                   |
                   K'
                   |
                   #P
                   |
                   #'
        NP ------------------ #
        |              # ---------- K
        |              |            |
        N'         [+plural]     +direct
        |                        -subject
        N                        ....
        |
    "APPLE"
```

The subsequent application of merger between the merged Kase Phrase-Number Phrase heads and the NP head will produce (14):

```
(14)              KP
                   |
                   K'
                   |
                   #P
                   |
                   #'
                   |
                   NP
                   |
                   N'
                   |
                   N
        N ------------------- #
        |              # ---------- K
        |              |            |
    "APPLE"        [+plural]     +direct
                                 -subject
                                 ....
```

In (14) Merger joins the newly formed #P head node with the NP head. Thus the head of #P and the head of KP are realized as suffixes of the NP head. Therefore they are part of the word containing this head.

After Vocabulary Insertion we have (15), and thus we account for Case marking in Turkish:[2]

(15)

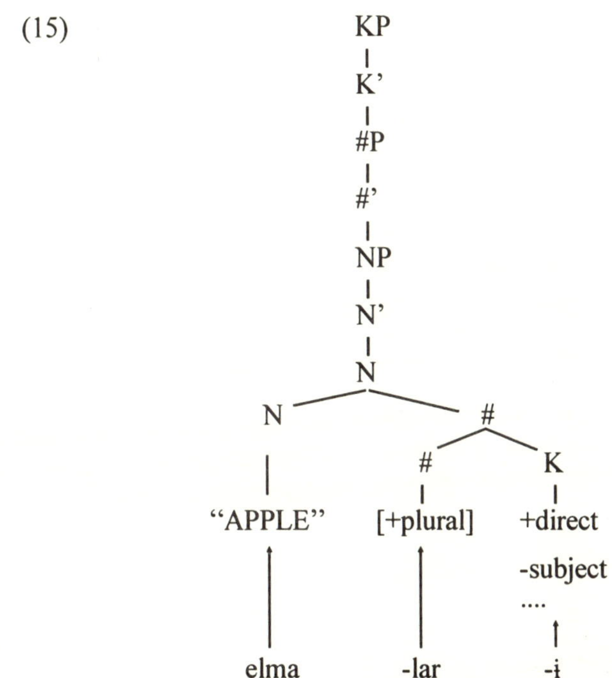

We can turn to Latin now. In Latin, number and Case features are morphologically realized with a single suffix. We can account for this by assuming that in addition to merger, fusion between the head of the Number Phrase and the head of KP also occurs. Thus the syntax provides the structure in (16) in the case of the genitive plural form "frūctuum" 'of the fruits':

[2] It is interesting to observe that Case merging seems to occur only when the KP is head final. Blake (1994) reports of only one language, Nungali, with clear case prefixes. He argues that these prefixes are better treated as independent prepositions. Thus there seems to be a total absence of case prefixes (see also Cutler, Hawkins, Gilligan (1985)). Limits of space prevent me from discussing this very interesting fact further.

(16)

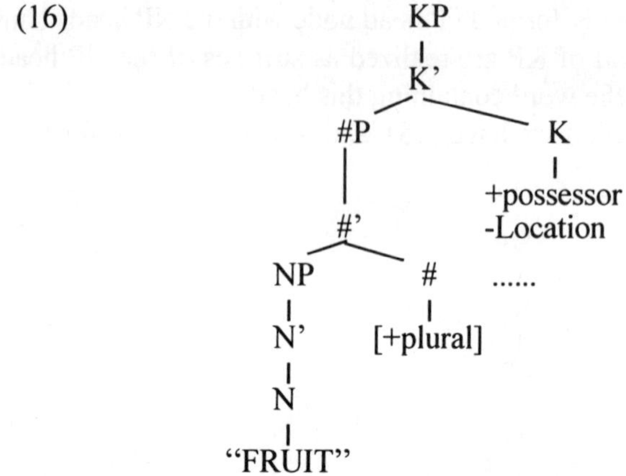

Recursive merger as in Turkish will produce (17):

(17)

KP
K'
#P
#'
NP
N'
N
N
#
#
K
"FRUIT"
[+plural]
+Possessor
-Location
.....

Fusion will create (18). Fusion takes two terminal nodes that are sisters under a single category node and fuses them into a single category node.[3] Only one lexical item may now be inserted, an item that must have a subset of the mor-

[3] Observe that the presence of merger, as in the case under discussion, is not a formal prerequisite for fusion, structural adjacency is enough (see Halle and Marantz (1993)).

phosyntactic features of the fused node, including the features from both input terminal nodes. Unlike merger, fusion reduces the number of independent morphemes (stem and affixes) in a tree:

(18)

KP
K'
#P
#'
NP
N'
N
N
#
"FRUIT"
[[+plural]
+Possessor]
- Location
....

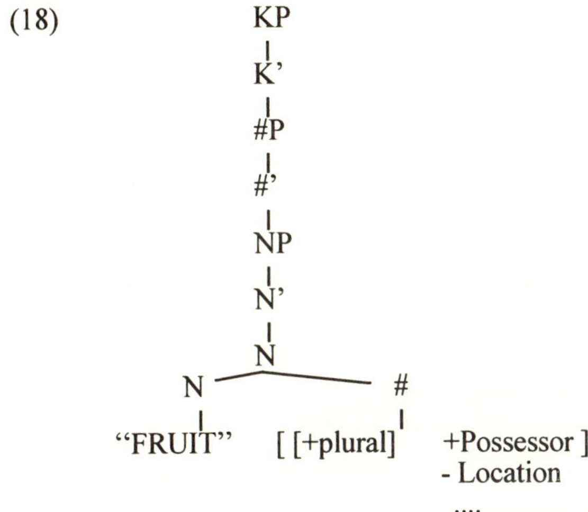

In (18) fusion takes the head of KP and the head of #P which are sisters under the head of #P node and fuses them into a single terminal node. Only one suffix will be inserted now, a suffix that must have Kase and number features.

Vocabulary Insertion will then give us (19):

(19)

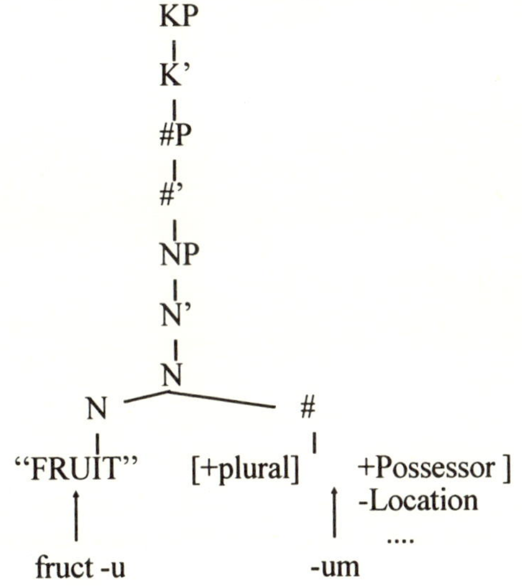

KP
K'
#P
#'
NP
N'
N
N
#
"FRUIT"
[+plural]
+Possessor]
-Location
....
fruct -u
-um

We thus have an account for why Case in Latin is realized with a suffix which also represents number distinctions.

We now have to explain why Case features are found on all the dependents of the head noun in a language like Latin. Latin is characterized by concord. Concord inside NP requires that all of the dependents of the head noun are assigned the number features of the head (I will not deal with the issue of gender concord which has some peculiarities of its own.[4] I will also omit discussion of concord in predicative constructions). Observe that the presence of concord in a language is independent of the presence of Case, as is shown by the fact that it is required in Case-less languages like Italian or Spanish. I hypothesize that concord is implemented by copying. In particular, concord targets the Number Phrase head merged with the Nominal head and copies its features onto all of the dependents of the head noun. In Latin, the fused number phrase head also contains Case features, as we see in (19). Thus, if we copy the features of the fused Number Phrase head in (19) we also assign Case features to all the dependents of the noun, as shown in (20):

(20)

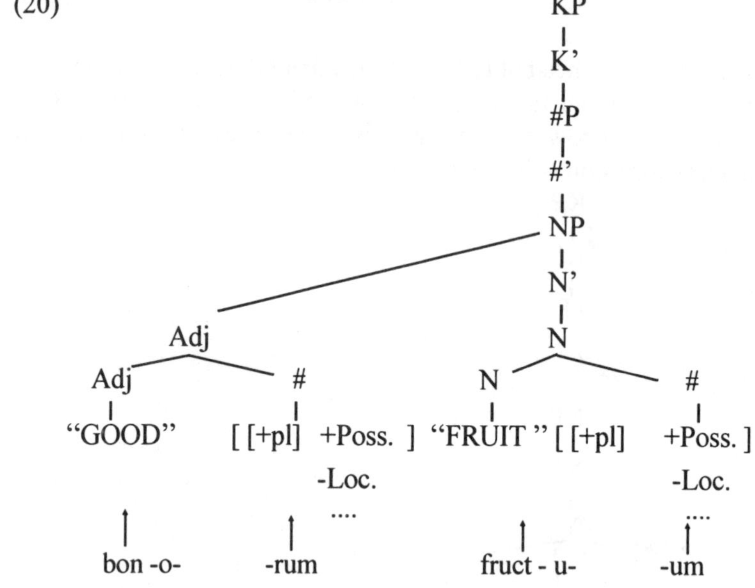

[4] Gender features are idiosyncratic features of the stem. Therefore, in order to be copied by concord, lexical insertion of the stem must occur before concord. This raises several technical problems that I cannot discuss here.

We thus have a straightforward account of why Case marking in a language like Latin is found on the head noun and all of its dependents. It is because of concord.

2.1 *Case features and syncretism*

In this section we will deal with the notions of Case system, Case features and Case syncretism. Since the last of these notions is of fundamental importance to understand the other two, we begin by discussing it. If one studies the syncretisms that are observed in Case systems, one can observe that they are neither accidental, nor random, but rather follow precise generalizations.[5] I would like to account for these generalizations.

Along the lines of Jakobson (1936), one can hypothesize that the elements of a Case paradigm are to be analyzed as belonging to an abstract system of contrasts analogous to that found in phonological inventories. Following Jakobson (1936), I assume that the first step in understanding syncretic changes is that of conceiving of Cases as bundles of feature specifications. I hypothesize that if the use of an exponent of a certain Case is extended so that it becomes the exponent of another Case, the two Cases share the same general meaning, i.e., a "gesamtbedeutung" in Jakobsonian terms, which is formally expressed as a distinctive feature.

I propose the feature system in (21) for the seven Cases that are most commonly found crosslinguistically —I do not include the features needed to account for the different locational Cases and other special Cases. Also I will not discuss Ergative Case systems. The features used in (21) are defined in (22). With the features in (21) I try to account for syncretism on a syntactico-semantic basis. Needless to say, the features in (21) are tentative and open to revision.[6]

---

[5] I refer only to syncretic phenomena which are not due to phonological changes —or other adjustments of the surface shape of morphemes such as paradigmatic levelling— but which are arguably due to morpho-syntactic reasons. Limits of space prevent me from elaborating on this important point further (see Ringe (1995) for more discussion of it.)

[6] The correct set of features will be established by developing a general theory of Case features through a cross-linguistic study of Case sytems. The development of such a theory is not a viable endeavor to undertake in this paper.

(21)

	Nom.	Acc.	Gen.	Dat.	Loc.	Abl.	Inst.
Subject	+	-	-	-	-	-	-
Direct	+	+	-	-	-	-	-
Possessor	-	-	+	+	-	-	-
Location	-	-	-	+	+	+	+
Source	-	-	+	-	-	+	+
Association	-	-	-	-	-	-	+

(22) Structural features:

[Subject] = This feature is assigned to the subject of the Predication

[Direct] = This feature is assigned to a KP governed by a [-N] head (Verb or Preposition).

Concrete Features (cf. Kurylowicz (1964)) (They are selected by a governing head):

[Possessor] = This feature is associated with grammatical functions expressing a relation of belonging.

[Location] = This feature is associated with grammatical functions expressing spatial reference.

[Source] = This feature is associated with grammatical functions expressing point of origin.

[Association] = This feature is associated with grammatical functions expressing the means associated with an action.

If we hypothesize that when there is syncretism between two Cases, they share a feature value, the system in (21) accounts for the syncretism cases commonly found in the Indo-European languages and listed in (23) (cf. Luraghi (1987), Meillet and Vendryes (1966)).

(23)

Syncretism		Languages in which it is found:
Accusative - Genitive: Common feature:	[-Location]	Russian animate plurals of all declensions and singulars of *o-declension.
Dative - Genitive: Common feature:	[+Possessor]	Romanian. Armenian. Italian dialects pronominal clitics.
Genitive - Ablative: Common feature:	[+Source]	Ancient Greek. Romance pronominal clitics.

Ablative - Locative:		Latin Common nouns.
Common feature:	[+Location]	
Dative - Ablative		Ancient Greek. Old Germanic.
Common feature:	[+Location]	
Dative - Locative		Ancient Greek. Italian dialects
Common feature:	[+Location]	pronominal clitics. Hittite.
Ablative - Instrumental		Latin.
Common feature:	[+Location]	
Nominative - Accusative		Latin Neuters.
Common feature:	[+Direct]	Russian inanimate plurals of all declensions and singulars of *o- declension. Armenian.
Accusative - All other Cases		Proto-Romance
Common feature:	[-Subject]	(seen in Old French).

Given the number of features proposed in (21) there will be some overgeneration, and some unattested Cases will be created. I hypothesize that they are ruled out by unviolable constraints disallowing certain combinations of features such as those sampled in (24). As we will see the constraints in (24) govern the wellformedness of the Case feature bundles in morphological derivations:

(24) a. *[+direct, +location]
b. *[+direct, +possessor]
c. *[+direct, +source]
d. *[-location, -source]/[+possessor, ______]
e. *[-direct, -possessor]/[-location, ____]

Not all Cases have the same status. Some Cases are less frequent than others. For example, the ablative is less frequently found than the genitive. Also, as observed by Blake (1994), there are clear implicational relationships between the different Cases with nominative, accusative, genitive present in all systems allowing three or more Cases. Thus, Case systems seem to be structured in a totally regular manner following the implicational hierarchy in (25) (See Blake (1994)):

(25) NOM < ACC < GEN < DAT < LOC/ABL/INST < OTHERS

The list of Case systems in (26) is evidence for the hierarchy in (25):

(26) Case systems (The lowest Case in the system usually has the functions of the other Cases appearing in the hierarchy. When this occurs we say that it is Obl (=Oblique):

a. Two Cases:
NOM - ACC(Obl) (e.g. in Chemehuevi, Kabardian)
b. Three Cases
NOM - ACC - GEN (e.g. in Classical Arabic, Modern Greek)
c. Four Cases
NOM - ACC - GEN - DAT(obl) (e.g. in Ancient Greek, Nuer)
d. Five Cases
NOM - ACC - GEN - DAT - ABL(Obl) (e.g. in Latin)
NOM - ACC - GEN - DAT - INST(Obl) (e.g. in Old High German)
e. Six Cases
NOM - ACC - GEN - DAT - LOC - ABL (e.g. in Turkish)
NOM - ACC - GEN - DAT - LOC - INST (e.g. in Slavic lgs)
f. Seven Cases
NOM - ACC - GEN - DAT - LOC - ABL - INST
(e.g. in C. Armenian)
g. Systems with more Cases may include differentiations in the local Cases (allative/perlative, etc.), the comitative, the purposive, the comparative, and some other special Cases:
e.g. Tamil: NOM - ACC - GEN - DAT - LOC - ABL - INST - COM
Toda: NOM - ACC - GEN - DAT - LOC - ABL - INST - COM - PURP

As we have seen, what is peculiar about what we traditionally call Case in opposition to what we call a postposition is that it is morphologically realized as a suffix on the adjacent NP head. Given (25), we can say that the realization of certain Cases as suffixes is disliked. Languages seem to prefer affixal Case-marking for grammatical relations such as subject and object but not for grammatical relations expressing location or instrument. For the latter, other morphosyntactic means are usually employed such as prepositions or postpositions. In terms of the theory of markedness, we can say that the affixal realization of Cases such as the ablative or the instrumental is complex from a morphological point of view.

Following Calabrese's (1995) analysis of markedness in phonological systems (see also the important work of Noyer (1993) on the use of constraints in morphological systems), we can account for the structure of the Case systems in (26) and for the implicational relationships in (25) as follows. Each Case is characteristically identified by a Case restriction, i.e., marking condition that constrains a Case feature. These Case restrictions represent Case feature combinations whose morphological expression is marked. Case restrictions may be active or inactive in a language. If a Case restriction is active in a language the relevant Case is not present in the language. If it is inactive, the relevant Case is present. The Case restrictions are organized hierarchically. The lower a restriction in the hierarchy, the more probable is that it is active across languages. Thus the restriction characterizing the instrumental is in a low position in the hierarchy. This expresses the fact that the instrumental is more rarely found across languages. I assume that a Case restriction can be deactivated only if the Case restrictions in higher positions in the hierarchy are also deactivated. This accounts for the implicational relationships observed above. The hierarchy of Case restrictions is given in (27):[7,8,9]

(27) a. [+Subject,+Direct] (Nominative)
b. [-Subject,+Direct] (Accusative Case)
c. [+Possessor, -Location] (Genitive Case)
d. [+Possessor, +Location) (Dative Case)

---

[7] Each Case restriction is constructed in such a way not only to identify the relevant Case uniquely, but also to characterize its idiosyncratic behavior. For example the Case restriction governing the dative contains the feature [+Location, +Possessor] to account for the fact that the dative tends to be replaced by Cases such as the genitive or the locative, as we will see later. The correct formulation of the Case restrictions is an empirical issue open to disconfirmation.

[8] The constraints in (27) are violable. Observe that the constraints in (24) are instead unviolable. Calabrese (1995a) proposes that the same distinction between violable and unviolable constraints is found among constraints governing the combination of phonological features. The violable constraints —called marking statements in that work— identify phonologically complex configurations which although found in some phonological inventories, are not found in others. The unviolable constraints —called prohibitions— identify configurations which are never possible because of articulatory and acoustic reasons. An example of the former constraints is the marking statement *[+low, -back] governing the appearance of low front vowels in phonological systems. An example of the latter is the prohibition *[+high, +low] disallowing the simultaneous use of the features [+high] and [+low].

[9] As in other markedness theories, violations of the implicational relationships predicted by the hierarchy in (27) must be allowed (see note 9 for an example). However, these violations must be considered as exceptional or marginal. Further research must establish under what conditions these violations are possible.

Observe also that probably the best way to represent the hierachy in (27) is not as the simple list given in the text, but as a tree, as proposed by Calabrese (1988, 1995) for phonological marking statements. The hierarchy in (27) could then be restated as in (i). In (i) there is an implicational relationship only between Case restrictions belonging to the same branch. Therefore the presence of the ablative does not involve the presence of the locative and vice versa. The same would be true for the instrumental:

e. [-Possessor, -Source]/[___, +Location] (Locative Case)
f. [+Location, +Source] (Ablative Case)
g. [+Source, +Association] (Instrumental Case)

Observe that given the analysis proposed here we have to say that the Case restrictions in (27) constrain Case feature bundles only when they are merged with other constituents, that is when they are morphologically realized as affixes or in any other morphologically bound form. Thus, the morphological realization of Case features in prepositions or postpositions is not governed by the restrictions in (27).

We now consider how Case restrictions can account for syncretism. The pronominal system of the Italian dialects is characterized by various phenomena of syncretism (see Calabrese (1995b and c) for more discussion). The syncretism phenomena targeting the 3rd person dative clitic are among the most interesting ones. In some dialects, this clitic is replaced by the exponent of the locative clitic, and in others by the exponent of the genitive clitic as exemplified in (28).

(28) a. In the Pugliese dialect of Bari, the clitic /ngə/, which is originally a locative (< Latin HINC), is now the exponent of the dative, as well as of the locative.
b. In the Salentino dialect of Otranto, the clitic /nde/ which was originally genitive (< Latin INDE), in addition to retaining its original function, has also become the exponent of the dative.

The changes in (28) can be expressed as in (29) where the system on the left of the arrow is proto-Romance:

(i) a. [+Subject,+Direct]
|
b. [-Subject,+Direct]
|
c. [+Possessor, -Location]
|
d. [+Possessor, +Location)
|
e. [-Possessor, -Source]/[___, +Location]
|
f. [+Location, +Source]
|
g. [+Source, +Association]

I adopt the simplified hierarchy in (27) only for expository reasons.

(29)

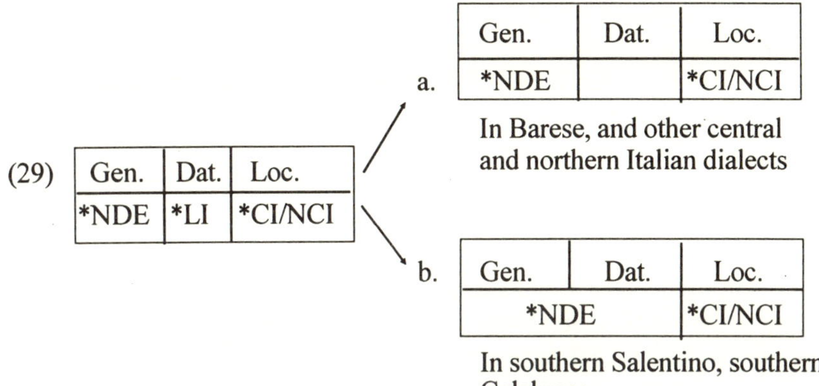

Gen.	Dat.	Loc.
*NDE	*LI	*CI/NCI

a.

Gen.	Dat.	Loc.
*NDE		*CI/NCI

In Barese, and other central and northern Italian dialects

b.

Gen.	Dat.	Loc.
*NDE		*CI/NCI

In southern Salentino, southern Calabrese

The following account of the changes in (29) can be proposed (see below, section 2.2, for discussion of other aspects of these changes). The syntactic feature bundles of the grammatical categories that are playing a role in the change in (31), those of 'dative', 'locative', and 'genitive', are given in (30)

(30)

a. 'Genitive'	b. 'Dative'	c. 'Locative'
-subject	-subject	-subject
-direct	-direct	-direct
-location	+location	+location
+possessor	+possessor	-possessor
+source	-source	-source

As discussed in the following section, the lexical items in (29) are to be represented as in (31):

(31) a *NDE ↔ -location
+possessor

b. *LI ↔ +Location
+possessor

c. *CI/NCI ↔ +location
-possessor
-source

I propose that syncretisms are the result of the reactivation of Case restrictions. These newly activated Case restrictions trigger repair operations that adjust the disallowed feature configurations in terminal nodes. As a consequence, the lexical items characterized by the disallowed configurations can no longer be inserted. Instead, the lexical items characterized by the configurations of the modified terminal nodes are inserted. Thus the exponents identified by the disallowed feature configurations are eliminated and replaced by the exponents of allowed configurations. The relevant morphological contrasts are therefore eliminated. Syncretism can be diagrammatically represented as in (32). As shown in (32), I assume that active Case restrictions and morphological operations are included in a morphosyntactic component which changes the underlying Case configurations into surface ones through various morphological operations, some of which are triggered by active case restrictions. A fundamental assumption is that all types of Case distinctions are present in the syntax in underlying Case configurations. It is the duty of the morphosyntactic component to filter out the Case configurations which have morphological realization in a given language.

(32)

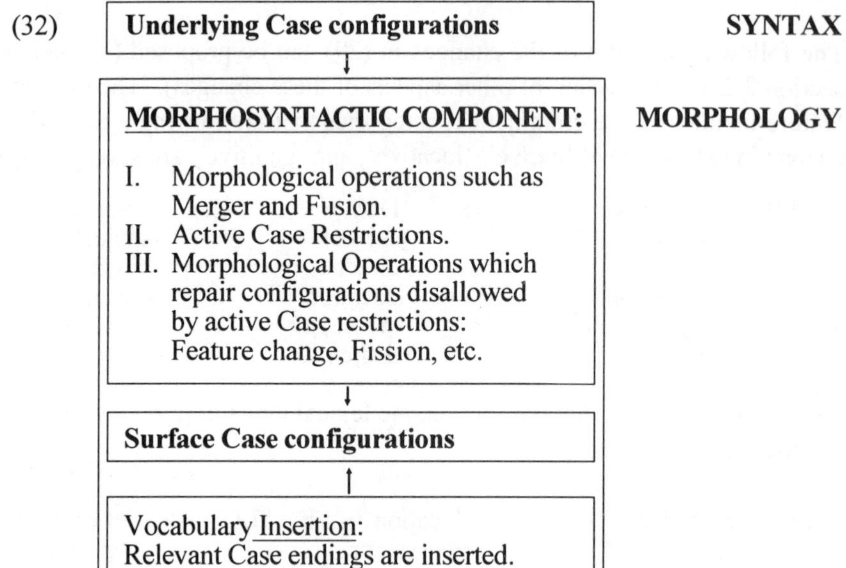

The changes affecting the dative pronominal clitic in Italian can now be accounted for in the following way. In the inventory of the proto-Romance clitics, two of the Case restrictions in (27) were active —in particular (27f) and (27g) disallowing the ablative and the instrumental—; but all of the others were inactive. In particular, the restriction in (27c) disallowing the dative (repeated here as (33)) was inactive. This system is preserved in many Romance varieties such as Sardinian and Standard Italian. Dialects like Pugliese and Salentino, however, are characterized by the activation of (27c=that is (33)).

The restriction in (33) will trigger the application of either the feature change in (34a) or the feature change in (34b).

(33) *[+location, +possessor]

(34) a. [+possessor]→ [-possessor] / [+location, ________]
b. [+location] → [-location] / [+possessor, ________]

The application of (34a) will change the feature complex of the dative in (30b) into that of the locative, whereas the application of (34b) will change it into that of the genitive. If we assume the lexical items in (31), the application of (34a) accounts for the case in which the locative takes over the function of the dative,[10] and the application of rule (34b) will account for the case in which the genitive takes over the function of the dative.

Observe that the application of the feature change in (34a) does not give immediately the feature bundle of the genitive. In order to obtain that feature bundle, the features [-source] characterizing the dative must be changed into [+source]. We can assume that this is an instance of the feature changes in (35) triggered by the unviolable filter in (24d). This is an automatic adjustment needed to obtain well-formed Case feature bundles:

(35) -source → +source / [____, +possessor, -location]

This is shown in (36):

(36) a. 'Dative'				'Genitive'
-subject		-subject		-subject
-direct		-direct		-direct
+location	→(34a)→	-location		-location
+possessor		+possessor		+possessor
-source		-source	→(35)→	+source
-association		-association		-association

---

[10] Here as in other instances the hierarchy in (27) is violated. The Case restriction in (27d) becomes active, but not the Case restriction in (27f). In addition the feature bundle of the less marked dative is changed into that of the more marked locative. Faced with this type of facts, one could be tempted to give up the idea of an implicational hierarchy among Case restrictions. However I believe that this would be the wrong move. As shown by Blake (1994) Case systems seem to be organized according to clear patterns (see the implicational hierarchy in (25)). Following what proposed in note 8, however, we could say that (25) represents just a tendency and that limited exceptions are thus allowed. Thus a less marked Case restriction can become active even though a more marked one still remains inactive. Such a situation is possible, but to be considered exceptional.

2.2 *The feature assignments of lexical items*

Before going on to discuss the Latin Case system and its evolution into Romance, we need to address two important theoretical issues: 1) what features are assigned to the different lexical items, in particular Case endings, in synchronic Case systems? and 2) how do these assignments relate to synchronic patterns of syncretism?

Two different types of Case syncretism can be recognized from the synchronic point of view: absolute and contextual syncretism.[11] Absolute syncretism involves replacing a given Case exponent with another Case exponent across all nominal classes and nominal categories. The cases discussed in the preceding section were cases of absolute syncretism. Contextual syncretism, in contrast, involves replacement of a given Case exponent with another Case exponent only in certain nominal classes or in certain nominal categories. As will be discussed below, the former type of syncretism always implies synchronic activation of a restriction against the former Case, whereas the latter type doesn't.

To illustrate the different types of syncretism and to discuss their treatment, I consider the Latin fifth declension. In this declension we observe various cases of contextual syncretism, for example that between the genitive and the dative in the singular or between the dative and the ablative in the plural. We also observe a case of absolute syncretism: in fact, in this declension as in all other Latin declensions, the exponent of the ablative is also used to represent a variety of other grammatical function such as that of the instrumental and of the locative.[12]

[11] See Meiser (1992), Ringe (1995) on this distinction. Meiser (1992) distinguishes between functional syncretism (my absolute syncretism), which he characterizes as the falling together of two morpho-syntactic categories into a single one across the morphology of a language, and formal syncretism (my contextual syncretism) which he characterizes as the use of the same form to express morpho-syntactic categories which are otherwise morphologically contrasting in a language.

[12] In this paper, I have omitted the marginal locative and vocative Cases from my analysis of Latin. Symplifying quite a bit for the sake of the exposition, I assume that the locative is always represented by the ablative, and the vocative by the nominative. See Joseph and Wallace (1984) for a brief discussion of the status of these two cases in Latin.

		Sg.	Pl
(37)	Nom.	di-ē-s	di-ē-s
	Gen.	di-ē-ī	di-ē-rum
	Dat.	di-ē-ī	di-ē-bus
	Acc.	di-ĕ-m	di-ē-s
	Abl.	di-ē-∅–	di-ē-bus

The issue is now that of establishing the feature assignments of the different Case suffixes in (37). We can account for the distribution of the Case suffixes in (37) by minimizing the number of features assigned to them. The principle in (38) could govern this feature minimization:

(38) For each lexical item I, the minimal common set of features able to account for the maximal distribution of I must be chosen.

As we will see below, feature minimization must be used to account for contextual syncretism, but not to account for absolute syncretism.

The synchronic contextual syncretism observed in (37) could be accounted for by assuming the Case suffixes with the minimized feature assignments in (39) (I consider only the genitive, dative and ablative, and abstract away the thematic vowel from the desinence. See section 3 for a different and more complete discussion of the Latin declensions):

(39) a. /-rum/ ⟷ -location, +possessor, +plural
b. /-∅/ ⟷ +location, +source, -plural
c. /-ī/ ⟷ +possessor
d. /-bus/ ⟷ +location

But the distribution of the Case suffixes is not the only property that needs to be accounted for in the case of a system like that in (37). We also have to decide which Case restrictions are deactivated in it and which thus determine the Case system that it has. In fact, in the model proposed here, for each language we have to decide which Cases, if any, are morphologically present in its Case system. I propose that the following principle governs the determination of the structure of Case systems:[13]

[13] The principle in (40) is still tentative and many issues related to it are still unclear to me. Further research will try to clarify them. What is needed is an in-depth study of the morphology of Case systems across languages. Notice that any type of morphological exponence can be evidence for the deactivation of Case restrictions. For example two cases having the same desinence could be distinguished by the shortening or lengthening of the thematic vowel. In DM, such shortening or

(40) a. Given a language L, for each Case restriction R it must be determined if R is active or deactivated in L.

b. A Case Restriction [∝F, βG] is deactivated in a language L

i) directly iff there is a lexical item I in L identified by the features [∝F, βG]

or

ii) indirectly if there are lexical items S and T (S≠T) in L, where S is inserted in a terminal node containing [∝F, βG] and T is inserted in a terminal node containing either [∝F, -βG] or [-∝F,βG].

Principle (40) requires that feature minimization of Case suffixes is possible only in situations of contextual syncretism, i.e., when a suffix in a declension represents two or more Cases which are otherwise represented by different suffixes in other declensions.

Thus Principle (40) is satisfied in (38) directly for the Case restrictions in (27c) (genitive) and (27f) (ablative) given the Case suffixes in (39a) and (39b), and indirectly for the Case restriction in (27d) (dative), since there is the Case suffix /-i:/(=(39c)) inserted in the terminal node containing the features [+possessor, +location] and the Case suffix /-rum/(=(39a)) which is inserted in a terminal node containing the features [+possessor, -location]. Notice that it is the presence of the latter Case suffix that creates a morphological contrast between the dative and genitive in (37), although this contrast is present only in the plural. This is the function of (40bii): it establishes the conditions under which we obtain a morphological contrast between Cases in a Case system, i.e., the conditions under which two Cases are considered to be morphologically distinct in a Case system.

The problem is now to account for the fact that the ablative is also the exponent of the instrumental and the locative, as well as of the ablative. In this case we are dealing with a case of absolute syncretism.

Should we account for absolute syncretism by minimizing the feature assignments of the Case suffixes or not? If we do, we should then try to find the minimal common set of features among the ablative, the locative and the instrumental. The suffix/-∅/ should then be represented as in (39b')—[+loca-

lengthing would be expressed by a readjustment rule. Therefore also the presence of a readjustment rule may trigger the deactivation of a Case restriction. Both (40bi- ii.) should be modified accordingly. I will not do it here for expository reasons.

tion] being the minimal common feature shared by the ablative, locative and instrumental:

(39) b.' /-∅/ ⟷ +location, -plural

This suffix would then essentially have the same features as the suffix /-bus/ in (39d). Is this the correct move? I propose that it is not.

The reason is the following. Remember that given (40) the presence of the lexical item in (39b) indicates that the Case restriction (27f) is deactivated, so that we can say that we have the ablative in the system. In contrast (27e) and (27g) are not deactivated since there are no lexical items characterized by the features included in these case restrictions. If we decide to account for absolute sincretism by encoding it in the lexical items, and thus we replace (39b) with (39b'), we obtain the result that principle (40) can no longer be satisfied. In fact, given the algorithm in (40b) we would fail to determine which Case restriction among (27e,f-g) is deactivated: specifically, the lexical item in (39b) does not trigger the deactivation of any of these Case restrictions —either directly or indirectly. Thus we would be unable to establish what Case system characterizes the declension in (37). Hence a system replacing (39b) with (39b') to account for absolute syncretism is rejected by (40a).

The question is now whether or not principle (40) is needed. Synchronic evidence is difficult to construct. Here I will consider some historical evidence (see also section 5 for more historical evidence from the evolution of Latin into Romance.) Take into consideration the change exemplified in (29a) again. An aspect of this change that was not discussed earlier involves the fact that the pronominal *NDE in Proto-Romance, in addition to being the exponent of the genitive, was also the exponent of the ablative, whose terminal node is given in (41). Thus, in this case there was an absolute syncretism between the ablative and the genitive:

(41) "Ablative"
-subject
-direct
-possessor
+location
+source
+association

Suppose that principle (40) does not hold. Lexical minimization could, and obviously should, then be used to account for this case of absolute neutralization. Therefore the lexical item *NDE of Proto-Romance should be characterized as having the feature [+source], the minimal feature shared by the genitive and ablative, as shown in (42):

(42) nde ←→ [+source]

But now we would have a problem in trying to account for the change we observe in (29). We have to account for why the lexical item *NDE characterized as in (42) took over the function of the dative, We can repeat the feature bundle of the dative as in (43a). In order to insert (42) in that terminal node, we would then have to change the feature [-source] of the dative into [+source] as shown in (43b):

(43)	a. 'Dative'		b.
	-subject		-subject
	-direct		-direct
	+location		+location
	+possessor		+possessor
	-source	→	+source
	-association		-association

But the feature change in (43) is totally unmotivated and arbitrary. There is no reason for hypothesizing the feature change in (43). By using lexical minimization to account for absolute syncretism, we would then be forced to arbitrary moves in our explanation of the change in (29a).

Also any other approach to the change in (29a) trying to account for why the minimized lexical item in (42) takes over the function of the dative is doomed to be unmotivated and arbitrary, as the reader can check.[14] This is not true, however, if we assume an analysis based on the principle in (40). In this case, in fact, we would not have any problem in accounting for the evolution of *NDE in a motivated and simple way.

The following analysis could be proposed. Before the change in (29a), Proto-Romance *NDE is the exponent of both the genitive and ablative. Given principles (40), it must be determined if it is the exponent of one or the other, i.e., it must be determined which Case restriction between (27c) and (27f) is

[14] The same is true for an analysis assuming that the lexical item *NDE is totally unspecified, i.e. the elsewhere case of the system. See Calabrese (1995b) for a detailed criticism of such an approach.

deactivated. Let us suppose that it is the less marked one to be deactivated, i.e., that of the genitive. Therefore *NDE is assigned the features of the Case restriction in (27c), i.e the features in (44). The Case restriction in (27f) repeated here in (45) is instead assumed to be active. The feature bundle in (41) is then repaired by the feature change in (46) which, followed by the other automatic adjustment shown in (47), transforms the terminal node of the ablative into that of the genitive. The clitic *NDE is then inserted in this terminal node, and thus we account for why *NDE is the exponent of both the genitive and the ablative.

(44) a *NDE ←→ -location
+possessor

(45) *[+Location, +Source]

(46) [+location] → [-Location]/ [_____, +source]

(47)	'Ablative'				'Genitive'
	-subject		-subject		-subject
	-direct		-direct		-direct
	+location	→(44)→	-location		-location
	-possessor		-possessor	→(by(24e))→	+possessor
	+source		+source		+source
	-association		-association		-association

Given the feature assignments in (44) for *NDE, which are identical to those in (31a), we can then account for the replacement of the dative as done in section 2.1. Thus principle (40) leads to a straightforward analysis of the evolution we see in (29a). Crucially this evolution involves an instance of absolute neutralization. In contrast, in a case with contextual syncretism such as that exemplified in (39), principle (40) allows an analysis characterized by the minimization of the lexical items feature assignments such as that shown in (39). The difference is that in this case principle (40) is satisfied. Therefore we can conclude that contextual syncretism can be accounted for by minimizing the number of features assigned to lexical items, but absolute syncretism cannot.[15]

---

[15] Contextual syncretism is usually the consequence of phonological changes and other adjustments in the surface shape of morphemes (see Meiser (1992), Ringe (1995)). However, I would like to suggest that in some cases it might be due to the 'local' activation of Case restrictions. Thus, for example, in the case of the syncretic patterns we observe in (37), the syncretism between the

3. *The latin case system*

After the long theoretical exposition of the preceding section, we can start addressing the main topic of this paper: the evolution of the Latin Case system into Romance. I begin by discussing Latin. Latin is characterized, by five Cases and five declensions. The desinences of the Latin cases are listed in (48):

(48)		I	II	III		IV	V
				C-stems and Mixed	i-stem		
SG.	NOM	a	us/ __	e:s/s/__is		us	ẹ:s
	GEN	ae	i:	is	is	us	e:i:
	DAT	ae	o:	i:	i:	ui:	e:i:
	ACC	am	um	em	im	um	em
	ABL	a:	o:	e	i:	u:	e:
PL	NOM	ae	i:	e:s		u:s	e:s
	GEN	a:rum	o:rum	um	ium	uum	e:rum
	ACC	a:s	o:s	e:s		u:s	e:bus
	DAT	i:s	i:s	ibus		ibus	e:s
	ABL	i:s	i:s	ibus		ibus	e:bus

The Latin nominal system is characterized by widespread contextual syncretism. Given the analysis proposed in the preceding section and relying on Halle (1996), the following account based on feature minimization of the lexical items can be proposed for the Latin nominal system. First we have to segment the sound strings composing the desinences. We know that each word class is characterized by a common vocalic element which is traditionally called the thematic vowel. The thematic vowels of Latin are given in (49):

(49)	TV	→	a	in the env. [I]
	TV	→	o	in the env. [II]
	TV	→	i	in the env. [III]
	TV	→	u	in the env. [IV]
	TV	→	e:	in the env. [V]

---

genitive and the dative in the singular could have been the outcome of the activation of the Case restriction (27d) but restricted to the singular and the syncretism between the dative and ablative could have been the outcome of the activation of the Case restriction (27f) but restricted to the plurals (see Sommer (1914: 327-8), Leumann (1977: 417-420) for alternative views). I propose, however, that although this could be historically correct, the synchronic syncretic patterns created by these local activations of Case restrictions —in the same way as those created by sound changes— are better represented by simplifying the lexical items as in (39). (see section 5 for other cases of contextual syncretism developed through the local activation of Case restrictions).

There are various processes of lengthening, lowering, raising and deletion affecting the thematic vowel. These processes are the outcome of different readjustment rules (see Halle and Marantz (1993) and Halle (1996) on readjustment rules). Limits of space, however, prevent me from discussing these readjustment rules. I will only mention, as an example, the readjustment rule lengthening the thematic vowel in the ablative and dative of the II declension stated in (50):

```
(50)   X   →   X    X   /____ [V= Thematic vowel, II, +Location]
       |        \  /
       V         V
```

Once we subtract the thematic vowel from the desinences, we can recognize two different types of elements: the augments and the endings. By recognizing the presence of an augment in some desinences, a simpler analysis of the endings can be proposed. The augments are given in (51) and the endings in (52). According to this proposal, the desinence of the ablative/dative plural of the III declension is analyzed as /-bu-s/, that of the ablative /dative of the I-II declension as /-i:-s/, that of the genitive plural of the I-II and III declension as /-r-um/, where /-bu-, -i:-, -r-/ are the augments and /-s, -um/ the endings.

The featural assignments of the different lexical items in (51)-(52) follow from the principle (38) stating that, for each lexical item, the minimal common set of features able to account for the maximal distribution of the lexical item is chosen. The principle (40) is satisfied by a combined action between endings, augments and readjustments rules. Lack of space prevents me from discussing how this is implemented;

(51) Aug ↔ /-r-/ in env.___ + [+plur., +possessor, -location]
if dominated by a stem of I, II, V class.

Aug ↔ /-bu-/in env.___ + [+plur., +location]
if dominated by a stem of III, IV, V class.

Aug ↔ /-i:-/ in env.___ + [+plur., +location]
if dominated by a stem of I, II class.

Aug ↔ /–∅-/elsewhere

(52)	/-um/	↔	[+possessor, -location, +plural]	<PLGEN>
	/-i:/	↔	[+subject, +plural]	<PL, NOM>
			in the environment dominated by a stem of I, II class.	
	/-i:/	↔	[+possessor, -plural]	<SgGEN/DAT>
	/-a/	↔	[+direct, +plural, neuter]	<Pl.NT>
	/-m/	↔	[+direct, -plural]	<Sg.ACC>
	/-∅ /	↔	[-pl]	<Sg default>
	/-s/	↔	Elsewhere11W1C1	

The correct insertion of these lexical items will be governed by the assumption, fundamental in DM, that in a competition among different lexical items, the most highly specified one whose identifying (syntactic/semantic) features are a subset of the features of the terminal node wins the competition and is inserted (see the Subset principle in (10)). The ending /-s/ is not assigned a set of features and is inserted wherever other lexical items fail to be inserted. It is called the elsewhere case (see Halle (1996), Harris (1995) for discussion of the status and function of elsewhere cases).

Once we decide that /s/ is the elsewhere case, we need to account for the shape of the nominative and genitive singular. According to the list in (52), in these cases we should expect the null morpheme which is the default ending of the singular. Following Halle's analysis, we can say that this is obtained by having the operation of impoverishment which deletes certain relevant features. Under these conditions the next relevant lexical item will be inserted. The two operations of impoverishment needed to account for the shape of nominative and genitive singular are given in (53):[16]

---

[16] The function of Impoverishment is to block the insertion of more specified lexical items which are replaced by less specified ones. In this sense, impoverishment doesn't need to involve deletion and could be replaced by a statement disallowing the use of certain features in lexical insertion.

Limits of space prevent me from discussing the issues related to impoverishment in detail in this paper. However, an important issue that needs to be considered even though briefly is that of the relationship between impoverishment and feature change. These two operations share the same result of preventing the insertion of a given lexical item. I would like to assume that they are both needed, although there is some overlap in their function that needs to be eliminated. The issue is then what is the correct division of labor between them. A possibility is that impoverishment plays a role in accounting for patterns of contextual syncretism in conjunction with the notion of elsewhere case. However, as argued in Calabrese (1995b)(see also 2.2 and 5 of this paper), impoverishment cannot be used to account for changes involving absolute syncretism, where instead feature change must be used.

From the diachronic perspective, impoverishment could account for the morphological extension of forms which are more general from the distributional point of view, in particular for the

(53) a. The feature [-plural] is deleted in lexical insertion in the context of [+subject] in the II-IV declensions.

b. The feature [-plural] is deleted in lexical insertion in the context of [+possessor -location] in the III-IV declensions.

Therefore the null morpheme ∅ cannot be inserted in this cases, and the elsewhere case /-s/ is inserted.

To account for the shape of the dative of the second declension where instead of the expected/-i:/ we have -∅, we can assume the impoverishment in (54):

(54) The feature [+possessor] is deleted in lexical insertion in the context of [+location] in the II declension

After having provided an account of the Latin endings, we can consider the grammatical functions of the Latin nouns and their relationship to Cases. The grammatical function of Latin nouns was expressed in two different ways, as we can see in (55)-(56):

(55) Only with the Case ending:
amicum salutare 'greet a friend'
plenus vino (or *vini*) 'full of wine'
gladio occidere 'kill with a sword'

(56) With the Case ending and a preposition:
ad pugnandum aptus 'fit to fight'
in vino veritas
de amico fabulam narrare
'to tell a story about a friend'

Only the accusative and the ablative are used with prepositions. Dative and genitive do not admit prepositions. This is shown in (57):

(57) a. *liber petri*	'the book of Peter'
do librum amico	'I give a book to a friend'

extension of elsewhere cases. For example, impoverishment could be used to account for the diachronic spreading of the plural in /-s/ in English or the plural in /-i/ in Italian. To use feature change for cases like these is simply awkward. I will end this note by admitting that many aspects of this issue are still unclear to me. Future research will address them.

b. *ferire gladio* 'wound with a sword'
epistulam scribo 'I write a letter'
maerore conficior 'I am consumed by sorrow'

c. *eo in urbem* 'I go to the town'
venio ex urbe 'I come from the town'
per fines contendit 'he went through the territory'
ambulare cum amico 'walk with a friend'

As already mentioned in section 2.2, a characteristic property of the ablative in Latin is that it is used to represent a variety of grammatical functions. In some instances, for example, when the ablative is used to represent spatial roles, it is accompanied by a preposition. Otherwise it appears without a preposition, for example when it is used to represent the instrumental role.

As discussed in section 2.2, in all of these cases, we are dealing with a situation of syncronic absolute syncretism where the exponent of the ablative, in addition to the proper "ablative" function, also represents across all declensions grammatical functions associated to other Cases such as the instrumental, the locative, etc. As we saw in section 2.2, this type of syncretism should be accounted for by assuming that the morphosyntactic component contains active Case restrictions blocking the Cases which do not have a morphological expression, together with morphological operations converting the feature bundles of the disallowed Cases into those of allowed ones. Let us see how this is done with the ablative. I begin to account for the use of the ablative with the grammatical function of the instrumental that we see in the Latin phrase in (58):

(58) ferire gladio 'wound with a sword'

In the case of (58) the syntax will provide a KP that has the features of the instrumental in its head —as proposed in section 2.1, all types of Cases are present in the syntax. After merger and fusion, this KP will have the structure in (59):

(59)

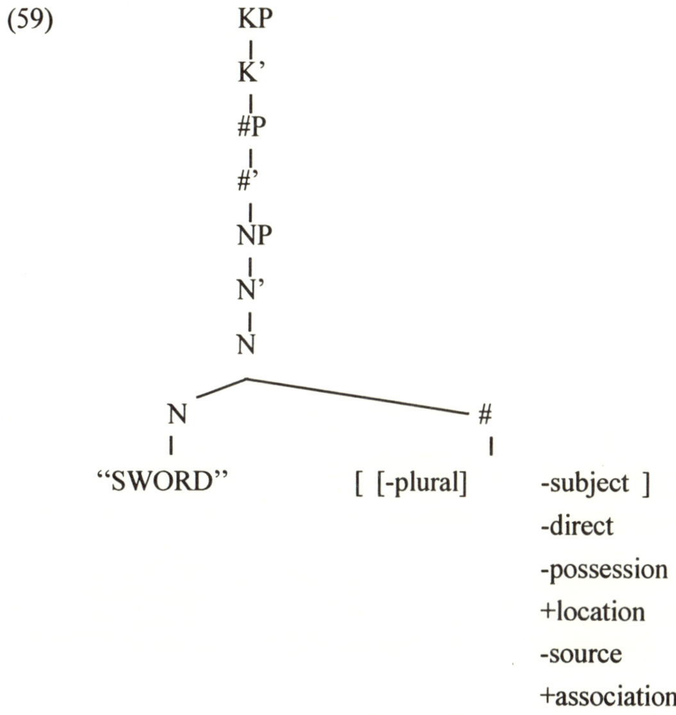

Latin disallows the morphological realization of the instrumental as an independent Case. This means that the Case restriction in (27g), repeated here as (60) is active in Latin:

(60) *[-source, +association]

This active Case restriction disallows the feature bundle in (54). Let us hypothesize that feature change is used to repair the disallowed configuration in (54) in the morphological component. This feature bundle is therefore modified by changing the feature [+association] into [-association] as in (61):

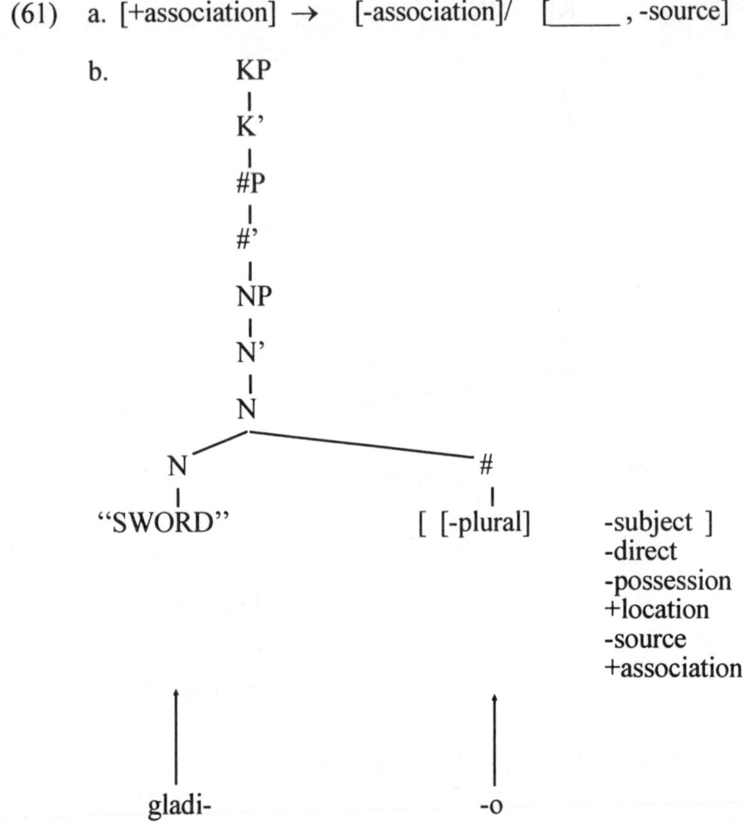

The Case feature bundle in (61b) is that of the ablative. Thus, by feature change, the instrumental provided by the syntax is replaced by the ablative in the morphological component.

At this point we have to address the status of the prepositions in Latin. Prepositions appear with Case-marked nominals in Latin. Now, Case-marking indicates that the KP is head-final. At the same time, the presence of prepositions indicates that the KP is head-initial. Latin is thus a problem since it apparently displays two contradictory properties.

Within DM, however, we have a simple solution for this problem. One of the operations that can repair a disallowed configuration is fission, which is formally represented in (9e). When fission applies to a disallowed Case configuration, it takes a feature from the disallowed bundle and adjoins it to the

KP. It thus creates a new position for lexical insertion in the morphology. This is shown in (62) (Using simplified tree structures):[17]

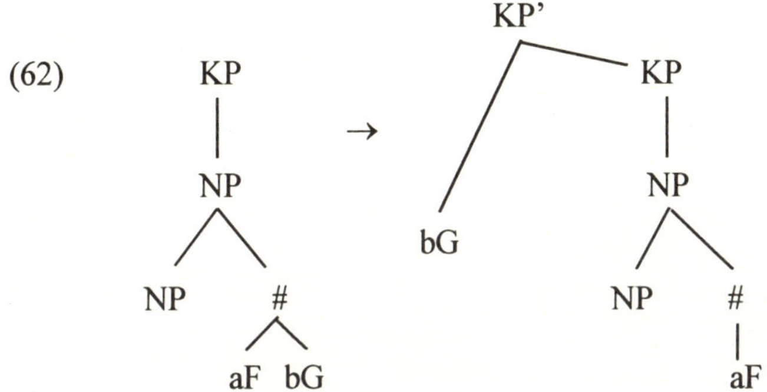

(where aF, bG are Case features)

This procedure accounts for the Latin Cases appearing with prepositions. Consider the example in (63):

(63) ex urbe "out of the town"

Let us assume that Latin disallows the configuration [+location, +elative[18]]. Thus the Case restriction in (64) is active in Latin:

(64) *[+location, +elative]

Let us suppose that fission is chosen to repair configurations disallowed by (64). Therefore, from the feature bundle in (65), we obtain the feature bundle in (66):

---

[17] As you can see in (62), the adjunction site of the fissioned element is at the side opposite to that of the fused Case head. I would like to suggest this follows from a general principle governing morphological fission. This principle should state that the landing site of morphemes fissioned from a head is always to the side opposite to the side of the head. Further research should determine if this principle is correct and whether or not this is the correct approach to the position of the fissioned element in (62).

[18] I am stipulating that the elative Case is characterized by the feature [+elative] just for the sake of the argument. The theory of Case features (which is still to develop) should determine the correct set of features that needs to be used to distinguish between local Cases, and therefore establish which feature is to be used in this case.

(65)

KP
K'
NP
N'
N
N
#
"ROME"
[..... -subject]
-direct
-possessor
+location
+source
+elative

(66)

KP'
KP
K'
NP
N'
N
K
N
#
+elative
"ROME"
[..... -subject]
-direct
-possessor
+location
+source
ex
Rom-
a

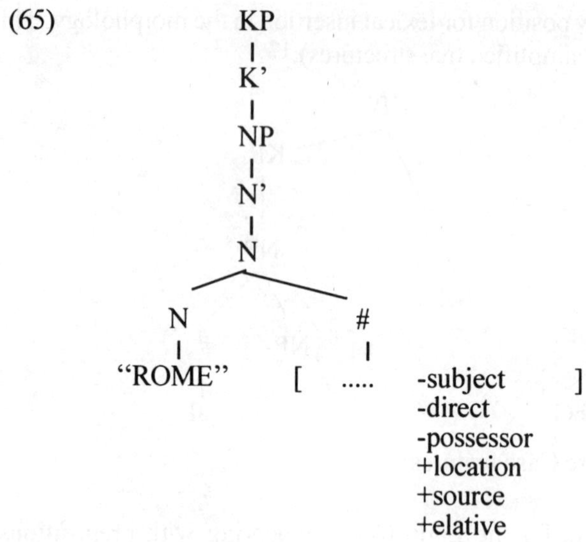

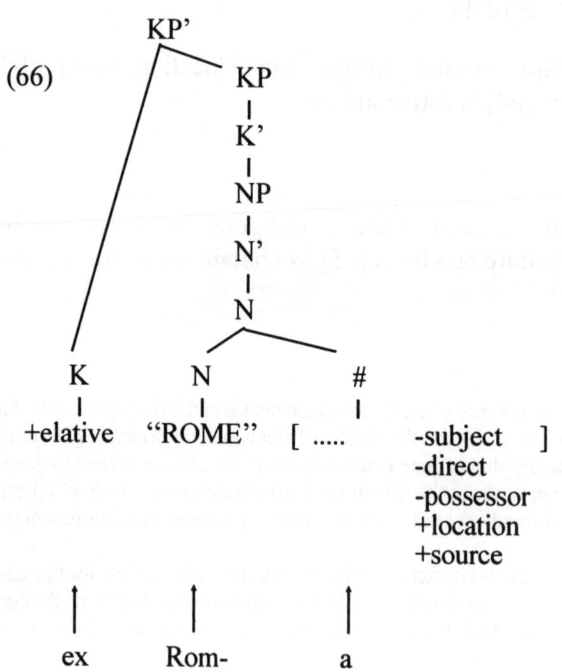

It appears that in Latin, fission is the preferred strategy for Cases which characterize different spatial relations such as the elative, allative, perlative, etc.), and for the other special Cases of (25)-(26), that is, the comitative, the purposive, the comparative and so on.[19]

Observe that by assuming fission we can analyze Latin as being a consistently head final language.

4. *The evolution of the latin case system*

In this section the developments of the Case system that are attested in Late Latin are discussed. First of all, there is a widespread syncretism between accusative and ablative. In particular, we see the appearance of the accusative after prepositions that took the ablative in the classical language. This is illustrated in (67):

(67) cum:
cum filios suos tres (CIL, VIII, 3933) 'with his three children'
(instead of *filiis suis tribus*)
ab:
posita a fratres (CIL, VIII, 20296) 'put by the brothers'
(instead of *fratribus*)
pro:
pro se et suos ((CIL, XII, 1185) 'for himself and his...'
(instead of *se et suis*)

Furthermore, there is widespread syncretism between the genitive and the dative. Characteristically it is the genitive that replaces the dative, as we can see in the cases in (68):

(68) *quod vinclum, quaeso, deest nostrae coniunctionis*
(instead of *nostrae coniunctionii*)(Cic. ad Fam. v, 15, 2)
'What bind, I ask, is absent from our relationship?'
ille tunc imber.. mortem intulit corporum (instead of *corporibus*)
(Chrisost. Ho. 7, 7)
'...the rain brought death to their bodies'
qui eorum (instead of eis) *auxiliare presumpserat* (Fredeg., sec.VI or VIII, 3, 51)

[19] There are also cases in which prepositions take the accusative. To account for them I would like to suggest that in addition to fission, these cases are also characterized by an operation of feature change which replaces the feature [-direct] with the feature [+direct]. Limits of space prevent me from developing this idea further.

'he who had taken help to them'
viriliter eorum (instead of *eis*)*resistens* (Chronicum Salernitanum, 747-974)
'...resisting corageously to them'

Eventually all prepositionless Case-marked NPs were replaced with prepositional constructions as shown in (69):

(69)	*ad carnuficem dabo*	in place of	*carnufici dabo*
	'I will give ___ to the executioner'		
	dixit Iesus ad discipulos		*dixit Iesus discipulis*
	'J. said to the disciples'		
	ostentare ad digitum		*ostentare digito*
	'to indicate with the finger'		
	monasterium de castas (Theodosius De situ terrae sanctae)		
	'monastery of young girls"		
	in hoc tempore		*hoc tempore*

Putting aside pronominal forms where a residual Case system was preserved, the majority of the Romance languages eliminated all expression of Case. There are two exceptions listed in (70):

(70) a. Old Gallo-Romance has a two Case system with an opposition between the subject and the oblique Case.
b. Rumanian has a two Case system. But here we have an opposition between Nominative/Accusative vs Genitive/Dative.

In the two languages in (70), the Case contrasts are best represented by the definite article (see section 5 for discussion of the nominal systems of these languages.)

In old French, which I take as representative of Old Gallo-Romance, the definite article has the 3 forms shown in (71):

(71) Old French definite articles:

	Singular	plural
Subj.	li < (IL)LI	li <(IL)LI
Obl.	le, lou <(IL)LU	les <(IL)LOS

In Rumanian where the definite article is enclitic, it has the 4 forms shown in (72) for the masculine and the feminine:

(72) Rumanian definite articles:

Masculine:	Singular	plural
Nom./Acc	lupul < LUPU (IL)LU	lupii < LUPI(IL)LI
Gen./Dat.	lupului <LUPU (IL)LUI	lupilor <LUPI (IL)LORUM
Feminine:	Singular	plural
Nom./Acc	casa <CASA (IL)LA	casele <CASAE (IL)LAE
Gen./Dat.	casei <CASAE (IL)LAEI	caselor <CASAE (IL)LORUM

In Old French, the subject Case is etymologically based on the Latin nominative, whereas the oblique is based on the Latin accusative. In Rumanian, the plurals seem to indicate that the etymological base for the nominative/accusative is the Latin nominative, whereas the basis for the genitive/dative is the genitive.[20]

5. *Account of the evolution of the latin case system*

A purely neo-grammarian type of explanation of the loss of the Case system in a language argues that it should be due to the phonological developments that this language underwent. In the case of Latin, the sound changes in (73) could have affected the Case system. By these changes, the Case distinctions in (74) were neutralized.

(73) a. Loss of /m/ in word final position.
b. Merging of short / ī , ū/ with /long /ē,ō/
c. Loss of quantity (Romā (nom.) cannot be distinguished from Romā (abl.) any longer)

	NOM	ACC	ABL		
(74)	terra	terram	terrā	→	terra
	campus	campum	campō	→	campo
	panis	panem	pane	→	pane

---

20 The evidence from the Rumanian singulars is more ambiguous. In particular, the Proto-Romance forms /*(IL)LUI/*(IL)LAEI/ from which the genitive/dative forms /-lui/-i/ derive are traditionally considered to be datives (cf. Lausberg (1977)). I would like to submit that they are actually genitives which replaced the classical form /ILLIUS/. Two morfological changes are relevant: I) the rule that deleted the thematic vowel before the genitive ending was lost; ii) the genitive ending /-i:/ of the nominal declension was extended to the pronominal declension. These two changes should give us forms such as *(IL)L-O-I/*(IL)L-A-I. Other minor phonological and morphological adjustments should produce the forms /*(IL)LUI/*(IL)LAEI/. Lack of space prevents me from developing the analysis of these forms in detail here.

However, a purely phonological explanation of the loss of the Case system in Latin does not work. First of all, observe that the system of inflectional endings in verbs was not lost, although these endings were affected by the changes in (73) in the same way as the nominal ones. Furthermore, given the changes in (73) in a language like Spanish where final vowels and final /s/ were preserved, all the Case distinctions in the plural should have been maintained, as we can see in (76). If they were lost, it must have been because of some non-phonological reason.

	Plural			
	Nominative	Genitive	Dative/Ablative	Accusative
(75)	terrae	terrarum	terrīs	terrās
	campi	camporum	campīs	campōs
(76)	*terre	*terraro	*terris	*terras
	*campi	*camporo	*campis	*campos

The same is true for the genitives and datives characterized by a long /-ī/ in languages like Italian where final vowels were preserved.

In Old French, where low vowels were raised but not lost in word final position, in contrast with non low vowels that were lost, we should find an alternation between /e to realize a genitive/dative of the Rumanian type, as in (77):

(77)	rose <	ROSA and ROSAM
	*ros <	ROSAE/ROSE

The absence of this Case contrast in Old French, as well as the other arguments mentioned above, demonstrates that a purely phonological account of the evolution of the Latin Case system is not satisfactory (see Renzi (1993) for more discussion of these points).

The traditional morphosyntactic account of the evolution of the Latin Case system relates the loss of Case-marking to the change in word order that occurred from Latin to Romance. Following Fillmore (1968), we can say that that Cases and prepositions are the morphological spell out of the same category Kase. We have prepositions when the KP is head-initial and Cases when the KP is head final, as shown in (78):

(78) a. Postposition/Case suffixes: b. Prepositions:

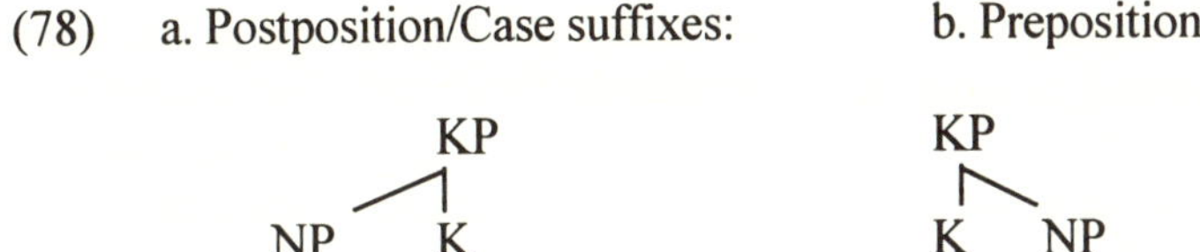

One could then propose that when Latin word order changed from head-final to head-initial, Case suffixes disappeared and became prepositions:

(79)

This account, though correct in its general effect, is obviously too simplistic. In fact, according to this analysis, it is not clear how to explain the various stages of the development of the Latin Case system. The proposed analysis could explain the replacement of the ablative with a prepositional construction. But it cannot account for why there is still accusative Case marking in this instance. Furthermore it cannot account for why there is the syncretism between dative and genitive which eventually leads to the Rumanian Case system. In the same way, it cannot account for the development of the two Case system subject vs. oblique attested in Gallo-Romance.

The theory of Case systems presented earlier provides an answer to these questions. We can then assume that concomitant with the trend to switch head position from final to initial, there was also a process of simplification of the Case system obtained by the activation of Case restrictions. It is this process of activation of Case restrictions that more strikingly accounts for the evolution of the Case system we see in Romance.

Before discussing an analysis of the syncretic changes based on the activation of the case restrictions, we need to explore another possible analysis of these changes. One could hypothesize that syncretic changes are due to the simple loss of lexical items, in this instance Case endings, with concomitant extension of the use of other lexical items. Assuming the lexical minimization proposed earlier, one could propose that more marked Case endings are lost and replaced by less marked ones. Such an analysis would simply not work. For example, consider the analysis for the Latin nominal system proposed in (52). In such analysis, the ending /-s/ has a special status being the elsewhere case, the least marked lexical item. If we assume that syncretic changes are due to the loss of lexical items, we should expect this ending to play a crucial role in the development of the system. We should then expect the ending /-s/ to be extended to uses that it did not have before. For example it should have become the exponent of the genitive of the second declension or of the dative, or of the genitive plural. No such change is attested, or can be reconstructed in the history of the Romance nominal system. Both Gallo-Romance and Rumanian preserve the exponents of Latin and their distribution intact. The changes that we observe in these Case system do not involve exponents, but the actual Cases. Thus for example, we have syncretic changes between ablative and accusative and between genitive and dative, regardless of the exponents that they have. The genitive plural /-ōrum/ replaces the dative plural /-īs/ in the second declension, regardless of the internal constituency and featural assignments of these exponents. The same is true for the replacement of the ablative /-īs/ by the accusative /-ōs/ where they both share the same ending/-s/ but differ in the quality of the thematic vowel —which is changed into /-i-/ in the ablative plural by a special rule (see Halle (1996)).

The evolution of these case systems seems to operate only through operations on Cases, regardless of the lexical items composing the Case system. The best way of representing these changes is therefore by modifications in the morphosyntactic component, i.e., through the activation of Case restrictions, as proposed earlier.

Two syncretic processes are observed in late Latin as shown in (67)-(69): the syncretism between ablative and accusative and the syncretism between genitive and dative.

I begin by considering the widespread syncretism between dative and genitive that characterized Late Latin. In the Case hierarchy in (27), the dative is more marked than the genitive. Let us suppose that the Case Restriction in (27d), repeated here as (80), is activated at a certain point in the history of Late Latin.

(80) *[+possessor, +location]

Therefore, a terminal node such as that in (81) must be repaired.

(81)

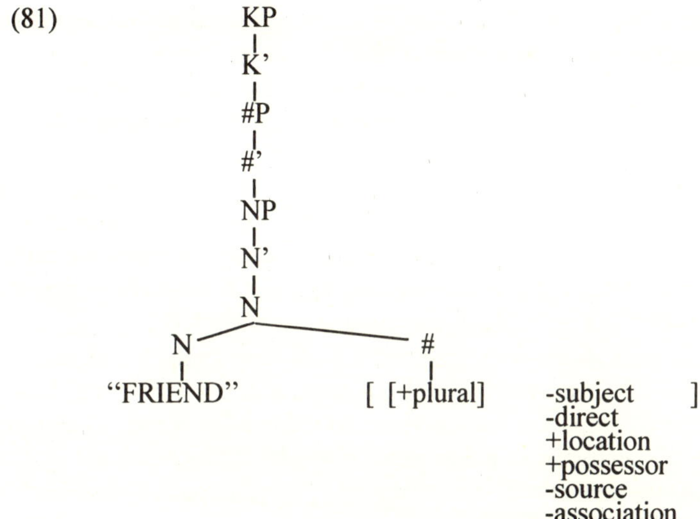

If it is repaired by changing the feature [+location], in conjunction with the other adjustments shown in (36), (81) will be changed into (82):

(82) a. [+location] → [-location]/ [___ , +Possessor]

b.

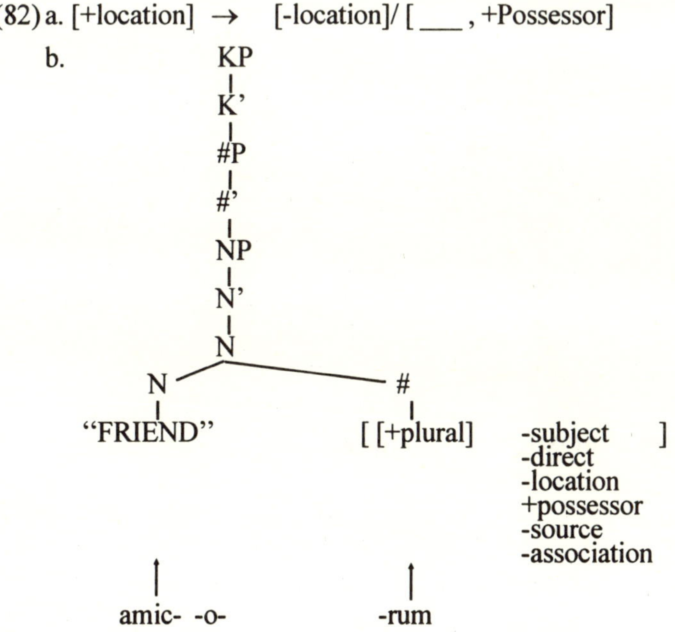

The exponent of the genitive will thus be inserted instead of the exponent of the dative. We have thus an account of the syncretism between genitive and dative. Notice that, at this point, the exponent of the genitive will also have the function of the dative, given that no preposition or other marker can distinguish the two.

Let us now consider the syncretism between ablative and accusative after prepositions. Observe that a further simplification of the Case system could be obtained if the leftmost K in (61) is reanalyzed as a head governing the embedded KP. As head of the higher KP, in fact, the leftmost K would be assigned all of the features that were previously assigned to the lower KP.

Now, as already discussed, Case restrictions only apply to merged Case feature bundles, i.e Cases that are realized as affixal, but not to morphologically free feature complexes such as those found in adpositions. Therefore if the leftmost K is analyzed as a free head, it would not be restricted by Case restrictions. At the same time, if the leftmost K is reinterpreted as a Head, the feature [+direct] must be assigned to the lower KP since it would be governed by a [-N] head. The result of this is that the ablative is eliminated after prepositions. The structure resulting from this change is represented in (83):

(83)

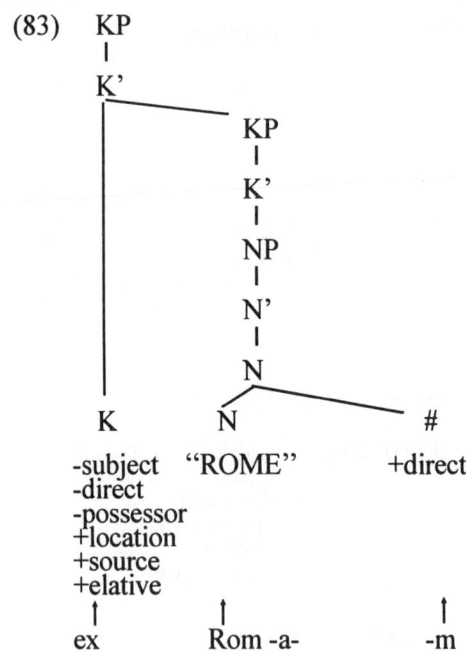

I hypothesize further that the elimination of the ablative after prepositions led to the activation of the Case restriction in (27f). Thus, prepositionless ablatives were also eliminated. They were repaired by fission. The fissioned Case feature was reinterpreted as the head as discussed above. Therefore the ablative was replaced in all situations with a prepositional construction employing the accusative.

Thus I propose that in Late Latin the Case restrictions in (27f) disallowing the ablative and that in (27d) disallowing the dative were activated. The ablative was replaced with prepositional constructions with accusative and the dative with prepositionless constructions with the genitive. For Proto-Romance, we can thus assume a system with the Cases in (84):

(84) I Declension Class

	Singular	plural	
Nom.	*porta	*porte	'door'
Acc.	*porta(m)	*portas	
Gen/Dat	*porte	*portaro(m)	

II Declension Class

	Singular	plural	
Nom.	*muros	*muri	'wall'
Acc.	*muro(m)	*muros	
Gen/Dat	*muri	*muroro(m)	

III Declension Class

	Singular	plural	
Nom.	*canes	*canes	'dog'
Acc.	*cane(m)	*canes	
Gen/Dat	*canis	*cano(m)?[21]	

The presence of a three Case system such as that in (84) for proto-Romance is predicted by the theory developed up to this point. Observe that the same system for proto-Romance has been independently argued by Burger (1943), de Dardel (1964), and Zamboni (1990).

21 At this point of my research, I am unable to decide what form should be reconstructed for the genitive plural of the third declension. Instead of the form given in (84) we could also propose **canoro* with extension of the suffix of the II declension. Further research should solve this problem.

Given the three Cases we see in the system in (84), we must suppose that the only Case restrictions that were inactive in Proto-Romance were those in (85):

(85) a. [+subject, +direct] (Nominative Case)
b. [-subject, +direct] (Accusative Case)
c. [+possessor, -location] (Genitive Case)

Now we can account for the difference in Case systems between Gallo-Romance and Rumanian. In the course of the development from Proto-Romance to Gallo-Romance, the Case restriction in (85c) became active, as shown in (86) and thus the genitive was removed from the system.

(86) a. [+subject, +direct] (Nominative Case)
b. [-subject, +direct] (Accusative Case)
c. *[+possessor, -location] (Genitive Case)

The feature [+possessor] was changed in the feature bundles of the genitive.[22] Thus, accusative exponents took the place of the genitive ones. We thus create a two Case system based on the contrast +/- subject, and obtain the system Subject vs. Oblique of Gallo-Romance, where the oblique forms are etymologically those of the accusative, and the subject ones those of the nominative. For Proto-Gallo-Romance we can then assume the system in (87):

(87) I Declension Class

	Singular	plural	
Subj.	*porta	*porte	'door'
Obl.	*porta	*portas	

II Declension Class

	Singular	plural	
Subj.	*muros	*muri	'wall'
Obl.	*muro	*muros	

III Declension Class

	Singular	plural	
Subj.	*canes	*canes	'dog'
Obl.	*cane	*canes	

---

22 This change is followed by the automatic adjustment of the features [-direct], [+source] into [+direct], [-source] because of the contraints in (24).

The Old-French system in (88) is obtained from that in (87) by the regular sound changes occurring in this language such as deletion of final non low vowels and raising of low vowels.[23]

(88) OLD FRENCH

I Declension Class

	Singular	plural	
Subj.	porte	portes	'door'
Obl.	porte	portes	

II Declension Class

	Singular	plural	
Subj.	murs	mur	'wall'
Obl.	mur	murs	

III Declension Class

	Singular	plural	
Subj.	chiens	chiens	'dog'
Obl.	chien	chiens	

---

[23] Observe that the ending of the plural Subject Case of the Old French first declension is identical to that of that of the oblique. I suggest that this might be a case of contextual syncretism triggered by a local activation of the case restriction (86a) in the plural of the first declension. This is the restriction that is activated across all declensions in a later stage of the language, as discussed below.

The phonological changes mentioned in the text and the local activation of the Case restriction (86a) created the complex pattern of contextual syncretism we observe in (88). As discussed in section 2.2, this pattern of syncretism should be accounted for by minimizing the feature assignment of the lexical items. The following system could be proposed (from M. Halle (p.c.)):

Vocabulary:

Thematic vowels:

(i) TV → /-e-//in envir. I declension
TV → ∅ /elsewhere

Case endings

(ii) /∅/ ↔ ∅[-plural]
/-s/ ↔ elsewhere

Morphological readjustments:

Impoverishment:

(iii) [-plural] → ∅ / [___, +subject, II, III]

Feature Change (ordered after (iii)):

(iv) [+plural] → [-plural]/ [___, +subject, II]

The peculiarity of Rumanian is that (85b) instead of (85c) was activated. Thus the accusative was removed from the system:

(89)	a.	[+subject, +direct]	(Nominative Case)
	b.	*[-subject, +direct]	(Accusative Case)
	c.	[+possessor, -location]	(Genitive Case)

We thus obtain the two Case system of Rumanian. Crucially the feature [-subject] was changed in the feature bundles of the accusative. Thus nominative exponents took the place of the accusative ones, giving a system nominative vs. genitive. This accounts straightforwardly for the forms that we find in the plurals of the definite article and of pronominals in Rumanian, as we can see in (90):

(90)					
a.	lupi-i	< LUPI(IL)LI	:	lupi-lor	<LUPI (IL)LORUM
	case-le	<CASAE (IL)LAE	:	case-lor	<CASAE (IL)LORUM
b.	ei	< ILLI	:	lor	<(IL)LORUM
	acesti	<ECCE+ISTI	:	acestor	<ECCE+ISTORUM
	acei	<ECCE+ILLI	:	acelor	<ECCE+ILLORUM

The situation in the nominal system is slightly more complicated. We can see the nominal system in (91)(Neuters are omitted)[24]

(91) RUMANIAN

I Declension Class (Feminine)

	Singular	plural	
Nom./Acc	capra*	capre	'goat'
Gen./Dat.	capre	capre	

---

[24] I also omitt discussion of endings whose form is different because of phonological changes. There are two classes of neuters. In the singular they behave like masculine nouns. In the plural, one class takes the suffix /-uri/. The other class is characterized by a change of gender and declension class so that the feminine plural suffix /-e/ of the I declension is found in this case. The behavior of the second class of neuters can be accounted for by assuming the lexical item in (93), the Redundancy rule in (i) proposed by Harris (1992) for Spanish, but which holds for Rumanian as well, and the feature change in (ii):

(i)	[+feminine]	→	[I]	
(ii)	[-feminine]	→	[+feminine]/	[___ , -masculine, +plural]

(i) assigns feminine nouns to the I declension. It does not apply to nouns of the III declension because they are idiosyncratically marked for declension class, as in Harris (1992) analysis of Spanish nominal morphology. The historical reasons for the feature change in (ii), which Rumanian share with Italian, are complex and cannot be discussed here.

II Declension Class (Masculine)

	Singular	plural	
Nom./Acc	codru	codri	'forest'
Gen/Dat.	codru	codri	

III Declension Class (masculine)

	Singular	plural	
Nom./Acc	câne	câni	'dog'
Gen/Dat.	câne	câni	

III Declension Class (feminine)

	Singular	plural	
Nom./Acc	vulpe	vulpi	'fox'
Gen/Dat.	vulpi	vulpi	

Observe first of all that in the nominal system, Rumanian displays contextual syncretism between nominative and genitive in the singular of the non-feminine declensions and in the plurals. In the feminine of all declensions, in contrast, the exponent of the genitive/dative is identical to that of the plural. Here I will sketch a possible analysis of the development of this pattern. The first change leading to this syncretic pattern could be the local activation of the case restriction (89c) in the plural. This is an expected change; it is well known that in many languages the plural is characterized by less Case distinctions than the singular. By this local activation all the genitive plural exponents were replaced by the nominative plural exponents and we thus obtain the syncretic pattern we observe in the plurals in (91).

A further local activation of this Case restriction also in the singular followed. I propose, however, that before this activation occurred, another change took place. In the first declension, the expected etymological ending of the genitive/dative singular(=/-e/) was homophonous to the ending of the plural (=/-e/) (at this point no case distinctions appeared in the plural). I propose that this homophony was eliminated by assuming that the same exponent appeared in both cases. This led to the stipulation of the feature change rule in (92), which in conjunction with the lexical item in (93), accounts for the distribution of the suffix /-e/ in the first declension in an optimal way (I = first declension):

(92) [-plural] → [+plural]/ [___, +nominal, I, +possessor]

(93) /-e/ ↔[+plural, I]

Subsequently, since the first declension contains only feminine nouns, the rule in (92) was extended as in (94) so that it applied to all feminine nouns, in particular to the feminine nouns of the third declension:

(94) [-plural] → [+plural]/ [___, +nominal, +feminine, +possessor]

This explains the syncretic pattern we observe in the feminines of the third declension. The other lexical items that are needed to account for the Rumanian nominal system and its contextual syncretism are given in (95):[25]

(95) /-i/ ↔ [+plural]
/∅/ ↔ elsewhere

We thus have an analysis of the synchronic situation of Rumanian. At this point we can consider the synchronic situation of the other Romance languages. In western Romance we have a further development. The two Case system subject/oblique is eliminated. I propose that it is eliminated by activating (86a). The nominative is therefore replaced by the accusative. We thus have an account of why the plural ending is /-s/ in western Romance. This is what we expect if the accusative is the base for the development of the plural morpheme as illustrated in (96):[26]

(96) Plurals

Proto-Western Romance	Western Romance (attested in Old French)	
*case		'house'
*casas	casas	
*campi		'field'
*campos	campos	
*dentes		'tooth'
*dentes	dentes	

[25] In addition, we need to assume that Rumanian nominal stems are characterized by the thematic vowels in (i) and that there is the readjustment rule in (ii) deleting the thematic vowel before another suffixal vowel:

(i) TV → e/ in the envir.[III]
TV → a/ in the envir. [I]
TV → u /elsewhere
(ii) V → ∅/ ___V

[26] See Wetzels (1981) for an interesting alternative analysis of the same facts. Observe also that given the system discussed in note 15 where /-s/ is the elsewhere case in Old French, there is no simple way to account for why the elsewhere /-s/ becomes the marker of the plural in modern French.

Let us consider Italian. We know that Italian has the old nominative ending as the marker of the plural. This is clearly shown by the plurals of the second declension as in (97):

	Sing.	Plur.
(97)	amico	amici
	campo	campi

We can account for this fact in two ways: We could propose that Italian shared the same development in the Case system as Rumanian. Therefore we could assume a two Case system N/A : G/D. Italian would be further characterized by the activation of (89c). The configurations disallowed by (89c) would be repaired by changing the feature [+possessor]. The feature [+possessor] was changed in the feature bundles of the genitive, followed by the automatic change of the feature [-direct] because of the unviolable constraint (24e) and of the change of [-subject] because of the active Case restriction (89b). Therefore the exponent of the genitive/dative would be replaced with that of the nominative. This is shown in (98):[27]

(98) Plurals

Proto-Eastern Romance	Italian	
*case	case	'house'
*casaro		
*campi	campi	'field'
*camporo		

Alternatively we could also propose that Italian shared the same development in the Case system as Western Romance. Therefore we could assume a two Case system Subject vs Oblique. However, instead of activating (86a), Italian would have activated (86b). Thus the configuration disallowed by (86b) would be repaired by changing the feature [-subject], and the exponent of the accusative would be replaced with that of the nominative. This is shown in (99):

---

[27] I do not consider the third declension where the nominative plural morpheme which we expect from Lat. /-es/ was replaced by the nominative plural morpheme of the II declension /-i:/. This happened in Italian and Rumanian. Therefore we have plural *cani* instead of *cane* (from Lat. *canes* with expected drop of final /-s/).

(99) Plurals

Proto-western Romance	Italian	
*case	case	'house'
*casas		
*campi	campi	'field'
*campos		

Evidence that the first alternative is the correct one may be found in the pronominal system. If we compare Italian plural stressed pronouns to those of Gallo-Romance and of Rumanian, we observe that in Italian the exponent of the genitive has taken over the function of the nominative:

(100)

	Plural			
	Nom.	Gen.	Dat.	Acc.
Class. Latin	ILLI	ILLORUM	ILLIS	ILLOS
Proto-Romance (cf (87))	ILLI	ILLORU	ILLORU	ILLOS
Italian	loro	loro	loro	loro
Rumanian	ei	lor	lor	ei
O.French	il	eus	eus	eus
O.Provencal[28]	il	lor	lor	els
		els	els	

The Italian system could be easily accounted for if we assume the Rumanian system and hypothesize that instead of activating (89c) and thus replacing the genitive with the nominative, we activate (89a) and replace the nominative with the genitive.

Further research will help in deciding which is the best reconstruction for the Italian system. Under both hypotheses, however, the forms in (101-2) would be the expected Italian outcomes:

(101)	*homo - homine	→	uomo	'man'
	*mulier - muliere	→	moglie	'wife'
	*latro - latronis	→	ladro	'thief'
	*sartor - sartoris	→	sarto	'tailor'
(102)	*pietas - pietate	→	pieta	'piety'
	*mel - melle	→	miele	'honey'
	*cor - corde	→	cuore	'heart'
	*fel - felle	→	fiele	'bile'

28 The Old Provencal pronominal system /il, lor, els/ preserves the three Case distinction of the Proto-Romance Case system as reconstructed in (84).

The forms in (103) that are usually reported as evidence of generalizations of the accusative Case in Italian can now be accounted for by assuming that the special allomorphy rules needed to account for the shape of the nominative forms of the so called "imparisillabi" were eliminated in Proto-Romance:

	Late Latin		Italian	
(103)	*mons - monte	→	monte	'mountain'
	*-ator - atore	→	-atore	'-suffixal element'
	*paries - pariete	→	parete	'wall'
	*pecten - pectine	→	pettine	'comb'
	*iudex - iudice	→	giudice	'judge'
	*pulex - pulice	→	pulce	'flea'
	*cardo - cardine	→	cardine	'pivot'

Evidence that this is correct is provided by Mayerthaler (1981) who demonstrates that the elimination of allomorphy in the case of the so-called imparisillabi is already attested in late Latin, as shown in (104):

(104)	nepotis	'grandson-NOM'	instead of Cl. nepos
	montis	'mountain-NOM'	instead of Cl. mons
	floris	'flower-NOM'	instead of Cl. flos
	mentis	'mind-NOM'	instead of Cl. mens

6. *Conclusions*

We thus have an account of the the loss of the Case system from Latin to Romance. My analysis is based on the idea that Case systems are structured in the same way as phonological systems. In particular, they are governed by Case restrictions that disallow the combinations of certain Case features.

Simplifications in the structure of Case systems involve the activation of Case restrictions. An active Case restriction disallows a given feature combination in the feature bundles of the terminal nodes provided by the syntax. Disallowed feature bundles can be repaired either by changing one of the disallowed features or by fissioning it. Both strategies were used in the historical development of the Latin Case system. Fission accounts for the appearance of prepositions at a stage when Latin Kase phrases were consistently head final. Feature change accounts for simple Case syncretism. By the combined effect of these two strategies, I have shown how the five Case Latin system was reduced to a three Case system in proto-Romance by eliminating the ablative and the dative. I have then shown how this three Case system evolved differently in western and eastern Romance, and why the plural morphemes in languages such as French, Spanish and Portuguese are etymologically based on the Latin accusative, whereas the plural morphemes of a language like Italian are etymologically based on the Latin nominative.

REFERENCES

Bittner, Maria & Ken Hale. 1996. "The Structural Determination of Case and Agreement." *Linguistic Inquiry* 27.11-69.

Blake, Barry. 1994. *Case*. Cambridge: Cambridge University Press.

Bonet, Eulalia. 1991. *Morphology After Syntax*. Ph.D. dissertation, MIT.

Burger, André. 1943. "Pour une théorie du roman commun". *Mémorial des études latines offert à J.Marouzeau*, 162-169. Paris: Les belles lettres.

Calabrese, Andrea. 1995a. "Marking Statements, Complexity and Simplification Procedures." *Linguistic Inquiry* 26.2.

———. 1995b. "Syncretism Phenomena in the Clitic Systems of Italian and Sardinian Dialects and the Notion of Morphological Change." *Proceedings of NELS 25,* 151-173. GLSA, University of Massachusetts.

———. 1995c. "I sincretismi fra pronominali clitici nei dialetti italiani e sardi e la teoria della morfologia distribuita" To appear in *Atti del XXI Congresso Internazionale di Linguistica e Filologia Romanza,* Palermo, 18/24 September 1995.

Calboli, Cesare. 1972. *La linguistica moderna e il latino*. Bologna: Patron.

Carstairs-McCarthy, Andrew. 1987. *Allomorphy in Inflection.* London: Croom Helm.

Comrie, Bernard. 1991. "Form and Function in Identifying Cases". *Paradigms, The Economy of Inflection* ed. by F. Plank, 41-56. Berlin: Mouton de Gruyter.

Cutler, A., J.A. Hawkins & G. Gilligan. 1985. "The suffixing preference: a processing explanation". Linguistics 723-758.

de Dardel, Robert. 1964. "Considerations sur la déclinaison romane à trois cas". *Cahiers Ferdinand de Saussure* 21.7-23.

——— & Paul A. Gaeng. 1991. "La declinaison nominale du Latin non classique: essai d'une méthode de synthèse". *Probus* 4. 91-125.

Ernout, Alfred et F. Thomas. 1972. *Syntaxe Latine*. Paris: Klincksieck.

Fillmore, Charles J. 1968. "The Case for Case." *Universals in Linguistic Theory* ed. by Emond Bach & R.T. Harms, 1-88. London: Holt, Rinehart & Winston.

Halle, Morris. 1990. "An Approach to Morphology." *Proceedings of NELS 20*.150-84, GLSA, University of Massachussetts.

———. 1996. "Class Notes, Spring 1996." Ms. MIT.

——— & Alec Marantz. 1993. "Distributed Morphology and the Pieces of Inflection". *The View from Building 20: Linguistic Essays in Honor of Sylvain Bromberger* ed. by Kenneth Hale & Samuel J. Keyser. Cambridge, Mas.: MIT Press.

———. 1994. "Some Key Features of Distributed Morphology." *MIT Working Papers in Linguistics* 21.275-288.

Harris, James. 1992. "The Form Classes of Spanish Substantives". *Yearbook of Morphology 1991* ed.by G. Booij & J. van Marle. Amsterdam: Kluwer.

———. 1994. "The Syntax-Phonology Mapping in Catalan and Spanish Clitics". *MIT Working Papers in Linguistics* 21.321-354.

Herman, Jozsef. 1967. *Le latin vulgaire.* Paris: Presses Universitaires de France.

Hjelmslev, Louis. 1935. *La catégorie des cas: Etude de grammaire générale I:* Copenhagen: Munsksgaard. [Acta Jutlandica: Aarsskriftmfor Aarhus Universitet 9.3].

Kurylowicz, Jerzy. 1964. *The Inflectional Categories of Indo-European.* Heidelberg: Carl Winter Universitätsverlag.

Jakobson, Roman. 1936. "Beiträge zur allgemeinen Kasuslehre". *TCLP* 6.240-288. (English Translation in R. Jakobson, *Russian and Slavic Grammar,* Berlin: Mouton, 1984).

———. 1958. "Morphological Inquiry into Slavic Declension: Structure of Russian Case Forms." *Selected Writings II: Words and Language* ed. by Roman Jakobson, 23-71. The Hague: Mouton.

Joseph, Brian & Rex Wallace. 1984. "Latin Morphology: Another Look." *Linguistic Inquiry* 15.319-28.

Lausberg, Heinrich. 1977. *Linguistica Romanza.* Milano: Feltrinelli.

Leumann, Manu. 1977. *Lateinische Laut - und Formenlehre.* 2nd ed. Munich: Neck.

Löfstedt, Einar. 1942. *Syntactica. Studien und Beiträgen zur historischen Syntax des Lateins. 1. Teil: Uber einige Grundfragen der Lateinischen Nominalsyntax.* Lund: Gleerup.

Luraghi, Silvia. 1987. "Patterns of Case Syncretism in Indo-European Languages". *Papers from the 7th International Conference on Historical Linguistics* ed. by A. Giacalone Ramat et al., 355-371. Amsterdam: John Benjamins.

Mayerthaler, Willi. 1988. *Morphological Naturalness.* Ann Harbor: Karoma Publishers.

Meillet, Antoine et Joseph Vendryes 1966. *Traité de grammaire comparée des langues classiques.* Paris: Champion.

Meiser, Gerhard. 1992. "Syncretism in Indo-European Languages- motives, processes, and results". *Transactions of the Philological Society* 90.187-218.

Norberg, Dag Ludvig. 1944. *Beiträge zur spätlateinischen Syntax.* Uppsala.

Noyer, Rolf. 1992. *Features, Positions, and Affixes in Autonomous Morphological Structure.* Ph.D. dissertation, MIT.

Renzi, Lorenzo. 1987. *Nuova introduzione alla filologia romanza.* Bologna: Il Mulino.

———. 1993. "Vestiges de la flexion casuelle dans les langues romanes". *XXe Congrés International de Linguistique et Philologie romanes, t.II. Sect. 6.* Bern: Francke.

Ringe, Don. 1995. "Nominative-Accusative Syncretism and Syntactic Case". *Penn Working Papers in Linguistics* 2.45-81

Rohlfs, Gerhard. 1966-69. *Grammatica storica della lingua italiana e dei suoi dialetti.* Torino: Einaudi.

Serbat, Guy. 1981. *Cas et Fonctions,* Paris, Puf.

Sommer, Ferdinand. 1914. *Handbuch der lateinschen Laut- und Formenlehre.* 2nd and 3rd ed. Heidelberg: Winter.

Tekavcic, Pavao. 1972. *Grammatica storica dell'italiano.* Bologna: Il mulino.

Väänänen, Veikko. 1972. *Introduzione al latino volgare.* Bologna. Patron.

Weerman, F. 1995. "On the Relation between Morphological and Syntactic Case." Ms. Utrecht University.

Zamboni, Alberto. 1990. "Premesse morfologiche e tipologiche del composto italiano «capinera», «pettirosso»". *Parallela 4. Morfologia/Morphologie*, 97-109. Tübingen, Niemeyer.

THE WH-FEATURE AND THE SYNTAX OF RESTRICTIVE AND NON-RESTRICTIVE RELATIVES IN FRENCH AND ENGLISH[1]

RÉJEAN CANAC MARQUIS
Université du Québec à Montréal
&
MIREILLE TREMBLAY
Queen's University

0. *Introduction*

Two types of relative clauses have been identified in the literature: restrictive relatives such as (1a), which restrict the reference of the antecedent, and appositive relatives such as (1b), which do not.

(1) a. The woman (whom/that) Mary saw works at UQAM.
    b. Marianne, who Mary saw, works at UQAM.

A number of syntactic and semantic arguments have been put forth in favor of a non-unified analysis of restrictive and appositive relatives. However, this paper claims that there is only one type of relative clause, which is restrictive, and that the observed differences follow from independant constraints on the identification of null pronominals and the syntax of unmerged objects. We argue that appositive relatives are in fact restrictive relatives in apposition.

---

[1] This research was supported by a post-doctoral fellowship from the Fonds FCAR (#940574) attributed to Réjean Canac Marquis and by a post-doctoral fellowship from the SSHRC (#756-94-0487) attributed to Mireille Tremblay, by the SSHRC grant # 411-92-0012 (La modularité de la grammaire) attributed to A.M. DiSciullo, and by the FCAR grant # 94ER0401 (Interfaces, invariants et relativisation) attributed to A.M. DiSciullo, M. Lemieux et M.T. Vinet. Preliminary versions of this paper were presented at the annual congress of the Association canadienne-française pour l'avancement des sciences (ACFAS) held at the Université du Québec à Chicoutimi in May 1995, and at Queen's University in February 1996. The authors wish to thank the participants to ACFAS as well as the members of the above mentioned projects for their helpful comments. We would also like to thank the SSHRC General Research Grant program for a conference travel grant from Queen's University. We also thank Jeff Gruber for judgements on the English data.

Such a unified analysis eliminates unnecessary complexity in the grammar, and should thus be considered the null hypothesis.

We further propose that relatives are not always derived by movement: Movement is only triggered by feature checking but base-generation, the basic use of the operation Merge, remains an option for convergence (e.g. Full Interpretation). Cross-linguistic differences between English and French are argued to follow from variation in the morphological feature [±Wh], which must be distinguished from the semantic feature [±Q].

The discussion is organized as follows: Section 1 provides arguments in favor of a unified analysis of restrictive and non-restrictive relatives and shows that non-restrictive relatives are licensed by a general strategy of apposition. Sections 2 and 3 discuss the role of the feature [±Wh] in the distribution of Wh-elements in questions and relatives and the observed variation in that respect between French and English.

1. *Appositive relatives are restrictive*

We begin with the general observation that appositive relatives, but not restrictive relatives, allow the relative expression to have its own head noun.

(2) a. Jane, a woman whom Mary met at the party, is brillant.
b. *The candidate a woman whom Mary met at the party is brillant.

The so-called appositive relative in (2a) is in fact a restrictive relative: it restricts the reference of its head *a woman*, which is itself in apposition with respect to its antecedent (*Jane* in this case). Such appositive relatives are (mere) instances of a general strategy of apposition, which is needed independently to account for examples such as (3).

(3) John, $[_{DP}$ an absent-minded man], came late.

We extend this analysis of headed appositive relatives to non-headed appositive relatives: non-headed appositive relatives are in fact restrictive relatives with a covert pronominal head coreferential with an antecedent.

(4) $John_i$, $[_{DP}$ pro_i $[_{CP}$ who Mary knows well]], came late

Example (5) shows that the covert pronominal has an overt counterpart.

(5) John, $[_{DP}$he $[_{CP}$who is usually not late]], came in at 10 o'clock.

This analysis provides a simple account for a number of intriguing differences between restrictive and appositive relatives. First, only appositive relatives can take a proper name as an antecedent.

(6) a. *John who I know well ...
b. John, who I know well, ...

Under our proposal, this follows from the more general constraint according to which proper names cannot be modified or restricted in the syntax (by a relative or an adjective) unless a determiner is present, in which case such proper names must be treated as common nouns (see Longobardi 1994 for discussion). The only strategy available to qualify a proper name is apposition, in which case the modifying element is not part of the DP containing the proper name and does not restrict its reference.

(7) Marianne, a very good linguist, provided a new account of WCO effects.

For cases such as (6b), we argue that the proper name is not the head of the relative. The head of the relative is a covert pronominal, coreferential with the antecedent.

(8) $John_i$, pro_i who I know well,....

This analysis explains a related fact. It has been noted that restrictive clauses must precede non-restrictive clauses.

(9) a. The girl who won the prize, whom you know, will go to college.
b. *The girl, whom you know, who won the prize, will go to college.

This follows from the general property that parentheticals can only be inserted between constituents (see Emonds 1979): it is impossible to separate the relative from its head.

We thus argue that all appositive relatives are in fact restrictive relatives contained in an appositive DP. The head of the restrictive relative in apposition may be overt or covert. Covert heads must be licensed by an adjacent antecedent, as will be shown in section 1.2.

1.1 *Appositive relatives are unmerged syntactic objects*

We claim that appositive DPs are unmerged syntactic objects, as evidenced by the break in intonation characteristic of parentheticals. In writing, this is indicated by the commas on each side of the parenthetical, as shown in the examples in (10) ((10a)=(3)).

(10) a. John, $[_{DP}$ an absent-minded man], came late.
b. Jane, $[_{DP}$the woman Mary met at the party], is a brillant professor.

Unmerged objects are independent phrase-markers to which the operation Merge has not applied. Strictly speaking, they do not belong to the same structure as the main clause to which they are associated, and thus are not visible to relations that are structure-dependent, such as operator-variable dependencies and scope. Rather, we argue that unmerged objects (and therefore appositive DPs) are only visible at the discourse level and appositive DPs must be licensed by coreference to satisfy the Principle of Full Interpretation.

Various evidence supports this conclusion. First, it is a well-known fact that appositives relatives, unlike restrictive relatives, cannot have a quantifier as their antecedent. If no c-command relation holds between the antecedent and the empty pronominal, the bound variable relation is blocked, just like it is blocked between independent clauses (11b). Since quantifiers have no reference, they may not act as discourse-antecedent of the pronominal either.

(11) a.*Everyone/no one$_i$, pro$_i$ who attended the party, had a good time.
b.*Everyone/no one$_i$ came to the party. He$_i$ left.

Secondly, as noted in McCawley (1988), VP anaphora does not include the non-restrictive relative, an expected fact if appositive DPs do not belong to the same syntactic object as the VP gap.

(12) John sold a violin, which had once belonged to Nathan Milstein, to Itzhak Perlman, and Mary did [e] too.
[e] = ... sell a violin to Itzhak Perlman.
*[e] = ... sell a violin, which which had once belonged to Nathan Milstein, to Itzhak Perlman.

Finally, the fact that non-restrictives are not in the scope of verbs like "think" (Srivastav 1990, cited in Dermidache 1991) also follows from their unmerged status. (13) does not imply that John thinks that Bill is a genius, showing that no c-command relation holds between the verb *thinks* and the relative, an expected consequence if appositive relatives are not merged.

(13) John thinks that Mary loves Bill, who is a genius.

1.2 Pro *identification and appositive relatives*

The analysis of appositive relatives as restrictive relatives with a covert head accounts for a number of properties associated with appositive relatives: 1) the obligatory presence of a Wh-element; 2) the structural adjacency of the antecedent; 3) the impossibility to stack or extrapose them. We will show that these properties are to be related to the presence of the null pronominal head and do not pertain to the syntax of appositive relatives *per se*. Under our analysis, such properties follow from licensing conditions on the identification of *pro*, as evidenced by the fact that they are not found when the appositive relative has an overt head.

First, it has long been noted that Wh pronouns may be omitted in restrictive relatives (14a), but not in appositive relatives (14b).

(14) a. The woman (who/that) Mary saw works at UQAM.
b. Marianne, *(who) Mary saw works at UQAM.

Interestingly, the restriction disappears if the head of the relative is overt.

(15) Marianne, $[_{DP}$ the woman $[_{CP}$ (who/that) Mary saw]], works at UQAM.

We propose that these facts reflect a more general, though English specific, rule of Deletion under Recoverability along the lines of Riemsdijk and Williams (1986): a Wh-pronoun can be deleted only if its content can be recovered, that is when the head of the relative is overt (in restrictive and headed appositive relatives), but not when the head of the relative is covert.

(16) Marianne$_i$, pro$_i$ who$_i$ Mary saw, works at UQAM.

A second property associable to the presence of the null head is linear adjacency with the antecedent: it is not required in the case of restrictive relatives (17a,b), while it is required in the case of appositive relatives (18a,b).

(17) a. A man Mary knows came. b. A man came who Mary knows.
(18) a. Peter, who Mary knows, came. b. *Peter came, who Mary knows.

Following Kayne (1994), we assume that the non-adjacency with restrictive relatives results from relative clause stranding after raising of the direct object.

(19) Something$_i$ just happened [[e]$_i$ that you should know about].

Such analysis is not possible with appositive relatives, assuming that *pro* identification in appositives always requires strict linear adjacency.

(20) *Peter$_i$ came [e]$_i$, *pro* who Mary knows.

Again, the sentence is grammatical if the head of the appositive relative is overt, in which case the construction is not restricted to ergative verbs.

(21) I lent my copy of the Minimalist Program to Jane,
a book which I bought last year.

A third difference imputable to a constraint on *pro* identification is that only restrictive relatives may be stacked (examples from McCawley 1988).

(22) a. The student who took the qualifying exam who failed it
wants to retake it.

b. *Sam Bronowski, who took the qualifying exam who failed it,
wants to retake it.

The impossibility to stack appositive relatives is expected if the head of such relatives is *pro*. We have already seen that *pro* identification requires the antecedent to be linearly adjacent: stacking would necessarily break such adjacency. The fact that stacking is allowed when the head is overt provides empirical evidence in favor of this proposal.

(23) Sam Bronowski, the student who took the qualifying exam who
failed it, wants to retake it.

Another property distinguishing restrictive and non-restrictive relatives is that while the former are always headed by an NP, the latter may take an antecedent that is not an NP ((24a) is an AP, (b) a PP, and (c) an IP).

(24) a. John is **afraid of snakes**, which I'm sure that Mary is too.
b. Senator Snerd is **in Bermuda**, where most of his colleagues
are too.

c. It has been reported that **Senator Snerd is in Kuwait**,
which can't be right.

Given that restrictives can never take anything but a nominal head, and given our analysis of appositive relatives as restrictives, we propose that appositive relatives are always headed by a (pro)nominal, be it overt or not.

(25) a. ...afraid of snake, pro which I'm sure Mary is not.
b. ...in Bermuda, pro where most of his colleagues are too.
c. ...Senator Snerd is in Kuwait, pro which can't be right.

French provides overt evidence for this structure as it requires an overt (pro)nominal head in all instances.

(26) a. *Marcelle est très fatiguée,* ***ce*** *que Marie n'est pas.*
b. *Marcelle est au Mexique, (**endroit**) où elle avait toujours voulu aller.*
c. *Marcelle est arrivée en retard,* ***ce/chose*** *qu'elle ne fait jamais.*

Having established that there is only one type of relative clause, we now turn to the question of the derivation of relatives and cross-linguistic variation.

2. *Wh-feature value and variation*

A central hypothesis of recent reductionist programs locates the source of variation in the properties of lexical items, in particular the nature of morphological/formal features and how they are verified through the derivation. An important question therefore lies in determining what are the features involved in variation and how they operate in syntax. For instance Chomsky (1995) adopts a privative system where the "value" of a feature corresponds to a "strong" versus "weak" distinction, which amounts to stipulating at which point of a derivation feature-checking operates (i.e. in the computational system or at an interface level). We do not exploit this distinction here but maintain a different, though not incompatible, approach whereby a feature must be lexically determined as to its PLUS or MINUS value and, if the case occurs, agrees w.r.t to this value. Given such a system, we argue that variation in the syntax of relatives and Wh-questions in French and English follows from basic processes of feature checking. In spirit with recent reductionist approaches, our assumptions include a strict feature-value sharing spec-head agreement as shown in (27).

(27) Strict Spec-head agreement: agreeing features share values.

$[_{YP}$ XP $[_{Y'}$ Y ...]]
* (αF) (βF)

2.1 *Wh-feature value and the distribution of Wh relative pronouns*

We claim that just as questions are characterized as [+Wh] or [-Wh] (Wh-questions vs. yes-no questions), relative clauses may also vary w.r.t. the value of the feature Wh: relative clauses are [+Wh] in English but [-Wh] in French (arguably also in Italian and Spanish). Next we show that this difference in feature value accounts for discrepancies in the distribution of Wh-words in the two languages.

Kayne (1976) made the observation that in French, no bare Wh-word may occupy spec of CP (see Cinque 1982 for a similar observation in Italian). Let us refer to this fact as the *[DP,CP] restriction.

(28) a. **L'homme lequel/qui je connais bien.*
b. **l'homme lequel connaît bien Marie.*

This restriction directly follows from the proposed [-Wh] status of relatives in this language in conjunction with Strict Spec-head agreement: Wh-words, which are inherently [+Wh], are ungrammatical in the SPEC of a [-Wh] COMP. The remaining option available to French to prevent a clash in feature-value is the systematic use of a [-Wh] null operator (see Browning 1987). Notice that, as argued convincingly in Kayne (1976), Pesetsky (1982) and Guéron (1986), *que* and *qui* are not bare Wh-words but complementizers in these contexts.

(29) a. *La table* [O_i [*que Marie a achetée* e_i].
'The table that Mary bought.'
b. *La table* [O_i [*qui a été achetée par Marie* e_i].
'The table that has been bought by Mary.'

The examples in (30) show that the *[DP, CP] restriction does not hold in English.

(30) a. The man [$_{CP}$whom I know well].
b. The man who knows Mary.

Under our approach, the possibility of having a bare Wh-word in the spec of relatives in English follows from the [+Wh] status of COMP in this language.[2]

---

[2] We assume that English relatives without an overt Wh-word result from an English-specific rule of PF deletion of Wh-word in relatives, as proposed for instance by Williams & Riemsdijk's (1985) *Deletion in COMP up to recoverability*.

Interestingly, the difference between French and English disappears when the Wh-word is embedded in a PP.

(31) a. *Je me demande* $[_{CP}[_{PP}$*à qui*$]$ $[_{C'}$ C $[_{IP}$*Marie parle t*$]]]]$
b. *L'homme* $[_{CP}[_{PP}$*à qui*$]$ $[_{C'}$ C $[_{IP}$*Marie parle t*$]]]$ *est intelligent.*

This is explained assuming that percolation of features across maximal projections is optional, as proposed for instance for Romanian in Dobrovie-Sorin (1993). In the case of Wh-questions involving pied-pipping in French or English, the Wh feature percolates for agreement with the [+Wh] COMP. A parallel analysis applies to English [+Wh] relatives: the [+Wh] feature must percolate. On the other hand, percolation in French relatives does not apply, which prevents a feature-value clash with the [-Wh] COMP.

In sum, a natural implementation of the [+/-Wh] distinction allows us to capture the main contrasts in the distribution of Wh-elements between French and English. In the next section, we consider some theoretical consequences of our proposal and present independent support for it. Finally, in section 3, we discuss apparent exceptions to the *[DP, CP] restriction in French appositives.

2.2 *Feature-driven movement versus base-generation*

Our proposal raises a theoretical question concerning the motivation for movement in syntax. In particular, a strong hypothesis of the Minimalist program (Chomsky 1995) maintains that movement is strictly triggered by morphological or formal feature checking, i.e. Last Resort. In this light, our claim that relatives are [-Wh] in French would seem to leave no trigger for movement of a Wh relative pronoun (under pied-pipping) or a Null operator. And indeed, this is the position we adopt, i.e. relative clause formation does not imply operator movement per se in French, while it does in English.

More precisely, along the lines of Canac Marquis (1996), we follow Chomsky (1995) in assuming that movement is strictly triggered by feature checking but depart from Chomsky's strictly derivational approach in allowing for base-generation through Merge of non feature-related A-bar operators. Notice that base-generation of operators requires no stipulation as the Merge operation is part of the computational system. In addition, chain construal seems required in a number of constructions. For instance in (32), left dislocation and resumptive pronouns in certain relatives in English (Safir 1986) must allow for base-generation of A-bar operators.[3]

(32) (Examples b and c from Safir 1986:682)
a. John, I am sure that my mother likes him.
b. That guy [who$_i$ I know his$_i$ sister] just phoned.
c. We were talking about the guy [who$_i$ Mary was wondering whether she should hire him$_i$].

In sum, we maintain that while syntactic movement is strictly triggered by feature checking, base-generation through Merge is always an option for convergence (e.g. Full interpretation). For instance in the case of relatives, the presence of an operator in spec of CP is required for Full interpretation independently of [-Wh]; the CP of a relative must contain an operator defining a set intersecting with the relative head, yielding the restrictive reading. Such operators must therefore be generated directly in spec of CP through Merge prior to or at spell out for convergence at LF.[4] For concreteness, we adopt Safir's notion of R(elative)-Binding.

(33) R-binding (Safir 1986)
The head of a relative must bind an operator in COMP
(R-binding cannot be vacuous in COMP).

Canac Marquis (1996) proposes independant support in the form of WCO effects for the distinction between base-generated versus derived A-bar operators. In Lasnik & Stowell (1991), it is suggested that WCO effects only surface with "true" operators, i.e. operators with intrinsic quantificational force such as quantifiers and Wh-words, but not topics and null operators. However, Canac Marquis discusses cases where "true" operators in the sense of Lasnik & Stowell do not show WCO effects and conversely, following an observation from Postal (1993), cases where pseudo operators do show WCO effects. As an alternative to Lasnik and Stowell's proposal, Canac Marquis argues for a direct correlation between the emergence of WCO effects and feature-triggered movement, i.e. any type of operator actually involved in

3 As proposed in Canac Marquis, (late) insertion of operators with an associated gap applies at SPELL OUT where the Wh-feature is checked.

4 An assumption here is that no feature checking applying at LF could trigger LF movement of the relative operator. This is one way in which [-Wh] is different from the Strong/Weak distinction.

movement triggered by feature checking displays WCO. The correlation is not only more appropriate for the English paradigm, but captures otherwise unexpected linguistic variations, e.g. the absence of WCO effects with long distance scrambling of "true" operators (Saito 1992) and the repair strategy of resumptive pronouns even with "true" operators.

Coming back to relative clauses in this perspective, there is a striking WCO contrast between French and English which falls directly under the [+/-Wh] distinction that we maintain. As noted by many others (such as Higginbotham 1980, Safir 1986, Lasnik & Stowell 1991 and Postal 1993), restrictive relatives trigger WCO in English, as show the examples in (34) from Lasnik and Stowell (1991). This is expected given that relatives are [+Wh] in English and must therefore involve movement. In contrast in (35), French restrictive relatives do not trigger WCO effects, as was first noted in Sportiche (1983, footnote 48 chap. 3).

(34) a. *Every man_i [O_i that his_i mother rejected t_i]
b. *The man [who_i his_i mother loves t_i]
(35) a. *Chaque enfant*$_i$ *que ses*$_i$ *parents ont aidé* t_i *a réussi*
b. *Aucun élève*$_i$ *que ses*$_i$ *parents ont aidé n'a réussi* t_i

This contrast follows without stipulation from our [+Wh]/[-Wh] distinction. English relatives are [+Wh], thus involve feature-driven movement and are expected to trigger WCO. In contrast French relatives are [-Wh], involve no movement but base-generation and just like topics and null operators, are not expected to trigger WCO.

3. *Some distinct properties of appositive relatives*

As Kayne (1976) noticed, the *[DP, CP] restriction in French relatives seems to be partially relaxed with appositives. First as the contrast (36a) vs (36b) shows, there is a subject/object assymmetry: a subject relative seems to evade the *[DP,CP] restriction by apparently allowing a [+Wh] relative pronoun in CP, while an object relative remains marginal but contrastively better than an object restrictive relative (cf. 28a/36b). Second, as the contrats (36a/c) and (36b/d) indicate, only discourse-linked Wh-pronoun allow such relaxation of the *[DP, CP] restriction.

(36) a. *Cette table, laquelle a été vendue pour $3, ...*
b. *??Cette table, laquelle Pierre a vendue pour $3, ...*
c. **Cette table, quoi a été vendue pour $3]], ...*
d. **Cet homme, qui*$_i$ *Marie connaît* t_i *bien, ...*

These intriguing facts find a natural explanation within the two main proposals in this paper, namely i) that appositives are unmerged syntactic objects and ii) that the distribution of Wh-elements is constrained by the [+Wh]/[-Wh] agreement in CP. The logic of our analysis implies that the Wh-pronoun in (36a) cannot be in [spec, CP] (otherwise a Wh feature-value clash would occur) but remains in [spec, IP]. Consequently, we propose that (36a) (and (b) by extension) are not actual relative structures, but apposition of bare CPs, i.e. without a relative head.

(37) a. *Cette table*, [$_{CP}$ [$_{IP}$*laquelle a été vendue pour $3*]],...
b. *??Cette table*, [$_{CP}$ *laquelle* [$_{IP}$ *Pierre a vendue pour $3*]],...

Let us consider the grammaticality of (37a). First, since there is no relative head, there is no need for the Wh-pronoun to occupy [spec, CP] for R-binding, thus no feature clash ensues. Second, the structure is perfectly interpretable as an apposition. In particular, *laquelle* following Cinque (1982), is a discourse-linked anaphor which is able to refer back to the antecedent *cette table* in the main clause. This property of *laquelle* distinguishes it from bare Wh-operators such as *qui* and *quoi* which are not discourse-linked and, we assume, may not be used anaphorically in the discourse. Hence, the contrasts (36a/c) and (36b/d) are directly captured.

This analysis seems to create an apparent problem for the (marginal) object case (37b). Notice that we locate *laquelle* in [spec, CP]. This seems motivated since, contrary to the subject case, there is obviously a displacement from the argument position, and [spec, CP] is a natural landing site for Wh-elements. However, we just mentioned that such a configuration should yield a Wh-disagreement with the [-Wh] COMP of French relatives. To capture this subtle contrast, we first need to look more closely at the structure of Wh-elements such as *laquelle*. In particular, as illustrated in (38), the morphology of relative pronouns such as *laquelle* and *lequel* strongly suggests that they are composed of a determiner and a Wh-element (see Cinque 1982) and contrast structurally in that respect with bare Wh-words. Percolation of the Wh-feature to DP in (38a) is optional, while it is necessary in (38b) since the Wh-word is the head of DP.

```
(38) a.     DP                        b.     DP [+WH]
           /  \                               |
         le    Wh [+WH]                      Wh [+WH]
```

Secondly, along with the notion of R-binding we adopted in (33) we assume the locality condition on R-binding in (39) argued for by Safir.

(39) Locality Condition on R-binding (Safir 1986)

If X is locally R-bound, X is the structurally highest element in COMP.

Safir presents convincing evidence that at LF, the Wh-pronoun must occupy the highest position in CP and proposes that this is accomplished through LF-raising.[5] Assuming Safir's proposal, our analysis of restrictive relatives with complex Wh-pronouns such as *laquelle* must be updated as in (40).

(40) LF: $[_{DP}$*Cette table*$[_{CP}$ $[_{DP}$ *quelle*$_i$$[_{D'}$ *la-t*$_i$]] $[_{C'}$ $[_{IP}$*Jean a achetée*]]]

R-binding requires the Wh-word *quelle* to occupy the structurally highest position in [spec,CP], which is [spec, DP]. Once in this position, spec-head agreement with the determiner head *le* applies necessarily and the whole DP becomes [+Wh], correctly triggering a Wh-disagreement. As for non-retrictive relatives, our proposal that they are bare CP appositions without a relative head implies that no R-binding applies at LF. Consequently, the Wh-element need not reach the highest position and stays embedded under the determiner as in (38a), the whole DP remaining [-Wh] and no Wh-disagreement ensuing with the [-Wh] COMP of relatives. Also, this analysis directly predicts why (36d) with the bare Wh-word *qui* is out and contrast with (36c): as indicated in (38b) *qui*, contrary to *laquelle*, is always [+Wh] and cannot occupy [spec, CP] of relatives without Wh disagreement.

---

[5] For one, the Wh-element can overtly occupy such position as examples in (1b) indicates. In addition, examples (2a,b) can be analyzed as typical WCO configuration after raising of the Wh-element in (2c,d) respectively. Finally, (3a) from Ishiara (1984) reflects a *that-t* effect while examples (3b,c) from Kayne (1984) illustrate a typical subject/object assymetries under extraction.

(1) a. Those reports, [the height of the lettering on which] the governement prescribes, are tedious.
 b. ?Those reports, [which$_i$ the height of the lettering on t$_i$] the governement prescribes, are tedious.

(2) a. *Any man [his$_i$ portrait of whom$_i$]
 b. ?*Any man [[his$_i$ mother's] portrait of whom$_i$]
 c. *...$_{CP}$ [whom$_i$ [his$_i$ portrait of t$_i$]]
 d. *...$_{CP}$ [whom$_i$ [[his$_i$ mother's] portrait of t$_i$]]...

(3) a. *The men [$_{CP}$ [$_{CP}$for whom to be invited to the parties was a privilege]
 b. ??the man [the possibility of you marrying whom] became a reality only yesterday.
 c. *the man [the possibility of you marrying whom] became a reality only yesterday.

The final point to consider is then Why the object relative (36c) is merely marginal and not simply grammatical as the subject case (36a)? Our answer relies in previous assumptions about movement. Recall that relatives being [-Wh] in French, base-generation of operators in CP is motivated for convergence at LF, namely R-binding. Since we assume no R-binding in (36b), there is no motivation for the presence of the operator *laquelle*. Hence, the marginality can be imputed to the lack of motivation for base-generation of the object in CP, yet no output condition is violated and the structure is interpretable.

4. *Conclusion*

In this paper, we have proposed a unified analysis of restrictive and appositive relatives: appositive relatives are in fact unmerged restrictive relatives with an overt or covert head. We further argued that English and French relatives differ with respect to the Wh-feature: English relatives are [+Wh] and therefore involve movement for feature-checking, while French relatives are [-Wh] and therefore are base-generated.

REFERENCES

Bouchard, Denis & Hirschbühler, Paul. 1987. "French QUOI and its Clitic Allomorph QUE" *Studies in Romance Languages 25*, ed. by C. Neidle & Rafael Nuñez. Dordrecht: Foris.

Brody, Michael. 1995. *Lexico-logical Form*. Cambridge, Mass.: MIT Press.

Browning, Margaret & Ezat Karimi. 1991. "Scrambling to Object Position in Persian". Paper presented at University of Massachusetts, Amherst.

Canac Marquis, Réjean. 1996. "Weak and Weakest Crossover are Configurational". *Configurations* ed. by Anna-Maria Di Sciullo. Somerville: Cascadilla Press.

Chomsky, Noam. 1977. "On Wh Movement". *Formal Syntax* ed. by Peter W. Culicover, Tomas Wasow, & A. Akmajian. New York: Academic Press.

———. 1986. *Barriers*, Cambridge, Mass.: MIT Press.

———. 1995. *The Minimalist Program*, Cambridge, Mass.: MIT Press.

Cinque, Guglielmo. 1982. "On the Theory of Relative Clauses and Markedness". *The Linguistic Review* 1.247-294.

Dermidache, Hamida. 1991. *Resumptive Chains in Restrictive Relatives, Appositives and Dislocation Structures*. Ph.D. dissertion, MIT.

Emonds, Joseph. 1979. "Appositive Relatives Have No Properties". *Linguistic Inquiry 10*.211-243.

Godard, Danielle. 1988. *La syntaxe des relatives en Français*. Paris: Editions du Centre National pour la Recherche Scientifique.

Goodall, Grant. 1991. "On the Status of SPEC of IP". *Proceedings of WCCFL X*. Stanford. Center for the Study of Language and Information.

Jackendoff, Ray. 1977. *X' Syntax: A Study of Phrase Structure*. Cambridge, Mass.: MIT Press.

Kayne, Richard. 1976. "French Relative QUE". *Current Studies in Romance linguistics* ed. by Frank Hensey & Marta Lujan, 255-299. Washington, D.C.: Georgetown University Press.

———. 1994. *The Antisymmetry of Syntax*, Cambridge, Mass.: MIT Press.

Lasnik, Howard & Timothy Stowell. 1991. "Weakest Crossover". *Linguistic Inquiry 22*.687-720.

Lefebvre, C. 1982. "Qui qui vient? ou Qui vient: Voilà la question". *La syntaxe comparée du français standard et populaire: approches formelle et fonctionnelle*. Office de la langue française, Gouvernement du Québec.

Longobardi, Giuseppe. 1994. "Reference and Proper Names". *Linguistic Inquiry 25*.609-665.

McCawley, James D. 1988. *The Syntactic Phenomena of English*. Chicago: The University of Chicago Press.

Pesetsky, David. 1982. *Paths and Categories*. Ph.D. dissertation, MIT.

Postal, Paul. 1993. "Remarks on Weak Crossover Effects". *Linguisic Inquiry* 24.539-557.

Reinhart, Tanya. 1983. *Anaphora and Semantic Interpretation*. London: Croom Helm.

Riemsdijk, Henk C. van & Edwin S. Williams. 1986. *Introduction to the Theory of Grammar*. Cambridge, Mass.: MIT Press.

Safir, Ken. 1986. "Relative Clauses in a Theory of Binding and Levels". *Linguistic Inquiry* 17.4.

Saito, Mamoru. 1992. "Scrambling as Semantically Vacuous Movement". *Alternative Conceptions of Phrase Structure* ed. by Mark Baltin & Anthony Kroch. Chicago: University of Chicago Press.

Sells, Peter. 1984. *Syntax and Semantics of Resumptive Pronouns*. Ph.D. dissertation, University of Massachusetts, Amherst.

Speas, Margaret. 1993. "Null Arguments in a Theory of Economy of Projection", *UMASS Occasional Papers in Linguistics*. GLSA, Amherst: UMASS.

Sportiche, Dominique. 1983. *Structural Invariance and Symmetry in Syntax*. Ph.D. dissertation, MIT.

Koopman, Hilda & Dominique Sportiche. 1983. "Variables and the Bijection Principle". *The Linguistic Review 2*.139-160.

Vergnaud, Jean-Roger. 1974. *French Relatives Clauses*. Ph.D. dissertation, MIT.

Williams, Edwin. 1992. *Thematic structure in Syntax*. Cambridge, Mass.: MIT Press.

A CONSTRAINT-BASED APPROACH TO SPANISH SPIRANTIZATION

MARIA M. CARREIRA

California State University, Long Beach

1. *Introduction*

Spanish spirantization, the alternation between voiced obstruent stops and fricatives, has been the subject of countless papers and discussions. This paper will differ from previous work on this topic in two important ways; first, in the theoretical model employed, in this case, Optimality Theory, and second, in the data under consideration. Regarding the latter, any analysis of spirantization must account for the fact that the distribution of voiced obstruents is invariant across dialects in the environments listed in (1), while it is subject to a great deal of cross-dialectal variation in others, namely, (2). The latter range, by and and large, from all spirants in Castilian Spanish, to all stops in Honduran and Salvadorian Spanish, to a combination of the two in Mexican and Caribbean varieties of Spanish.

(1) a. [-continuant] b. [+continuant]
N__ V__V
ld__

(2) Variable environments
G__ r__ s__ Obstruent___ l___(for [b,g])

Previous analyses of this phenomenon as a process of assimilation involving the feature continuant have had limited success with the data in (1), but have failed to explain (2) as part of the same process.

2. *Previous analyses*

By and large, assimilation analyses of spirantization fall into three categories: 1) those that allow assimilation of [-continuant] to take place between homorganic clusters, 2) those that allow [+continuant] to spread between non-homorganic clusters, and 3) those that allow both values of this feature to spread.

Analyses of the first type, such as Lozano (1979) and Hualde (1988) argue that [-continuant] spreads from a nasal consonant or [l] onto a homorganic voiced obstruent that follows. Voiced obstruents in nonhomorganic clusters such as [lb] and [lg], as well as those that are not part of a consonant cluster, receive the default specification [+continuant].

The problem with analyses such as these, however, is that in some dialects of Spanish it is indeed possible to get nonhomorganic consonant clusters that are [-continuant], as shown in (3a). Moreover, it is also possible for [b] and [g] to surface as [-continuant] following continuants like [r] and [l], as in (3b). Clearly, homorganicity is not a necessary or sufficient condition for adjacent consonants to agree on the value [-continuant].[1]

(3) a.

u[nd]edo	'a finger'	(Lozano 1979:72)
ané[kd]dota	'anecdote'	(Harris 1984:150)
a[bd]omen	'abdomen'	
ami[gd]alas	'tonsils'	

b.

a[rb]ol	'tree'	(Malmberg 1965:63, 70, 77)
ve[rd]e	'green'	
a[lg]o	'something'	

Harris (1984) posits a rule that spreads the feature value [+continuant]. Since this analysis assumes that [l] is [+continuant], it must explain why in some dialects the lateral spreads its continuancy to [b] and [g], as in ar[β]ol 'tree' and al[γ]o 'something', but not to [d] (*cal[δ]o).

Harris' solution to this problem invokes the Adjacency Identity Constraint, more recently known as Geminate Inalterability. According to Harris, this principle blocks the rule of continuancy assimilation from applying to partially linked clusters such as nasal-obstruent clusters and [ld].

However, as Martínez-Gil (1992) points out, features that are not shared by adjacent consonants fall outside the scope of Geminate Inalterability. For example, in Spanish, voicing assimilation applies between homorganic /sd/, yielding a voiced sibilant as in des[δ]e 'since'. Thus, Geminate Inalterability does not block voicing assimilation from applying to a partially linked structure such as that of the cluster [sd]. Crucially, then, if Geminate Inalterability

---

[1] In Catalan, a language with a similar stop/spirant alternation as Spanish, stops always occur after nasals, even if the nasal is not homorganic with the stop.

can only block a phonological rule from altering the place node of homorganic clusters, it cannot account for the failure of [+continuant] to spread to the voiced obstruents in clusters such as [mb], [nd], [ld], etc.

Mascaró's (1984) solution to the problem presented by the lateral involves a rule of continuancy assimilation that spreads either value of the feature continuant to a voiced obstruent. For example, [s] spreads the feature [+continuant] to a following voiced obstruent, while [m] spreads [-continuant] to such a segment. The segment [l] is able to spread both values of this feature because "...the narrowing of the vocal tract characteristic of laterals counts as blocked for the region where laterals are articulated, but as unblocked for other regions, just as nasals are fricatives in the nasal cavity but stops in the oral cavity." (p. 292). This means that for purposes of the continuancy assimilation rule, laterals are [-continuant] before coronals and [+continuant] elsewhere.

However, as Hualde (1988) observes, this solution suffers from circular reasoning since in order to know the continuancy value of [d] we must first determine whether or not [d] is preceded by an [l]. But in order know the continuancy value of [l] we must determine whether or not a [d] follows.

A second drawback of this solution is its inability to extend to Basque, a language with the same stop/spirant distribution as that assumed for Spanish by most analyses of spirantization.

(4) Basque spirantization (Mascaró 1984: 288-289)

a.	#____	[beso]	'arm'
b.	N___	[isango]	'will be'
c.	ld	[saldi]	'fear'
d.	[-cons]____	[eɣo]	'south'
e.	{r,r}____	[erβi]	'hare'
f.	l {B,G}____	[alβoa]	'the side'
g.	[-son, +cont]___	[ezβay]	'doubt'

Hualde (1988) presents strong evidence in favor of the non-continuant status of Basque [l] in the presence of coronals and non-coronals alike. Since Mascaró's solution hinges on the dual nature of the lateral with respect continuancy, this solution cannot apply to Basque.

A review of the literature on dialectal variation reveals yet a more serious challenge to this, as well as other assimilation analyses of spirantization. Canfield (1981:5) states:

> In the stream of speech of Colombia (except Nariûo), El Salvador, Honduras, and Nicaragua, the occlusive allophone of the consonants /b/, /d/, and /g/, is heard after any consonant or semivowel... Lacayo (1954) noted the same consistency in Nicaragua, as I did (Canfield 1962b) during six months of teaching at the Instituto Caro y Cuervo, Bogotá, with trips to many parts of the country... Resnick (1976) rightly points out that nonstandard occlusive pronunciations are common in many regions others than those noted, but it has been my observation that, although recordings reveal occlusives where not expected in some speakers from Ecuador, Bolivia, Guatemala and Costa Rica, they do not show the consistent pattern of the four countries indicated... Many nonstandard occlusives are heard in the Caribbean area...

Similar observations are also made by Malmberg (1965) and Castillo and Bond (1972). Sabino and Persinotto (1975) note as well that in Mexico City Spanish /b/ and /g/ are frequently occlusive after /l/ and /r/, and /d/ is also often a stop after /s/. Resnick's (1975) extensive analysis of Spanish dialects documents occlusive voiced obstruents after fricative consonants and occlusive [b] and [g] after [l] in dialects as varied as those of Costa Rica; Jalisco, Mexico; Cuba, Puerto Rico, Colombia, Ecuador and Argentina.

Amastae (1986) reports a high incidence of stops after these and other consonants in Colombian, Mexican, and Mexican-American Spanish. According to his data, the only environment showing across-the-board consistency with respect to continuancy is the post-nasal context and the [ld] sequence. The former context invariably yields a stop, while the former nearly always results in a stop.[2]

3. *The analysis*

Padgett (1991, 1994, 1995) examines the question of why consonant clusters that have undergone assimilation must agree with respect to continuancy. Such work argues for a representation such as (5a), where the feature continuant is a dependent of the articulator node. It follows from this that when two consonants share Place of articulation features, they will also have the same value of continuancy, as shown in (5b).

---

[2] Though these environments appear to be the most resistant to spirantization across all dialects, Hammond (1976) and Murillo (1978) both report cases of spirants in post-nasal position.

(5)

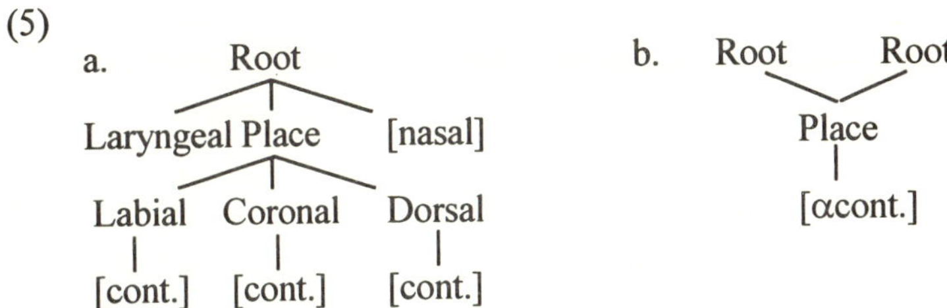

Let us assume then, that the feature [continuant] is a dependent of the articulator node, as in (5a). Let us also assume the marking conditions below which prevent nasals and [l] from being continuant.

(6) *Nasal-Continuant: if [nasal] then not [continuant]
*Lateral-Contin: if [lateral] then not [continuant]

Given these assumptions, it follows that voiced obstruents that are homorganic to a nasal or lateral consonant will be [-continuant]. This is because having a continuant voiced obstruent in this environment would entail a violation of the marking conditions in (6).

Padgett's representation then, takes us a long way in explaining why homorganic clusters having a nasal or lateral consonant must agree with respect to continuancy. However, it does not explain three important questions: 1) Why do nasals and [l] undergo place assimilation to begin with? Crucially, if there were no place assimilation, then nasal-obstruent sequences and the sequence [ld] would be free to exhibit opposing values of continuancy. 2) How it is possible for nasal assimilation to take place in homorganic sequences consisting of a nasal consonant and a fricative as in *enfermo*, and *manso*? Aren't the assimilated nasals in these words in violation of the nasal marking condition? and 3) How it is possible to obtain a fricative-stop sequence in a homorganic cluster such as [sd]? The literature attests to the relative frequency of these clusters, yet Padgett's model, as presented thus far, predicts that these clusters should not be possible.

Before addressing these issues, let us return to the environments where spirantization exhibits cross-dialectal variation. Consider the consonant clusters listed in (7A). Column (B) shows the sonority difference between each of the clusters, assuming the sonority scale in (8). Column (C) shows the probability of obtaining a fricative C_2 for each of the consonant clusters listed in (A), as given in Amastae (1986). Note that as we move down the vertical axis in (7C), the probability of obtaining a fricative decreases in proportion to the sonority distance between the clusters. This probability ranges from 45% in glide-obstruent sequences, to 5% in obstruent-obstruent sequences.

(7)

A	B	C
C1C2	Sonority distance C1-C2	prob. C2 is cont. where C2={B,G,D}
G__	4	45%
r__	3	35%
l__ (not [d])	2	17%
N__	1	0%
s__	-1	14%
b,d,g__	0	5%

(8) Sonority Scale (in increasing value from left to right)

voiceless stops < voiced stops < voiceless continuants < voiced continuants < nasals < l < r < glides < vowels

I formalize the relationship between sonority and spirantization observed in the above data, by means of the Sonority Distance rule in (9). The Sonority Distance rule states that the probability that the second of a two consonant sequence is continuant grows along an S-shaped curve, as the sonority difference Delta S increases. What differs between dialects is the value of Delta S, where the S-curve takes its upswing towards 1. We call this value of Delta S, Theta.

(9) Sonority Distance: Given C1\$C2, P[C2 is cont] = Sigmoid (θ, ΔS), where S= |C2| -|C1| and |C|= sonority value of C.

In dialects such as Castilian, Theta is near zero, implying that C2 is always a fricative (10a). In the dialects of Colombia, El Salvador, Honduras, and Nicaragua described by Canfield, Theta is very large, implying that C2 will never be a fricative (10b). In the dialects studied by Amastae, Theta assumes an intermediate value, such that the probability of finding a spirant ranges from 0 to 1 (10c).

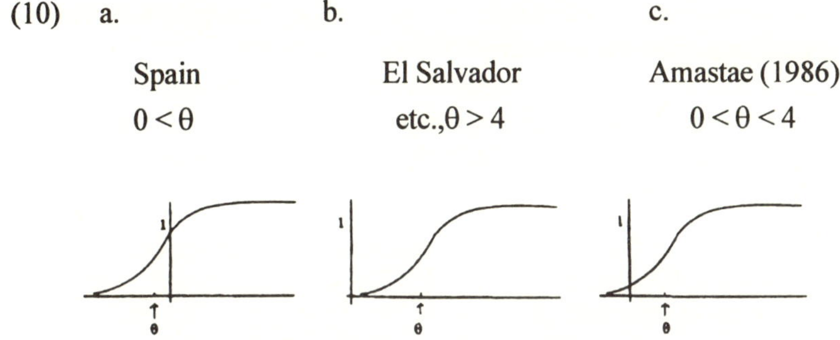

It is not surprising that the notion of sonority distance should be a factor in the distribution of heterosyllabic consonant clusters. This is, in fact, what Murray and Vennemann's Syllable Contact Law predicts:

11) The preference for a syllabic structure A$B, where A and B are marginal segments and a and b are the consonantal strength values of A and B respectively, increases with the values of b minus a.
(Murray and Vennemann 1983: 520)

Since stops are less sonorous than fricatives, the Syllable Contact Law tells us we should expect a preference for onset stops over fricatives in consonant clusters. Our Sonority Distance Rule, then, represents a parametrized version for Spanish of the universal principle captured in the Syllable Contact Law. This rule allows us to capture the inherent variability of spirantization in non-homorganic clusters.

Let us now recapitulate our analysis as it stands. First, we have accounted for the invariant environments listed in (1a) by appealing to Padgett's model of feature representation, where continuant is dominated by Place. I write this in the form of a constraint in (12a). Second, we have proposed the Sonority Distance Rule as an account of the variation inherent in some consonantal clusters. This rule is repeated in (12b). However, not all voiced obstruents can be accounted for by these two principles. Intervocalic voiced obstruents, which in all dialects are continuant, must receive the feature continuant by means of a constraint such as (12c). This constraint will also be applicable to voiced obstruents in consonant clusters that are outside the scope of (12a) and (b). Given the nasal and lateral marking conditions in (6), Voice-Continuant must not apply to nasals or laterals. And of course, no constraint interaction can result in spirants in homorganic clusters such as [mb] and [ld]. In Optimality Theoretic terms, this means that the constraints below must be ranked as in (13). Since Continuant-Dep is undominated, all homorganic clusters will agree with respect to continuancy. Moreover, since Voice-Continuant is dominated by the marking conditions, all voiced obstruents following a nasal or a homorganic lateral will be [-continuant].

(12)	a. Continuant-Dep:	continuant is place dependent
	b. Sonority Distance:	P[C2 is cont] = g(θ, ΔS)
	c. Voice-Continuant:	if [voice] then [continuant]
	d. *Nasal-Continuant:	if [nasal] then not [continuant]
	e. *Lateral-continuant:	if [lateral] then not [continuant]

(13) Continuant-Dep >> Sonority Distance, *Nasal-Continuant, *Lateral-Continuant >> Voice-Continuant

This leaves us with the three questions we posed earlier. For insight into these issues, I turn now to Optimality Theory as set forth in Prince and Smolenski (1993), McCarthy and Prince (1995), Ito, Mester and Padgett (1995), and Inkelas (1995). Briefly, Optimality Theory holds that the output of phonology or morphology is determined by wellformedness constraints that select among some candidate set of forms considered in parallel. The set of constraints is provided by Universal Grammar and an individual grammar is obtained by imposing a strict dominance order on the constraints. All constraints are in principle violable, though violation is always minimal.

Let us turn our attention to the first question, namely, why nasals and [l] assimilate to the point of articulation of a following consonant. We remarked earlier that if nasals and [l] were not constrained to assimilate to a following segment, then they could differ from a following segment with respect to continuancy. The question we need to answer then, is, why is assimilation obligatory for syllable-final nasals and for [l] before the segment [d]? Ito, Mester & Padgett (1995) propose the principle of Licensing Cancellation which states that "if the specification F implies the specification G, then it is not the case that F licenses G". Given the predictable nature of coda features in Spanish, we extend the concept of Licensing Cancellation to the syllable so as to rule out the licensing of place features in coda position. Onsets, on the other hand, exhibit a greater range of Place features, suggesting that they are allowed to license such features more freely.

(14) *Coda-Place: The coda does not license Place features.

In (15) I illustrate how a nasal that does not share its place features with a following consonant (15a) violates CODApl and loses out to one which takes its place from a following onset (15b). Therefore, (15b) is more harmonic than (15c) by virtue of the fact that it does not involve a violation of CODApl.

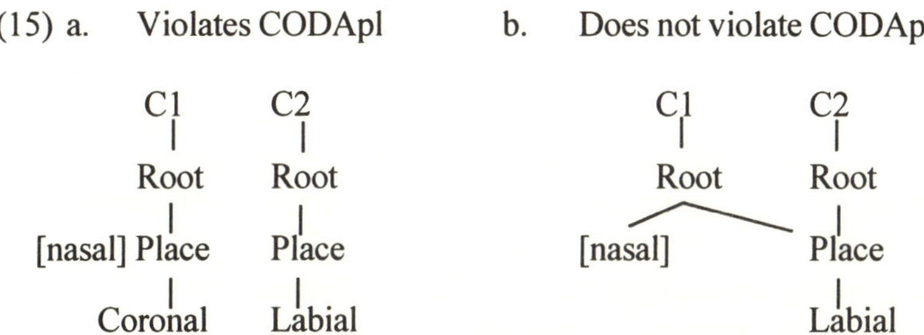

Below, we see why the lateral, unlike nasals, does not always have the option of undergoing Place assimilation so as to comply with CODApl. Essentially, we assume the existence of a marking condition which prevents laterals from being anything but coronal (16c). This marking condition dominates *Coda-Place, thus preventing place assimilation from taking place in clusters such as [lb] and [lg]. Therefore, (16a) will be more harmonic than (16b).

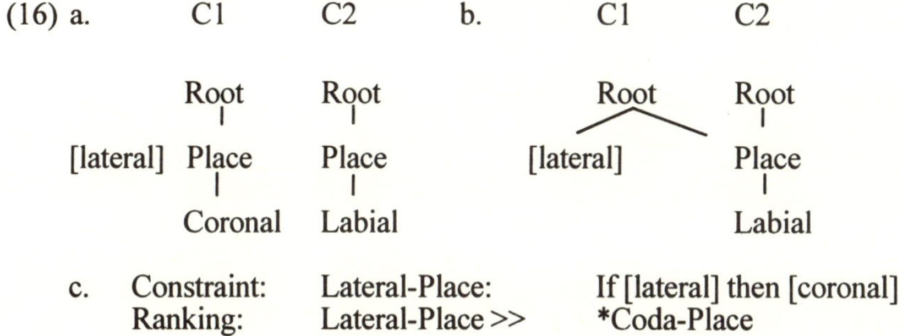

c. Constraint: Lateral-Place: If [lateral] then [coronal]
Ranking: Lateral-Place >> *Coda-Place

Regarding our first question then, consonants assimilate to a following segment so as to comply with CODApl. However, assimilation does not take place when there's a higher ranked constraint ruling out certain feature combinations. For example, the lateral marking condition prevents [l] from undergoing place assimilation to anything but a coronal consonant. Other similar constraints keep segments such as [r] and [s] from being anything but coronal.

This brings us to our second question, namely, if there's a marking condition that prohibits nasals and [l] from being continuant, how is it possible for these consonants to undergo place assimilation to a continuant in words like *e[mf]ermo, ma[ns]o*, and *a[ls]ar?* Padgett's answer to this question is simply that the marking conditions ruling out continuant nasals and laterals are not enforced in these cases. Optimality Theory provides insight as to way this should be so. If CODApl is ranked higher that the nasal and lateral marking conditions, syllable-final nasals and laterals will take on the feature continuant rather than violate CODApl. In other words, continuant nasals and laterals are consistent with a grammar that prefers to violate the nasal and lateral marking conditions rather than to leave nonlicensed Place features in coda position. Regarding our second question then, nasals assimilate to a continuant and consequently become continuant so as not to incur a violation of the higher ranked CODApl.

However, if nasals can take on the feature continuant, why don't we get voiced spirants after assimilated nasals. The reason, of course, is that a cluster consisting of a nasal plus a voiced spirant (17a) must always compete with a nearly identical one that consists of a nasal plus a voiced stop (17b). Since the latter does not violate the marking condition for nasals, it will always win over the cluster with the spirant. The same argument applies to the sequence [ld]. As mentioned earlier, a non-homorganic nasal-obstruent sequence will be ruled out for being in violation of CODApl.

(17)

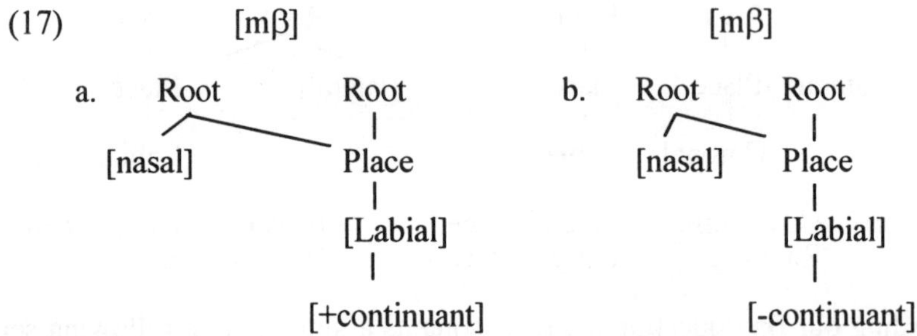

Let us now turn to the final question, namely, how it is possible to obtain a fricative-stop sequence in the cluster [sd]. Given Padgett's claim that continuant is Place dependent, we expect the cluster [sd] to obtain a voiced stop only if there is no sharing of Place.

A review of the literature reveals some disagreement regarding whether or not [s] assimilates to a dental point of articulation. According to Quilis (1962), [s] does not undergo assimilation. Martínez Celdrán (1989) however, makes the opposite assertion.

Let us assume for a moment that Quilis is right, and [s] does not assimilate to a following dental. That being the case, we might posit a constraint such as (18) which mandates the presence of the feature [distributed] in an alveolar fricative. If this constraint is ranked higher than CODApl, there will be no assimilation to a dental point of articulation. If there is no assimilation, then, the consonants [s] and [d] may disagree with respect to continuancy.

(18) *Non-Distributed [s]: *[-voice, +cont., +coronal, -distributed]

However, if we assume that Martínez Celdrán is right and that [s] does assimilate to a following dental segment, then we are back to our original question of how an assimilated [s] can differ in continuancy from the segment that follows it. Padgett (1991, 1994, 1995) argue that the coronal articulator dominates a Site node with includes the features anterior and distributed, as shown in (19a). That being the case, assimilation of [s] to a dental consonant can take place at the Site articulator without affecting the feature continuant, as shown in (19b). This assumes, of course, that in dialects where [s] takes on a dental point of articulation, the constraint in (18) is not operative.

(19) a. b.

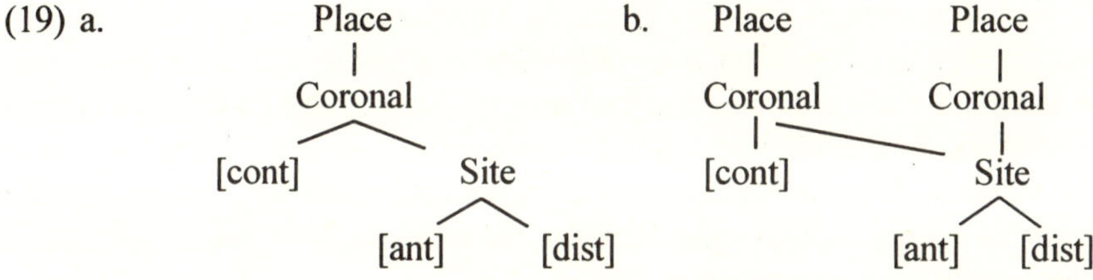

However, on what grounds can we justify assimilating to Site, when assimilating to the Coronal node will better satisfy the CODApl constraint? The answer lies in the interaction of the CODApl constraint with the Sonority Distance rule. Recall that the Sonority Distance Rule tries to maximize the sonority distance between heterosyllabic clusters. If this constraint is higher ranked than CODApl, then we expect to get a stop rather than a fricative onset in the [sd] cluster. This is accomplished by assimilating at the Site node, as shown below:

(20)

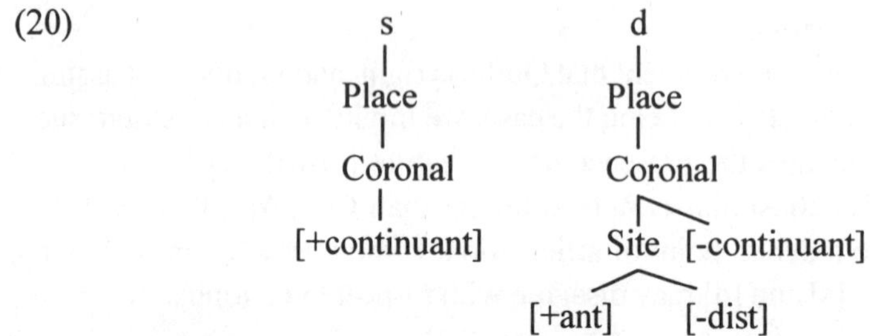

The above representation leaves some place features in coda position as it strives to comply with the Sonority Distance Rule by having a stop in onset position. Assimilating at the Site node represents an advantage over not assimilating at all in that it allows the feature anterior to be licensed by the onset [d]. The distribution of voiced spirants in dialects such as those studied by Amastae is consistent with a relative ranking of CODApl and the Sonority Distance Rule where the latter dominates the former (ie. Sonority Distance >> CODApl). Recall that in such dialects the probability of obtaining a fricative goes up in direct proportion to the the sonority distance between the voiced obstruent and the preceding consonant.

In dialects, such as Castilian, which consistently yield a spirant [δ] after [s] we can assume that either one of two conditions holds. One possibility is that CODApl dominates Sonority Distance. That being the case, the locus of assimilation will be the Place node rather than at the Site node, since assimilation at the Place node provides maximal compliance with the CODApl constraint. Therefore, the dental obstruent will be continuant. A second alternative is that the value of Theta in the Sonority Distance rule in dialects such as Castilian assumes a large enough value such that the sequence [sδ] meets the minimum sonority distance requirement. That being the case, assimilation will take place at the articulator node, yielding a spirant.

Having now answered all questions, let us conclude my summarizing the analysis presented.

4. *Conclusion*

The present analysis accounts for the variant and invariant distribution of Spanish spirantization in an Optimality Theoretic framework. The constraints and relative rankings proposed for the three classes of spirantizing dialect presented are summarized below. The fact that continuant is place dependent explains why assimilated consonants to agree with respect to continuancy. The CODApl constraint accounts for why syllable-final consonants assimilate in point of articulation to a following consonant. Marking conditions on feature co-occurence however, keep some consonants from assimilating. The Sonority-Distance Rule accounts for the effects of the sonority hierarchy on spirantization, and finally, the voice-continuant constraint creates spirants in intervocalic environments.

In keeping with Optimality Theory, the constraints posited are universal in nature with dialectal variation resulting from the parametrization of some variables, as well as from the relative rankings of constraints.

(21) *Constraints*

a. Continuant-Dep: Continuant is place dependent
b. Sonority Distance: P[C2 is cont] = $g(\theta, \Delta S)$
c. Voice-Continuant: if [voice] then [continuant]
d. *Nasal-Continuant: if [nasal] then not [continuant]
e. *Lateral-continuant: if [lateral] then not [continuant]
f. Lateral-Place: if [lateral] then [coronal]
g. *Coda-Place: The coda does not license Place features
h. *Non-distributed [s]

Rankings

Castilian Spanish: a >> f >> g >> b, d,e >> c, and $\theta > 4$

Other dialects: a >> f >> b >> g >> d,e >> c
In dialects where C2 is always a stop, $\theta > 4$
In dialects where the probability of C2 being continuant varies, $0 < \theta < 4$.

REFERENCES

Amastae, John. 1986. "A Syllable-based Analysis of Spanish Spirantization". *Studies in Romance Linguistics* ed. by Osvaldo Jaeggli & Carmen Silva-Corvalán, 3-21. Dordrecht: Foris.

Blevins, Juliette. 1995. "The syllable in phonological theory". *The Handbook of Phonological Theory* ed. by John Goldsmith. Cambridge, Mass.: Blackwell.

Canfield, D. Lincoln. 1981. *The Pronunciation of Spanish in the Americas*. Chicago: University Press.

Clements, G. Nick. 1985. "The Role of the Sonority Cycle in Core Syllabification". *Working Papers of the Cornell Phonetics Laboratory* 2.1-68.

Harris, James. 1984. "La espirantización en castellano y la representación fonológica autosegmental". *Universitat Autónoma de Barcelona, Estudis Gramaticals* 1.149-167.

———. 1989. "Our Present Understanding of Spanish Syllable Structure". *American Spanish Pronunciation* ed. by P.C. Bjarkman & R.M. Hammond, 151-169. Washington D.C.: Georgetown University Press.

Hooper, Joan. 1976. *An Introduction to Natural Generative Phonology*. New York: Academic Press.

Hualde, José Ignacio. 1988. *A Lexical Phonology of Basque*. Ph.D. dissertation, University of Southern California, Los Angeles.

Inkelas, Sharon. 1994. "The Consequences of Optimization for Underspecification". Ms., Berkeley: University of California.

Ito, Junko, Mester, Armin & Jaye Padgett. 1995. "NC: Lincensing and Underspecification Theory". *Linguistic Inquiry* 26.3.

Lozano, Ma. del Carmen. 1979. *Stop and Spirant Alternations: Fortition and Spirantization Processes in Spanish Phonology*. Ph.D dissertation, University of Indiana, Bloomington.

Malmberg, Bertil. 1965. *Estudios de fonética hispánica*. Madrid: C.S.I.C.

Martínez Celdrán, Eugenio. 1989. *Fonética*. Barcelona: Editorial Teide.

Martínez-Gil, Fernando. 1991. "The Insert/Delete Parameter, Redundancy Rules, and Neutralization Pocesses in Spanish". *Current Studies in Spanish Linguistics* ed. by Héctor Campos & Fernando Martínez-Gil, 495-571. Washington D.C.: Georgetown University Press.

Mascaró, Joan. 1984. "Continuant Spreading in Basque, Catalan, and Spanish". *Language Sound Structure* ed. by Mark Aronoff & R.T. Oehrle, 287-298. Cambridge, Mass.: MIT Press.

McCarthy, John, & Alan Prince. 1993. "Generalized Alignment". *Yearbook of Morphology* 6.79-153.

Menéndez Pidal, Ramón. 1980. *Manual de gramática histórica española*. Madrid: Editorial Espasa-Calpe.

Murray, Robert W. 1987. "Preference Laws and Gradient Change: Selected Developments in Romance". *Canadian Journal of Linguistics* 32.115-132.

Murray, R.W. & Theo Vennemann. 1983. "Sound Change and Syllable Structure in Germanic Phonology". *Language* 59.514-528.

Quilis, Antonio. 1982. *Curso de fonética y fonología españolas*. Madrid: Consejo Superior de Investigaciones Científicas.

Padgett, Jaye. 1991. *Stricture in Feature Geometry*. Ph.D. dissertation, University of Massachusetts, Amherst.

———. 1994. "Stricture in Feature Geometry". *Natural Language and Linguistic Theory* 12.465-513.

——— .1995. *Stricture in Feature Geometry*. Standford: CSLI Publications.

Prince, Alan, & Paul Smolensky. 1993. "Optimality Theory: Constraint Interaction in Generative Grammar". Ms., Rutgers University and University of Colorado.

Sabino Giorgio & Antonio Persinotto. 1975. *Fonología del español hablado en la ciudad de México: Ensayo de un método sociolingüístico*. México: El Colegio de México.

A SYNTACTIC ACCOUNT OF PERFECTIVE AND POSSESSIVE VERB SELECTION IN ROMANCE LANGUAGES[1]

JUAN CARLOS CASTILLO
University of Maryland

Introduction

The goal of this paper is to show that copulas, auxiliary verbs in perfective tenses, and possessive verbs are formed in the morphology and do not have their own lexical entries. Following the ideas on perfective auxiliary selection developed by Kayne 1993, I want to extend his analysis to the Spanish verb *tener* '(possessive) have'. Some previous analyses have overlooked the morphological difference between *tener* and the auxiliary *haber,* absent in many languages. I want to explain why these two verbs are the same in English and Italian, but different in Spanish.

This paper supports the view that there is a morphological component acting after the point of Spell-Out, in the course of the derivation towards PF, which has no effect on interpretation. This component determines the form of the auxiliary verb in perfectives (Spanish *haber*, English *have*, Italian *avere/ essere*) and possessives (Spanish *tener*, English *have*, Italian *avere*). All of these verbs are assumed to represent different combinations of the same set of heads (BE, D^0, $Poss^0$) at the point of Spell-Out. However, both their initial structures and their LF outputs are the same and, we hope, universal.

This paper also assumes that part of the morphological component is determined at the initial numeration. Thus, the difference between simple and compound perfective tenses (Spanish *preparé* versus *he preparado*) is already present when selecting the numeration, and it will lead to a simple or multiple clausal structure respectively.

A modular analysis of auxiliary/possessive verbs is more accurate and covers more cross-linguistic data than a purely lexical one, even though it brings a higher level of complexity into the structure. It has been observed that auxiliary

[1] I wish to thank Norbert Hornstein, David Lightfoot and Juan Uriagereka for comments on this paper. This work has been made possible by a Scholarship from the Basque Government's Department of Education, BFI94.036.

verbs are very abstract entities, different from lexical verbs in this sense. The fact that auxiliaries show a great deal of homogeneity in their cross-linguistic behavior, and their general lack of lexical content suggest that they may be the Spell-Out of functional categories. The capture of generalizations across languages always compensates for the abstractness of the approach to specific languages.

The structure of the paper will be as follows: the remainder of the introduction will give a brief outline of the analysis. Section 1 will study the analysis of perfective tenses in general, and Section 2 will talk about the auxiliary verb "have" in particular. Section 3 will consider an analysis of the possessive verb in its different versions. Section 4 will discuss auxiliary selection in some Romance languages. Finally, Section 5 will be devoted to issues of learnability of the parameters involved in the analysis.

In Spanish, we find two verbs equivalent to the English 'have', possessive *tener*, and auxiliary *haber*. Tensed perfective clauses are formed using the verb *haber* 'have', and the past participle of the main verb, as shown in (1a).[2]

(1) a. *Te he preparado la cena.*
you-D have-1S prepare-en-∅ the dinner-FS
'I prepared dinner for you.'
b. *Homer tiene un buen trabajo.*
H has-3S a good-MS job-MS
'Homer has a good job.'

Notice that the English equivalents use the same verb *have*.

(2) a. I have prepared dinner for you.
b. Homer has a good job.

The structures I want to propose for (1a) and (1b) are similar, in order to explain the use of the same verb in the English (2a) and (2b).

Kayne 1993 follows ideas present in Szabolcsi 1983 to suggest that all instances of possessive and auxiliary 'have' are in fact formed by incorporation into BE of the head of the DP selected by the copula. Evidence for this fact comes first from languages where possessive sentences use the copula equivalent to 'be', such as Hungarian (example from Szabolcsi 1994):

[2] I will use the following abbreviations in the English glosses: en: participial affix; 1: first person; 2: second person; 3: third person; M: masculine; F: feminine; S: singular; P: plural; N: nominative; E: ergative; O: objective (accusative or absolutive); D: dative; ∅: default form (3,m,s in Spanish).

(3) a. *Mari-nak van-nak kalap-ja-i*
Mari-D be-3P hat-Poss.3S-NP
'Mari has hats.'
b. *Mari-nak*$_i$ [$_{VP}$ *van-nak* [$_{DP}$ t$_i$ [$_{D'}$ D^0 [$_{NP}$ t$_i$ [$_{N'}$ *kalap-ja-i*]]]]]

The structure in (3b) roughly corresponds to that of an existential 'be' with a single argument. In sentence (3a) the possessor raises from the existential DP, after being marked dative in the [Spec,DP] position, as shown in the derivation in (3b).

Kayne 1993 extends the analysis to English, claiming that the structure of a possessive sentence with 'have' starts out with a similar structure, as shown in (4).[3]

(4) a. John has a sister.
b. BE [$_{DP}$ D^0 [$_{AGR\text{-}P}$ John [$_{AGR'}$ AGR^0 a sister]]]

In order to derive (4a) from (4b), 'John' has to move first to [Spec,DP] and then to the upper projections of the matrix clause. Since [Spec,DP] is assumed to be an A'-position, the incorporation of D^0 into BE is required in order to turn it into an A-position and avoid a case of improper movement of the possessor.

Following the Szabolcsi 1983,1994 / Kayne 1993 analysis, both sentences (1a-b) contain a big DP selected by BE.

(5) a. BE [$_{DP}$ [$_{D'}$ D^0 [$_{TP}$ [$_{T'}$ T [$_{VP}$ *yo* [$_{V'}$ *preparado* [$_{DP}$ *la cena*]]]]]]]
b. BE [$_{DP}$ [$_{D'}$ D^0 [$_{PossP}$ *Homer* [$_{Poss'}$ $Poss^0$ [$_{DP}$ *un buen trabajo*]]]]]

The compound tense sentence (5a) (=(1a)) includes a full VP, where all thematic relations are realized. (5b) includes a small clause headed by $Poss^0$. By LF, both the embedded T^0 in (5a) and $Poss^0$ in (5b) have to reach the matrix T^0, in order to check their features and render the appropriate interpretations. However, the morphological differences among languages will arise from the strength of those features and the overt derivations that they force, as well as the licensing conditions on D^0.

[3] The same idea is present in Freeze (1992), who studies languages where the structure of a possessive sentence is exactly that of an existential locative. The details of Freeze's analysis diverge greatly from those in Kayne's.

1. ***Perfective tenses***

According to this analysis, compound tenses are formed by incorporation of the embedded T^0 in (5a) into the matrix T^0. Spanish has two types of evidence in support of this hypothesis.

The participle in compound tenses in Spanish has to incorporate into the auxiliary. Notice the adjacency effect between the auxiliary verb and the participle shown in cases of inversion, like (6).

(6) *¿Cuándo he preparado yo la cena?*
when have-1S prepare-en-∅ I the dinner-FS
'When have I prepared dinner?'

I want to propose that (6) shows incorporation of the participle into the auxiliary verb. This incorporation is obligatory, as the ungrammaticality of (7) shows.

(7) **¿Cuándo he yo preparado la cena?*
when have-1S I prepare-en-∅ the dinner-FS

Incorporation in Spanish compound perfective tenses is forced by tense-aspect reasons. The construction is interpreted as a single verb, rather than as a multiclausal sentence.

Another piece of evidence for this fact is the existence of simple perfective tenses such as (8).

(8) *Yo preparé la cena.*
I prepared-1S the dinner-FS

The so-called simple perfect preterit is used in some varieties of Spanish in place of the compound perfective past shown in (1a). Let us assume that, by the minimalist hypothesis of the universality of LFs, all perfective tenses must end up being a single head. The participial T^0 must then have a feature that forces it to incorporate into the matrix T^0. In Spanish this feature must be strong, since the incorporation is overtly realized, as we have just seen. In languages like English, where adjacency is not required, as shown in (9), the feature must be weak, and, by Procrastinate, incorporation must be covert.

(9) When have I prepared dinner?

The conclusion of this section is that all perfective tenses must end up being a single T^0 at LF. When a languages chooses a biclausal structure for such tenses, the embedded T^0 must incorporate into the matrix T^0. Some languages must complete this process by Spell-Out.

2. *Auxiliary 'have'*

I want to propose that the Spanish auxiliary verb *haber* is formed by the incorporation of the head of the big DP into the copula BE (as in Kayne 1993), rendering a complex head [BE[D^0]]. The D^0 head of the big DP selects for a TP, following Szabolcsi's 1983 intuition that the functional head D^0 has a similar nature to that of C^0. The structure in (5a) is repeated below:

(10) a. BE $[_{DP}$ $[_{D'}$ D^0 $[_{TP}$ $[_{T'}$ T $[_{VP}$ yo $[_{V'}$ preparado $[_{DP}$ la cena]]]]]]]

b. BE $[_{DP}$ $[_{D'}$ D^0 $[_{TP}$ yo_i $[_{T'}$ $preparado_k$ $[_{VP}$ t_i $[_{V'}$ t_k $[_{DP}$ la cena]]]]]]]

c. BE+D^0_m $[_{DP}$ $[_{D'}$ t_m $[_{TP}$ yo_i $[_{T'}$ $preparado_k$ $[_{VP}$ t_i $[_{V'}$ t_k $[_{DP}$ la cena]]]]]]]

d. BE+D^0_m+$preparado_k$ $[_{DP}$ $[_{D'}$ t_m $[_{TP}$ yo_i $[_{T'}$ t_k $[_{VP}$ t_i $[_{V'}$ t_k $[_{DP}$ la cena]]]]]]]

(11)

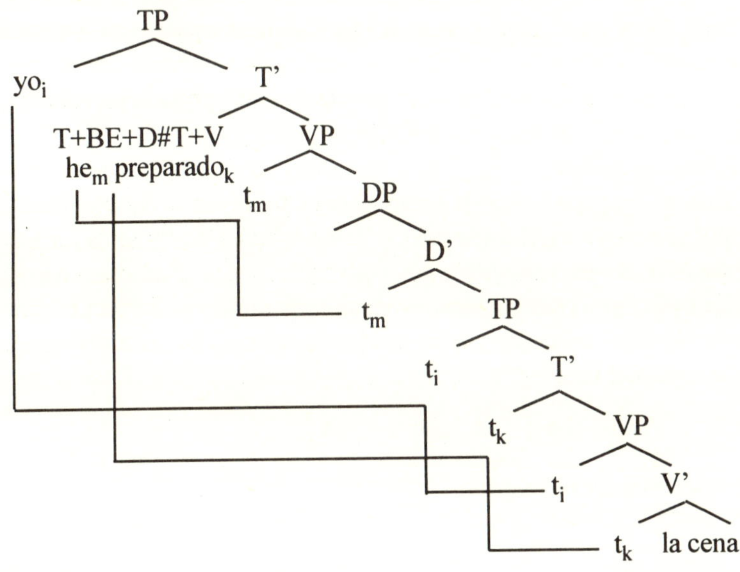

The derivation proceeds as follows: (10a) is the initial structure, which includes BE, D^0, the main verb inflected as a participle, and the arguments of the main verb. In (10b) the participle raises to the embedded T^0 to check its tense/aspect features, and the external argument raises to [Spec,TP] to check the EPP. Since the embedded clause is non-finite, the subject cannot check case or agreement there. (10c) represents the incorporation of D^0 into BE, which in fact yields *haber*. Once the auxiliary verb is formed, as we will see, the participle has to incorporate to support the matrix T^0. That is the step in (10d). This step does not violate minimality, provided that traces are not visible to the computational component, as argued for by Chomsky 1995. (11) is the tree that shows all the movements.

According to Kayne 1993, this movement is necessary to turn [Spec,DP] into an A-position where the subject may stop on its way to the matrix TP. I want to propose that the subject need not stop in this position at all, since it does not check any features there.

Let us assume that D^0 has strong nominal features. These features can be satisfied by spec-head agreement with a DP. Since the position of [Spec,DP] is an A'-position, the movement of a caseless DP to that position will inevitably yield improper movement, given that the DP must move to an A-position later to get case. D^0 only has a way to check its features: namely, incorporating into BE, which eventually will be in a Spec-head configuration with a DP.

3. *Possessive 'have'*

Spanish possessive verb *tener* always involves a double incorporation [BE[D^0 [$Poss^0$]]] (cf. Kempchinsky 1995), where $Poss^0$ stands for the head of a Possessive phrase (roughly equivalent to AGR-O in Szabolcsi/Kayne).[4] The subject of PossP is the possessor, which will end up as subject of *tener* in the matrix TP. The possessed theme will be its object. The sentence under discussion is repeated here:

(12) *Homer tiene un buen trabajo.*
H has-3S a good-MS job-MS
'Homer has a good job.'

[4] Szabolcsi (1983) points out that the possessor theta-role is unlikely to be assigned by the possessed noun. Some nouns in possessive relations, such as kinship terms or cases of inalienable relations, may be inherently relational, but in most alienable possessions there must be an additional way to assign the possessor role.

The derivation must proceed as follows:

(13) a. $[_{TP}$ T $[_{VP}$ BE $[_{DP}$ $[D^0$ $[_{PossP}$ Homer $[Poss^0$ $[_{DP}$ un buen trabajo]]]]]]]

b. $[_{TP}$ T $[_{VP}$ BE $[_{DP}$ $[D^0+Poss^0{}_i$ $[_{PossP}$ Homer $[t_i$ $[_{DP}$ un buen trabajo]]]]]]]

c. $[_{TP}$ T $[_{VP}$ BE+$[D^0+Poss^0{}_i]_k$ $[_{DP}$ $[t_k$ $[_{PossP}$ Homer $[t_i$ $[_{DP}$ un buen trabajo]]]]]]]

d. $[_{TP}$ Homer$_m$ T+[BE+$[D^0+Poss^0{}_i]_k]_n[_{VP}$ $t_n[_{DP}[t_k[_{PossP}$ $t_m[t_i$ $[_{DP}$ un buen trabajo]]]]]]]]

(14)

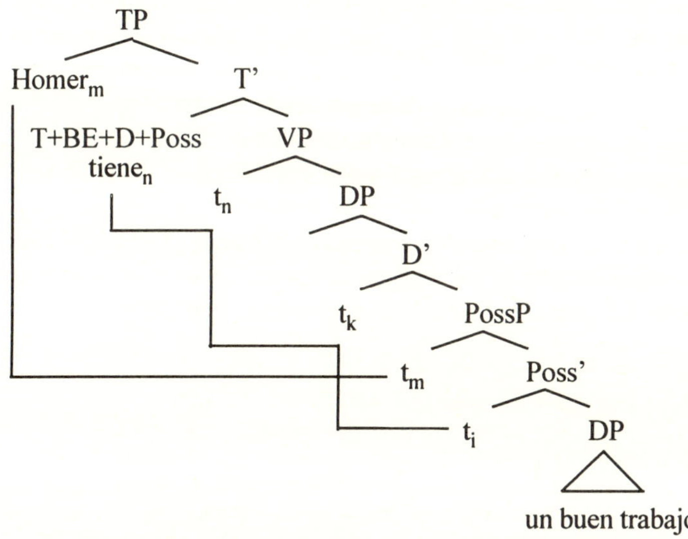

$Poss^0$ must raise to D^0, and this compound head raises further to BE, yielding the possessive verb *tener*. Now, the possessor DP may move to the matrix TP to check nominative case.

Given that the movement of $Poss^0$ in Spanish must be overt, the feature that forces it has to be strong. Otherwise, we would expect the verb to be spelled out as *haber*. It is difficult to establish what the nature of $Poss^0$ is. It must have verbal features in order to assign accusative case. On the other hand, it may not be a regular verb, given that it may not support a clause on its own. If it were a regular transitive verb, we would expect it to allow passivization. It does not:[5]

(15) a. **Un buen trabajo es tenido por Homer.*
b. *A good job is had by Homer.

What seems at stake here is the fact that *tener* is both a raising and an ECM verb at the same time, since it takes two arguments out of a small clause and assigns case to both of them. Raising verbs such as 'be' or 'seem' do not assign accusative case, but ECM verbs like 'believe' or 'consider' have their own external argument, so by Burzio's generalization the two classes exclude each other. Remember that this generalization states that a verb must have an external argument in order to assign accusative, and vice versa. Even causative verbs, which may be considered a type of ECM verb, have a subject of their own. The peculiarity of tener is mixing characteristics of both types of verbs.

If we want to keep Burzio's generalization straight, we must attribute the raising and ECM properties to different heads. I want to propose that the raising properties of *tener* come from the matrix head BE, whereas its ECM properties come from the embedded $Poss^0$. Furthermore, if we assume that this head is assigning the theta-roles in this construction (as suggested by Szabolcsi 1983), then it follows that $Poss^0$ in fact is not always an ECM head, since it assigns accusative to its own object. In some cases, this head will assign a genuine ECM, when its object is a small clause, as in (1b).[6]

---

[5] When being part of an idiom, these verbs may passivize, as in (i).

(i) a. A good time was had by everybody.
b. *Tu opinión será tenida en cuenta.*
your opinion-FS will.be-3S have-en-FS in account
"Your opinion will be taken into account."

I will take these idioms to be regular verbs, grammaticalized as a lexical unit, and the analysis in the text will not cover them.

[6] Freeze (1992) shows that in those languages that use the same copula for existential and possessive clauses, such as the Finnish sentences under (i), the theme receives whatever case the associate gets in an existential.

(i) a. *pöydä-llä on kynä*
table-ADESSIVE COP pencil-NOM
'There is a pencil on the table.'
b. *Liisa-lla on mies*
L.-ADESSIVE COP man-NOM
'Lisa has a husband.'

The English possessive verb is not overtly distinguishable from the auxiliary ‘have’. I want to propose that this overt identity corresponds to similar structures before Spell-Out. In the covert component, $Poss^0$ will incorporate into the matrix T^0, where it provides the possessive interpretation of ‘have’, ending up in a structure equivalent to that of Spanish, as shown in (16).

(16)

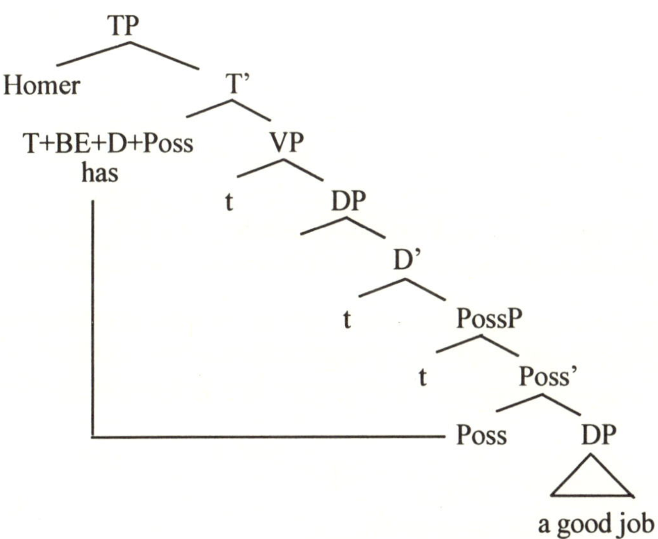

This covert movement is also not blocked because traces are not subject to movement, under current assumptions. Notice that the Spell-Out of the verb does not change, given that this movement occurs covertly and has no effect on the PF output.

Thus the morphological component simply has to decide the form of the possessive verb according to the incorporations that have occurred by Spell-Out, following the paradigm in (17).

According to Freeze (1992), the interpretation as an existential or a possessive will be determined by the [human] character of the locative/possessor noun. It seems clear that the account for case-assignment in languages like Finnish should be the same for both constructions.

(17)	Auxiliary	Possessive
Spanish	[BE[D^0]] *haber*	[BE[D^0[$Poss^0$]]] *tener*
English	[BE[D^0]] *have*	[BE[D^0]] *have*

In this section we have seen that possessive verbs have a uniform LF, which requires the incorporation of the embedded $Poss^0$ into the matrix T^0. Once again, this incorporation may occur covertly or overtly, giving rise to the differences observed between Spanish and English.

4. *Auxiliary selection*

It is a well-known fact that Romance languages show a very wide range of variation in their treatment of perfective tenses. Here I will consider two types of languages: Spanish-like languages, and Italian-like languages.

With a certain level of idealization (see Kayne 1989, for some cases of agreement in the presence of 'have'), let us assume that there exists the correlation in the paradigm in (18).

(18)	Auxiliary	Agreement
a.	have	no
b.	be	yes

(19) a. *Maria e arrivata.*
M. be-3S arrive-en-FS
'Maria has arrived.'
b. *Maria ha conosciuto Gianni.*
M. have-3S meet-en-∅ G.
'Maria has met Gianni.'

Spanish will always use (18a), whereas Italian will use (18a) for transitives and unergatives and (18b) for unaccusatives. There is an obvious correlation between agreement and presence of 'be'. It seems that when agreement is present incorporation of D^0 into BE is not necessary. Therefore, an agreeing participle licenses D^0. On the other hand, if no agreement occurs, D^0 must incorporate into BE.

This analysis proposes that the two verbs previously discussed, the Spanish possessive *tener* and the perfective auxiliary *haber/have/avere*, plus the cases of perfective auxiliary *essere* are in fact morphological realizations of different Spell-Outs of the same projections. The lexical entries for the heads (BE, D^0,

$Poss^0$) are assumed to be universal, as well as their LF interpretations. However, different languages will group them in different ways according to their formal features to give a variety of morphological outputs in the Spell-Out form:

(20)

	Unaccusative verbs	Transitive/Unergative verbs
Italian	[BE] *essere* [D^0[+AGR]]	[BE[D^0]] *avere* [-AGR]
Spanish	[BE[D^0]] *haber* [-AGR]	[BE[D^0]] *haber* [-AGR]
English	[BE[D^0]] *have* [-AGR]	[BE[D^0]] *have* [-AGR]

For Kayne 1993, the real reason for the variation is the shift of [Spec,DP] into an A-position, but we already rejected this proposal on grounds that this position is not necessary for any movement. We want the licensing of D^0 to be the reason why heads move around the way we have seen.

What is common to all instances of agreement between the participle and the internal argument (including those in Kayne 1989) is that the latter appears overtly in front of the former. Therefore, agreement must have been established through a spec-head configuration at some point of the derivation. This position must not be [Spec,TP], since we know that external arguments of transitive and unergative verbs stop at that position to check the EPP of T^0, and they do not trigger agreement with the participle. The object may stop at [Spec,VP] for two reasons. One is that this position is empty in the case of an unaccusative verb. However, assuming the multiple spec approach to case assignment in Chomsky 1995, it may stop at this spec on its way out of the VP. The lack of participle agreement with the external argument may be explained if, as suggested in Chomsky 1995, checking can only be done through movement and never through merge.

The kinds of agreement will be determined specifically for each language by its morphological properties. Spanish verbal heads never have ϕ-features; only T^0 does. Italian participles, on the other hand, may have ϕ-features, but they are activated by overt movement of the internal argument only.

Some proposals (Nunes 1993, Kempchinsky 1995) treat the participle as a kind of nominal element. I do not agree with this view, given that even some cases of agreeing participles may assign accusative case and accusative is largely assumed to be an exclusive feature of verbs.

One further option is to assume that agreement with the participle happens in the T-projection, and that the AGR-O features are carried by the participial inflection rather than V^0. The proposal is interesting, especially because it would allow us to propose the absence of nominal features in verbal heads across the board for the languages studied here. However, this proposal leaves open the question of why then external arguments in that position do not trigger agreement. I will continue to assume that a perfective sentence includes a full-fledged embedded clause, and that every clause with a T-projection has an EPP feature to be checked by its subject. Also, I will keep assuming that the subject is generated inside VP. I do not see a way to reconcile these assumptions with the lack of agreement between external arguments and participles. Thus, the safest hypothesis seems to be that agreement occurs inside VP, where the positions of subject and object may still be distinguished.

The agreement of the participle licenses D^0 without the need to incorporate into BE. Recall that D^0 has strong nominal features. These features could be checked by spec-head agreement with a DP. Another way to check them would be the incorporation of a head that contains those features, such as an agreeing participle. When the participle bears no nominal features, D^0 can only satisfy the requirement by incorporating into BE.

Thus, the simple proposal of a strong nominal feature of D^0, and the parameterization of the presence of ϕ-features on participial V-heads are enough to give an introductory account of Romance auxiliary selection and past participle agreement.

5. *Learnability issues*

In this section I will discuss the type of evidence that children learning different languages receive from their environment in order to set the parameters involved in this paper.

I will assume that only overt differences are learned through experience, and that the linguistic input does not provide any evidence for LF-processes. I will also assume that both the initial array of heads (including BE, D^0, $Poss^0$, T^0 and V) and the final interpretation at the interface are given by UG and common to all languages. This much is not learned by children. What they have to learn is how particular morphologies of languages resolve the PF-outputs of their derivations. The overt differences to be explained are presented in (21) to (25). English happens to be the null case in all three parameters: it has a single verb for all three functions (auxiliary for all kinds of verbs and possessive) and shows no adjacency effect between auxiliary and participle.

5.1 *Auxiliary selection between* essere *and* avere *and participle agreement (Italian)*

The contrast in (21) shows how Italian children may acquire the paradigm of auxiliary selection.

(21) a. *Maria e arrivata.*
M. be-3S arrive-en-FS
'Maria has arrived.'
b. *Maria ha conosciuto Gianni.*
M. have-3S meet-en-∅ G.
'Maria has met Gianni.'

When hearing *essere,* their morphological component deduces that the nominal feature of D^0 must be satisfied without incorporation into BE. Then, the presence of overt participle agreement permits Italian children to deduce a different way to license the requirement of D^0. On the other hand, when the verb is not unaccusative, Italian children hear the verb *avere,* which includes D^0, so that the requirement is licensed as well. Upon hearing *avere,* children perceive no participle agreement, and hypothesize that agreement is realized only when absolutely necessary.

Spanish or English children will not hear any difference between the sentences equivalent to (21) that they receive as input. Therefore, they hypothesize that D^0 has been properly licensed by incorporation into BE and do not apply any agreement to the participle. (22) shows the outcome of the parameters involved in (21).

(22)	Unaccusative verbs	Transitive/Unergative verbs
Italian	[BE] *essere* [D^0[+AGR]]	[BE[D^0]] *avere* [-AGR]
Spanish	[BE[D^0]] *haber* [-AGR]	[BE[D^0]] *haber* [-AGR]
English	[BE[D^0]] *have* [-AGR]	[BE[D^0]] *have* [-AGR]

5.2 *Difference between* haber *and* tener *(Spanish)*

Spanish children receive overt evidence of the difference between *haber* and *tener*:

(23) a. *Yo he preparado la cena.*
b. *Yo tengo la cena preparada.*

Therefore, they hypothesize in their grammars that there is a different overt realization of the possessive and the auxiliary verb. This means that Spanish children can hypothesize the overt incorporation of the third head $Poss^0$ into the complex $[BE[D^0]]$.

Italian and English children, on the other hand, will not make this hypothesis, since the input they receive is the same for both verbs. The principles of UG will determine the incorporation of $Poss^0$ at LF. The parameter system is shown in (24).

(24)	Auxiliary	Possessive
Spanish	[BE[D⁰]] *haber*	[BE[D⁰[Poss⁰]]] *tener*
Italian	[BE[D⁰]] *avere*	[BE[D⁰]] *avere*
English	[BE[D⁰]] *have*	[BE[D⁰]] *have*

5.3 *Adjacency effect between auxiliary and participle (Spanish/Italian)*

The last parameter involves the adjacency effect between the auxiliary verb and the participle. UG requires that this incorporation occurs before LF, but the morphology of Spanish requires that the incorporation is overt.

(25) a. *¿Cuándo [he preparado]*$_i$ *yo* t_i *la cena?*
b. When [have]$_i$ I t_i prepared dinner?

The data that Spanish children need in order to acquire this requirement cannot arise from negative evidence such as the fact that in adult's language no words ever intervene between the auxiliary and the participle. However, I take a sentence like (25a) to be a genuine example of positive evidence, since the auxiliary verb and the participle have moved together as a constituent. From evidence like this, the child may hypothesize that Spanish has overt incorporation of the participle into the auxiliary.

Of course, English children get evidence for their analysis very easily, when they see movement of the auxiliary alone, as in (25b), or elements intervening between the auxiliary and the participle, such as adverbs.

I think I have provided evidence that the overt structures for the main points of deviation from UG are easily learnable by children acquiring Spanish, Italian and English. This evidence makes the analysis more tenable.

6. *Conclusion*

The idea that auxiliary verbs have a purely functional nature has been entertained in linguistic research for a long time. Pollock 1989 made use of this intuition to explain the ability of English auxiliaries to move even when they appear to be main verbs. The proposal made here is that in fact auxiliaries are never main verbs, in the sense of having a V-head of their own in the numeration, not even when they do not auxiliate another verb. The main advantage of this approach is that it has an enormous potential for cross-linguistic coverage, going well beyond Indoeuropean languages, as suggested by Freeze 1992. It opens itself to a high level of complexity in the specific analysis of each language, but with two virtues that fit very well into the Minimalist Program. First, numerations and LFs are universal, a very desirable result when talking about functional categories. Second, morphology is language specific, but, at least in part, predictable from the syntax. The morphological component that depends on syntax is the one that applies after Spell-Out, and will connect syntactic facts like participle agreement with purely morphological ones, such as the form of the auxiliary. Other morphological decisions seem to precede syntax. The choice between a monoclausal or a biclausal perfective construction will determine the syntactic derivation radically. A system like this, where some morphology precedes syntax, and syntax determines some of the morphology could be the way to solve the complicated interactions between these two components of the grammar.

REFERENCES

Chomsky, Noam. 1995. *The Minimalist Program.* Cambridge, Mass.: MIT Press.

Freeze, Ray. 1992. "Existentials and Other Locatives". *Language* 68.553-595.

Kayne, Richard. 1989. "Facets of Romance Past Participle Agreement". *Dialect Variation and the Theory of Grammar* ed. by Paola Benincá, 85-103. Dordrecht: Foris.

_____. 1993. "Toward a Modular Theory of Auxiliary Selection". *Studia Linguistica* 47.3-31.

Kempchinsky, Paula. 1995. "Perfective Auxiliaries, Possession and Existence in Romance". Paper presented at LSRL 25. Seattle: University of Washington.

Nunes, Jairo. 1993. "English Participle Constructions: Evidence for a [+PF,-LF] Case". *University of Maryland Working Papers in Linguistics* 1 ed. by C. Mason, C., S. Powers and C. Schmitt, 66-79. Department of Linguistics, College Park.

Pollock, Jean-Yves. 1989. "Verb Movement, Universal Grammar, and the Structure of IP". *Linguistic Inquiry* 20.365-424.

Szabolcsi, Ana. 1983. "The Possessor that Ran Away from Home". *The Linguistic Review* 3.89-102.

———. 1994. "The Noun Phrase". *Syntax and Semantics 27: The Syntactic Structure of Hungarian*, 179-274. Academic Press.

TWO TYPES OF PREDICATE MODIFICATION

EVIDENCE FROM THE ARTICULATED ADJECTIVES OF ROMANIAN

DOMNITA DUMITRESCU
CSLA
MARIO SALTARELLI
USC

0. *Introduction*

Among the Romance languages Romanian is unique in exhibiting definite modified nominal constructions in which either the noun or the modifier incorporates a definite article in the form of an enclitically bound morpheme, as illustrated in (1).[1] The alternative order in (1a) and (1b) identifies a semantically variable reading of the lexical adjective sărac "poor," as can be gathered from the glosses.

(1) a. săracul om (*sărac omul) "the poor (pitiable) man"
b. omul sărac (*om săracul) "the poor (indigent) man"

As a contribution toward an understanding of the semantic alternation in (1) and the relative syntactic issues, we outline in this paper a predication hypothesis of Romanian adjective constructions. We begin with a discussion of relevant aspects of the determiner system of the language.

1. *Determiners*

In comparison with other Romance languages the determiner system of Romanian is unique in its morphological, syntactic and semantic nature.

1.1 *Definite articles*

The Romanian definite article -l (2a) is morphologically bound to the noun as an inflectional or enclitic form, in contrast with the indefinite article un (2b) which precedes the noun as in Spanish and Italian. The inflectional paradigm

---

[1] The genesis of the enclitic definite article is a debated topic in the Romanian philological tradition. For an authoritative assessment and an evaluation of the issues see Renzi (1995).

of the definite article for nominals like copac "tree" and carte "book" is reported in (3).[2]

(2) a. copacul -(u)l enclitic definite article
tree-the
"the tree"

b. un copac **un** prenominal indefinite article
a tree
"a tree"

(3)

	NOM ACC SING	NOM ACC PLUR	GEN DAT SING	GEN DAT PLUR
masculine	copacu-**l**	copaci-**i**	copacu-**lui**	copaci-**lor**
feminine	carte-**a**	cărţi-**le**	cărţi-**i**	cărţi-**lor**

Regarding the structural status of (3), it should be noted that, in current analyses, the Romanian definite article is not base-generated in its enclitic position. Rather, it is projected as the head of the functional category DP.[3] Departing from the standard view, we assume that the Case and φ-features of the inflectional paradigm (3) are included in the numeration of the noun, except for their choice and morphological form, following Chomsky (1995:237).

1.2 *Possessives*

With respect to the morphologization of the determiner, it should be noted that in Romanian, the definite article is not the only element which is encliticized to the noun. Possessive elements also occur in a similar morphologically bound form with kinship terms (4) as well as with other lexical classes.

1.2.1 *Enclitic possessives*. This fact is relevant for the analysis of the determiner system if we consider that in Romanian possessives occur as adnominal adjectives usually in postnominal position, as in fratele său (4b), and only in conjunc-

[2] Figure (3) is adopted from Cornilescu (1992:205). In addition to the case distinctions given in (3), there is also a vocative case: băiatule "boy!", fato "girl!".
[3] Cornilescu (1992; cf. also 1995) follows Dobrovie-Sorin's (1987; cf. also 1994) DP analysis (Abney 1987). She also argues, following Giusti (1992), for the existence of a Case Projection in Romanian which selects DP as its complement (1992:196).

tion with an obligatory (cliticized) article on the preceding constituent.[4] Hence, a complementary distribution can be established between the enclitic possessive in (4a) and the enclitic article in (4b). If our analysis is correct, the determiner system of Romanian includes enclitic possessives as definite determiners along with articles.

(4)	a. soru-sa	(sister-his)	"his sister"
	frate-su (-său)	(brother-his)	"his brother"
	mamă -ta	(mother-your)	"your mother"
	tată -su (-său)	(father-his)	"his father"
	b. sora sa	(sister-the his)	"the sister of his"
	fratele său	(brother-the his)	"the brother of his"
	mama ta	(mother-the your)	"the mother of yours"
	tatăl său	(father-the his)	"the father of his"

The approximation of the Romanian (enclitic) definite article to the analysis of (enclitic) possessives is important for their common semantic property as logical binders. This property is required to actualize the referential potential of the noun. In fact, in the presence of the clitic possessive the expression (4a) does not admit any article, suggesting that the clitic possessive is an instance of the category D^0 along with the article -l.[5] Under this analysis, then, a separate functional projection for possessives other that D in the determiner system of Romanian would not be justified. Moreover, postnominal (non-clitic) possessives are semantically analyzed as adnominal complements, functioning as modifiers, whose nominal head requires an independent determiner to actualize the reference potential of the head noun, as the examples in (4b) illustrate.[6]

---

[4] In addition to the enclitic (4a) and adjectival form (4b), Romanian has a third possessive construction in which a so called "possessive article" (al, a, ai, ale) is inserted before the possessive: al meu, a mea.

[5] The morphological status of the Romanian enclitic possessive is reminiscent of the French prenominal possessive determiner leurs in leurs chevaux "their horses" which is analyzed as a conflation of the definite determiner le(s) and the possessive eux and derived by a special rule of suppletion (Vergnaud and Zubizarreta 1992:623).

[6] This behavior of enclitic possessives is also found in Marsian, a southern Italian dialect (Dumitrescu and Saltarelli 1966).

1.3 *Demonstratives*

Like definite articles, Romanian demonstratives acest [m.] "this" and acel [m.] "that" are inflected for Case and φ-features, namely nominative/genitive, singular/plural, and masculine/feminine.

1.3.1 *Prenominal and postnominal demonstratives*. The following paradigm (5) is the nominative/accusative singular/plural for acest om "this mam."

(5) Nominative forms of acest(a)

Singular

a. acest om	"this man"
b. omul acesta	(man-the this)
c. *acest/acesta este Ion	"this is Ion"
d. Ion este acesta	"Ion is this"

Plural

e. aceşti oameni	"these men"
f. oamenii aceştia	(the men these)
g. *aceşti/aceştia sunt oamenii	"these are the men"
h. oamenii sunt aceştia	"the men are these"

As illustrated in (5a/b,e/f), Romanian exhibits prenominal as well as postnominal demonstratives, a distribution this language shares with Spanish,[7] but not Italian.[8]

1.3.2 *Two morpho-syntactic classes of demonstratives*. A unique feature of Romanian demonstratives is their dual morpho-syntactic nature: a "short" form found prenominally (5a,e) and a second form, which is "longer" by a vowel [a]. The long form is found generally postnominally (5b,f) and in predicate contexts (5d,h). It's important to observe that the short demonstrative cannot be used as a (referential) pronoun as in other Romance languages or English. In fact, we see in (5c,g), that expressions structurally equivalent to

[7] The postnominal position of the demonstrative in Spanish in an expression like la casa esta as opposed to esta casa has been recently analyzed in Juan Martín's dissertation (1995:259-60). His analysis assumes a double articulation of DP along the lines of Cornilescu, but with clear theoretical advantages.

[8] This variation between Romanian and Spanish vs. Italian is also in need of a principled parametric distinction within Romance.

English "this is Ion" and "these are the men" are only possible in Romanian with the long form of the demonstrative ending in [**a**].[9]

1.3.3 *The dual nature of demonstratives*. The distribution of Romanian demonstratives we have just discussed suggests a distinct syntactic-semantic link with a different function in prenominal and postnominal position. Specifically, the prenominal short form acest functions as a determiner. As such its semantic role is to bind (or saturate) the referential variable of the noun. Nominals are analyzed here as a simple predicates.[10] In contrast, the postnominal longer form acesta does not function as the determiner of the noun. This is demonstrated by the fact that the noun requires an independent binder. Following the same arguments as for possessives (cf. (4)), the data suggests that the short demonstrative is an instance of the same functional projection D^0. In the context of our analysis, then, a separate functional projection for Romanian prenominal demonstratives is not justified.[11]

As in the case of postnominal possessives (4b), the postnominal longer forms of the demonstrative acesta/acestia (5b,f) and its semantic function cannot be derived from the same underlying syntactic position as prenominal demonstratives. Rather like postnominal (non-clitic) possessives, postnominal demonstratives merge as complements of the noun. Under this syntactic condition, their deixis is extensionally identified as a property of a modifier in conjunction with the preceding noun.

1.3.4 *Binding relations between determiners and nominals*. A preliminary assessment of the binding relations between determiners and nominals is given in (6). In Romanian, as in other Romance languages, nominals may function as predicates, as in Ion este profesor "Ion is [a] professor," in which

---

9 With respect to the role of this vowel morpheme our understanding is only speculative. Its distribution would suggest that -[a] grammaticizes the marked property function of deixis in postnominal position, as opposed to an inherent determiner function of the demonstrative in prenominal position.

10 The predication theory we are following is roughly identified with an understanding of the terms predication and saturation in the tradition of Frege's work (Geach and Black 1952:108,132).

11 The analysis we present here is in contrast with previous analyses (cf. Cornilescu (1992:206) in which demonstratives head their own projection, and N raises to D^0 in overt syntax. See Juan Martín (1995:252) for a discussion of this analysis.

the theta-grid of profesor contains an open position <1> which must be "saturated" <*1> for its interpretation, in this case by the subject Ion.[12] In a parallel manner, we are assuming that in noun phrases the noun is a simple predicate and the semantic role of the determiner is to saturate (by theta-binding) an open position,[13] along the lines of Higginbotham (1985, 1987) thematic theory.[14]

(6) Thematic theory (after Higginbotham 1985, 1987)

a.

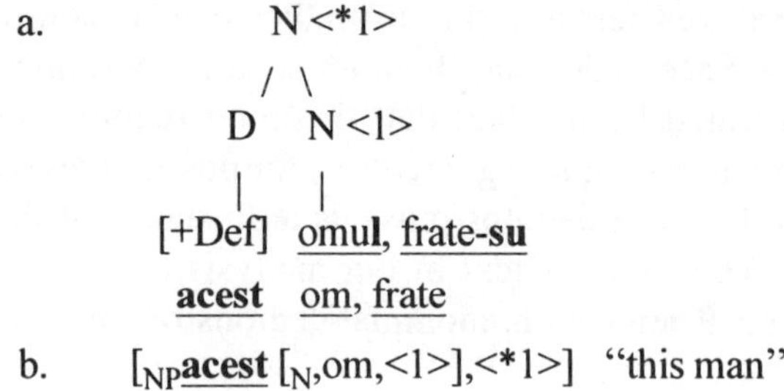

b. [$_{NP}$**acest** [$_{N}$,om,<1>],<*1>] "this man"

Accordingly, in (6), acest binds om or frate thus saturating the open variable in the theta-grid of the noun turning the expression into an argument.[15] Note further that, in this analysis, the demonstrative determiner acest conflates both definiteness and deixis. Lexical conflation accounts for the non co-occurrence of the definite article in deictic noun phrases.[16]

1.4 *Cardinals and adjectives*

Unlike demonstratives Romanian cardinals are invariable for case, but, like demonstratives, they are inflected for gender and number. Like demonstratives, cardinals may appear postnominally, which points out another unique

---

[12] In effect, in copular contexts the open position of the nominal profesor is licensed by the head of IP (arguably Tense, as its binder) and only 'remotely' identified with Ion for referentiality, hence the more open-ended interpretation of the predicate nominal.
[13] It has also been argued that determiners contain their own (special type of) variable, rather than binding directly the nominal variable.
[14] See also the work of Michel Degraff and Deborah Mandelbaum (1993) for a similar thematic analysis of adnominal adjectives in Romance.
[15] Rothstein (1983) proposes the principle that syntactic predicates are unsaturated. Semantic interpretation of syntactic predicates requires saturation.
[16] Conflation of semantic features is stipulated here as a lexicalization process (cf. Talmy 1985), rather than the result of a morphological or syntactic rule.

feature of the cardinal system of this language in comparison with other Romance languages. Their basic distribution is found in (7).

As a first observation we note that the plural cardinal numeral doi "two (m.)" can bind an indefinite plural noun (7ai), but not a definite noun (7bi). Such a quantified expression, in fact, requires a preceding definite demonstrative-like plural determiner cei (sing. cel) in order to actualize the referential potential of the noun.[17] It should be observed, in contrast, that cei is optional (colloquially, but not in prose) in (7bii), where the noun copacii takes an obligatory enclitic plural article -i. These facts support the analysis we have been discussing so far, according to which postnominal (non clitic) possessives, demonstratives, and now cardinals, are of a category other than Determiner, in contrast with their prenominal counterparts.

(7)
a. (i) doi copaci/*copaci "two trees"
(ii) *copaci doi "(trees two)"
b. (i) *(cei) doi copaci "the two trees"
(ii) copacii (cei) doi "(trees-the (the) two)"
c. (i) acești doi copaci "these two trees"
(ii) copacii aceștia doi "(trees-the these two)"
(iv) *doi acești*doi aceștia copaci (vs. 7ci)
d. (i) acești doi vechi prieteni "these two old friends"
(ii) ?acești vechi doi prieteni "?these old two friends"
(iii) prietenii aceștia doi vechi "(friends-the these two olds)"
(iv) *prietenii aceștia vechi doi "(friends-the these oldss two)"
e. (i) acești doi bieți vechi prieteni "these two poor old friends"
(ii) acești bieți doi vechi prieteni
(iii) ?acești bieți vechi doi prieteni
(iv) *doi acești bieți vechi prieteni

A second observation regarding Romanian cardinal numbers is that they follow the demonstratives (7civ), as expected. Their order with respect to adjectives differs in complex and yet unclear ways. Cardinals may weakly bind a nominal (7ai), and therefore have a determiner-like function. In the presence of a determiner, however, cardinals do not differ from adjectives, with which they may combine. For example, in prenominal constructions and in combi-

---

[17] Although our grammatical treatment of cel differs from Cornilescu's (1992:232-237), we are in general in agreement with her empirical assessment. We analyze prenominal cel as a definite article subcategorized for quantifiers (cf. (9)).

nation with only one adjective like (7d), the cardinal doi can precede the adjective (7di) but not follow (7dii) vechi. The same strict cardinal+adjective order is maintained (7diii,iv). For reasons which remain obscure, in combination with two adjectives (7di-iii) there is much more flexibility.

A third observation is in order between cardinals and adjectives. As noted earlier (7ai,8a), cardinals can weakly bind a noun. This is a function which unarticulated adjectives do not possess in this language, as we illustrate in ((8b): *bieţi elevi au lipsit ieri "poor pupils were absent yesterday."[18] In contrast with simple adjectives, however, Romanian articulated adjectives do saturate the nominal expression (8c). In accordance with our analysis this binding function of articulated adjectives is made possible by the presence of the nominal enclitic **-i**, which checks its [+def] feature of the functional category Determiner in [Spec,NP].

(8) a. doi (bieţi) elevi au lipsit ieri
"two (poor) students were absent yesterday"
b. *bieţi (doi) elevi au lipsit ieri
(poor (two) students ...
c. bieţii (doi) elevi au lipsit ieri
"(poors-the two students ...)"

Our brief discussion of the determiner system of Romanian has argued that the particular distribution of prenominal elements in this language is narrowly determined by their morphological and lexical properties in conjunction with semantic principles of predicate structure. In the remainder of the paper we attempt to show how a predication analysis of Romanian adjectives can contribute to an understanding of their semantics and syntax.

2. *The predicate structure of adjectives*

In the context of the predication theory we assume in (6), the theta-grid of prenominal adjectives also contains a variable <1> which must be bound by a determiner. We suggest that this is indicated by the morphology of Romanian articulated prenominal adjectives (8b/c). An extension of (6) is given in (9).[19]

---

[18] Cf. Cornilescu (1992:208, (39)) for a different argumentation.

[19] As noted in (9) and in 1.4 prenominal cardinals appear to have a dual function as weak binders (7ai) and may combine with prenominal adjectives (7e) to some degree (cf. Cornilescu 1992:209).

```
(9)              N <*1>
                  / \
                D    N <1>
               / \
             D    A <*1>
             |    |
        [+Def] bieţi-i, sărac-ul      (cf. examples (8b, 1b))
           cei    doi                 (cf. example 7bi)
```

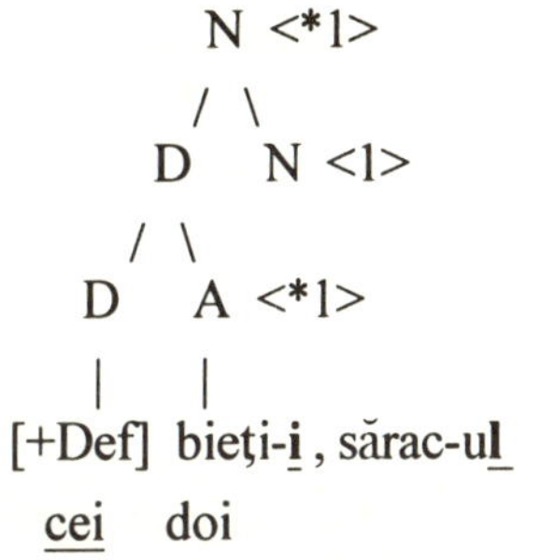

2.1. *Two types of predicate saturation*

A generalized assessment of noun phrases is illustrated in (10).

```
(10)             N <*1>
                 /    \
                D      N<*1>
              /   \     /   \
             D  A<*1> N<1>  A<*1>
                         |_____|
```

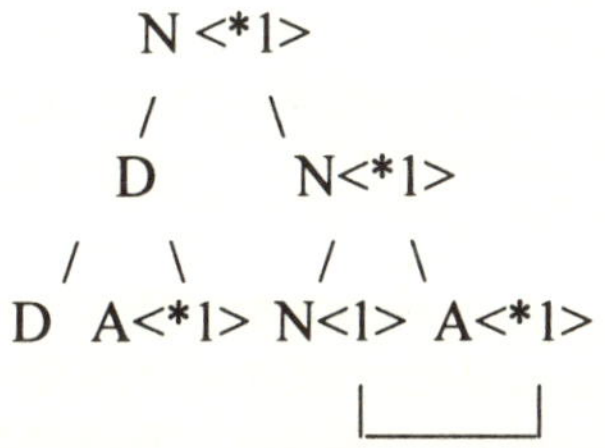

2.2 *Theta binding and prenominal adjectives*

Focus first on prenominal adjectives. In this case, the determiner D binds the open variable of the predicate adjective A<*1>. Theta-binding occurs as prenominal adjectives are assumed to be merged as complements of the functional head D. Theta-binding represents one way predicate adjectives are saturated. (10a) is a partial representation of the example (1a): săracul om "the poor (pitiable) man".

(10) a. $[_{DP}$ $[_{D'}$ D $[_{AP}$ săracul,<1>],<*1>] ...

2.3 *Theta-identification of prenominal adjectives*

The second type of saturation involves postnominal adjectives, which like prenominal adjectives, are uniformly merged as complements of a head, in this second case the lexical head Noun. In this syntactic context composition proceeds by "identification" (Higginbotham 1987:46), understood as "identifying" the positions in the thematic structure of the modifying adjective and of the modified noun, as shown by the connecting lines in (10). Identity reduces the two variables of N and A to one variable for the modified phrase N'<1>.

This is understood as the syntactic condition for an extensional interpretation of noun phrases. An illustration of the second type of predication is represented in (10b) for the example (1b): omul sărac “the poor (indigent) man”.

(10) b. ... [$_{N'}$ omul,<1> [$_{AP}$ sărac,<1>],<1>]

2.4 *Intensions and extensions of adjectives*

Assuming predication theory as bootstrapping for semantic analysis, how do we construe that “the poor (pitiable) man” (1a) is not interpreted the same as “the poor (indigent) man” (1b), given the fact that we posit in both noun phrases a single lexical entry for the Romanian adjective sărac “poor”.[20] We take the conceptualist view that adjectives have a concept, as their intention, associated with the lexical item. The intension is what is common to all uses of the word. But from the intension itself nothing follows, as the expression is only interpretable under saturation. Technically the intension identifies the conceptual properties of the adjective prior to saturation. Based on this premise, the difference in interpretation derives from the two types of predicate saturation: namely, theta-binding and theta-identification. Specifically, under this view, the distinct readings for (1a) and (1b) are anchored to the manner in which the predicate variable is saturated.

2.4.1 *Referential interpretation*. With theta-identification as the function composition of the noun and the adjective, we obtain the extensional interpretation of the noun phrase with reference to the objects in the mind world the noun identifies for an individual concept. Thus, in the example in question (10ci) omul sărac “the poor (indigent) man” the interpretation differs from that of (10cii) pământul sărac “the poor (infertile) land” as the object of reference differs. This gradation in extensionality is further observable in (10c).

---

[20] In a DP analysis postnominal sărac may derive from N movement to head of DP where om amalgamates with ul (i). Prenominal sărac must be generated in a position higher than the landing site of N, from which position it raises to amalgamate with the Determiner (ii).

(i) [$_{DP}$ [$_{D}$ om$_{i}$-ul ... [$_{NP}$ sărac [$_{NP}$ [$_{N}$ t$_{i}$]]]]
“this poor (indigent) man”

(ii) [$_{DP}$ [$_{D}$ sărac$_{j}$-ul [$_{AP}$ t$_{j}$ ... [$_{NumP}$ [$_{Num}$ om$_{i}$ [$_{NP}$ [$_{N}$ om$_{i}$]]]]]
“this poor (pitiable) man”

(10) c. (i)	omul sărac	"the poor (indigent) man"
(ii)	pământul sărac	"the poor (infertile) land"
(iii)	pământul virgin	"the virgin land"
(iv)	femeia virgină	"the virgin woman"
(v)	[e] virgină	"the virgin"
(vi)	o maşină veche	"an old car"
(vii)	un prieten vechi	"an old friend"
(viii)	o idee veche	"an old idea"

2.4.2 *Prenominal adjectives as specifiers.* In contrast with theta-identification, under the syntactic conditions of theta-binding (10a) the predicate variable is syntactically saturated, but referentially unidentified with respect to the head noun. Hence, we take it that prenominal adjectives function as nominal specifiers, rather than strictly modifiers of the head noun. This position implies that theta-bound adjectives will not exhibit the referential gradation observed with extensional expressions. In fact, note that the interpretation of Sp. viejo "old" does not vary in correlation with the head noun(10di): un viejo coche, un viejo amigo, una vieja idea. Consider, in addition the ironical meaning of Romanian dulce in eşti un dulce copil "you are a sweet (dumb) child" or the Italian adjective bella "beatiful" with a speaker-oriented flavor in (colloquial) expressions such as mi sono mangiata/o una bella pizza, "I ate a beautiful (satisfying) pizza", mi sono fatta/o una bella dormita "I took a beautiful (restoring) siesta". The equivalent of these noun phrases in Spanish might be better conveyed by the adjective rico "rich" as una rica pizza, una rica siesta . What these examples show is that the use of prenominal adjectives is rather free from the referential extensions of the nominal head in the noun phrase. We have noted that the Italian bella is idiomatically parallel to Spanish rica in prenominal contexts and in no way related to the referential extensions of the noun phrase. Rather prenominal adjectives are uniformly used epithetically or evaluatively of the noun. It is, we suggest, the particular referentially unidentified type of predicate saturation which lends itself to a speaker-oriented, subject-oriented, sometimes ironical or metaphorical use of adjectives.

2.5 *Deriving phrase structure*

From the object in (10) constructed out of projections of lexical categories, predicate adjectives are uniformly defined by their "most local" relation to a head, the Head-Complement relation, where the head is either a Determiner or a Noun (cf. Chomsky 1995:245). From the thematic analysis developed in this paper the phrase structure of the examples (1) is derived in (11), as the minimal or null hypothesis. Although we assume that the structure is bare (roughly as in (10)), the representations (11a',b') are given in X-bar conventions for syntactic concreteness.

(11) a. săracul om "the poor (pitiable) man"
a'. $[_{NP} [_{DP} D_i [_{AP} e_i [_{A'}$ săracul$]]]][_{N'}$ om$]]$
b. omul sărac "the poor (indigent) man"
b'. $[_{NP} [_{DP} D]][_{N'}$ omul$_i$ $[_{AP} e_i [_{A'}$ sărac$]]]$

Note that the predicate variable e is represented as a constituent in Spec of AP. APs appear as Complements of the Determiner (prenominally) or of the Noun (postnominally). On inspection, the structure of the noun phrase which follows from this analysis is rather anti-climactic as to the stipulation that DP is in Spec of NP. We assume this a priori on considerations of economy. We leave however the debate open and without discussion (cf. Stowell 1989:236).[21] Nevertheless, a restored NP hypothesis of noun phrases has interesting implications for an understanding of the basic syntactic properties distinguishing prenominal versus postnominal adjectives. We will discuss briefly word order and modification.

2.5.1 *On the apparent mobility of adjectives*. It is said that Romanian adjectives come mostly after the noun. This approximation is in fact true in comparison with many other Romance languages, except Marsian where practically no adjective precedes the noun. Nevertheless, Romanian has the usual classes of prenominal adjectives, including the class which can only occur prenominally like alt (12a) and biet (12b). As in other Romance languages, there are adjectives of origin like italiană (12c) and deverbal ad-

---

[21] Two competing analyses are possible in a generalized X-bar theory of the noun phrase. An endocentric hypothesis (i), in which N is the maximal projection of the nominal phrase, and an exocentric hypothesis (ii), in which the D is the maximal projection of the nominal phrase and NP is a complement in the Determiner Phrase.

(i) $[_{NP}$ DP $[_{N'}$ N$]]$
(ii) $[_{DP} [_{D'}$ D ... NP$]]$

A DP hypothesis compatible with the syntactic conditions for the function composition (10) would require a sort of "NP internal" theory of the noun phrase reminiscent of the "VP internal" theory of subject (Koopman and Sportiche (1988) 1991).

jectives like căzute, bă tut (12d,e), which only occur postnominally. Similarly, we find the movable class which includes sărac in the initial example of this paper (1), as well as the less obviously contrastive brutală in (12f).

(12) a. un alt cuvânt/*un cuvânt alt
"another word"
b. bietul bătrân/*bătrânul biet
"the old man"
c. invazia italiană a Albaniei/*italiana invazie a Albaniei
"the Italian invasion of Albania"
d. nişte frunze căzute/*nişte căzute frunze
"some fallen leaves"
e. lapte bătut/*bătut lapte
"cultured milk" ("buttermilk" as a compound)
f. brutala agresiune contra Albaniei/agresiunea brutală...
"the brutal aggression of Albania"

Regarding (12) and in particular the last example (12f), in the present analysis prenominal and postnominal expressions do not receive the same thematic form, which implies different semantic interpretations. This categorial duality of adjectives is also generally assumed on syntactic bases in most current studies, although not in a uniform way.[22]

2.5.2 *Theta-marking and "defective" adjectives.* The first issue which needs a statement in any theory of adjectives is the status of those adjectives which can occur only in one position (12a-e). The predication analysis makes available a natural account for this class of adjectives which would otherwise have to be defined simply as "defective." Theta-marking seems to be the mechanism through which the members of the "defective" class can be derived. Take, as an example, the adjective italiană in (12c). Arguably italiană , as a referential adjective, includes an implicit referent (-ană) and an argument of origin (Italia). Given this thematic specification, saturation of the predicate variable can only occur under the syntactic conditions for theta-identification, namely as complement of the head noun. Hence, adjectives of origin can only occur postnominally. A similar analysis is applicable to deverbal adjectives like căzute "fallen", bătut "beaten" (12d,e).

---

[22] There is no general agreement as to the syntactic category of theta-identified (postnominal) adjectives: they are assumed to be either adjuncts or specifiers of NP.

If the theta-marking analysis of strictly postnominal adjectives is correct, adjectives which may appear either before or after the noun, like brutala "brutal" (12f) should fall under a class of predicates which does not theta-mark for a referent and, therefore, can be saturated as specifiers of the head noun or as modifiers.

2.5.3 *Modification.* Another well known syntactic distinction between prenominal and postnominal adjectives is that the latter but not the former can be modified by a complement, as we illustrate in (13).

(13) a. ce mere [e bune [de e mâncat]]!
"(what apples good to eat)!"
b. *ce [bune [de e mâncat]] mere!
"(what [good [to eat] apples)!"

The predication hypothesis offers a straightforward account for this syntactic phenomenon as well. The argumentation is virtually the same as for the cases discussed in relation to the examples in (12).[23] Specifically in (13), the variable of the complement [de e mâncat] must be referentially bound by the variable of the predicate adjective [e bune]. For this to occur, the adjective must be in a syntactic position in which its own variable can be referentially saturated. As we have been arguing, this is possible only under theta-identification, which requires a head-complement relation. Hence, complements of predicate adjectives can only appear with the adjective bune in post nominal position (13a).

---

[23] It should be noted that in Romanian the complement [de e mâncat] "to eat" is a non-finite form of the verb and that the variable e is the theme.

[24] Genitives in Romanian come in two types: (i) N+AL+N-genitive case and (ii) N-enclitic article+N-genitive case. The alternation is characterized by the occurrence of the definite article either (i) suffixed to a (dummy) preposition AL (analyzable as a stem a and a suffixed article l according to Grosu 1988:933) or (ii) simply encliticized to the head noun. The two strategies are mutually exclusive in Romanian, although a sort of "doubling" strategy is found in the Aromanian dialect of Olympus (A. Androutsopoulou, paper presented at the Linguistic Symposium on Romance Languages 26).

2.6 *Romanian genitives*

We wish to briefly mention a final point which refers to genitives. Under this interpretation of noun phrases, the well studied case of the Romanian genitive nominals (Grosu 1988; Cornilescu 1995) receives a uniform account along with possessive adjectives. Our hypothesis is illustrated in the paradigm (14).[24]

(14) a. (i) portretul regelui/*portretul al regelui
"the king's portrait/the portrait of the king"
(ii)*un portret regelui/un portret al regelui
"*a king's portrait/a portrait of the king"
b. (i) portretul meu/*portretul al meu
"my portrait"
(ii)*un portret meu/un portret al meu
"a portrait of mine"

In (14a) we have the classic scenario, in which a genitive case-marked noun phrase regelui modifies an articulated nominal phrase portretul.[25] In this respect it's important to note that the distribution of the genitive construction is parallel to the distribution of the possessive construction (14b), in which a possessive adjective phrase meu modifies the same articulated noun phrase portretul.

As proposed earlier (cf. 4b), adjectival possessives are, like nouns, analyzed as predicates whose open variable requires an independent determiner as a "local" binder. In (14b) either the enclitic article -(u)l or the possessive article al (but not both) fulfill the theta binding requirements and narrowly account for the morpho-syntactic distribution of the expressions. A similar reasoning is necessary and sufficient to characterize the genitive construction (14a).[26] The evidence in favor of a theta-binding account is syntactically concrete in the case of genitive nominal modifiers like regelui, whose reference is independent of that of its head noun.

---

[25] (14ai) is adopted from Grosu (1988:933-935).

[26] There is a typologically larger issue involved with the concept "genitive" viewed, in one sense, as a morphological case and, in an another sense, as a syntactic construction. We leave this issue unexplored in this paper.

3. *Conclusions*

In conclusion, the goal of this paper has been to tease out the fine tension between the "attributive" and the "predicative" system within the Romanian noun phrase, with special attention to an understanding of the time-honored distinction between the so-called attributive and predicative function of adjectives. The results which follow from a Fregean-inspired thematic approach lead to an endocentric view of the noun phrase which relies on strictly local binding conditions between determiners (the referential binders) and lexical-conceptual predicates. A major consequence of this perspective reclaims the integrity of the NP construct, in which DP is within the projection of N. Under such a hypothesis the strictly local relations reduce to two: Head-Complement and Specifier-Head. One relevant empirical result of this minimal assumption is the local role the Romanian definite article plays in the context of a unified hypothesis of genitives and possessives.

The attributive versus predicative hypothesis which follows from this paper is supported by grammaticized features of the language which attest to the attributive/predicative adjectival categories. The articulated adjectives of Romanian narrowly define the "attributive" category. As a direct consequence of the extended predicative analysis of adjectives we have been able to outline a derivation of the semantic variation observed with respect to articulated (1a) vs. unarticulated (1b) adjectives for an otherwise undefined order of semantic variation in the interpretation of adjectives. The analysis is extendable to other Romance languages, which do not exibit the unique morphosyntactic property of Romanian while retaining prenominal/postnominal distribution. It is evident, however, that the semantic variation in question could not be a function of word order, since the phenomenon is also found in English where adjectives usually occur prenominally.

The distribution of the short versus long form of the demonstrative (acest/acesta) is morphological evidence, we speculate, for the "predicative" (modifying) function of a canonical determiner, whose distribution would remain otherwise unexplained. This last trait of Romanian is reminiscent of the residual case-marked predicative adjectives well studied in the tradition of Rhaeto-Romance (Haiman and Benincà 1992), whose relevance to predication theory and the structure of adjective phrase is discussed by Yves Roberge (1989).

REFERENCES

Abney, Steven. 1987. *The English Noun Phrase in Its Sentential Aspect.* Ph.D dissertation, MIT.

Bernstein, Judy. 1993. *Topics in the Syntax of Nominal Structures Across Romance*. Ph.D. dissertation, CUNY.

Chomsky, Noam. 1995. *A Minimalist Program.* Cambridge, Mas.: MIT Press.

Cinque, Guglielmo. 1993. "On the Evidence for Partial Movement in the Romance DP". Ms., Università di Venezia.

Cornilescu, A. 1992. "Remarks on the Determiner System of Romanian: The demonstrative al and cel". *Probus* 4.189-260.

———. 1995. "Rumanian Genitive Constructions". *Advances in Roumanian linguistics* ed. by Guglielmo Cinque & G. Giusti, 1-54. Linguistik Aktuell, Volume 10. Amsterdam: John Benjamins.

Degraff, M. and D. Mandelbaum. 1993. "Why is My Old Friend Not Old?". *Papers from the 29th Regional Meeting of the Chicago Linguistics Society*, ed. by Beals, K., et al. 121-136. Chicago: Chicago Linguistics Society.

Dobrovie-Sorin, Carmen. 1987. "A propos de la structure du groupe nominal en Roumain". *Rivista di Grammatica Generativa* 12.

Dumitrescu, Domnita & Mario Saltarelli. 1996. "El adjetivo en el sintagma nominal: posición y predicación". *Signo y Seña* 6. Special issue on linguistic theory, edited by N. Múgica and M. L. Freyre. Buenos Aires: University of Buenos Aires.

Geach, P. & M. Black (eds.) 1952. *Translations from the Philosophical Writings of Gottlob Frege*. Oxford: Blackwell.

Giorgi, Alessandra & Giuseppe Longobardi. 1991. *The Syntax of Noun Phrases*. Cambridge: Cambridge University Press.

Giusti, G. 1993. *La sintassi dei determinanti*. Padova: Unipress

Grosu, Alexander. 1988. "On the distribution of genitive phrases in Rumanian." *Linguistics* 26.931-949.

Haiman, J. and P. Benincà 1992. *The Raetho-Romance Languages*. New York: Routledge.

Higginbotham, James. 1985. "On Semantics". *Linguistic Inquiry* 16.547-594.

———.1987. "Indefiniteness and Predication". *The Representation of (In)definiteness* ed by Erich J. Reuland & Alice ter Meulen, 43-70. Cambridge, Mas.: MIT Press.

Kayne, Richard. 1994. *The Antisymmetry of Syntax*. Cambridge, Mas.: MIT Press.

Koopman, Hilda & Dominique Sportiche. 1991. "The Position of Subjects". *Lingua* 85.211-258.

Martín, J. 1995. *On the Syntactic Structure of Spanish Noun Phrases*. Ph.D. dissertation, USC.

Renzi, Lorenzo. 1995. "A proposito della teoria di Graur sulla posposizione dell'articolo rumeno". *Studi Rumeni e Romanzi: Omaggio a Florica Dimitrescu e Alexandru Niculescu* ed. by Coman Lupu and Lorenzo Renzi. Padova: Unipress.

Roberge, Yves. 1989. "Predication in Romontsch". *Probus* 1/2.225-229

Stowell, Tim. 1989. "Subjects, Specifiers and X-bar Theory". *Alternative Conceptions of Phrase Structure*, ed. by Michael Baltin & Anthony Kroch. Chicago: University of Chicago Press. 232-262.

Vergnaud, Jean Roger & María Luisa Zubizarreta. 1992. "The Definite Determiner and the Inalienable Constructions in French and English". *Linguistic Inquiry* 23.595-652.

ALIGNMENT AND SONORITY IN THE SYLLABLE STRUCTURE OF LATE LATIN AND GALLO-ROMANCE

RANDALL S. GESS
University of Utah

1. *Introduction*

This paper provides an Optimality Theoretic (OT) treatment of two types of simplification in the syllable structure of Late Latin and Gallo-Romance (henceforth LL and GR, respectively). The reduction of complex codas is seen as resulting from an alignment requirement, while the elimination or sonorization of simple obstruent codas is described as a sonority-based constraint on which segments could be moraic.

I am assuming that, before the changes to be discussed, the maximal expansion of the syllable was to bimoraicity, with any additional material appended directly to the syllable node, as shown in (1) (see Sherer (1994:191-193) for a discussion of possible appendix adjunction sites).

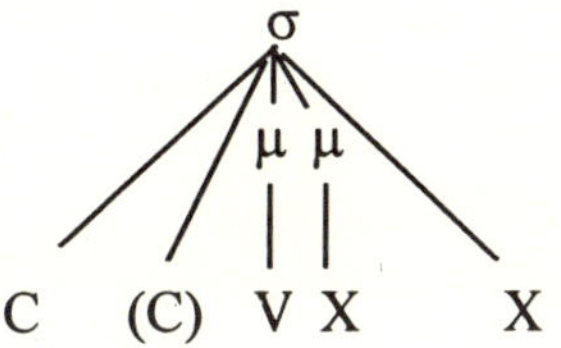

(1) Maximal expansion of the syllable in Latin.

Notice that I am not assuming a coda constituent and use the term "coda" simply for convenience, and in the traditional sense of "syllable-final consonant or consonant cluster".

2. *The data*

The first type of simplification to be discussed, shown in (2), is in terms of number. (Examples are from Jacobs (1992).)

(2) Complex coda simplification in LL

a. Appendix Probi

auctor	non autor	
auctoritas	non autoritas	
obstetrix	non obstetris	
locuples	non locuplex	(hypercorrection)
miles	non milex	(hypercorrection)

b. Inscriptions

scultus	<	sculptus	'to sculpt (partc.)'
temtaverit	<	temptaverit	'he would have touched'
cunti	<	cuncti	'together'
mers	<	merx	'merchandise'

Very early on in LL, based on evidence from the Appendix Probi (a list of correct and incorrect spellings composed approximately in the 3rd century), and from inscriptions, we can see that the number of syllable-final consonants permitted was reduced from two to one.

Developments following the process of syncope in GR show that the constraint on the number of syllable-final consonants was still active at this later period. This is shown in (3). (Examples are again from Jacobs (1992).)

(3) Complex coda simplification in GR

LL		GR	Latin origin	Gloss
*[kɔmptarɛ]	>	*[kɔmter]	compŭtāre	'to count'
*[dɔrmtorju]	>	*[dɔrtojr]	dormĭtōrĭum	'(bed)room'
*[džalbnu]	>	*[džalnɛ]	galbĭnum	'yellow'
*[fɔrtmɛntu]	>	*[fɔrmɛnt]	fortĭmentum	'strongly'
*[ɔsptalɛ]	>	*[ɔstel]	hospitālis	'residence'

The second type of simplification to be discussed, which took place in GR, is shown in (4).

(4) Simple coda simplification in GR

LL		GR	Latin origin	Gloss
*[faktu]	>	*[fajt]	factum	'deed, act'
*[rɔktarɛ]	>	*[rɔtter]	rŭctāre	'to belch'
*[debtə]	>	*[dettə]	dēbĭta	'obligation'
*[tsivtatɛ]	>	*[tsittɛ]	cīvĭtātem	'city'
*[advenirɛ]	>	*[avvenirɛ]	advenīre	'to arrive'
*[admirarɛ]	>	*[ammirer]	admīrārī	'to admire'

The sonorization of /k/ to [j] applied when that segment was in a stressed syllable, although there are counter-examples to this generalization, such as traitier < tractāre. Otherwise, the offending segments were subject to deletion, with a concomitant process of regressive gemination.

This type of simplification has been described as resulting from illicit syllable contacts, but I will attempt to show that it is best seen as resulting from syllable-internal, rather than syllable-external, considerations. My analysis will proceed, however, by looking first at the simplification of complex codas, and then at the simplification of simple codas.

3. *Analysis*

3.1 *Complex coda simplification*

The simplification of complex codas can be seen as the result of an alignment requirement, as suggested by Sherer (1994:11,193), and independently by Gess (1996). Specifically, we may view the process as resulting from a requirement of syllable-to-mora alignment such that every syllable must have a mora aligned at its right edge. This constraint is stated in Generalized Alignment terms as in (5) (where I follow Itô and Mester (1994:4) in factoring out common edges of alignment constraints).

(5) Right-edge syllable-to-mora alignment

Align-R(ight) (σ,μ)

That deletion was preferred to right-edge syllable-to-mora alignment violation suggests the ranking Align-R (σ,μ) >> PARSE. We can see how these constraints work with respect to the example *[kɔmter] in the tableau in (6), where only the first syllable shown is of relevance.

*[kɔmter]	Align-R (σ,μ)	PARSE
a. 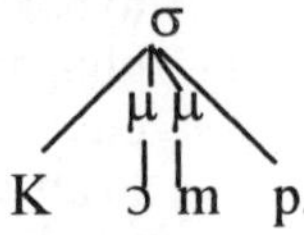 σ μ μ K ɔ m p. ter	*!	
b. 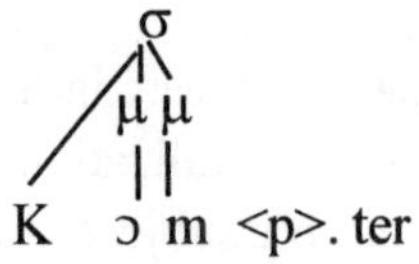 > σ μ μ K ɔ m <p>. ter		*

(6) Alignment and PARSE in GR *[kɔmter]

I assume that a surface form with the second coda element adjoined to the preceding mora is ruled out by a constraint proposed by Rosenthall (1994:30), against branching moras. This constraint is stated as shown in (7), where @ = root node.

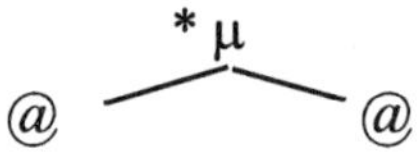

$$ * \mu $$
@ —— @

(7) Branch-μ

This constraint must also have been ranked above PARSE, as shown in (8).

/kɔmter/	Branch-μ	PARSE
a. 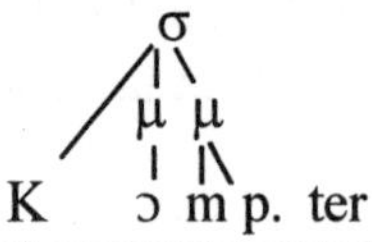 σ μ μ K ɔ m p. ter	*!	
b. 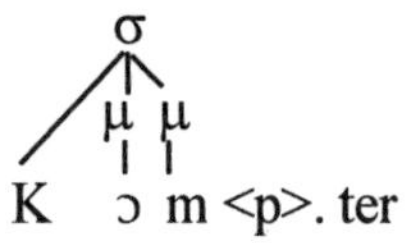 > σ μ μ K ɔ m <p>. ter		*

(8) Branch-μ >> PARSE

3.2 *Simple coda simplification*

Since the resulting configurations of simple coda simplification were predominantly geminates, a convenient starting point in finding an explanation for this process is in a previous treatment of Romance regressive gemination. Steriade (1988), proposes the rule in (9) to account for this process.

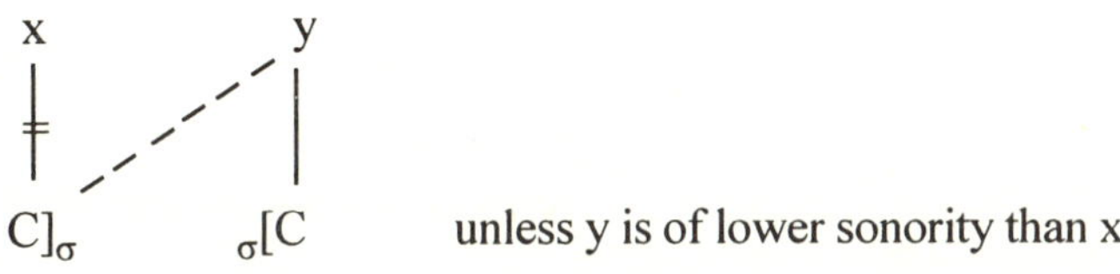

(9) Romance regressive gemination (Steriade (1988:389)).

According to Steriade's analysis, the general process of Romance regressive gemination was triggered by heterosyllabic sequences of equal or increasing sonority. The rule was obligatory in derived environments, as a cyclic rule, and optional postcyclically. While I agree that the process was the result of sonority considerations, I believe that, in the case of Gallo-Romance at least, those considerations were syllable-internal, rather than syllable-external. Specifically, I believe that the process at hand was due to a sonority-based constraint on which segments could occur in syllable-final position.

First of all, if the requirement for gemination to occur was equal or increasing sonority across heterosyllabic sequences, we would not expect to have seen gemination in certain instances in which it did occur, as in the examples in (10).

(10) Gemination in sequences of decreasing sonority

LL	GR	Latin Origin	Gloss
*[tsivtatɛ]	*[tsittɛ]	cīvĭtātem	'city'
*[mɔvtə]	*[mɔttə]	mŏvĭta	'move, fem.pp.'
*[gravtatɛ]	*[grattɛ]	grăvĭtātem	'weight'

If we assume the same GR relative sonority scale as Jacobs (1992:71), shown in (11), where /v/ must be either equal to or more sonorous than /f/, then these are clearly cases of decreasing sonority where gemination nevertheless resulted.

(11) GR sonority scale (Jacobs (1992:71))

r
l
n,m
s,z
f
p,t,k,b,d,g

This case can be explained if we assume a syllable-internal constraint according to which only segments of sonority equal to or greater than /s/ were permitted in syllable-final position.

There are also examples of heterosyllabic sequences of increasing or equal sonority which consistently did not result in geminates, suggesting that GR was a dialect which took advantage of the optionality of the rule and opted out of gemination in certain, very predictable contexts. Since Steriade's rule is optional in non-derived environments, this is not problematic for her analysis, but it is important to note that in each case, the heterosyllabic sequences which failed to undergo regressive gemination consisted of two sonorant consonants, or /s/ followed by a sonorant consonant. Such sequences did geminate in many Romance dialects, as can be seen in (12).

(12) Geminating sequences of increasing or equal sonority
(2 sonorants) - other Romance

a. increasing sonority

pōnĕre	>	*[ponrɛ]	>	It. porre	'to put'
*[volero]	>	*[volro]	>	It. vorrò	'want,1sg.fut.'

b. equal sonority

scamnum	>	*[skannu]	>	Sp. escano	'type of bench'
ma[ŋ]num	>	*[mannu]	>	Sard. mannu	'great'

In GR, there are a multitude of examples such as these, where gemination did not occur. Examples include both sequences of increasing sonority and those of equal sonority.

(13) Non-geminating sequences of increasing or equal sonority (2 sonorants or sonorant + /s/) - GR

a. increasing sonority

*[kozere]	>	*[kozrɛ]	>	O.F. cosdre	'to sew'
genĕrum	>	*[dženru]	>	O.F. gendre	'son-in-law'
cumŭlum	>	*[kumlu]	>	O.F. comble	'top'
*[volerajo]	>	*[volrajo]	>	O.F. voldrai	'want,1sg.fut.'

b. equal sonority

sēmĭnāre	>	*[semnarɛ]	>	O.F. semmer	'to sow'
fēmĭna	>	*[femnə]	>	O.F. femme	'woman'

Notice in these cases that the heterosyllabic sequence is still not maintained, but it is eliminated by a mechanism other than regressive gemination. In the examples in (a), an epenthetic element breaks up the illicit sequence, and in the examples in (b), gemination is progressive rather than regressive. What is important to note is that these alternative mechanisms differ from gemination and the sonorization of /k/ in allowing the syllable-final element of the first syllable to remain intact in its original position. Again, of specific interest to us is that these are cases in which a sonorant consonant or /s/ is in syllable-final position.

To summarize thus far, while Steriade's analysis is fairly adequate on a descriptive level, a more explanatory account is available, for the GR data at least, if we focus on syllable-internal, rather than syllable-external, sonority considerations. Such an account can, for example, explain why obstruents were subject to deletion even when the following consonant was of lower sonority, and why regressive gemination failed to apply when the first member of a heterosyllabic sequence of equal or increasing sonority was a sonorant or /s/.

It is also the case that an account in terms of syllable-internal sonority considerations is formally simpler than one in terms of syllable-external considerations. If we were to specify the contexts in which regressive gemination occured in GR, in terms of heterosyllabic sequences (and even ignoring cases like *[tsivtatɛ] > *[tsittɛ]!), we would get the two environments shown in (14).

(14) Heterosyllabic environments for regressive gemination

X [-son] X is of sonority greater than /s/
X [+son] X is of sonority greater than /s/

The redundancy is immediately apparent — the first member in each case is a segment of sonority greater than /s/. This redundancy is eliminated if we state the environment in intrasyllabic terms, i.e. a [-son] segment in syllable-final position. From this perspective, the environment is seen as a target for deletion, and regressive gemination is simply a by-product of that deletion. The environment for deletion is shown in (15).

(15) Intrasyllabic environment for deletion

$[\text{-son}]]_{\sigma}$

Now, given our assumptions concerning syllable structure, as shown in (1), our formal OT account will entail a sonority-based constraint on which segments could surface as moraic. Such a constraint will allow a sonorant consonant or /s/ to be dominated by a mora, but not other obstruent consonants. Note, however, that I do not assume that moras are present underlyingly. Rather, I assume that candidate analyses are considered in which moras dominate any and all segments. Analyses are then rejected via the effects of other constraints, i.e., for example, one forbidding moraic onsets (perhaps a negative alignment constraint), and the one just mentioned forbidding moraic obstruents (other than /s/).

Another mora-related constraint that I assume to have been active in Gallo-Romance was one which pushed for a maximal expansion of the syllable to bimoraicity (cf. Broselow (1992) for several dialects of Arabic, and Sherer (1994) for Wiyot, a native language of California). This constraint can be stated as in (16).

(16) $\sigma = [\mu\mu]$

A syllable is optimally bimoraic

The constraint that was operative in GR, and which ruled out moraic obstruents other than /s/ can be stated as in (17).

(17) A sonority-based constraint on moraicity

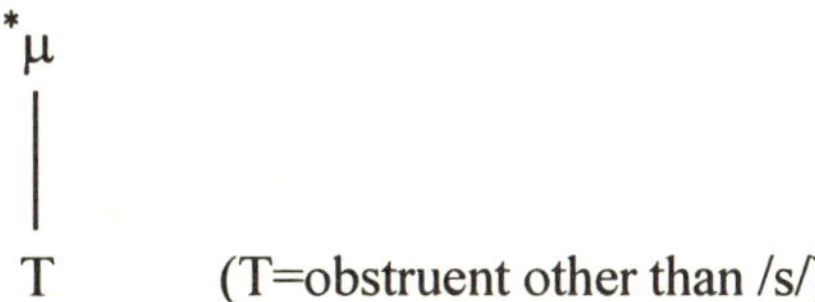

Notice that it is crucial to our analysis that the representation in (17) be subject to Hayes' (1986) Linking Condition, whereby all association lines in structural descriptions are interpreted as exhaustive. That is, this constraint must allow linked structures in which a consonant is doubly linked to a mora and a following onset in order to license geminate consonants (cf. Itô's (1989) Coda Condition).

We can think of the constraint in (17) as only part of a sonority-based family of constraints based entirely on the GR sonority scale shown in (11) above (cf. Prince and Smolensky (1993:Ch.8). The entire family of constraints on moraicity can be represented as in (18).

(18) A sonority-based family of constraints on moraicity

*μ/p,t,k,b,d,g >> *μ/f >> *μ/s,z >> *μ/m,n >> *μ/l >> *μ/r

It is important to recall that in any sub-hierarchy of this type, unrelated constraints may intervene at any point. My proposal is that the surface phonotactics of GR can be captured by assuming that the PARSE constraint was ranked below *μ/f, and above *μ/s,z. Just as we subsumed all obstruents other than /s/ under the label T, let us subsume /s/ and the sonorants under the label R. The ranking of PARSE with respect to the sonority-based constraints on moraicity can then be represented rather simply as in (19).

(19) PARSE in the scheme of things

*μ/T >> PARSE >> *μ/R

These constraints are illustrated in (20), with the form *[rɔktarɛ] > *[rɔtter]. (Changes other than the deletion of the syllable-final obstruent are ignored in this tableau.)

/rɔktarɛ/	*(μ/T)	PARSE	*(μ/R)
a. 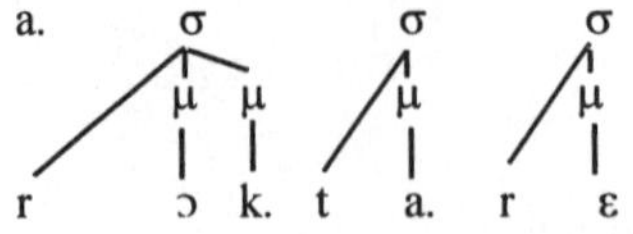 σ σ σ / μ μ μ μ / r ɔ k. t a. r ɛ	*!		
b. 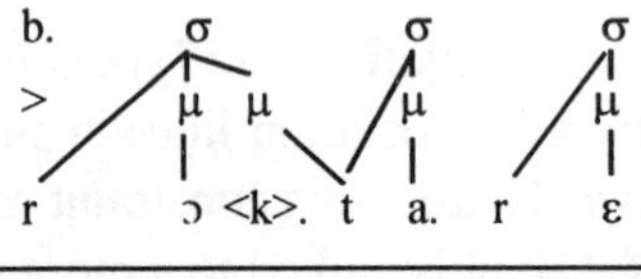 > σ σ σ / μ μ μ μ / r ɔ <k>. t a. r ɛ		*	

(20) *[rɔtter] < *[rɔktarɛ]

An analysis in which the mora potentially attached to /k/ is instead attached to the preceding vowel is ruled out by a structure-preserving constraint against long vowels. (Length had ceased to be phonemic rather early on in LL.) The constraint against long vowels, again from Rosenthall (1994:30), is stated as shown in (21).

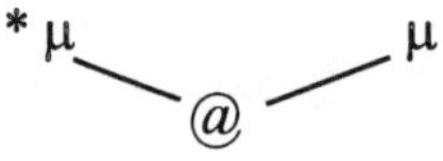

* μ μ
@

(21) No Long Vowels (NLN)

The effects of this constraint can be seen in the tableau in (22).

/rɔktarɛ/	NLV	PARSE
a. 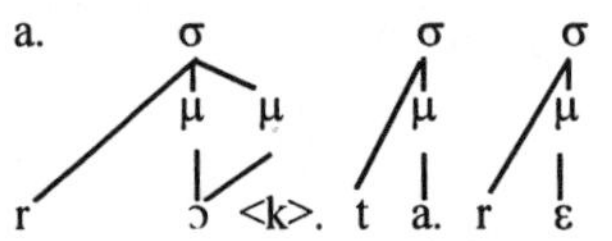 σ σ σ / μ μ μ μ / r ɔ <k>. t a. r ɛ	*!	*
b. 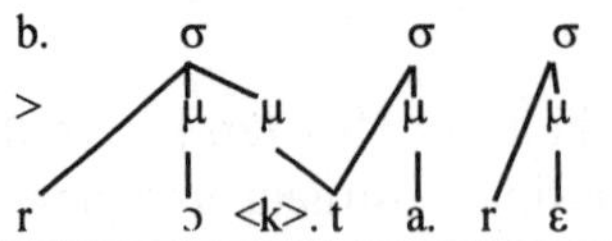 > σ σ σ / μ μ μ μ / r ɔ <k>. t a. r ɛ		*

(22) *[rɔ: ter] ≮ *[rɔktarɛ]

Notice that since both candidates violate PARSE equally, we have no evidence as to the ranking of the two constraints with respect to each other. The candidate in (a) will be ruled out either way since it entails an additional violation.

Recall that the second mora itself is motivated by the constraint pushing for a bimoraic expansion of the syllable, σ = [μμ]. The practical effects of this constraint can be seen in the tableau in (23).

/rɔktarε/	σ = [μμ]	PARSE
a. 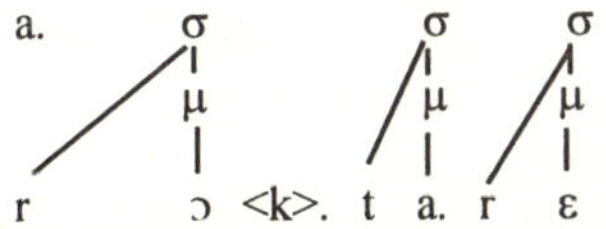 σ σ σ μ μ μ r ɔ <k>. t a. r ε	*!	*
b. 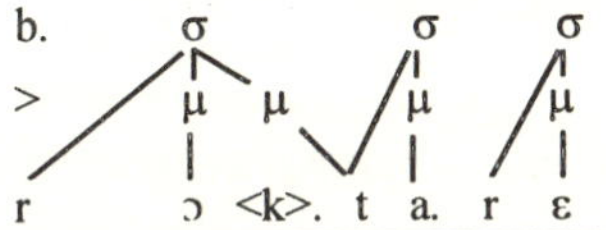 > σ σ σ μ μ μ μ r ɔ <k>. t a. r ε		*

(23) *[rɔter] ≮ *[rɔktarε]

This is again a case in which both candidates violate PARSE equally, so we have no evidence as to the ranking of these two constraints with respect to each other either. Notice, however, that since the constraint σ = [μμ] did not cause epenthesis, it must have been ranked below FILL.

4. *Conclusion*

According to what we have seen, two crucial changes in constraint ranking must have occurred in the development of LL into GR. First, the ranking PARSE >> Align-R (σ,μ) which must have held in LL in order to allow syllable appendices, as in *[kɔmptarε], must have reversed, producing forms like *[kɔmter] instead. Second, the ranking PARSE >> *μ/T which must have held in LL in order to allow moraic obstruents, as in [rɔktarε], must have reversed, producing forms like [rɔtter]. These crucial changes in constraint rankings are illustrated in (24), where the semi-colon between two constraints indicates that those constraints are indeterminately ranked with respect to each other.

(24) Constraint rankings in LL and GR

a. LL: PARSE >> *μ/T;Align-R (σ, μ)

b. GR: *μ/T;Align-R (σ, μ) >> PARSE

REFERENCES

Broselow, Ellen. 1992. "Parametric Variation in Arabic Dialect Phonology". *Perspectives on Arabic Linguistics IV* (Papers from the Fourth Annual Symposium on Arabic Linguistics), ed. by Ellen Broselow, Mushira Eid and John McCarthy, 7-45. Amsterdam: Benjamins.

Gess, Randall. 1996. *Optimality Theory in the Historical Phonology of French.* Ph.D. dissertation, University of Washington.

Hayes, Bruce. 1986. "Inalterability in CV Phonology". *Language* 62. 321-351.

Itô, Junko. 1989. "A Prosodic Theory of Epenthesis. *Natural Language and Linguistic Theory* 7.217-260.

Itô, Junko & Armin Mester. 1994. "Reflections on CodaCond and Alignment". Ms., University of California, Santa Cruz.

Jacobs, Haike. 1992. "The Interaction Between Syllable Structure and Foot Structure in the Evolution from Classical Latin to Old French". *Theoretical Analyses in Romance Linguistics* ed. by Christiane Laeufer & Terrell A. Morgan, 55-79. Amsterdam: Benjamins.

McCarthy, John J. & Alan S. Prince. 1993. "Generalized Alignment". Ms., University of Massachusetts, Amherst and Rutgers University.

Meyer-Lübke, W. 1972. *Romanisches Etymologisches Wörterbuch.* Heildelberg: Carl Winter Universitätsverlag.

Prince, Alan S. & Paul Smolensky. 1993. "Optimality Theory". *Technical Report #2 of the Rutgers Center for Cognitive Science*. Rutgers University.

Rosenthall, Sam. 1994. *Vowel/Glide Alternation in a Theory of Constraint Interaction.* Ph.D. dissertation, University of Massachusetts at Amherst.

Sherer, Tim. 1994. *Prosodic Phonotactics*. Ph.D. disseration, University of Massachusetts at Amherst.

Steriade, Donca. 1988. "Gemination and the Proto-Romance Syllable Shift". *Advances in Romance Linguistics*, ed. by David Birdsong & Jean-Pierre Montreuil, 371-409. Dordrecht: Foris.

LOCATIVE AND TEMPORAL WEAK PROFORMS

JAVIER GUTIÉRREZ REXACH
&
LUIS SILVA VILLAR
University of California, Los Angeles

0. *Introduction*

Nominal proforms or pronouns constitute a well established and exhaustively studied grammatical category in Romance languages. Nevertheless, the properties of other types of proforms have not received much attention to date. The existence of locative and temporal proforms has been observed by several traditional grammarians and dialectologists: Badía (1947), Corominas and Pascual (1985), Cuervo (1886), DHLE (1972), Espinosa (1946), Menéndez Pidal (1904), Navarro Tomás (1926), Place (1930), Tiscornia (1930), among many others. These studies normally assume a prosodic characterization of the class, without making explicit any theory, and provide some examples of the forms in earlier or dialectal documents. Nevertheless, none of them attempt to determine systematically the morphosyntactic and semantic properties of the forms. In this paper, we show that modern Spanish has a system of locative and temporal weak proforms. We also study their syntactic and semantic properties, with particular emphasis on the latter. Finally, we demonstrate that this system has been active since early Spanish and we compare it to the situation in other neighbouring languages.

1. *Weak and strong proforms*

In general, locative and temporal proforms can be classified, as either weak or strong from the prosodic point of view Strong forms can receive phrasal stress, whereas weak forms are never assigned phrasal stress. As shown in table 1, the strong proform [a.í] is bisyllabic whereas the weak locative form is monosyllabic ([áj]). In parallel, the strong proform [a.ó.ra] is trisyllabic, contrasting with the weak [áo.ra], which is bisyllabic. Notice also the contrast in the stress pattern.There are also other temporal weak proforms, such as *ya* or *aun* [áun] (vs. the prosodically strong *aún* [a.ún].).

MEANING	PROSODIC TYPE	GRAPHIC REPRESENTATION	PHONETIC REPRESENTATION
– Locative	strong	ahí	[a.í]
	weak	ahi / ay	[áj]
– Temporal	strong	ahora	[a.ó.ra]
	weak	ahora, aora, ara	[áo.ra] / [á.ra]

Table 1

Strong proforms are syntactically full adverbial phrases. On the other hand, weak proforms behave syntactically as clitics. They meet the criteria for clitichood in any of the current syntactic theories of clitics, from Kayne (1975) to Sportiche (1992). First, weak and strong proforms cannot be coordinated (1b, 2b), nor can weak proforms by themselves (3b). Strong proforms are full constituents and can be coordinated (1a, 2a, 3a).

(1) a. *ponlo allí y [a.í]*
'put it there (next to it) and there (next to you)'
b. **ponlo allí y [áj]*

(2) a. *hay que hacerlo [a.ó.ra] y siempre*
must that do-it now and always
'One must do it now and ever'
b. **hay que hacerlo [áo.ra] y siempre*

(3) a. *[a.í] y [a.ó.ra]*
there and now
'over there and (right) now'
b. **[áj] y [áo.ra]*

Weak proforms are part of prosodic phrases but do not constitute prosodic phrases by themselves. As a consequence, they cannot attract focus stress (4, 5) nor they occur as constituent answers to questions (6, 7).

(4)	*anda por [áj]/*AJ* walk-2p.sg over there 'go away'	vs.	*anda por [a.í]/AHÍ* walk-2p.sg. over there 'walk over THERE'
(5)	*[áo.ra]/*AHORA(w) llega* now arrive-3p.sg 'S/he is arriving now/NOW'	vs.	*llega [a.ó.ra]/AHORA(s)* arrive-3p.sg. now

(6) *—¿Dónde lo llevaste?—* *[a.í]/*[áj]*
where it take-2p.sg. there
— ' Where did you take it?'— 'There'

(7) *—¿Cuándo lo hago?—* **[áo.ra]/[a.ó.ra]*
when it make-1p.sg now
— 'When may I do it?'— Now/Right now'

Further evidence for the syntactically dependent nature of weak proforms is that they are not modified neither by appositives (8, 9) nor by precision adverbs (10). Notice that modification by an adverb of the latter class is perfectly natural in the case of strong forms, since the adverb acts as a sort of intensifier.

(8) **[áj]/[a.í] entre ellos*
'there among them'

(9) **[áo.ra]/[a.ó.ra] tras la película*
'now after the movie'

(10) a. *lo dejé exactamente *[áj]/[a.í]*
it left-1p.sg. exactly there
'I left it right there'
b. *¿Te vas precisamente *[áo.ra]/[a.ó.ra]?*
you leave precisely now
'¿Are you leaving right now?'

Weak adverbial proforms have the same distribution with respect to the verb as pronominal clitics. Therefore, they are proclitic to finite verbs (11) and enclitic to non-finite verbs or imperative forms (12).

(11) a. *[áj] viene* vs. **viene [áj]*
there come-3p.sg. vs. come-3p.sg. there
'there s/he comes'
b. *[áo.ra] llega* vs. **llega [áo.ra]*
now arrive-3p.sg. vs. arrive-3p.sg. now
'S/he is arriving now'

(12) a. *no sé que puede haber [áj]* vs. **no sé que puede [áj] haber*
not know-1p.sg. that can be there vs. not know-1p.sg. that can there be
'I don't know what there is in it'

b. *eso se arregla yendo [áj]* vs. **eso se arregla [áj] yendo*
that SE settle going there vs. that se settle there going
'That is settled going there'

c. quédate [áj] vs. **[áj] quédate*
stay-2p.sg.-you there vs. there stay-2p.sg.-you
'Stay there'

d. *véngase [áo.ra]* vs. **[áo.ra] véngase*
come-2p.sg.-SE now vs. now come-2p.sg.-SE
'Come over now'

Weak proforms have emphatic variants with *mismo* and *mero* (13a) but not with *precisamente*, in contrast to strong forms which admit modification by *mismo* and by *precisamente*. Finally, we observe that weak proforms cannot be nominalized (13b).

(13) a. *[áj] mismo / mero*
there self
'right there'

b. *hay que vivir el *[áo.ra]/[a.ó.ra]*
must that live the now
'One must live the present'

2. ***Syntactic and semantic properties***

There are some properties of adverbial weak proforms that set them apart from pronominal clitics.

1. They can be attached to non-verbal hosts.

(14) a. *¡hele [áj] los poetas!*
HE-LE there the poets
'Here are the poets!'

b. ¡[áj] mi niño! (cf. *¡Ay de mi niño!*)
there my son (cf. oh of my son!)
'This is my (true) son!' (cf. 'Poor my son!')

c. *¡[áo.ra] mi niñ a!*
now my dear
'Your turn, my dear'

2. Selectional restrictions/requirements. Torrego (1989) and Bosque (1990) have observed that weak proforms occur in unaccusative constructions as in (15) in contrast to other constructions (16). In the next section we will see how this generalization can be refined.

(15) a. *[áj] viene/corre/llega ella*
there come/run/arrive-3.p.sg. she
'There she is coming/runing/arrives'
b. *[áo.ra] viene/corre/llega ella*
now come/run/arrive she
'She is about coming/runing/arriving'

(16) a. **[áj]/*[áo.ra] comen patatas tus amigos* (OK with [a.í]/[a.ó.ra])
there/now eat potatoes your friends
b. **[áj]/*[áo.ra] (les) dan las gracias a los invitados*
(OK with [a.í]/[a.ó.ra])
there/now (to-them) give the thanks to the guests

(17) a. **[áj]/*[áo.ra] sonríe Pepe* (OK with [a.í]/[a.ó.ra])
there/now smile-3p.sg. Pepe
b. **[áj]/*[áo.ra] ladra el perro* (OK with [a.í]/[a.ó.ra])
there/now bark-3p.sg. the dog

3. Progressive Aspect alters the grammaticality of (16) and (17):

(18) a. *[áj]/[áo.ra] están comiendo patatas tus amigos* (cf. 16a)
there/now are eating potatoes your friends
'Your friends are eating potatoes there/now'
b. *[áj]/[áo.ra] está sonriendo Pepe* (cf. 17a)
there/now is smiling Pepe
'Pepe is smiling now'

4. Negation. Weak proforms introduce polarized'' constructions:

(19) *¡[áj] (*no) te quedas!* vs. *¡[a.í] (no) te quedas!*
there (not) you remain vs. there (not) you remain
'Gotta hell!' vs. 'You must (not) remain there!'

(20) a. *[áj] (*no) te la mando (la carta)* vs.
[a.í] no te la mando
there (not) to-you it-f.sg. send-1p.sg. (the letter) vs.
there not to-you it send
'I am sending it to you' vs. 'I am not sending you it there'

(21) *[áj]/[áo.ra] (*no) llega Pedro* vs. *[a.í]/[a.ó.ra] no llega Pedro*
there/now (*not) arrives Pedro vs. there/now not arrives Pedro

3. *The semantics of weak proforms*

Strong *ahí* is a locative deictic pronoun. Similarly, strong *ahora* is a deictic temporal pronoun referring to the speech time or utterance time. The weak locative *ahi* is semantically more complex. It can be used in some occasions to deictically refer to a specific location, but in most of its uses its content is not that restricted. In general it denotes a contextually determined modifier linked to the speech time (t_{NOW}). Therefore, it can refer to locations but also denote a contextually relevant modifier, obligatory adjunct or argument function:

(22) ahi = $\lambda P \lambda e \lambda t\, [t = t_{NOW} \wedge CUL(e,t) \wedge M(P(e))]$

Thus, there are two essential ingredients in the semantic definition of *ahi*. First, the proform denotes a modifier function M (type <<e,t>,<et>>), or an argument function M (type <<et>,t>). The denotation of the variable M is context dependent. The modifier function has to be 'compatible' with or coerced (Pustejovsky 1995) by the denotation of the verb (with the property P). Consider the variety of interpretations associated with *ahi* in the sentences in (23). For instance, in (23d) *ahi* denotes the argument of *ir a parar*, namely the contextually relevant subject or topic of the conversation. In (23g) *ahi* acts almost like a pure temporal deictic, which has to be necessarily *ahora* in order to satisfy the temporal condition in its definition ($t = t_{NOW}$). The same happens in (23h) where *ahi vengo* is semantically equivalent to *ahora vengo*.

(23) a. *[áj] hay mucho de que hablar*
there HAY much of that talk
'There is much to say about that subject'
b. *Por [áj] se llega a una solución*
by there SE arrive to a solution
'Doing that we arrive at a solution'
c. *Por [áj] de ancho* vs. **de ancho por [áj]*
by there of wide vs. of wide by there
'approximately of that width'
d. *Ya sabía yo que [áj] vendríamos a parar*
Already know I that there would-arrive-3p.pl. to stop
'I knew that we would get into that'
e. *[áj] me saludas a tu padre*
there me greet to your father\
'give my greetings to your father'
f. *[áj] verás que no miento*
there will-see-2p.sg. that not lie-1p.sg.
'You see that I am not lying with respect to that issue'

g. *[áj] está llegando Pedro*
there is arriving Pedro
'Pedro is arriving now'
h. *[áj] vengo*
there come-1p.sg.
'I am coming (now)'

The second essential ingredient in the semantics of weak proforms is that the culmination point of the event denoted by the verb has to be the speech time. We use here the predicate CUL, introduced by Parsons (1985). The culmination predicate is also used by Moens and Steedman (1988) , and is related to Dowty's (1979) BECOME operator. The modifier denoted by *ahi* can take the verb denotation as its argument if and only if the culmination property holds between the event denoted by the verb and the speech time. As we stated before, *ahi* can co-occur with unaccusative verbs. The majority of the verbs comprised into the syntactic class of unaccusative verbs denote achievements. Unaccusative verbs describe events where the internal argument undergoes some kind of change. Vendler's classification of verbs in states, activities, acomplishments and achievements can be partitioned along the culmination dimension: achievements and accomplishments have a culmination point whereas states and activities do not have a culmination point. The distinction between culminated/ non-culminated events is captured in most event typologies. Achievements have a definite terminus but no duration (they are instantaneous). Accomplishments have duration (they are not instantaneous).

The combination of event type and tense determines the licensing of *ahi*. An achievement verb in the present form describes an event whose culmination point coincides with the speech time. Therefore, the denotational requirement imposed by the weak proform is met, and it becomes licensed. The sentences in (15) become ungrammatical if the present tense is interpreted as generic or habitual. Similarly, if we shift the tense to past, pluperfect, etc. the sentences become ungrammatical (24a). The latter is a property which is apparently absent in some dialects of Spanish like North Western Spanish or Mexican Spanish that lack the present perfect form *haber-pres.+past participle*. In these dialects, some uses of the simple past cover what is the interpretation of the present perfect is Castillian Spanish. Therefore, (24a) is grammatical since the simple past form may be connected to the speech time. Similarly, in most dialects there exists a use of the future in which this tense behaves like the present (future for present interpretation). For example, sentence (24b) can be interpreted as 'now you see that I am not lying' rather than as 'there you will see that I am not lying'

(24) a. **[áj] llegó/había llegado ella*
there arrived/has arrived she
b. *[áj] verás que no te miento*
there will-see-you that not you lie-I
'now you see that I am not lying to you'

Transitive verbs describe events in any of the four vendlerian types. Consider (16a), where the VP comer patatas describes an activity event. In this case, the event is non-culminating. Therefore, the denotational requirement of *ahí* is not satisfied and the sentence becomes anomalous. Consider the contrast between sentence (16a) and sentence (18). Progressive aspects makes sentence (16a) grammatical. This is due to the action of the progressive operator. This operator —as defined by Dowty (1979), etc.— allows for the culmination of compatible subevents of the event described by the verb. As a consequence, the denotational requirement of the weak proforms is satisfied, and the resulting sentence is not anomalous.

The culminativity requirement of weak proforms makes them specially sensitive to negation. The verb *llegar* denotes an achievement, but when it is negated —*no llegar*—, the event described loses its culminativity or termination property. Thus, it can no longer be characterized as an achievement. This explains, why whereas the sentence in (15a) is O.K., sentence (21) *ahí no llega Pedro* is anomalous. The reason is again that the presence of negation triggers a violation of the denotational requirements of the weak proform.

4. *History of locative and temporal proforms*

4.1 *Historical development*

MEANING	PROSODIC T YPE	ORIGIN
Locative	strong	*ahí* < *a* + strong *y* < IBI / HIC
	weak	*ay, aj, ahi* < *a* + weak *y*
Temporal	strong	*ahora, aora* < *agora* < HAC HORA / AD HORAM
		ahora, aora < *a* + *hora* (adv.)
	weak	*ahora, aora, ara* < *a* + *hora* / stress shift from *ahora*

Table 2

The weak status of locative and temporal proforms is not a recent phenomenon in Spanish since they are found with the same status throughout the history of the language. In Menéndez Pidal (1908, Cid , I, II, section 30), it is stated without empirical support that *The change in stress from [a.í] to [áj] occurs in Spanish from the beginning of the language*. Although there is not a unanimous agreement among scholars about the Romance development of these forms, two main theories have been presented in the past by traditional grammarians. The first one conceives of weak proforms as coming from their strong locative and temporal counterparts after applying a stress shift or weakening operation (Corominas and Pascual 1985, Cuervo 1886, Menéndez Pidal 1904). The second theory sees their formation as a late Romance combination of the preposition *a* 'to' and the locative and temporal weak adverbs *y* 'there' and *hora* 'now' (Badía 1947, Place 1930).

The stress shift theories are forced to postulate the initial existence of the strong forms in order to create the input for the stress shift. We will show that independently of their frequency in old texts, weak forms are present in Spanish and related languages from early times as a consequence of the existence of dual strong and weak locative and temporal *y* and *ora*. Within the context of Romance languages, we are dealing with a distinctive (and unique) phenemenon unattested among the other Romance languages. If we are right, and both strong and weak variants are attested from the origin of the Romance languages, the stress shift theory approach is wrong because the weakening of the strong variants should have happened in Latin too. This is a very doubtful claim since, for instance, *ahí* —the strong deictic locative—, is unattested out of the Western Iberian domain. We present some evidence that supports Menéndez Pidal's observation about the medieval origin of weak proforms, although not as a consequence of stress shift, but as the product of a word formation process yielding complex units from the combination of weak *y* and weak *ora* with the preposition *a*.

4.2 *Iberian distribution of locative* y, i, hi, hy

An initial partition is necessary in order to clarify the history of these proforms: locative and temporal proforms will be differently treated in Eastern and Western Iberian languages since there are differences in the syntactic behavior with respect to the strength of the features of the proforms. Within the domain of Eastern Languages, locative and temporal proforms are always weak (Badia 1947). On the other hand, the situation in the Western domain is not so clear and we have to go case by case. The first step is to show the existence of strong and weak locative *y* in Western Romance Languages. We start with Old Spanish.

The strong status of locative *y* is shown by its behavior within well known medieval syntactic structures. Example (25), taken from 12th C. Spanish, shows the inversion of the past participle in perfect constructions. In the corresponding derivation, the past participle *ganado* 'earned' moves beyond the auxiliary *an* 'have-3p.p'. Both sets, clitics as well as the group made by pronominal clitics and an auxiliary participate as an unbreakable complex unit in this type of constructions. Since locative *y* is out of the clitic cluster domain, we conclude that *y* is not a clitic. Inverted Conjugations provide a similar test in (26) and (27).

(25) ... *ganado se an y algo*
... earned SE have-3p.pl. there something
'They have earned something there' (12th, Cid, 1779)

(26) *et fallarlas hades y*
and find-them have/will-2p.sg. there
'and you will find them there' (13th, Crónica Gral.:610, 15, a)

(27) *et darvos he y de las nueses*
and give-you will-1p.sg there PART. the walnuts
'and I will give you there some of the walnuts'
(14th, Arcipreste de Hita, I, 290, 861)

Inverted conjugations build up future and conditional tenses in Old Western Iberian Languages (Lema 1991, Rivero 1991, 1993; Lema & Rivero 1990a, 1990b, 1992; Roberts 1993, Silva-Villar 1995). In (27), the infinitive *dar* 'to give', the pronominal clitic *vos* 'you', and the auxiliary clitic *he* 'have-1p.sg.' merge to form the analitic future. In this construction, again, clitics cannot be split at all. Since locative *y* contributes to the derivation independently of the clitic domain/group, we conclude that these data do not support its clitic status.

A well known property of early Romance grammars is that clitics cannot occupy the initial position of their prosodic domain (Saco e Arce 1868; Tobler 1875; Mussaffia 1886). From the syntactic point of view, clitics cannot close derivations. They trigger a final operation that protects them from being in that uncomfortable position (Silva-Villar 1995, 1996, in preparation). Weak locative *y* is not an exception. That is why we can conclude that locative *y* in the 12th C. Old Spanish examples (28), (29) and (30) cannot be weak.

(28) *tornos a Carrion, I lo podrie fallar*
came-back to Carrion, There him could-3p.sg. find
'He made his way to Carrion. There he could find him'
(12th, Cid, 1313)

(29) *Hy en os primeros el rey fuera dio salto*
there in the first the king out gave jump
'The king jumped outside with the first ones' (12th,Cid, 1833)

(30) *Busco algun lugar de gran religion I sovo escondido faziendo oracion*
looked-for-3p.sg. some place of great religion there was hidden making pray
'He looked for a very religious place. There he was hidden praying'
(12th-13th, Berceo, Mil., 87, 350)

Subordinate constructions headed by the complementizers que 'that' and *desque* 'since' have the property of attracting clitics. In fact, they are often clusterized with them. Since that is not what the sentences show, we must reject the clitic status of *y* in both sentences. We conclude that strong locative *y* is part of the grammar of Old Spanish.

(31) *que faga I cantar mill missas*
that make-3p.sg. there to-sing one-thousand Masses
'that he orders thousand masses' (12th, Cid, 225)

(32) *e desque llegaron y ...*
and since arrived-3p.sg. there ...
'and since they arrived there ...'
(14th, L. de Ayala, Cron. de D. Pedro, 507a)

Weak locative y is also attested in Old Spanish texts. Partial evidence suggesting the existence of weak locative *y* is provided by negation. The negative marker *non* and the verb have a local relation only split by clitics at the spell-out. Since in (33) and (34) locative *y* intervenes in the Negation-Verb relation, we must conclude that *y* is a clitic. (35) and (36), in contrast to (31) and (32), show the expected derivation in which clitics and complementizers are involved. All in all, the data presented above shows the weak and strong dual status of locative *y* in Old Spanish.

(33) *dubda non y aura*
doubt not there will-have-3p.sg.
'He will not have any doubt about it' (12th, Cid, 1131)

(34) *non y ouo rapaz que ...*
not there had-3p.sg. boy that ...
'There was not kid that ...' (12th, Cid, 3289)

(35) *et dijo a un portero que y fallo que ...*
and said to a doorkeeper that there met that ...
'He said that ... to a doorkeeper that he met there'
(14th, Juan Manuel, Lucanor, 370, b)

(36) *... por quelos que y vjniessen ...*
... for that-those that there came-3p.pl. ...
'On account of those that came there' (14th, Doc. Lings., 262, 19)

Galegan is another Western Iberian Language that exhibits similar properties although they are attenuated in several respects. The behavior of *y* as a strong form is demonstrated by examples (37) and (38) where *y* is split from the verb by the noun *mesura* 'prudence' in (37), and the pronoun *ele* 'him' in (38). Although clitics can sometimes be split from the verb in Western Iberian Languages, a phenomenon called Interpolation, this never happens to the right (Wanner 1991). The locative *y* is modified by the appositive PP *en sua cidade* 'in his city' in (39). Clitics, as the prosodically weak items they are, cannot be modified as we have already shown in (8) and (9) above. Our conclusion is that locative *y* can be strong.

(37) *Faredes mesura i*
make-2p.sg. prudence there
'Be prudent on that!' (13th, Ioan Ayras, C.V., 554.26)

(38) *Et deu ele y muy bõas dõas*
and gave him there very good donations
'and he gave him very good donations'
(14th, Trans., Crónicas, 54.27-8)

(39) *Mandou Mahomet...fazer naues y en sua cidade*
ordered-3p.sg. Mahomet...to-make ships there in his city
'Mahomet ordered to construct ships in his city' (Trans., 48.35)

Weak *y* is the unmarked case in Galegan. In (40a) and (40b), the conjunctions *mas* 'but' and *et* 'and' head the derivation. It is well known that conjunctions do not host clitics in Old Romance, therefore *y* is placed in the potential clitic position. The clusterization between the complementizer *qu'* 'that' and *y* (41), which is even graphically written, shows the weak status of the locative. The same type of construction is illustrated in (43). Both (41) and (43) are similar to the Old Spanish examples (35) and (36). Examples (42) and (44) are instances of spell-outs in which pronominal clitics, locative *y* and the verb appear locally aligned. This local configuration is enough evidence in most Romance languages to conclude that they are clitics, but Western Iberian Languages have a potential alternative analysis. These languages have a type of derivation called Interpolation that allows intervening material between clitics and verb under restricted conditions. Derivations as the ones producing (42) and (44) have been described in Martins (1994) as instances of Interpolation. Crucially the status of locative *y* as strong or weak is what guarantees that we have instances of Interpolation or not, but as Martins recognizes, scholars do not agree about that status. We circumvent the problem showing that *y*, at least sometimes must be a clitic. Existential *hai* with the spelling *i ha*, as in French *il-y-a*, provides the evidence that we need. Locative *y* only can be weak in existential constructions (45). Thus, we can conclude that at least in some instances locative *y* is a clitic.

(40) a. *mas faliu-vos I o viso*
but failed-3p.sg-to-you there the sight
'but your eyes failed'
(12th. Paio Soares, tenso, in Justo Gil, 13)

b. *et tomou y muitos moros*
and captured-3p.sg. there many moors
'and he captured there/because of that many moors' (Trans, 22.8)

(41) *mas non sei tal qu'i estevesse*
but not know-1p.sg. such-a-person that'there was
'But I don't know anybody being there'
(13th, Ioan Ayras, C. V., 554.12)

(42) *et do eyxedo que llj y deu hũu seu caualleiro*
and from piece-of-land that to-him there gave a his knight
'and from the piece of land that one of his knights gave him'
(Trans, 49.2)

(43) *dos que y morreron*
of-those that there died
'of those that died there' (Trans, 19.39)

(44) *que lles y mandara*
that to-them there send
'that he send them there/ to do that' (Trans, 44.38)

(45) *tem auga quando a hi ha na fonte*
take water when it there is in-the fountain
'Take water whenever there is some in the fountain' (Martins 1994: 105)

If we compare Western Iberian Languages to French, we notice a clear asymmetry. In the *Chanson de Roland*, locative *y* obeys the same laws of distribution with respect to the verb as do Old French unstressed personal pronouns as studied by Jenkins (1924) and Foulet (1923). Jenkins has noted only two exceptions in the *Chanson*. On the contrary, in the *Cid*, 14 out of 43 instances of y obey different distribution as shown by Place (1930). The case of Aragonese and Catalan is similar to Old French: locative *y* follows the same derivational patterns as clitics (Badia 1947).

As an additional piece of evidence of the different status of locative *y* among Iberian languages, we see that Western Iberian Languages, as opposed to Eastern Iberian Languages, do not form pronominal and locative clitic clusters. The only exception we have found in Old Spanish is (46), taken from the Riojano dialect spoken at the East of the Western domain. On the other side, Aragonese (47) and (48) and Catalan (49) and (50) have had these complex units from their origins as Romance languages.

(46) *perdoneli (l' + i) Cristo*
forgive-3p.sg. (SE-it-m.sg. + there) C.
(13th, Berceo, Mil., 38, 143, in Badia 1947:92)

(47) *et aquellas que los y an*
and those that them there have-3p.pl. (13th, Arco, Ordenanzas, 119)

(48) *et si (se + I) desembargaban*
and SI (SE + there) raised-3p.pl.-the-embargo
(14th, Mora, Ordinaciones, I, 264)

(49) *...que ell li'n(l'+i+n) recomptave*
...that he it-there-of-it tell-3p.sg.
(13th-14th, Llull, Meravelles, I, 102, 11)

(50) *e vostra majestat... vage-hi-li ajudar*
and your Majesty... goes-there-him to-help (15th, Tirant, IV, 14, 21)

We can sum up this section by concluding that Old Spanish and Galegan have both strong and weak locative *y* co-variants. Aragonese, Catalan, and French only have weak (clitic) *y*.

4.3. *Weak and strong locative proforms in Western Iberian languages*

This section provides evidence of the existence of both strong [a.í] and weak [áj]. It follows from the properties of weak proforms we have presented in sections 1 and 2, that *ay* in (51) must be an instance of a strong locative since the verb *anda* 'go' is unaccusative. Metrical evidence helps us find strong [a.í] in (52) and (53). Both poems are octosyllabic and their metrical parsing demonstratess their two-syllable status.

(51) *...dixo: Quien anda ay?*
...said: who goes there
'He asked: who is there?' (14th, Lucanor, 290.28)

(52) *-aun. cre.d-en. A.do.na. y.'.* */ qu'el. vos. sa. na.ra. de-a.y.'.*
(14th, Ferrús, Canc. Baena, in DHLE)

(53) *A.do. es. el. gran. li.na.je.* */ a.y. son. lo. s-al.ca.mien.tos*
(14th, Juan Ruiz, LBA, 1901)

The weak status of *aj* is shown metrically in (54). Example (54) is one of the four alexandrine tetradecasyllabic (14-syllable) lines of a strophe called CUADERNA VÍA. But undoubtfully (56) is the most clear evidence of the weak status of *aj*. In (56), two different locatives *allí* and *aj* occur together. The two of them cannot be simultaneously strong in the same syntactic environment because they would add contradictory information to the event. Additionally, we know that *allí* cannot be monosyllabic. Therefore, we conclude that *aj* is weak. We can also mention that the proclitic position of *ay* and its semantic interpretation, which is non-demonstrative/deictic, support our conclusions. The weak status of *aj* in (57) can be argued on the basis of its semantic interpretation: *por-aj* does not mean in this specific example 'go in that direction' -i.e. the speaker is not giving directions- but rather 'go away!'.

(54) *gen.tes. de. to.do-el. mun.do. ay. e.ran. a.lle.ga.das.*
(14 syllables) (12th-13th, Berceo, Loor, 159, a)

(55) *... de un logar que dizen Aguilar, pero estaba ay Don Guido*
(14th, L. de Ayala, Cron. de D. Pedro, 505, a)

(56) *Alli ay fallaras de lo susodicho*
there there will-find-2p.sg. PART the above-mentioned
'in doing that you will find some of the above mentioned things'
(15th, Corbacho, 164)

(57) *Pues espera,/que por si o por no, no quiero/*
que por ahi te vayas.- Suelta
so wait,/ that because yes or bec. not, not want/
that by there you go.- Leave-it
'I don't want that you go away' vs.
*'I don't want that you go in that direction'
(17th, Calderón, No hay cosa como callar,1.4, in Cuervo 1886)

Galegan, as opposed to Old Spanish, seems to have only the strong variant (Mercedes Brea p.c). Consider examples (58) and (59) :

(58) *desejan sas terras assi / que non dormiron muit'ai*
(Brea 1988, Tavani, 115.10)

(59) ..., *que ben pode entender / quen quer o mal que ai lhe parece*
(Brea 1988, Tavani, 30.31)

4.4. *Temporal weak* ara, ora

The identification of strong and weak temporal *ara*, *ora* have additional difficulties since these two-syllable variants can be both strong and weak as we will show. The strong status of *ara* is illustrated in (60) where *ara* is part of a coordination structure. Since weak proforms cannot be coordinated as we have shown in (1b) and (3), we conclude that *ara* is strong. The 3-syllable status of *aora* in (61) must be attributed to the rhyme with the noun *hora*. In (62), the distributive sequence *cada dia en nuestros tiempos* 'every day in our times' modifies *ahora* 'now'. This modification was used in (8) and (9) to distinguish strong and weak proforms. *Ahora* is isolated in (63). Again that is impossible if we are right: isolated proforms cannot be weak (cf. (6) and (7)).

(60) *por ara τ todos tiempos*
for now and all times
'for now and ever' (14th, Doc. Alto Aragón, 96∃03∃ , 1957)

(61) *por aora/ subamos, que ya es hora*
for now/ let's-get-up that already is time
(16th., Güete, Vidriana, 210, 1207)

(62) *esto acontece ahora cada dia en nuestros tiempos*
this happens now every day in our times
(16th, Quevedo, Genealogía modorros, 35)

(63) *Mira, ahora/ Es ocasion, mientras veo*
look, now/ it's time, while see-1p.sg.
(18th, Fdz. Moratín, Viejo y ni a, II, VI, 89)

The existence of weak *ara* is uncontroversial. The history of Spanish is rich in instances of the distributive conjunction *ora* as in (69). Nevertheless, its status is unclear. In (67) it is again the metric parsing of the string what helps us. The first syllable of the second line only can be [jáo] to maintain the octosyllabic structure of the poem. Notice also that the meaning of the proform is not 'now' but 'ago': 'one year ago' instead of 'now one year'. In (66), it is the parallel rhyme of *Lau-ra* and *aho-ra* what shows the weak status of *ara*. Notice that with the parsing [a.ó.ra] , it is an eneasyllable (9-syllable) line. The rest of examples (64), (67) and (68) are examples with temporal conjunctions. In (68), taken from a Colombian writer, *ara* forms a cluster with the copulative conjunction *y* 'and'. It is not easy to imagine a stressed copulative conjunction *orY*.

(64) *ara escogi qual te quieras*
now select-2p.sg. which you want
(14th., Fdz. Heredia, G. Cron. de Espanya, 207)

(65) *Pues ara veredes, que Dios vos de bien*
(15th., Valencia, Canc. de Baena, 159, d)

(66) *Que. Lau.ra. aho.ra. no. pue.de.* (Octosyllabic)
(17th, L. de Vega, Pobreza no es vileza, I, 495, a)

(67) *No. di.ce. que. vi.ve. Cris.to./ y-aho.ra-un. a. o. lo. ne.ga.ba.?*
(Octosyllabic) (17th., Qui ones Benavente, El Borracho, 563, b)

(68) *Pues ory (=ahora+y(conj.)) vera*
then now+and see-will-2p.sg.
'You'll see...' (19th, Isaacs, María, 443)

There are 42 examples in DHLE of the weak conjunction *ora/ara/ao.ra* conjunction between 16th-17th. centuries.

(69) *Aora vengais vno a vno... ora todos juntos*
now come-2p.pl. one by one... now all together
(17th., Cervantes, Quijote, I, 4 fo, 14 vo)

Galegan is less conclusive than Spanish with respect to the status of temporal *aora/ara*. The form *agora* is the standard one in Western Iberian Languages. Since *agora* is a 3-syllable word, it is uncontroversially strong. Finally, the last set of examples —(70) to (74)— illustrate some exceptions to the standard occurrence of *agora* in Old Galician that behave like weak forms. In (70), metrical parsing shows the "weakness" of *ora*. In (71), we have a case of doubling between *ora* and *aquí* which is very similar to (56). In this example, *aquí* has a temporal interpretation with the meaning 'from this moment'. The rest of the examples are more opaque. (74) with two instances of *ora* is clearer.

(70) *ora-xa. me-i. po.de. en.ga.nar.*
now me-there can-3p.sg. deceive
'You can deceive me on that'
(Octosyllabic, both *ora* and *i* weak) (13th, Alfonso X, C. V., 63)

(71) *Mays ara/ora leyxamos aqui de fallar disto*
but now we-stop here of talk of-that
'From this moment on we stop talking about it
(14th, Trans. Crns., 95.65)

(72) *esperate, amjgo, ca ora he a sazõ*
wait-for-me-you, friend, because now have-1p.sg. the time
'Wait a second, my friend. Now I have the time'
(14th., Trans., 107.75)

(73) *Et ora soo traudo ao que rrey Pelayo me disso*
and now am attracted to that king Pelayo me told-3p.sg.
'I am now where King Pelayo told me'
(14th., Trans., 128-72)

(74) *Amjgos, ora teendes ora de me dar dereyto de...*
friends, now have-2p.pl. time of me to-give right of...
'My friends, it's now time to give me the right to ...'
(14th., Trans., 193.29)

We can partially conclude that weak and strong locative proforms are attested in early Old Spanish. Galegan is more opaque in general with respect to the weak proforms *aj/ara*.

5. *Conclusions*

Modern Spanish has prosodically weak and strong temporal/locative proforms. The weak proforms are clitics. In this respect they have the general properties of pronominal clitics. We analize the constraints on their distribution. Adjunct clitics denote contextually determined modifiers. This explains the variety of (related) interpretation. The contrast between weak and strong *y* has been active since medieval Spanish, in contrast with the rest of the Romania. Galegan/Portuguese shows a more restrictive distribution than Spanish. No stress shift theory is necessary to explain the origin of strong/weak proforms. We are dealing with a Romance phenomenon in which strong/weak proforms are combinations of *a* + strong/weak *y*.

REFERENCES

Alonso, Amado. 1930. *Problemas de dialectología hispanoamericana.* Biblioteca de dialectología hispanoamericana III. Buenos Aires: Instituto de Filología de la Universidad de Buenos Aires.

Badía Margarit, Antonio M.a. 1947. "Los complementos pronominalo-adverbiales derivados de *ibi* e *inde* en la península ibérica". *Revista de Filología Española,* Anejo XXXVIII.

Bosque, Ignacio. 1990. *Las categorías gramaticales.* Madrid: Síntesis.

Corominas, Joan. 1984. *Diccionari etimologic i complementari de la llengua catalana.* Barcelona: Curial edicions catalanes.

Corominas, Joan & José A. Pascual. 1985. *Diccionario crítico etimológico castellano e hispánico.* Madrid: Gredos.

Cuervo, Rufino J. 1886. *Diccionario de construcción y régimen de la lengua castellana.* Paris: A. Roger and F. Chernoviz.

Dowty, David. 1979. *Word Meaning and Montague Grammar.* Dordrecht: Reidel.

Espinosa, Aurelio. 1946. *Estudios sobre el español de Nuevo Méjico. Parte II. Morfología.* Trans. Angel Rosenblat. Biblioteca de dialectología hispanoamericana. Buenos Aires: Facultad de Filosofía y Letras de la Universidad de Buenos Aires.

Foulet, Lucien. 1930. *Petite syntaxe de l'ancien français.* Paris: Libraire ancienne Honor Champion.

Hayes, Bruce. 1990. "Precompiled Phrasal Phonology". *The Phonology-syntax Connection,* ed. by Sharon Inkelas & Draga Zec, 85-108. Chicago & London: The University of Chicago Press.

Jenkins, T. Atkinson. 1924. *La Chanson de Roland.* New York: Oxford.

Kayne, Richard S. 1975. *French Syntax: The Transformational Cycle.* Cambridge, Mas.: MIT Press.

Lema, José. 1991. *Licensing Conditions on Head Movement.* Ph.D. dissertation, University of Ottawa.

——— and María-Luisa Rivero. 1990a. "Inverted Conjugations and V-second Effects in Romance". *Proceeding of the 19th Linguistics Symposium on Romance Languages.* Amsterdam: John Benjamins.

——— and María-Luisa Rivero. 1990b. "Long Head Movement: ECP vs. HMC". *Proceedings of NELS* 20. GLSA. Amherst: University of Massachusetts.

——— and María-Luisa Rivero. 1992. "Types of Verbal Movement in Spanish: Modals, Futures and Perfects". *Probus* 3. 237-278.

Martins, Ana M. 1994. *Cliticos na historia do portugués.* Ph.D. dissertation, University of Lisbon.

Menéndez Pidal, Ramón. 1904. *Manual de gramática histórica.* Madrid: Espasa-Calpe.

Moens, Mark & Mark Steedman. 1988. "Temporal Ontology and Temporal Reference". *Journal of Computational Linguistics* 14.

Mussaffia, Alfredo. 1886. *Una particolaritá sintattica della lingua italiana dei primi secoli.* Miscellanea de filologia e linguistica. In memoria de N. Caix and U.A. Canello, 255-261. Firenze: Successori le Monnier.

Navarro Tomás, Tomás. 1926. *Manual de pronunciación española.* Madrid: Consejo Superior de Investigaciones Científicas.

Otero, Carlos P. 1996. "Head movement, Cliticization, Precompilation, and Word Insertion". *Current Issues in Comparative Grammar*, ed. by Robert Freidin, 296-337. Dordrecht: Kluwer Academic Publishers.

Parsons, Terence. 1985. "Underlying Events in the Logical Analysis of English". *Actions and Events: Perspectives on the Philosophy of Donald Davidson* ed. by Ernest LePore. Oxford: Blackwell.

Place, Edwin B. 1930. "Causes of the Failure of Old Spanish *y* and *en* to Survive. *Linguistic Review* XXI.223-228.

Pustejovsky, James. 1995. *The Generative Lexicon.* Cambridge, Mas.: MIT Press.

Real Academia Española. 1972. *Diccionario histórico de la lengua española.* Madrid: RAE.

Roberts, Ian G. 1993. *Verbs and Diachronic Syntax: A Comparative History of English and French.* Dordrecht: Kluwer Academic Publishers.

Saco e Arce, Juan A. 1868. *Gramática gallega.* Lugo: Soto Freire.

Silva-Villar, Luis. 1995. "Diachronic Interpolation Shift". Paper presented at the *Annual Meeting of the Linguistic Association of the Southwest* XXIV, Las Cruces.

———. 1996. "C- D-driven Derivations, Verb Movement and Clitic Closure". Paper presented at the *Meeting of the Linguistic Society of America*, San Diego.

———. In preparation. *Enclisis in North Western Iberian Languages. A diachonic perspective.* Dissertation, UCLA.

Sportiche, Dominique. 1992. "Clitic Constructions". Ms., UCLA.

Tiscornia, Eleuterio F. 1930. *La lengua de "Martín Fierro".* Biblioteca de dialectología hispanoamericana III. Buenos Aires: Facultad de Filosofía y Letras de la Universidad de Buenos Aires.

Tobler, Adolf. 1875. *De l'ordre des mots dans Chrétien de Troyes.* Review of J. le Coultre. Reprinted in A. Tobler. 1912. Vermischte Beiträge zur Französischte Grammatik. Leipzig: S. Hirzel.

Torrego, Esther. 1989. "Unergative-Unaccusative Alternations in Spanish". *MIT Working Papers in Linguistics* 10. 253-272.

Wanner, Dieter. 1991. "The Tobbler-Mussafia law in Old Spanish". *Current Studies in Spanish Linguistics*, ed. by Héctor Campos & Fernando Martínez-Gil, 313-378. Washington, D.C.: Georgetown University Press.

OPTIMALIZING IBERIAN CLITIC SEQUENCES

DAVID HEAP
University of Toronto
&
University of Western Ontario

The internal ordering of clitic pronoun sequences has been a matter of vigorous debate for over 25 years, without a wide consensus being reached. While derivational or principle-based approaches to this problem do not cover the attested data, template or surface structure approaches are unconstrained and ultimately predict nothing, and both have difficulty when faced with nonstandard and variable sequences. An alternative is to be found in a framework which allows for constraint interaction, such as Optimality Theory. In this account, unranked constraints and morphological underspecification are combined to produce just the range of variation which is attested in some nonstandard Iberian clitic sequences.*

1. *The problem*

How do clitic pronouns get arranged in a specific order? This is a problem which goes back at least to Perlmutter's (1971) initial proposal of surface structure constraints (or output filters) to account for clitic sequences. Since that time authors have argued against a filter-based approach as theoretically undesirable and/or empirically inadequate (Dinnsen 1972, Szabo 1974, Hetzron 1977, Wanner 1977). On the other hand, various attempts to represent clitic

* I am indebted to Eulàlia Bonet, who originally encouraged me to try an OT solution to the problems of clitic sequencing, and to Greg Lamontagne and Carrie Dyck, who walked me through the rudiments of Optimality Theory. Earlier versions of this work benefited from comments received at the Canadian Linguistics Association Annual Meeting (1995), at workshops in the University of Toronto Departments of French and Linguistics, at the LSRL XXI in Mexico City, and at the Grup de Gramàtica Teòrica of the Universitat Autònoma de Barcelona. Thanks are also due to my colleagues in the Groupe de recherches en dialectologie comparative (Sarah Cummins, Terry Nadasdi and Yves Roberge), as well as Naomi Nagy, Keren Rice, Elan Dresher and especially Dieter Wanner. Funding was received from the Social Sciences and Humanities Research Council of Canada (Heap 752-91-2167, Roberge 410-91-1307) and a Queen Elizabeth II Ontario Fellowship.

sequencing facts in purely syntactic terms (Bastida 1976, Pearce 1991, Laenzlinger 1993, Uriagereka 1995) have not completely succeeded either. Bonet (1991, 1995a&b) and Nadasdi (1995) return to templatic treatments of clitic linearization, while Harris (1994, 1996) uses 'precedence conditions' to achieve the same ends within the Distributed Morphology framework.

All of these proposals contain important insights (for at least some of the relevant data), but share the dual drawbacks that they are rigidly deterministic, in that they predict exactly one sequence of clitics will be permitted to surface in any given grammar, while at the same time being arbitrary, inasmuch as the same formalisms could easily be adapted to represent any output sequence, including many which are not attested in any Romance grammar. These twin drawbacks are really two sides of the same problem, one which can only be transcended by means of a formalism which retains the many different (at times contradictory) insights into clitic sequencing, while allowing them to interact in a variable fashion. In this paper I first examine some previous approaches to clitic sequencing in order to see how they would deal with some cases of variation in nonstandard clitic sequences, and then turn to an Optimality and underspecification treatment of the same facts.

1.1 *Some assumptions*

I will not be addressing the debate as to whether or not Romance pronominal clitics should be treated as syntactically active elements which are placed and moved in a syntactic component. Following among others Heap et al. (1993), Cummins & Roberge (1994), Auger (1994), Bessler (1994) and Nadasdi (1995), I assume that the mechanisms available in syntax and phonology are insufficient to account for the types of surface configurations attested in Romance varieties, and that it would be quite undesirable to extend the power and purview of these modules to cover such phenomena, in that it would simultaneously clutter up their respective formalisms with otherwise unmotivated ad hoc processes, and reduce their explanatory value by making them so powerful as to be vacuous (Harris 1994).

To put the point more positively, this thorny problem is not solely (or even primarily) the responsibility of syntacticians, but rather something which must be addressed in terms of interaction between the various components of a modular grammar (Wanner 1996:39). I therefore take as my starting point the necessity of positing some level of representation which mediates between the terminal nodes of syntax and phonological interpretation. I follow Auger

(1994) in adopting an 'Lexicon-Syntax Interace' (or LSI) analysis (Cummins & Roberge 1994, Bessler 1994), a slightly modified version of the Minimalist Program model. (Chomsky 1993) Note that in addition to the LSI, this model assumes a Morphophonological Interface (MPI) between syntax and PF.[1] It should be noted that I am not making any claims here about clitic placement with respect to the verb or within a phrase (i.e. proclisis, enclisis or clitic second phenomena), which may in fact be syntactic in nature.[2] The claim here is simply that the surface forms of Romance pronominal clitics, and in particular their linear order, cannot reasonably be accounted for without positing an MPI.[3]

So the crucial question now becomes: just what happens in this MPI? What sorts of mechanisms (representations and rules) are available there? In particular, how would available mechanisms deal with variable clitic sequences? Bonet's (1991, 1995a) and Harris' (1994, 1996) models share the same basic architecture: fully-specified feature matrices from the output of syntax are (partially) mapped onto morphological structures, where morphological rules operate on them before linearization and spell-out. Since the morphological rule subcomponent does not provide much empirical basis for choosing between the two models of the MC, we can concentrate on the more interesting substantive difference between Bonet's and Harris' accounts: the mechanisms chosen to account for the linear sequencing of clitic strings.

Bonet's template for Barceloní pronominal clitics in 1, with the six slots corresponding to the feature hierarchies of the different clitic structures, is in many ways a typical templatic treatment of sequencing facts (the example sentence illustrates all six slots filled):

(1) Bonet's template for Barceloní:

[ARG]	[ARG] II	[ARG] I	[ARG] III	[OBL] [GEN]	[OBL]

[1] I use the term MPI in contradistinction to the MC or Morphological Component, which is associated with the Distributed Morphology framework, a different proposal from the LSI-analysis (although similar in some respects). The term is also intended to stress the Minimalist idea that variation occurs at the interfaces.

[2] But see Anderson 1994 for a treatment of clitic placement in OT morphology.

[3] More detailed discussion and argumentation of this as well as other points can be found in Heap (1996).

e.g. [s t m lz n i] vas quedar tres.
'You took three of them from me' (Bonet 1995)

Unfortunately, as with Permutter's (1971) SSCs or output filters, this same formalism can easily be modified to encode any number of different clitic orderings, since there is no theory constraining the shapes which templates can take. Indeed, Bonet gives three other examples of templates with different clitic orderings, corresponding to different varieties of Catalan (1991:74, 1995b:73). We can of course devise a template reminiscent of Perlmutter's which captures the Standard Spanish facts using Bonet's features:

(2) Template for Standard Spanish:

[ARG]	II	I	III

Harris (1994, 1996) rejects the templatic approach in favour of precedence conditions or sequencing principles which refer to the actual phonological shapes of clitics after spell-out, thus 'filtering out' ungrammatical sequences:

(3) Harris' precedence conditions for Spanish:

* [X]-[s] i.e. nothing can precede a reflexive clitic.
* [l]-[X] i.e. nothing can follow a 3rd person clitic.
* [1per]-[2per] i.e. a 1st person clitic cannot precede a 2nd person clitic. (Harris 1996)

Both Bonet and Harris assume a syntactic movement account of clitic placement (such as Kayne 1975 or 1991), without anything crucial in either account depending on such an assumption. Indeed, Harris underlines his 'resolute agnosticism' with respect to the syntax of clitic placement: he holds that a morphological account of clitic sequencing should be compatible with whatever may eventually be decided about the syntax of clitics (1994:42). Furthermore, since the MC would in principle make any modifications necessary to achieve the required surface forms of the clitics in question, both of the accounts just outlined would in fact be compatible with any conceivable account of syntactic clitic placement. In fact, they would be equally compatible with no theory of syntactic clitic placement at all, which is precisely the position assumed in this paper and related work on the MPI. If we have a post-syntactic interface capable of doing this job, why burden the syntax with it as well? The output of syntax would then consist simply of feature-bundles which are spelled-out and linearized in the MPI, which allows us to assume a maximally general Computational Component.

1.2 *Some clitic sequencing data*

Let us now consider how these two linearization proposals would fare when faced with some nonstandard Spanish data. The 'inverted' clitic clusters *te se* and *me se* shown in 4 alternate freely with the Standard Spanish orderings *se te* and *se me* in Murcian:[4]

(4) *El hígado de conejo, lo puedo comer frito,*
pero en el arroz me se queda en la garganta.
'Rabbit liver, I can eat it fried, but in rice it sticks in my throat.'
Si no riego, me se seca todo.
'If I don't irrigate, everything dries up on me.'
La he atado para que no te se caiga.
'I tied it so that it wouldn't fall.'
Si soplas al fuego, igual te se apaga.
'If you blow on the fire, it is just as likely to go out on you.'

These data happen to be from rural Murcian (a Castilian-based southern Spanish variety similar to Eastern Andalusian), but similar data can be found from other regions: this 'inversion' would appear to be a widespread nonstandard feature: '... esta contrucción es estimada en todas partes como solecismo plebeyo.' (RAE 1973:427) It is of course straightforward to construct a Bonetian template which would represent the nonstandard or 'inverted' order, as in 5a, but unfortunately it is also equally staightforward to devise a similar template for unattested sequences, as in 5b:

(5) a. Nonstandard Spanish (me se, te se):

II	I	[ARG]	III

b. Unattested Romance: (* lo me se te):

III	I	[ARG]	II

[4] All these data consist of clitic sequences in proclisis: I have no data on the behaviour of these sequences in enclisis.

So in varieties like Murcian, the templatic approach leaves us with the problem of why a grammar should contain just the templates in 2 and 5a, but not any others, such as the one in 5b. Harris' precedence conditions, on the other hand, are clearly too rigid faced with data like those in 4, since *se* simply does not always precede all other clitics. What we evidently need is a 'middle ground' solution somewhere between the rigidity of precedence conditions and the unconstrained templatic notation.

1.3 *A first OT approximation*

Anderson's (1994) OT account of Serbo-Croatian second position clitics in terms of constraint interaction relies heavily on the use of the constraints of the EdgeMost family. Anderson (1995) suggests that the order in which clitics appear is determined by the dominance relation that obtains between their corresponding EdgeMost constraints. (Anderson 1995). These proposals suggest a first approximation of the internal sequencing of clitic clusters: replacing EdgeMost (cl,L,PrWd) with ALIGN (cl,L,PrWd,L), and ranking the different members of this family of related constraints appropriately, we obtain the tableau in 6, corresponding to the Standard Spanish sequence, and the one in 7, with the reverse ranking of the same constraints, corresponding to the nonstandard 'inverted' sequences:

(6) ALIGN (se,L) >> ALIGN (te,L) with inputs /se te/ and /se me/ (standard sequences):

candidates	ALIGN (se,L)	ALIGN (+1ps.cl.,L)
a. ☞ se te, se me		*
b. te se, me se	*!	

(7) ALIGN (±1ps.cl.,L) >> ALIGN (*se*,L) with inputs /se te/ and /se me/ ('inverted' sequences):

candidates	ALIGN (+1ps.cl.,L)	ALIGN (se,L)
a. se me, se te	*!	
b. ☞ me se, te se		*

We can thus describe the difference between the standard order and the nonstandard order of clitics in terms of the dominance relationships between the different parametrizations of ALIGN, an independently motivated constraint.

1.4 *Unranked constraints and variation*

This OT account has a further interesting consequence:the representation of variation within a given grammar. Note that clitic sequences like those in 4 are not the only grammatical options: it is quite common in Murcian to hear the same speaker use both the Standard Spanish and the nonstandard clitic sequences, even within a single utterance. The OT formalism offers us a built-in mechanism for representing such competing variants within a grammar: the nonranking of constraints that in principle conflict. (McCarthy 1993:6, also p.c. apud Reynolds & Sheffer 1994:105). Thus for those speakers for whom both orders are possible and natural, we need only posit that ALIGN (se,L) and ALIGN (1ps.cl,L) are unranked: nonranking, or an absence of dominance relationship between constraints, is represented by the dotted line separating the columns (McCarthy 1993:4), and leads to nonunique optimal candidates:[5]

(8) [ALIGN (+1ps.cl,L), ALIGN (*se*,L)] unranked with inputs /se me/ and /se te/:

Candidates	ALIGN (+1ps.cl,L)	ALIGN (*se*,L)
a. ☞ se me, se te	*	
b. ☞ te se, me se		*

This finding supports Anttila's contention that the nonranking of constraints is not just a 'technical quirk of OT', but rather corresponds emprically to attested variation within a grammar. (1995:12) But unfortunately, this use of parametrized ALIGN remains just as descriptive and ad hoc as the templates discussed earlier. And of course, as with templates, there is nothing to stop us from parametrizing ALIGN so as to describe any clitic sequence at all, including

[5] Given the obvious prestige of the standard clitic sequencing, it is of course more than likely that these alternations correlate in reality with sociolinguistic variables, but I do not have a sufficient corpus to arrive at quantitative results. Such variation suggests at least the possibility that the dotted line in (8) is in fact a crude stand-in for a more precise factor-weighting of the sort which would result from a variable rule analysis (this may also be the case for the asterisks and empty cells in the preceding tableaux). This fascinating possibility is beyond the scope of the present paper, but suggests a possible relationship between optimality and variable rules (both of which, after all, are concerned with non-unique outputs resulting from the interaction between linguistic constraints) which might bring a formal model of grammar closer to an actual model of linguistic performance (cf. Nagy & Reynolds, 1994; Anttila 1995; Nagy, 1996).

many nonattested ones. So unless we can formulate these ordering facts in terms of principles which are more motivated than ALIGN, we will have done little apart from creating a notational variant of the clitic template which is more 'harmonic' (for lack of a better term) with current trends in formalism.

2. *A more motivated OT account*

So what we need to do is translate the partially valid (but inflexibly deterministic) insights of earlier work on clitic sequencing into constraints, which can be placed in a framework which allows for more flexible constraint interaction, i.e. OT. As a starting point, let us consider Wanner's (1996:19) *binomios de linearización* or 'Two Term Sequencing Patterns' (TTSPs): these amount to positive statements of ordering relationships, i.e. a reformulation of the 'output filter' in terms of three simultaneously applied linear ordering restrictions:

(9)	a.	+R > X	[+reflexive precedes all other clitics]
	b.	+P > -P	[+person clitics precede -person (i.e. 3rd) clitics]
	c.	II > I	[second person precede first person clitics]

It should be obvious that these TTSPs state exactly the same information as Harris' 'precedence conditions' (1993) but in a positive rather than negative fashion (which is perhaps more plausible from an acquisition perspective). The principles involved have of course been around for a long time, dating at least from descriptive grammarians like Bello (1972). It is however crucial to understand that the interpretation of these constraints makes them different from previous formulations in two important ways. Firstly, they are compositional, i.e. the three constraints are independent and can interact variably; secondly, they are variably specified, i.e. the morphological vocabulary items which they refer to can be interpreted differently by different speakers/ varieties. Or as Wanner puts it: 'Lo propio de los binomios de secuencialidad es su libre cominación para producir efectos locales, en principio variables según hablantes, registros, regiones y periodos.' (1996:33) This leads to a certain amount of indeterminacy in the system: a form like *te* can be both reflexive [+R] with respect to 9a, and second person [II] with respect to 9c.

Wanner exploits this combination of syncretism and underspecification in the pronominal system to account for the *me se / te se* data: the clitic *se* is both +R (reflexive) and -P (third person), and as such can be fit into two different 'slots': 9a places it before everything (=standard sequences) while 9b places it after +P clitics such as *me* and *te* (=nonstandard sequences). In Optimality terms, we could simply not rank these two constraints, as in 10, and thus allow both candidates to surface as optimal:

(10) R > X and +P > -P unranked, with inputs /se te/ and /se me/:

candidates	R > X	+P > -P
a. ☞ se te, se me	*	
b. ☞ te se, me se		*

This is a tempting solution, in that it derives variation in the data from tensions inherent between the specifications of clitic pronouns and the ordering constraints in 9. Unfortunately, this approach predicts that *se* will also follow the plural +P clitics *nos* and *os*, as in 11:

(11) R > X and +P > -P unranked, with input /se nos/:

candidates	R > X	+P > -P
a. ☞ se nos		*
b. ☹ nos se	*	

Here the 'unfelicitous' 11b (which gets ☹ rather than ☞) is incorrectly selected as optimal: candidate forms such as **nos se* (and **os se*) are not attested in varieties where *me se* and *te se* are common, even predominant: 'esta posposición incorrecta sólo se da cuando dichas formas átonas están en singular; nunca alcanza al plural: *se nos quedó muerto* (y nunca *nos se quedó muerto*).' (García Martínez 1986: 117) Since such sequences cannot readily be excluded on purely phonological or pragmatic grounds, we need to find another motivated constraint which can in effect restate the ALIGN (+1ps.cl.,L) constraint. Just such a principle is suggsted by Wanner's discussion of the diachronic drift from the medieval ordering ILLUM MIHI to the modern Romance MIHI ILLUM, which he describes as a *metabinomio* (1996:27), a more abstract constraint on how argumental clitics tend to be ordered. The overall tendency is to place arguments with which one can empathize before those to which one simply refers:

(12) Empathy > Referentiality (or Empathy 1st) (Wanner 1996:27)

If we assume that the persons which receive the specification [+empathizable] can vary from variety to variety, then one of the plausible settings would be to specify the first and second person singular as [+empathizable]. Integrating this constraint into our analysis, we can of course draw a tableau in which the two relevant constraints are unranked, which leads to nonunique optimal forms and variation in sequencing:

(13) a. Empathy 1st and +R > X unranked, with inputs /se te/ and /se: me/:

candidates	II > I	Empathy 1st	+R > X
☞ se me, se te		*	
☞ me se, te se			*

b. Empathy 1st and +R > X unranked, with inputs /te me/:

candidates	II > I	Empathy 1st	+R >
☞ te me			
me te	*!		

c. Empathy 1st and +R > X unranked, with inputs /se nos/:

candidates	II > I	Empathy 1st	+R > X
☞ se nos			
nos se		*!	*!

Note that none of the optimal candidates violate the II > I constraint, but that any candidate containing **me te* is eliminated by this undominated constraint as in 13b, and that forms with [+plural] [+person] clitics in initial position satisfy neither of the unranked conditions, and are thus eliminated in favour of the standard order 13c.

2.1 *Templates: where do we draw the (dotted) line?*

It can of course be argued that, since the 'nonranking of constraints' convention represents a considerable increase in generative power, in order to make a fair comparison between the OT solution sketched above and its templatic counterpart, we must allow the templates to have an equally powerful device. In other words, would a template which has option of placing a 'dotted line' between columns (thus 'unranking' two classes of clitics) be able to produce just the same sequences as the OT tableaux? Consider the following template for Peninsular Spanish with the relevant clitic forms filled in:

(14) Standard Spanish

[ARG]	II	I	III
se	te os	me nos	lo(s) la(s) le(s)

In order to get just the orders in 13a (*me se* and *te se*) from the same template, where exactly do we draw the dotted line? One immediate problem is that the line has to enclose just the pronouns involved (*se, me* and *te*), and nothing else, since the standard orders involving plural first and second person pronouns do not vary: *se os* and *se* nos do not alternate with **os se* and **nos se*. To do this, the middle two columns have to be split horizontally along the feature [plural] (a division which otherwise plays no part in clitic sequencing). However, even this use of dotted lines cannot adequately represent the facts, since the relative order of the two middle columns must be maintained, despite the fact that *se* can follow either one of them: as already shown, we find the nonstandard orders *me se* and *te se* but never **me te* (nor **nos os*). So the nonstandard alternations require a special, highly stipulative version of the 'nonranking' convention: a dotted line that can include just three forms from three columns, while respecting the dashed line which maintains the strict order between two of them, as in 15:

(15) Nonstandard Spanish

[ARG]	II	I	III
se	te	me	lo(s) la(s) le(s)
	os	nos	

So in order to allow for variation in a template approach to clitic sequences, the nonranking convention has to be 'enriched' with the special 'permeable' dashed line, one which allows *se* to reorder itself with either *te* or *me*, while maintaining the fixed order of these last two. In contrast, our OT treatment of these same data avoids these pitfalls: the Empathy 1st constraint ensures that only the first and second person singular forms appear sequence-initially, while the II > I constraint remains undominated, thus preventing **me te* sequences from ever being selected as optimal. And the nonranking convention is maintained in its simplest (and independently motivated) form, i.e. simply expressing the absence of a hierarchical relationship between constraints, rather than a linear adjacency between clitics.

3. ***Variable sequences in Central Catalan***

Mascaró (1986:138) gives the following ordering variants from Central North-Eastern Catalan (all of which correspond to the combination of *em* + *et*, to which an 'extra' reflexive clitic *es* is added):

(16) *setem' escapes.*	*setem' escapo.*[6]
tesem' escapes.	*tesem' escapo.*
temes' escapes.	*temes' escapo.*
'You get away from me.'	'I get away from you.'

(Mascaró 1986:138)

Here again it is not difficult to devise a feature-based template based on Bonet's (cf. 5 supra):

(17) Partial template for Barceloní:

[ARG]	II	I
es	et us	em ens

which gives the relatively transparent order *setem'*. But if we want to allow for the other two variant orders in 16, where would we put the dotted lines in this template? Without even getting into the problem of drawing a line which excludes the 2nd and 1st persons plural, how do we maintain the order II > I? In the Spanish case (where *te* and *me* are in adjacent columns), one could argue for a special 'dashed line within a dotted line' which maintains the order of *te* and *me* while allowing *se* to follow either of them. But given that in the

[6] Note that the schwas (orthographic <e>) are inserted in these forms for syllabification (a process I have nothing to say about here), since the underlying forms of these clitics really only consist of the relevant consonants (the initial orthographic *e* in the isolated forms of pronouns does not necessarily surface).

Catalan data, persons II and I need not even be adjacent, how can a template represent the fact that *es* can appear before, after or between *et* and *em*, but *em* can never precede *et*? Any version of the template in 17 which allowed for the various orders in 16 would be hard pressed to exclude unattested orders such as those in 18:

(18) * *metes'* * *meset'*

In the OT treatment, of course, the adjacency of columns is irrelevant: the unattested candidates in 18 are violations of the undominated II > I (or 'politeness') constraint, and as such will never be selected as optimal, even when we leave R > X and Empathy 1st unranked, as in 19:

(19) Empathy 1st and +R > X unranked, with inputs /se me te/:

	candidates	II > I	Empathy 1st	+R > X
☞	*setem*		*	
☞	*tesem, temes*			*
	metes, meset	*!		

It should be clear by now that unranked constraints in an OT tableau interact in a more restricted fashion than unranked columns in templates, and it turns out that this more restricted grammar corresponds better to the range of variation attested in Romance clitic sequences. This means that, despite superficial similarities, OT tableaux are not simply notational variants of templates when it comes to clitic sequences, since they allow to make more restrictive statements and more specific predictions about possible clitic sequences.

If, on the other hand, it were the case that all mathematically possible combinations of clitic pronouns (including unattested ones such as those in 18, among others) in fact did surface in some Romance variety, there would of course be no need at all for anything like OT: it would suffice to have a free theory of templates which simply produced clitic sequences in an unconstrained fashion. This would be, in effect, the equivalent of the function GEN, capable of freely generating candidate outputs. But we know that some of these possible sequences never occur, which means that some constraints do apply across the board. What is more, some constraints can apply variably both within and across varieties, a fact which forces us to adopt some mechanism capable of evaluating their relative weight. Such a theory of constraint interaction is however crucially dependent on the constraints is uses, and constraints like Empathy 1st as used above are just too ad hoc to be retained: we still need to find more motivated constraints on which to base our analysis.

4. *The LLL constraint and underspecification*

Harris (1996) points out an interesting generalization which emerges when the clitics in his 'precedence conditions' (cf. 3 above) are associated with their respective feature matrices: *se* has the least specification (just [ARG]), first and second have a bit more (either II or I, and perhaps [plural]), while the third person clitics are most specified: they bear [ARG], III, [plural] and [fem] as well as morphological [kase] (either dative or accusative). This representation suggests a sort of 'crescendo effect' from least- to most-specified clitics, which Harris sums up in the slogan 'syncretism precedes contrast'. This generalization can be interpreted in arboreal terms as 'arrange clitics from smallest to largest [feature] trees', which, paraphrased more alliteratively, becomes the 'least leafy to the left' (or LLL) constraint shown in 20:

(20) Least Leafy to the Left (LLL):

Arrange clitics from the morphologically least specified to most specified.

```
[ARG]  >   [ARG]     >    [ARG]
             |             /  \
           II / I       III   DAT/ACC
           [pl]               [pl] [fm]
 se        te/me/nos          le(s)/lo(s)/la(s)
```

The LLL constraint in 20 simply restates the Standard Spanish order as given in various other notations, i.e. it replaces 9a, b but not 9c. If however we assume with Anttila that variation emerges in environments where the grammar underdetermines the output, (1995:24) then the LLL constraint (like Wanner's variably specified TTSPs) becomes more flexible in a potentially interesting way. Consider the underspecificied version of LLL in 21, where *me* and *te* require only the specification for I and II respectively, assuming that their status as [ARG] (or equivalent) can be supplied redundantly, and that number is only marked in the plural:

(21) Morphologically underspecificied LLL.

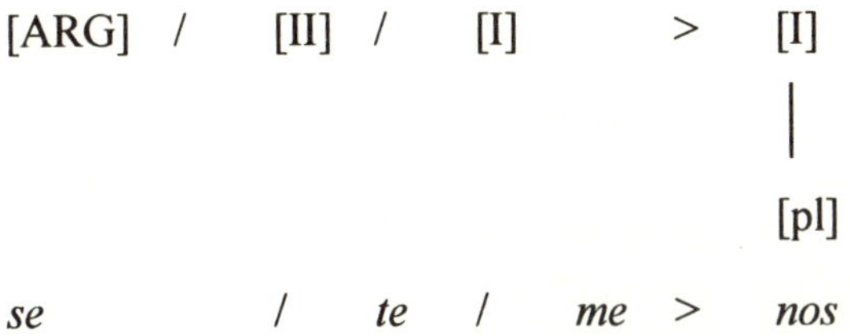

We can see from 21 that, properly underspecified, *se, me,* and *te* have the same minimal amount of feature 'leafiness', and thus can all be ordered leftmost by the LLL constraint. The clitics *nos* and *os* must always have one more feature, and so must be ordered after any of the first three, thus providing singular / plural asymmetries automatically. Note however that the LLL constraint on its own overgenerates, incorrectly predicting free ordering of the three least specified clitics (*se, me*, and *te*). It must therefore be dominated by the remaining 'politeness' constraint II > I (=Harris' 3c and Wanner's 9c). The interaction of these two constraints is shown is 22, where the underspecified interpretation of LLL allows for all (and only) the nonstandard orders to be selected as optimal:

(22) a. II > I dominates (underspecified) LLL with inputs /se te/ and /se me/:

	candidates	II > I	LLL
☞	se me, se te		
☞	me se, te se		

b. II > I dominates (underspecified) LLL with input /te me/:

	candidates	II > I	LLL
☞	te me		
	me te	*!	

c. II > I dominates (underspecified) LLL with input /se nos/:

	candidates	II > I	LLL
☞	se nos		
	nos se		*!

So we now have two possible representations of variation in clitic sequences: unranked constraints and variable morphological underspecification. The underspecification account entails an interesting prediction: there should exist Iberian varieties with just the standard sequences (*se me*), and varieties with both the standard sequences and the 'inverted' sequences (*se me / me se*), but no varieties with just the 'inverted' sequences (*me se*) since *me* can never have less morphological specification than *se* (only the same or more). This prediction seems to be borne out empirically by available data.[7]

5. *Other constraints on clitic sequences*

Having established that a formalism with approximately the power of OT is necessary to account for variable clitic sequencing facts, we should briefly consider how other well-known problems in clitic morphology can be expressed in this framework. What follows is not intended to be an exhaustive OT account of all the various peculiar phenomena associated with Romance clitics, but rather an indication that some of the most notorious problems can also be captured by a constraint-interaction account.[8]

5.1 *PARSE and OCP*

First of all, it is logical to assume that, all other things being equal, candidates which preserve the input features provided by the syntax are to be preferred over those which do not preserve these features. This preference falls into the general class of 'faithfulness' constraints, well-known from OT phonology, and which can be formulated (for the purposes of clitic morphology) as follows:

(23) PARSE: Spell out all input morphological features.

[7] This is the case for Iberian clitic sequences that I am aware of: obviously other constraints and/or rankings apply to other cases, such as the Italian facts.

[8] Specifically, I do not address the **Person-Case Constraint**, which is amply discussed by Bonet's (1994) pioneering treatment of OT pronominal morphology.

Naturally, this constraint refers only to those features which are passed on to the MPI, i.e. the subset of features retained after spellout, erasure and impoverishment rules etc. apply. Note that in most straightforwardly transparent cases there will be no violations of PARSE at all, and all the input features will be present in the optimal candidate. Where however a higher violation eliminates the completely faithful candidate, the minimal violation of PARSE ensures that the optimal forms is still as close as possible to the featural makeup of the input. Thus PARSE captures both the straighforward facts about 'normal' or transparent clitic strings, and the important insight about nontransparent or opaque clitic outputs expressed by Bonet's generalisation, i.e. that 'nontransparent output forms will have the same surface form as other clitics of the language instead of becoming an arbitrary phonological sequence.' (1991:2-3) As discussed elsewhere (Heap et al. 1993), there are a small number of exceptions to this generalisation, i.e. cases where the output sequence is not made up exclusively of other clitics from the inventory of the same language. But the generalisation is otherwise very robust, and thus it is a natural correlate of the type of 'soft universals' which flow automatically from violable constraints. Cases where the minimal violation of PARSE comes into play include the notorious spurious *se* facts of Spanish, which are the result of a conflict with another constraint familiar from phonology:

(24) OCP: *[α F [α F

This highly generalised version of the OCP constraint is intended to allow it to apply to a variety of facts, including morphological 'dissimilation' effects, depending on the exact features which conflict in a given variety. In the case we are interested in, the OCP is instantiated as a ban on sequences of third person clitics which concerns us: *[-P] [-P]. As pointed out by Bonet (1991:156,n18), the 'substitution' of *se* for *le* in fact represents the least possible change in features in order to 'dissimilate' the two clitics, or in OT terms, the minimal violation of PARSE. Changing the input *le* to another clitic in the inventory such as *me* would require the addition or changing of features, i.e. more violations of PARSE. Thus spurious *se* corresponds to a ranking of OCP above PARSE:

(25) OCP > PARSE, with input /le lo/:

	candidates	OCP	PARSE
	le lo	*!	
	me lo		**!
☞	se lo		*

Of course, the idea of a ban on sequences of third person clitics is nothing new, and whenever it is evoked, the problem comes up of how to allow for those varieties where such sequences do surface, such as Standard French. The OT framework accommodates these facts quite easily by simply reversing the ranking of the relevant constraints for those grammars: in Standard French, as in Valencian, PARSE outranks OCP. Other Romance varieties resort to other solutions when faced with cases of OCP violation, for example Standard Catalan li + *el* => *l'hi.* Such 'repair strategies' include deletion of the features involved in the OCP clash, as in some colloquial French haplology *le* + *lui* => *y*, or spelling out one of the offending clitics as a strong pronoun, as in certain varieties of Franco-Ontarian *je lui donne ça* (Nadasdi 1995). The optimal solution in each case will depend in part on the interaction of PARSE and OCP with grammar-specific constraints on the maximum allowable length of clitic sequences. There are obviously natural tensions between length constraints, OCP and PARSE, as well as other, as yet unformalized, constraints: such conflicts are resolved through grammar-specific constraint rankings (or, in the case of variation, nonrankings).

6. *Conclusions*

This analysis is primarily motivated by the need to account for the variable output of clitic sequences, a problem which requires, on the one hand, constraints on clitic sequences which are more motivated than just ALIGN (or its variants), and on the other hand, a framework which is sufficiently flexible to allow these constraints to interact in different ways, and to produce nonunique outputs. A theory of constraint interaction which allows for crucial nonranking gives us just the sort of variation which is attested in clitic sequences. The proposal outlined here is obviously not the final word on this longstanding problem, but it is worth noting that a nondeterministic theory of constraint interaction succeeds exactly where other (more categorical) accounts have failed, i.e. in dealing with variable clitic sequences. As Wanner says 'la idea generativista original de una restricción de salida única y global es poco iluminadora y completamente inflexible, en constraste con la elasticidad evidente de los datos.' (1996:38). The account presented here shows that the Optimality framework can constrain the MPI to cover just the range of clitic sequences which are actually attested, without either the rigidity of precedence conditions or the all-powerful open-endedness of templates. It also provides a built-in mechanism for encoding the alternations between competing variants in those cases where the data are noncategorical, which would seem to be a relatively common occurrence in the MPI.

The challenge is of course to extend this type of analysis to other clitic ordering facts, at least (initially) in other Romance languages. French alternations such as *donne-le-moi* and *donne-moi-le* merit further attention, as do Italian and Rumanian facts. Further constraints will undoubtedly be needed for some of these varieties, as well as for Catalan, which in many ways constitutes the test case for any account of Romance pronominal clitics: for example, the variable data in 16 involve only three of the six slots from Bonet's Barceloní template in 1.

Whatever the final inventory of constraints (and features) looks like, it should be clear that a theory of how such constraints interact will be necessary in order to account for the attested facts, and so something resembling Optimality Theory will thus play a key role in the MPI. This in turn has positive implications for the Minimalist program: with such idiosyncratic morphological phenomena relegated to the MPI, the syntax can be left unobstructed to do its work. There is also an important methodological lesson here: the formal superiority of the OT account only becomes clear when we take seriously the task of accounting for variable data. If we continue to idealise variable orders out of our data (as accounts since Perlmutter have tended to do, with a few notable exceptions), we lose valuable evidence about the internal organization of the grammar.

REFERENCES

Anttila, Arto. 1995. "Deriving Variation from Grammar: A Study of Finnish Genitives". Ms., Stanford University, (Rutgers Optimality Archive #63).

Anderson, Stephen. 1994. "How to Put your Clitics in their Place, or Why the Best Account of Second-Position Phenomena May be a Nearly Optimal One". Ms., Yale University.

Anderson, Stephen. 1995. "Rules and Constraints in Describing the Morphology of Phrases". *CLS Parasession on Clitics.*

Auger, Julie. 1994. *Pronominal Clitics in Québec Colloquial French: A Morphological Analysis.* Ph.D. dissertation, University of Pennsylvania.

Bastida, Salvador. 1976. "Restricciones de orden en las secuencias de clíticos del castellano: dos requisitos". *Estudios de gramática generativa* ed. by Víctor Sánchez de Zavala, 59-99. Barcelona:Labor.

Bello, Andrés. 1972. *Gramática de la lengua castellana destinada al uso de los Americanos.* Caracas: Ediciones del Ministerio de Educación.

Bessler, Paul. 1994. *Une analyse morphosyntaxique de l'accord grammatical en français.* Ph. D. dissertation, University of Toronto.

———, Sarah Cummins, David Heap, Terry Nadasdi & Yves Roberge. 1992. "Cliticisation morphologique ou catégories fonctionnelles?". *Proceedings of the 1992 Annual Meeting of the Canadian Linguistics Association,* ed. by Carrie Dyck, Jila Ghomeshi, and Tom Wilson, 29-42. Toronto: Toronto Working Papers in Linguistics.

Bonet, Eulàlia. 1991. *Morphology After Syntax: Pronominal Clitics in Romance.* Ph.D. dissertation, MIT.

———. 1994. "The Person-Case Constraint: A Morphological Approach". *MIT Working Papers in Linguistics* 22. *The Morphology-Syntax Connection,* 33-52.

———. 1995a. "The Feature Structure of Romance Clitics". *Natural Language and Linguistic Theory* 13.607-617.

———. 1995b. "The Where and How of Clitic Ordering". *Revue québecoise de linguistique* 24/1.61-81.

Chomsky, Noam. 1993. "A Minimalist Program for Linguistic Theory". *The View from Building 20,* ed. by Ken Hale & Samuel J. Keyser. Cambridge, Mass.: MIT Press.

Cummins, Sarah, & Yves Roberge 1994. "Romance Inflectional Morphology In and Out of Syntax". *MIT Working Papers in Linguistics* 22. *The Morphology-Syntax Connection.* 53-70.

Dinnsen, Daniel. 1972. "Additional Constraints on Clitic Order in Spanish". *Generative Studies in Romance Languages* ed. by B. Saciuk and J. Casagrande, 175-183. Rowley, MA: Newbury House.

García Martínez, Ginés. 1986 (1960). *El habla de Cartagena: palabras y cosas (Notas para el estudio del castellano vulgar actual y de la propagación del aragonés y del catalán por el Sur).* Murcia: Universidad de Murcia.

Harris, James. 1994. "The Syntax-phonology Mapping in Catalan and Spanish clitics". *MIT Working Papers in Linguistics,* ed. by A. Carnie & H. Harley, 21.321-353.

———. 1996. "The Morphology of Spanish Clitics". *Evolution and Revolution in Linguistic Theory: Essays in Honor of Carlos Otero,* ed. by Héctor Campos & Paula Kempchinsky. Washington D.C., Georgetown University Press.

Heap, David. 1995a. "The Morphophonological Interface: Optimalizing nonstandard Spanish Clitic Clusters". Paper given at *Canadian Linguistics Association Annual Meeting*, Université du Québec à Montréal.

———. 1995b. "Est-ce que la théorie de l'optimalité peut nous aider à évaluer les schèmes morphologiques?". Paper given at a Workshop on Postsyntactic Morphological Mechanisms, Department of French, University of Toronto.

———. 1996. "Variation, Optimality and Underspecification in some Iberian Clitic Sequences". Paper given at the *Grup de Gramàtica Teòrica,* Universitat Autònoma de Barcelona.

———, Silvana Mastromonaco, Terry Nadasdi, and Paul Bessler. 1993. "If a Template Fits...: Case Studies in Morphological Cliticization". *Proceedings of the Fourth Annual Canadian Workshop on Lexical-Syntactic Relations*, ed. by Carrie Dyck. *Toronto Working Papers in Linguistics* 12/1.109-124.

Hetzron, Robert. 1977. "Clitic Pronouns and Their Linear Representation". *Forum Linguisticum* 1.189-215.

Kayne, Richard. 1991. "Romance Clitics, Verb Movement, and PRO". *Linguistic Inquiry* 22.647-686.

Laenzlinger, Christopher. 1993. "A Syntactic View of Romance Pronominal Sequences". *Probus* 5.241-270.

Mascaró, Joan. 1986. *Morfologia*. Barcelona: Enciclopèdia catalana.

McCarthy, John. 1993. "Elements of Optimality Theory". Course notes.

——— & Alan Prince. 1993. "Generalized Alignment". Ms., University of Massachusetts at Amherst & Rutgers University.

Nadasdi, Terry. 1995. *Variation syntaxique et langue minoritaire: le cas du français ontarien.* Ph.D. disserttion, University of Toronto.

Nagy, Naomi. 1996. *Language Contact and Language Change in the Faetar Speech Community.* Ph.D. dissertation, University of Pennsylvania.

Nagy, Naomi, & Bill Reynolds (forthcoming). "Optimality Theory and Variable Word-Final Deletion in Faetar".

Perlmutter, David. 1971. *Deep and Surface Structure Constraints in Syntax.* New York: Holt, Rhinehart & Winston.

Prince, Alan & Paul Smolensky. 1993. "Optimality Theory: Constraint Interaction in Generative Grammar". Ms., Rutgers University & University of Colorado.

Real Academia Española. 1973. *Esbozo de una nueva gramática de la lengua española.* Madrid: Espasa-Calpe.

Reynolds, Bill & Hadass Sheffer. 1994. "Variation and Optimality". *University of Pennsylvania Working Papers in Linguistics* I.103-110.

——— & Naomi Nagy. 1994. "Phonological Variation in Faetar: An Optimality Account". *Chicago Linguistics Society* 30:2.

Szabo, Robert. 1974. "Constraints on Clitic Insertion in Spanish". *Linguistic Studies in Romance Languages*, ed. by R. Campbell, 124-138. Washington D.C.: Georgetown University Press.

Todolí, Júlia. *Aproximació a la sintaxi dels pronoms clitics catalans.* Ph.D. dissertation, Universitat de València.

Uriagereka, Juan. 1995. "Aspects of the Syntax of Clitic Placement in Western Romance". *Linguistic Inquiry* 26.79-123.

Wanner, Dieter. 1977. On the Order of Clitics in Italian". *Lingua* 42.101-128.

———. To appear. "El orden de los clíticos agrupados en castellano". *Thesaurus* 19.

THE DEVELOPMENT OF PROCLITICS AND ENCLITICS IN MIDDLE FRENCH[1]

KEN JOHNSON
Purdue University

In this paper I examine how the functional node Agr had a strong influence on the dissimilar grammaticalization patterns of Middle French (MidF) pre-verbal and post-verbal subject pronouns. I propose that the post-verbal subject pronouns grammaticalized more quickly than the pre-verbal variety because they had a closer relationship to Agr at a much earlier period. Section one is a brief outline of the subject pronouns and the basic sentence structure of Old French (OF) and MidF. In section two I review Vance's (1995a) analysis of OF post-verbal subject pronouns and embedded pre-verbal subject pronouns as syntactic clitics and her claim that the embedded subject pronouns decliticized in MidF. The divergent nature of this process and the structural changes associated with it provide an example of the types of factors which affect how a single item, in this case an atonic subject pronoun, may split into two elements which then proceed along different grammaticalization paths. A potential problem arises because decliticization implies a case of degrammaticalization, thus violating the principle which says that grammaticalization is a unidirectional process (Hopper and Traugott 1993). In section three I focus on Agr's role in the grammaticalization of the subject pronouns, making particular reference to Roberts' (1993) analysis of OF and MidF sentence structure.

1. *Subject pronouns in Old and Middle French*

First let's briefly look at the subject pronouns in OF. OF was a verb-second or V2 language, meaning only one constituent could precede the verb in matrix clauses. It also exhibited pro-drop tendencies because in cases of subject-verb

[1] My thanks go to Becky Brown, Robert Channon, Ronnie Wilbur, Mary Niepokuj and Victor Raskin for helpful comments on the structure and content of this paper. An earlier version was presented at a meeting of the Purdue Linguistics Group. Any and all mistakes are mine.

inversion, the subject pronoun was frequently, though not always, deleted as illustrated in the sentences in (1):

(1) Deletion of subject pronoun in subject-verb inversions (from Jensen 1990):

a. *a la cort furent ∅ venu*
to the court had (they) come
'They had come to the court.' (Erec et Enide)

b. *or revendrai∅ al pedre ed a la medre*
now shall-return (I) to-the father and to the mother
'now I shall return to the father and the mother.' (Saint Alexis)

At the same time, they could also be emphasized, coordinated with other pronouns as in (2a), modified by adjectives or relative clauses as in (2b), or separated from the verb as in (2c) (de Lage 1966, Jensen 1990):

(2) Examples of constructions using tonic subject pronouns (from Jensen 1990):

a. coordinated subject pronouns
*et **je** et **tu** avrons Rome a tenir*
and I and you will-have Rome to keep
'and you and I will have Rome to keep.' (La Couronnement de Louis)

b. subject pronoun modified by a relative clause:
*mes **je**, qui sui dehors le mur*
but I who am outside the wall
'but I who am outside the wall' (Le Roman de la Rose)

c. subject pronoun separated from verb
***je** meïsmes cil Yvain sui*
I myself that Yvain am
'I am that Yvain in person.' (Yvain)

In early OF, matrix clauses with non-subject constituents in first position were more common (Marchello-Nizia 1995), but by the late OF period subject pronouns were beginning to fill the pre-verbal slot more frequently and appearing in contexts where they were neither emphatic nor tonic (Price 1971). Since the verb was still inflected for person and number, subject pronouns were not necessary to mark verbs in this way, leading some to suggest that they were being used as obligatory space fillers to prevent verb-initial sentences (Ashby 1977, M. Harris 1978, Jensen 1990). Subject-verb inversion and pro-drop were substantially less common in embedded clauses, where the order was typically CSpXV (where C is a complementizer and X is some non-subject constituent) (Zwanenburg 1978, Vance 1995a, Roberts 1993).

This question of the subject pronouns' atonicity and apparent space-filling function becomes all the more relevant when looking at the developments of MidF. For one thing, the tonic forms of subject pronouns were being used less frequently during this period. There was also a decrease in the incidence of subject-verb inversion and pro-drop along with an increased use of sentences with pre-verbal subject pronouns even if some other constituent preceded the subject. The basic schematic change is illustrated in (3a) (where X may be a fronted adverbial or topicalized object. Parentheses indicate optionality). (Marchello-Nizia 1995, Zwanenburg 1978). Based on studies of six OF and MidF texts Vance (1995b) shows that inversions with subject pronouns after fronted constituents decreased from 97% in the mid 13th century to 15% in the late 15th century while those involving subject nouns remained relatively stable and highly frequent. The subject pronoun's position in embedded clauses also moved from being next to the complementizer (C) to being next to the verb as shown in (3b) (Vance 1995a).

(3) a. OF MidF
XV(Sp) → XSpV

b. OF MidF
CSpXV → CXSpV

By comparison, subject pronouns in ModF are obligatory pre-verbal phonological clitics. Subject-verb inversion may occur only in restricted contexts, particularly in interrogatives as either simple inversion involving just a pronoun as in (4a) or complex inversion involving both the noun and the pronoun as illustrated in (4b):

(4) a. *Connaissez-vous les parents de Françoise?*
know you the parents of Françoise
'Do you know Françoise's parents?'
b. *Paul travaille-t-il aujourd'hui?*
Paul_i work-he_i today
'Is Paul working today?'

These structures, leftover from processes occurring in MidF, include pronouns which have a unique syntactic status. The importance of these factors will become apparent as we proceed.

2. *Subject pronouns as syntactic clitics*

One important question here is how and when subject pronouns became clitics in French. The issue becomes more complex when we distinguish between syntactic and phonological clitics. Klavans (1985) focusses on this distinction as shown in (5):

(5)

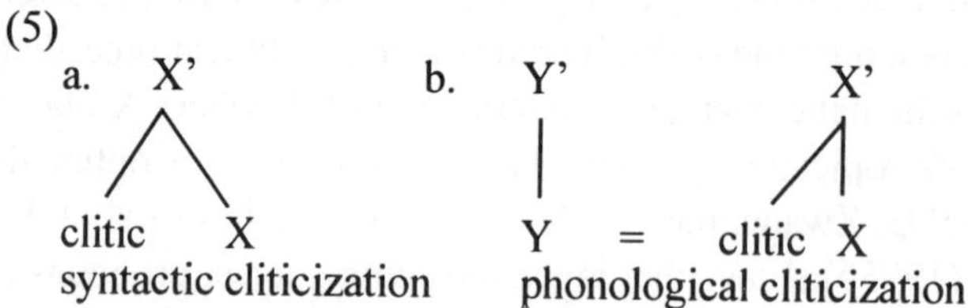

The clitic which is syntactically procliticized to X in (5a) is simultaneously phonologically encliticized to Y in (5b). The English possessive illustrates the difference between phonological and syntactic cliticization. In the sentence in (6) the clitic's phonological host is "to" (6a) the last word of the syntactic host noun phrase "The man whom I spoke to" (6b):

(6) The man whom I spoke to's wife is a doctor.
a. Phonological: The man whom I spoke to=s wife is a doctor
b. Syntactic: [NP The man whom I spoke to]=s wife is a doctor

In this case, cliticization is in the same direction for each type, but depending on the language, the two types of cliticization may or may not be in the same direction.

Vance (1995a) uses this hypothesis to argue that OF subject pronouns were phonological proclitics and syntactic enclitics in certain environments. As an example, Vance proposes that in embedded clauses such as in (7), the subject pronoun was syntactically encliticized to the complementizer containing "com" and phonologically procliticized to "es":

(7)	*Si*	*com*	*j'es*	*livres*	*sui*	*lisant*
	just	as	I-in-the	books	am	reading

'just as I am reading in books' (Chronique des Ducs de Normandie).

I will leave aside the issue of phonological cliticization for now. As for syntactic cliticization, Vance concludes that post-verbal subject pronouns in matrix clauses and pre-verbal subject pronouns in embedded clauses were syntactically cliticized to the complementizer slot C, the head of CP. She follows a common analysis of V/2 structures by claiming that in cases of inversion, such as in example (8), the verb had to move to C whenever any non-subject constituent was placed in Spec CP:

(8) a. (Vance's ex. 11)
Et *lors* *oste* ***il*** *son* *hiaume*
and then removes he his helmet
'and then he removes his helmet' (Queste 89, 15)
b. [CP lors [C' oste$_i$+il [AgrP [Agr' t_i [VP [V' t_i son hiaume]]].

Vance points out that in the case of OF, the obligatory placement of the pronoun next to the verb contrasts to the separation of a lexical noun from the verb in a similar inversion structure as shown in (9):

(9) (Vance's ex. 12a)
car cele aventure ne voult onques mes ***nus hom*** *achever...*
for this adventure neg wanted ever more no man to-accomplish
'for no man ever wanted to accomplish this mission...' (Queste 10, 9).

Embedded clauses, such as in (10), typically contained the order SpXV with the subject pronoun next to the complementizers:

(10) (Vance's ex. 4a)
que ***tu*** *cel* *cheval* *me* *prestes*
that you that horse to-me lend
'that you lend me that horse' (Queste 88, 33).

Once again, Vance contrasts this situation to a sentence containing a subject noun as in (11) where the subject noun is separated from the complementizer:

(11) (Vance's ex. 10a)
plus *que* *onques* ***fame*** *n'ama* *home*
more than ever woman neg-loved man
'more than woman ever loved man' (Queste 181, 4).

Vance proposes that the pre-verbal atonic subject pronouns in matrix clauses were only phonological clitics based on the assumption that C was not activated because matrix SVO sentences were AgrP or IP sentences as illustrated in (12a). This structure contrasts with a strict V2 analysis of SVO where the subject would move to Spec CP and the verb to C as illustrated in (12b) (cf. Adams 1987, Roberts 1993):

(12) a. [IP SVO]
b. [CP S_i [Vj [IP t_i t_j O]]].

In effect, Vance says that there was no host for syntactic cliticization in SVO sentences. For this reason, she proposes the condition in (13) which only includes cases of inversion and embedded clauses:

(13) Subject pronouns in OF must be syntactically enclitic to C, whenever a CP is projected.

Let's consider now the types of subject pronouns in OF based on Vance's analysis. Basically, it seems there were three types which are listed in (14):

(14) a Tonic subject pronouns which are totally independent and thus not clitics.
b. Pre-verbal subject pronouns in matrix clauses which are phonological clitics.
c. Post-verbal subject pronouns and embedded pre-verbal subject pronouns which are phonological and syntactic clitics.

Vance (1995a) claims that in the MidF period, the subject pronouns of embedded clauses decliticized from the C node and shifted towards the verb as in example (15) after the C node lost the capacity to act as a host:

(15) 13th century (Sp X V)
que ***tu*** *cel cheval me prestes*
that you that horse to-me lend
'that you lend me that horse' (Questes)

15th century (X Sp V)
que son seel et sa lettre ***il*** *advouoit*
that his seal and his letter he affirmed
'that he affirmed his seal and his letter' (Jehan de Saintr_)

The post-verbal subject pronouns apparently remained syntactically cliticized, although as we shall see, the host changed. The loss of the tonic subject pronouns left two types of subject pronouns as listed in (16):

(16) a. Pre-verbal subject pronouns in matrix and subordinate clauses which were phonological proclitics.

b. Post-verbal subject pronouns which were syntactic clitics and which were further restricted in where they could occur.

In effect, the decliticization of the subject pronouns in embedded clauses is more the result of a change in the nature of the host rather than in the nature of the pronoun itself.

From this point pre-verbal and post-verbal subject pronouns developed along different paths. By the end of the MidF period (the 16th century) pre-verbal subject pronouns were mostly, if not totally, atonic whether in matrix or embedded clauses, but here I am going to concentrate on the behavior of those of embedded clauses. Phonologically, they were already cliticized to whatever followed and apparently maintained this status. Syntactically, according to Vance's analysis, they decliticized. In this case, however, the decliticization was not the result of any changes in the subject pronoun's properties. Rather, it was more the result of changes in the complementizer node's properties.

The post-verbal subject pronouns, however, subsequently grammaticalized syntactically and phonologically even further as can be seen by the development of complex inversion beginning in the 15th century and the interrogative marker "ti" found in colloquial registers as early as the 16th century (Roberts 1993, M. Harris 1978). Modern French complex inversion, already exemplified in (4b), is restricted to interrogative structures and is the only context in the standardized language where a subject noun and pronoun may simultaneously be contiguous to the verb. Although differing on the details, Rizzi and Roberts (1989), (repeated in Roberts (1993)), Kayne (1983) and Zribi-Hertz (1994) claim that in this structure, the subject pronoun is an expletive generated somewhere in AgrP and syntactically distinct from pre-verbal subject pronouns which are generated in Spec VP, the base subject position, and moved to Spec AgrP.

The historically related interrogative marker "ti" could be suffixed to verbs regardless of the person or number as illustrated in example (17):

(17) Examples of use of interrogative element "-ti" (Foulet 1921: 278):

a. *Tu* *les* *avais* *ti* *vus?*
You them had ti seen
'Had you seen them?'

b. *vous* *vendez* *ti* *de* *la* *moutarde?*
you sell ti some the mustard
'Do you sell any mustard?'

This suffix was apparently still prevalent in the provincial (non-Parisian) popular language of central and eastern France in the early half of the 20th century (Foulet 1921), and continues to be used in some form in Canadian French dialects. M. Harris (1978) says that it began developing from interrogative inversion structures in the 15th century as a means to avoid using inversion in questions in conformity with SVO order. OF third person forms such as "aime il" began inserting a voiceless dental stop in analogy with other verbs already having this consonant such as "dort-il" (sleep-he "is he sleeping") or "est-il" (is-he) as illustrated in (18):

(18)	*aime il*	[ɛm il]>*aime-t-i*[ɛmtil]	likes-he	'does he like?'
	dort-il	[doʁtil]	sleep-he	'is he sleeping?'
	est-il	[etil]	is-he	'is he?'

At some point this form was further reduced to [ti]. Roberts (1993) proposes that this element was located in Agr, which would make sense considering its inflectional nature.

3. *Syntactic changes and grammaticalization in Middle French*

The divergent developments of the preverbal and postverbal subject pronouns present a situation where two segments originating from the same source subsequently followed different paths of grammaticalization. In this section I will examine how changes in MidF sentence structure affected this process. I am using grammaticalization in the sense of C. Lehmann's (1985) set of synchronically oriented grammaticalization parameters based primarily on the notion of *autonomy*. As a segment grammaticalizes, it loses its autonomy both paradigmatically (*what* elements it may combine with) and syntagmatically (*how* it may combine with other elements). Paradigmatically, a strongly grammaticalized form has lost semantic and phonological substance, has become part of a paradigm, and has become obligatory and the only choice where previously there were several. Syntagmatically, a strongly grammaticalized form may only connect to a very limited set of items, has become more closely bonded to whatever it attaches to, thus losing syntactic and morphological boundaries, has lost its independent semantic identity, and has been fixed in one spot. ModF subject pronouns for example have lost paradigmatic autonomy by becoming part of the verb's paradigm since they are the primary indicator of person and number; by becoming obligatory whenever the noun is not present; and by being the only choice of replacements for lexical nouns (as opposed to null-subjects as in OF). The fact that they are phonological clitics fixed in a pre-verbal position shows how they have lost syntagmatic autonomy since the OF period when there were tonic varieties which were mobile and able to combine with other types of constituents.

One potential problem comes from Vance's (1995a) conclusion that the subject pronouns in embedded clauses "decliticized" when the C node could no longer serve as a host. A clitic by definition is dependent; therefore, if an item decliticizes, it becomes independent and an apparent case of degrammaticalization. The decliticization of these particular subject pronouns, however, was the result of syntactic changes and not changes in the pronoun itself. Furthermore, the post-verbal subject pronouns did not undergo a similar process. On the contrary, they grammaticalized even further as can be seen in the development of expletive subject pronouns in complex inversion and the interrogative marker "-ti" in the colloquial language. It would seem, therefore, that the preverbal and postverbal subject pronouns were either different types of clitics or had different influences on their development.

Although the dissimilar fate of the post-verbal subject pronouns suggest other factors were involved in their grammaticalization, these factors may be related to the same syntactic changes going on at the time. Roberts (1993) provides an account of these syntactic changes in terms of verb movement, incorporation, case checking and pro-drop theory. He assumes that as a V2 language, OF had matrix CP sentences (see example 12) even in sentences with SVO order. The verb moved to Agr to get agreement features, and then the Agr-Verb combination moved to C. I will not go into detail about how this movement was motivated except to say that Roberts bases his claim on incorporation theory. The important point is that this movement occurred because of certain properties in Agr and in C. In embedded clauses, a complementizer filled the C node, so the verb could go no further than Agr.

As for case checking and pro-drop licensing, Roberts proposes that OF subject nouns and pronouns had a nominative case feature [F] which had to be checked by Agr either by Spec-head agreement (as in 19a) or by government (as in 19b).

(19)

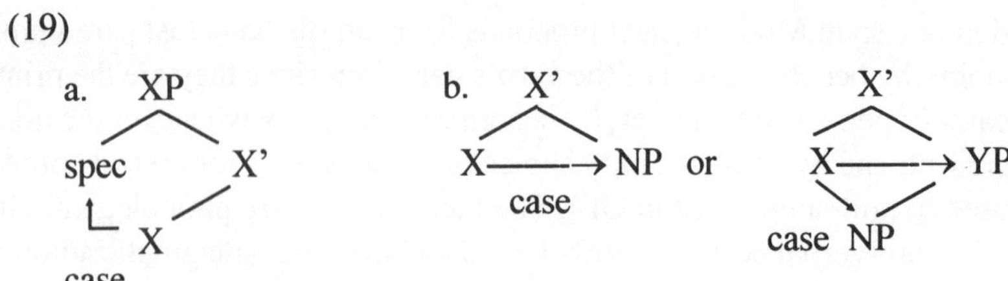

Roberts' modified version of Rizzi's (1986) licensing conditions on pro, repeated in (20), says that pro's licenser dominates or case-marks it, and provides it with content features:

(20) a. If X licenses *pro* in configuration Y, then X either dominates or is a potential Case-marker of *pro*'s position in Y (formal licensing)
b. *Pro* has the grammatical features of its licensing head X (content licensing).

Pro-drop licensing in OF apparently occurred only by government since the subject pronouns in Spec AgrP could be deleted only when Agr-V moved leftward into C in subject-verb inversion.

The loss of CP sentences in MidF was a major factor in how post-verbal subject pronouns subsequently grammaticalized. According to Roberts subject-verb inversions involving pronouns decreased in MidF because Agr-V stopped moving to C when people began reanalyzing CP sentences as AgrP sentences as illustrated in (21):

(21) [CP NP$_i$ [C' V+Agr$_j$ [AgrP t$_i$ [Agr' t$_j$...→
[AgrP NP$_i$ [Agr' V+Agr...

Vance (1995b) corroborates this analysis by showing that inversions with subject nouns, which do not rely on verb movement, were not affected in the same way. Roberts also proposes that the loss of case checking by government meant the loss of rightward pro licensing which at that time depended on case checking by government. Like Vance (1989) he proposes that null subjects in MidF were probably pre-verbal and depended partly on a weakening Agr and a decreasing set of verbal inflections.

These changes occurred mostly in the syntax. The changes in the pronouns themselves may involve Roberts' nominative feature [F]. He proposes that pronouns lost this feature before the 15th century. As a result, case checking by any means was no longer possible since there was no feature to check. The subject pronouns then began to incorporate by adjunction to Agr in order to gain case. Such an incorporation, he claims, was necessary for the development of complex inversion, one of few exceptional cases of Agr-V movement to C in ModF. This incorporation might also explain the further development of the interrogative marker "-ti" which Roberts claims was located in Agr. Since the semantically weakened pronoun was already in Agr, further grammaticalization to being an inflectional element would not be an extreme move.

It is clear, however, that the pre-verbal and post-verbal subject pronouns developed quite differently. For one thing, according to Vance (1995a), post-verbal subject pronouns were the only ones to remain syntactically cliticized after the shift from Old to MidF, and with the loss of subject-verb inversion, they no longer had much syntactic support except in special contexts such as questions. In fact, the modern colloquial language tends to use very few if any inversion structures, relying instead on question words and intonation patterns. The interrogative marker "-ti", which persists in Canadian French dialects, seems to be the last remnant of enclitics in the colloquial language. Furthermore, Roberts claims that as syntactic clitics, the post-verbal pronouns were incorporating into Agr in C before the pre-verbals had to with the loss of the case feature. Even if the post-verbals were not getting case by incorporation that early, they still obviously had a special relation to C which the subject pronouns in embedded clauses apparently did not have. The next question then is what did the C in inversion structures have that those of embedded clauses did not? By definition, the C node in inversions had Agr-V. For this reason, I would propose that even in OF, post-verbal subject pronouns were even more closely tied to C than the pre-verbal subject pronouns of embedded clauses. When the C node was no longer available, the post-verbal subject pronouns merely latched on to Agr itself, eventually becoming the expletive pronoun of complex inversion and the interrogative marker "-ti" in the spoken language. The embedded subject pronouns of OF did not undergo the same type of grammaticalization because the complementizer did not have the same type of relationship with the pronouns that Agr did and still does. The embedded subject pronouns did not stay close to C because there was nothing else holding them there once this node lost whatever feature allowed it to act as a host.

What does all this mean in terms of grammaticalization? After the loss of C as a host, the post-verbal subject pronouns began to undergo strong grammaticalization in several ways. According to Roberts' analysis of complex inversion, they had lost some of their referential properties as early as the 15th century since they were expletives and the subject noun was also present. The related development of the interrogative marker "-ti" in the 16th century shows a loss of paradigmatic variability in that the choice among subject pronouns expressing three persons in singular and plural was reduced to a form based on the third person singular "il". The fact that it was used strictly as an interrogative marker with no indication of person, number or semantic role implies a complete loss of the semantic properties they had as pronouns at an earlier stage.

The pre-verbal subject pronouns did not grammaticalize to quite the same extent, but they were already becoming phonological clitics in OF. The complete loss of tonic forms in MidF shows further evidence of phonological attrition. Their syntactic status in MidF, however, remains unclear. Roberts' claim that they incorporated into Agr could mean they became syntactic clitics with Agr as a host. Such an analysis is possible for two reasons. First, they became obligatory and part of the verb's paradigm since they were the primary markers of person and number. Second, recent analyses of the spoken language indicate that the subject pronouns have further reduced to the point of becoming prefixed agreement markers on the verb, marking the role of the subject noun which is topicalized through left or right displacement (Lambrecht 1981, M. Harris 1985, Matthews 1988, Zribi-Hertz 1994). The following example comes from Lambrecht:

(22) Examples of left (a) and right (b) displacement structures in spoken French

a. *Ces Romains ils sont fous*
These Romans they are crazy
"These Romans are crazy."

b. *Ils sont fous, ces Romains.*

Subject pronouns as agreement markers have less autonomy than clitics since they are more closely bound to the verb, having entered its morphological structure. This phenomenon indicates that they are inflections or agreement features found in Agr. As such, they have followed the same basic path as the post-verbal subject pronouns by moving closer to and then becoming part of Agr. In any case, they became a part of the verb's paradigm since they became the primary indicator of person and number in ModF. Furthermore, they have subsequently entered into the verb's morphological structure in the spoken language by becoming prefixed agreement markers.

4. *Conclusion*

I have proposed that Agr may have had a crucial role in determining how the OF enclitics went along separate paths of grammaticalization in MidF. The post-verbal subject pronouns encliticized to C may have developed an early relationship to Agr because of incorporation in OF and so grammaticalized more quickly at an earlier stage. The pre-verbal subject pronouns did not grammaticalize at the same rate, but they may have attached to Agr at some later time, particularly in the spoken language.

REFERENCES

Adams, Marianne. 1987. "From Old French to the Theory of Pro-Drop". *Natural Language and Linguistic Theory* 5.1-32.

———. 1989. "Verb Second Effects in Medieval French". *Studies in Romance Linguistics* ed. by Carl Kirschner & Janet Decesaris, 1-31. Amsterdam: John Benjamins.

Ashby, William J. 1977. *Clitic Inflection in French: An Historical Perspective.* Amsterdam: Editions Rodopi N.V.

Bailard, Joelle. 1982. "Le Français de demain: VSO ou VOS?" *Papers from the Fifth International Conference on Historical Linguistics*, ed. by Anders Ahlqvist, 20-28. Amsterdam: John Benjamins.

Baker, Mark. 1988. *Incorporation: A Theory of Grammatical Function Changing.* Chicago: Univ. of Chicago Press.

Brunot, Ferdinand. 1966. *Histoire de la Langue Française des origines à nos jours.* Vol. 1. Paris: Librairie Armand Colin.

de Lage, Guy Raynaud. 1966. *Introduction à l'Ancien Français.* Paris: Sedes.

Einhorn, E. 1974. *Old French: A Concise Handbook.* Cambridge: Cambridge University Press.

Foulet, Lucien. 1921. "Comment ont évolué les formes de l'interrogation?" *Romania* 47.243-348.

Harris, Martin. 1978. *The Evolution of French Syntax: A Comparative Approach.* New York: Longman.

———.1985. "Divergent Patterns of Word Order Change in Contemporary French". *Papers from the Sixth International Conference on Historical Linguistics* ed. by Jacek Fisiak, 235-49. Amsterdam: John Benjamins.

Hopper, Paul J. & Traugott, Elizabeth. 1993. *Grammaticalization.* Cambridge: Cambridge Univ. Press.

Jensen, Frede. 1990. *Old French and Comparative Gallo-Romance Syntax.* Tübingen: Max Niemeyer Verlag.

Kayne, Richard. 1983. "Chains, Categories External to S, and French Complex Inversion". *Natural Language and Linguistic Theory* 1:1.107-139.

Klavans, Judith L. 1985. "The independence of Syntax and Phonology in Cliticization". *Language* 61:1. 95-120.

Lambrecht, Knud. 1981. *Topic, Antitopic and Verb Agreement in Nonstandard French.* Amsterdam: John Benjamins.

Lehmann, Christian. 1985. "Grammaticalization: Synchronic Variation and Diachronic Change". *Lingua e Stile* 20:3.303-318.

———.1986. "Grammaticalization and Linguistic Typology". *General Linguistics* 26.3-22.

Marchello-Nizia, Christina 1995. *L'Evolution du français: Ordre des mots, démonstratifs, et accent tonique.* Paris: Armand Colin.

Matthews, Stephen J. 1988. "French in Flux: Typological Shift and Sociolinguistic Variation". *Synchronic and Diachronic Approaches to Linguistic Variation and Change* ed. by Thomas J. Walsh, 188-203. Georgetown University Round Table on Languages and Linguistics 1988. Washington, D.C.: Georgetown University Press.

Price, Glanville. 1971. *The French Language: Present and Past.* London: Edward Arnold Ltd.

Rizzi, Luigi. 1986. "Null Objects in Italian and the theory of *pro*". *Linguistic Inquiry* 17.501-557.

——— and Roberts, Ian. 1989. "Complex Inversion in French". *Probus* 1.1-30.

Roberts, Ian. 1993. *Verbs and Diachronic Syntax.* Dordrecht: Kluwer Academic Publishers.

Skårup, Povl. 1975. *Les Premières zones de la proposition en ancien français*. Copenhagen: Akademisk Forlag.

Vance, Barbara. 1989. "The Evolution of Pro-drop in Medieval French". *Studies in Romance Linguistics* ed. by Carl Kirschner & Janet Decesaris, 413-441. Amsterdam: John Benjamins.

———. 1995a. "On the Clitic Nature of Subject Pronouns in Medieval French". Paper given at *CLS 31 Parasession on Clitics.*

———. 1995b. "On the Decline of Verb Movement to Comp in Old and Middle French". *Clause Structure and Language Change* ed. by Adrian Battye & Ian Roberts, 173-199. New York: Oxford University Press.

Zribi-Hertz, Anna. 1994. "The Syntax of Nominative Clitics in Standard and Advanced French". *Paths Towards Universal Grammar: Studies in Honor of Richard S. Kayne* ed. by Guglielmo Cinque, Jan Loster, Jean-Yves Pollock, Luigi Rizzi and Raffaella Zenuttini. Washington D.C.: Georgetown Univ. Press.

Zwanenburg, Wiecher. 1978. "L'ordre des mots en Français Médiéval". *Etudes de Syntaxe du Moyen Français* ed. by Robert Martin, 153-171. Metz: Centre d'Analyze Syntaxique de l'Univ. de Metz.

LICENSING AND IDENTIFICATION OF NULL CATEGORIES IN SPANISH NON-NATIVE GRAMMARS*

JUANA M. LICERAS, BIANA LAGUARDIA,
ZARA FERNÁNDEZ, RAQUEL FERNÁNDEZ
University of Ottawa
&
LOURDES DÍAZ
Universitat Pompeu Fabra

1. *Introduction*

In this paper we incorporate recent reformulations of the null-argument parameter to provide a competence account of null subjects in the Spanish non-native grammars of speakers of Indo-European and Oriental languages. Central to the proposals are: 1) the need to refer to three different levels of structure (VP, IP and CP) as the locus for licensing, and 2) the identification requirements. Assuming that adult L2 learners access UG principles (directly or via L1) but do not reset parameters, and assuming that licensing is related to parametrization, we would like to argue that non-native null arguments are not sensitive to licensing requirements but only to identification principles.

We will show that: a) the distribution of null and subject pronouns in advanced intermediate and beginning speakers from Indo-European and Oriental languages is similar and does resemble the distribution in native Spanish; b) a qualitative analysis shows that there is non-native usage of pronominal subjects, that the distribution of null subjects originates non-native ambiguity and that there are morphological mismatches, all of which leads us to propose that

* A previous version of this paper was presented at the XXVI Linguistic Symposium on Romance Languages at UAM, Iztapalapa, March 28-30, 1996, Mexico City. We would like to thank the audience for helpful comments. We would also like to thank the Lycée Claudel for giving us access to the students who participated in the project, and very specially to Begoña Soloaga who has been instrumental at all stages. We would also like to thank the students at the Lycée Claudel and our own students for their collaboration. This research was supported with research grants from DGCYT (Spain), the Vice-Rectorship of the Universitat Pompeu Fabra (Barcelona, Spain), the Secretary of State for Multiculturalism (Canadian Heritage) of Canada, and the Faculty of Arts of the University of Ottawa (Canada).

non-native grammars are not sensitive to parametrized features but rather implement new L2 identification procedures which may co-exist with the L1's.

2. *Null arguments in adult language*

It has been systematically assumed that null arguments will occur provided they are licensed and identified (Rizzi 1986).

In languages such as Spanish and French licensing occurs at the level of Spec-IP and only in the case of subjects, as in (1) below.

(1) a. ___*estudian español (ellos)*
b. They study Spanish
c. *Ils étudient l'espagnol*

We will assume that this is due to the presence of a [+strong] feature in INFL, as shown in (2).

(2)

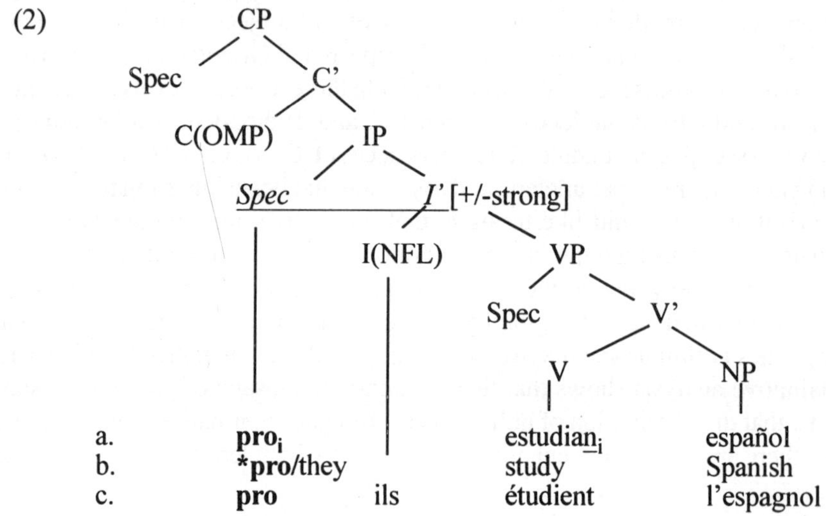

In Spanish, identification takes place through the f-features in AGR. In French, via the clitic subjects.[1] English does not licence pro due to the [-strong]

[1] Even though French has been traditionally analyzed as a [-pro-drop] language, strong arguments in favor of a [pro-drop] analysis have been put forward by Roberge (1986, 1990) and Authier (1992) among others.

feature. Huang (1984) argued that Chinese (the same can be said of Japanese and Korean) is a [pro-drop] language in spite of the fact that it lacks AGR entirely. According to Huang (1984) Chinese pro is licensed by a discourse-bound operator in the specifier of the root and identified by null topics. Thus INFL is not the only available licensing head.

3. *Null arguments in child language*

3.1. *Null constants*

In order to acount for null subjects in child grammars, Rizzi (1994) argues in favor of Hyams' (1986) original proposal that null subjects in child language are a genuine grammatical option and cannot be reduced to extragrammatical factors. Rather than comparing children's null subjects in English to null subjects in adult native Italian or Spanish, he maintains that early null subjects in English only appear in Spec-ROOT; namely, early English and French null subjects are said to present the following pattern:

a)They occur in matrix sentences such as (3)-(4).

(3) a. ___ want more
b. ___ is broken

(4) a. ___ *boit café*
b. ___ *est tombé*

b)They do not occur in *wh* questions such as (5), even though overt pronouns can appear post-verbally as in (6).

(5) *Where ___ go?

(6) Where he go?

This is not the pattern which is found in the adult or the child grammars of a null subject language such as Spanish, where the equivalent of (5) is possible, as shown in (7).

(7) *A dónde va* ___?

c) If the *wh* word appears *in situ,* null subjects are possible as in (8).

(8) a. ___ see what bear?
b. ___ have what?
c. ___ doing what?

d) Null subjects do not occur in embedded clauses as indicated in (9).

(9) a. ___ went in the basement #that what we do # after supper
b. ___ know what I maked

Since a similar pattern is found in the case of diaries (Haegeman 1990), Rizzi (1994) argues that these grammars do not implement the principle **ROOT=CP**. If a root sentence does not have to contain COMP, null subjects will be possible in the case of languages which do not allow them. However, Rizzi (1994) argues that it is a different type of null subject which is not pronominal (*we/pro*) but the empty option of a nominal, null constant (nc)—(*John and me/null constant*)-, which can occur when the CP projection is omitted as in (10).

(10)

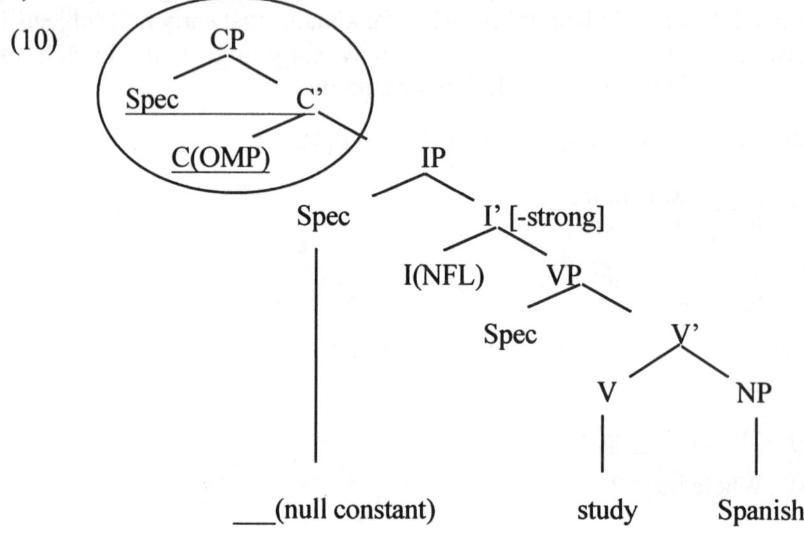

Following Lasnik and Stowell (1991), Rizzi (1994) argues that the null subject in (10) is not PRO or *t*, but a *null constant*, an empty category which is an R-expression with the features [-anaphoric], [-pronominal], [-variable], as shown in (11).

(11)

pro	[+pronominal] [-anaphoric]
PRO	[+pronominal] [+anaphoric]
NP-t	[-pronominal] [+anaphoric]
t	[-pronominal] [-anaphoric] [+variable]
n.c.	[-pronominal] [-anaphoric] [-variable]

3.2 *Subject-drop versus topic-drop languages*

From a somehow different and complementary perspective, Hyams (1994) proposes that the null argument parameter differentiates languages according to whether licensing of pro takes place at Spec-CP or at Spec-IP, as in (12)a and (12)b below.

(12) a. [topic-drop] (12) b. [pro-drop]

(12) a.: [CP **Spec** [C' C [IP Spec [I' I VP]]]]

(12) b.: [CP Spec [C' C [IP **Spec** [I' I VP]]]]

She assumes that pro accounts for null subjects both in topic-drop languages such as German and Dutch and in pro-drop languages such as Spanish. She does not attempt to justify her proposal and specifically states that she is not assuming that Chinese null arguments are also instances of pro.

In languages such as Chinese, arguments (subjects and objects) are licensed as in (12)a, and identified by discourse topics. In Spanish, licensing occurs at the level of Spec-IP—as in (12)b—and only in the case of subjects. Identification takes place through the f-features in AGR. German is a [topic-drop] language with pro licensed in Spec-CP under Spec-head agreement, thanks to the presence of V features in CP (the same as Dutch and other V2 languages). According to Hyams (1994), null subjects occur in colloquial German because they are identified by a discourse-identified operator. Null objects are also possible in German but only in the third person. Hyams (1994) and Rizzi (1994) provide different explanations for this phenomenon.[2]

In order to account for children's null subjects in English, Hyams (1994) proposes that they have pro in Spec-IP, the default position, where they can be licensed but not identified. Identification takes place by moving pro to topic

---

[2] There is no agreement with respect to the status of German null arguments. See Roeper and Rohrbacher (1995) for further comments on this topic.

position. Thus she proposes a hybrid explanation whereby licensing occurs as in Italian and identification as in German.

Even though Hyams (1994) does not relate licensing to the specific features of these functional categories, we will assume that this is the case. Specifically, we would like to propose that the [+strong] INFL features which differentiate English from Spanish and French in terms of V-movement (Pollock 1989) are also responsible for whether pro can be licensed or not, thus unifying French and Spanish in this respect (Roberge 1986, 1990). Consequently, in both French and Spanish, subjects will be licensed at Spec-I'. Identification will occur via the f-features in Spanish, and via the subject clitic pronouns in French, as in (2) above. Null subjects cannot be licensed in English. Within our framework, and probably Rizzi's (1994), German does not license pro because, unlike the Oriental languages, it does not have a [+] licensing feature in CP.

3.3 *Japanese-like pro*

Roeper and Rohrbacher (1995) argue that some null subjects which occur in early English cannot be Diary/Topic null subjects for at least two reasons: 1) Adam, one of the English speaking children in Brown's (1973) study, produces numerous wh-questions of the type illustrated in (5) above, as illustrated in (13); 2) Adam's data display a clear-cut distinction between finite and non-finite wh-questions (finite= modals, auxiliaries and -s marking).

(13) a. where go?
b. what doing?
c. why laughing at me?
d. what think

On the other hand, cases such as (14) have not been attested.[3]

(14) @where goes?

Consequently, they propose that these null subjects are instances of Japanese-like pro, which occurs because Japanese does not have an AgrSP projection as proposed by Speas (1994), whose account of the pro-drop parameter is illustrated in (15)a-c.

[3] We use @ rather than an asterisk (*) to indicate that a form has not been attested because, in the case of children's production data, it is not possible to declare a given sentence ungrammatical.

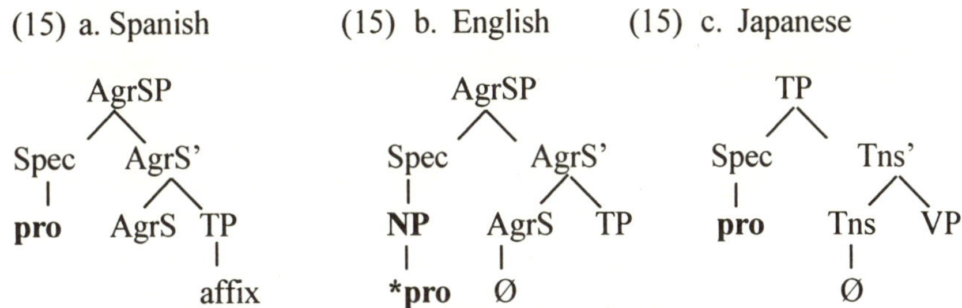

3.4 *Spec-VP pro*

Pierce (1992) proposes that a pro which is generated within the VP accounts for the occurrence of null subjects and verb subject inversion in early French and null subjects in early English. This pro does not move to Spec-I' category, which is projected already in the early grammar, and can license pro at Spec-VP, the default option according to Lebeaux (1988), as indicated in (16).

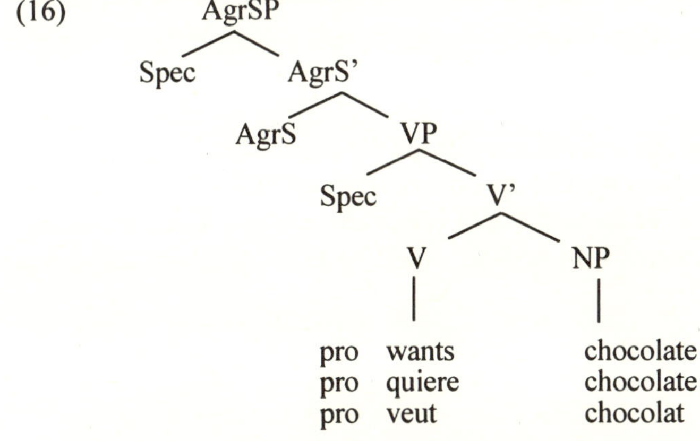

It is obvious that in order to accomodate child language and oriental languages within the null argument parameter, it is necessary to refer to different levels of structure and to the specific licensing feature located in a given category.

4. *Null subjects in non-native grammars*

From the above it is easy to infer that in order to account for null arguments in non-native grammars we have two options: 1) to dispense with the null argument parameter altogether; 2) to redefine the parameter as a subset of the V-movement super parameter (Pollock 1989, Chomsky 1992) in line with the proposal that parameters are to be defined as abstract features which are located in functional categories (Borer 1984, Lebeaux 1988, Chomksy 1992). We have opted for this second approach and for the proposal that there is a clear-cut difference between principles and parameters in linguistic theory so that adult L2 learners do not reset parameters.

4.1 *Re-structuring versus parameter resetting*

The possibility of access to UG but not resetting parameters is addressed in Tsimpli and Rousseau' s (1991) proposal concerning the nature of null subjects in the English IL of Greek speakers. They specifically propose that the grammatical representation which underlies a sentence such as (17) in the English IL contains a pro if the [+pro-drop] option of Greek is transferred, and PRO if the IL does not have the f-features which would account for the identification of pro.

(17) ___ live in Sitges (he)

Since both options (parametric transfer and the use of an empty category from the inventory provided by UG) are possible options for the L2 learner, the IL null argument may be an instance of either pro or PRO. Thus, according to Tsimpli and Rousseau, (18) or (19) would be possible grammatical representations for (17).

(18)

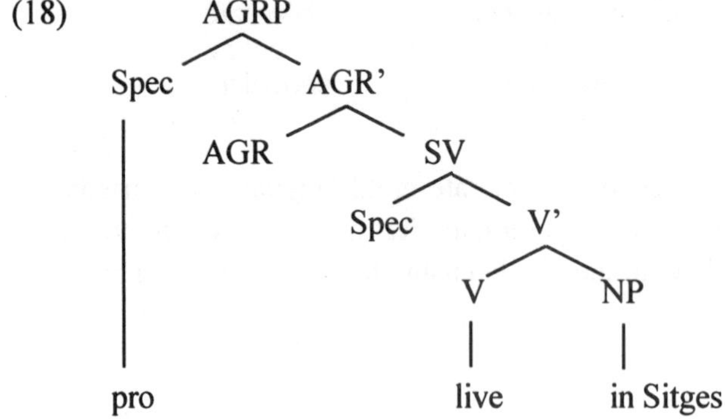

(19)

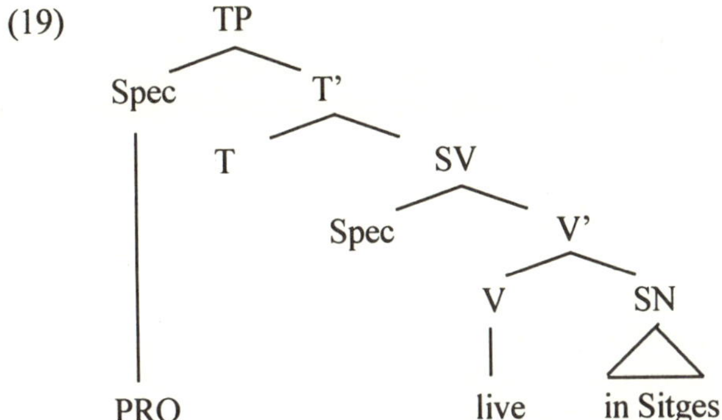

Since the [+pro-drop] option is supposed to be the only one available in the English IL of Greek speakers, examples such as (20), which occur at a more advanced stage, will not correspond to the native English grammatical representation in (21)a or the Spanish "equivalent" in (21)b.

(20) We eat a lot of fish

(21)

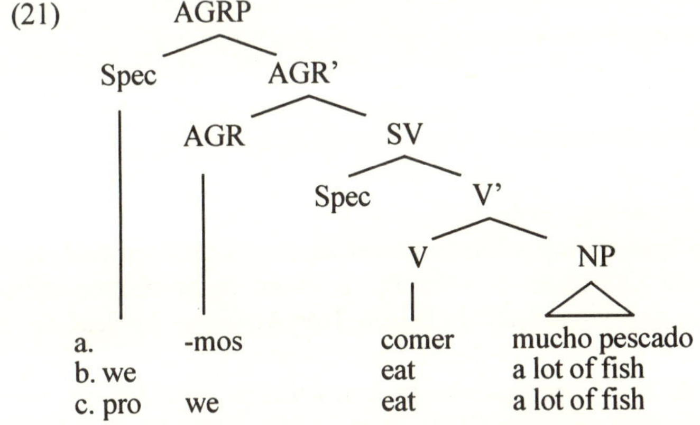

What Tsimpli and Rousseau (1991) actually propose is that a re-structuring process which consists of reanalyzing the L2 subject pronouns as f-features will create the IL representation shown in (21)c, so that both pro and the subject pronoun coexist. This grammatical representation is the one that accounts for the clitic nature of subject pronouns in French and other languages (Roberge 1986).

In the case of the Spanish non-native language, we have suggested (Liceras 1994) that evidence for the reanalysis of subject pronouns as AGR may come from sentences such as (22) which are systematically produced by some native speakers of Spanish.

(22) The girl *that she* is very nice

Torrego (personal communication) suggested that reanalysis could account for the fact that native speakers of [+pro-drop] languages systematically use *he* as the only third person pronoun. In fact, this would show that *he* does not have a referential value but an structural value.

4.2 *Non-native data*

We will discussed the results of two different sets of non-native Spanish data: 1) the spontaneous production of non-native speakers of Spanish from six different language backgrounds (Chinese, English, French, German, Korean, and Japanese). Sixteen advanced intermediate non-native speakers and three native speakers of Spanish were asked to tell a story based on one of their favorite movies. 2) Data obtained from an ongoing project (a longitudinal study) on the acquisition of Spanish by children, adolescents and adults in institutional settings. We will present data from the very first interview (50 hours of formal contact with Spanish); French/English bilingual speakers, only two of which are English dominant.

4.3 *Hypothesis I: null constants*

If non-native Spanish null subjects are instances of a null constant (Rizzi 1994), there should be a clear-cut difference between the production of null subjects in matrix and in embedded clauses. This would be the case for all non-native speakers, regardless of their L1 background.

If they transfer their L1 representation, a structure such as (10) will never be an option unless there is a simplification procedure (principle ROOT=CP) which resembles the one in the grammar of diaries (Haegeman 1990).

If we compare the production of null subjects in matrix and subordinate clauses for all non-native speakers, we come to the conclusion that these null arguments cannot be null constants: 1) tables I-IV for advanced intermediate show an almost even distribution of null subjects in matrix and subordinate clauses.

Table I
Advanced intermediate French speakers: production of null subjects in narratives

		Matrix	Subordinate	Total
F#1	pro	.43(19/44)	.37 (11/29)	.41 (30/73)
	s. pronoun	.11 (5/44)	.27 (8/29)	.17 (13/73)
F#2	pro	.50 (47/94)	.50 (15/30)	.50 (62/124)
	s. pronoun	.3 (3/94)	.06 (2/30)	.04 (5/124)
F#3	pro	.75 (62/82)	.74 (37/50)	.75 (99/132)
	s. pronoun	.02 (2/82)	—	.01 (2/132)

Table II
Advanced intermediate English speakers: production of null subjects in narratives

		Matrix	Subordinate	Total
E#1	null	.62 (15/24)	.52 (10/19)	.58 (25/43)
	s. pronoun	.12 (3/24)	—	.06 (3/43)
E#2	null	.28 (15/52)	.20 (1/5)	.28 (16/57)
	s. pronoun	.03 (2/52)	.20 (1/5)	.05 (3/57)
E#3	null	.56 (14/25)	.44 (11/25)	.50 (25/50)
	s. pronoun	—	.12 (3/25)	.06 (3/50)

Table III
Advanced intermediate German speakers: production of null subjects in narratives

		Matrix	Subordinate	Total
G#1	null	.50 (16/32)	.53 (8/15)	.51 (24/47)
	s. pronoun	—	.06 (1/15)	.02 (1/47)
G#2	null	.47 (17/36)	.38 (7/18)	.44 (24/54)
	s. pronoun	.19 (7/36)	.33 (6/18)	.24 (13/54)
G#3	null	.45 (9/20)	.33 (3/9)	.41 (12/29)
	s. pronoun	.05 (1/20)	—	.03 (1/29)

Table IV
Advanced intermediate Chinese, Japanese and Korean speakers: production of null subjects and subject pronouns in narratives

		Matrix	Subordinate	Total
Ch#1	null	—	.30 (3/10)	.30 (3/13)
	s. pronoun	—	.10 (1/10)	.07 (1/13)
Ch#2	null	.65 (39/60)	.56 (26/46)	.61 (65/106)
	s. pronoun	.05 (3/60)	.15 (7/46)	.09 (10/106)
Ch#3	null	.60 (12/20)	.60 (3/5)	.60 (15/25)
	s. pronoun	—	—	.0 (0/25)
J#1	null	.45 (29/64)	.34 (9/26)	.42 (38/90)
	s. pronoun	.19 (12/64)	.26 (7/26)	.21 (19/90)
J#2	null	.37 (26/70)	.57 (11/19)	.41 (37/89)
	s. pronoun	.45 (32/70)	.10 (2/19)	.38 (34/89)
J#3	null	.57 (19/33)	.40 (6/15)	.52 (25/48)
	s. pronoun	.15 (5/33)	.26 (4/15)	.18 (9/48)
K#1	null	.33 (8/24)	.50 (7/14)	.39 (15/38)
	s. pronoun	.12 (3/24)	.14 (2/14)	.13 (5/38)

2) same in the case of bilingual English/French beginners as shown in tables V-VI.

Table V
Beginning French/English speaking adults: production of null subjects and subject pronouns in interviews

		Matrix	Subordinate	Total
UB1	*null	.81 (36/44)	.92 (12/13)	.84 (48/57)
	s. pronoun	—	—	—
UB2	null	.34 (19/55)	.100 (7/7)	.42 (26/62)
	s. pronoun	.16 (9/55)	—	.14 (9/62)
UB3	null	.77 (37/48)	.100 (8/8)	.80 (45/56)
	s. pronoun	.06 (3/48)	—	.06 (3/48)
UB4	null	.58 (21/36)	.80 (4/5)	.60 (25/41)
	s. pronoun	—	.20 (1/5)	.20 (1/5)
UB5	null	.50 (17/34)	.66 (4/6)	.52 (21/40)
	s. pronoun	.08 (3/34)	.33 (2/6)	.12 (5/40)
UB6	null	.65 (32/49)	.71 (5/7)	.66 (37/56)
	s. pronoun	—	—	—

3) The data from the early IL of Chinese, Japanese and Korean speakers have not been quantified yet. We can already say that we have not come across subordinate clauses but that there are instances of wh-questions with null subjects, as indicated in 23.

(23) a. *¿dónde___ eres?*
b. *¿dónde___ vives?*

The fact that the English subjects (Table II), one of the English dominant subjects (Table VI) and two German subjects produced more null subjects in the matrix clauses does not provide evidence for a null constant analysis because several oriental speakers also did, as well as one of the native speakers. And, what is more compelling, the percentage of null subjects in embedded clauses is significant in all cases.

Table VI
Beginning French/English speaking adolescents: production of null subjects and subject pronouns in interviews

		Matrix	Subordinate	Total
SC1	*null	.27 (13/48)	.14 (4/27)	.22 (17/75)
	s. pronoun	.14 (7/48)	.29 (8/27)	.20 (15/75)
SC2	null	.71 (33/46)	.100 (6/6)	.75 (39/52)
	s. pronoun	.08 (4/46)	—	.08 (4/46)
SC4	null	.79 (41/52)	.87 (7/8)	.80 (48/60)
	s. pronoun	.03 (2/52)	—	.03 (2/52)
SC5	null	.46 (15/32)	.100 (2/2)	.50 (17/34)
	s. pronoun	.21 (7/32)	—	.21 (7/32)
SC6	null	.30 (12/40)	.50 (1/2)	.40 (13/42)
	s. pronoun	.10 (4/40)	—	.10 (4/40)

4.4 *Hypothesis II: AgrSP*

If non-native Spanish null subjects are instances of Japanese-like pro (Roeper and Rohrbacher 1995), there should be a clear-cut distinction between the production of null subjects in finite and non-finite clauses, and we would not find instances of wh-questions with an inflected verb such as (14) above. This would also be the case for all non-native speakers.

a) All subjects produced verbs with f-features (at least four different markers). There are some cases of lexical pronouns with infinitives (beginners) such as the one in (28). This could indicate that AgrSP is projected.

b) Even though there are null subjects in interrogatives such as (5), as shown in (23), they happen to be cases which were unattested in early English (14), because the verbs are inflected.

4.5 *Hypothesis III: VP internal pro and non-native identification principles*

A. Indo-European speakers. If pro is generated internal to VP, English, French and German speakers will transfer the AgrSP projection from their L1. This projection will license pro at the VP internal level (Pierce 1992, Lebeaux 1988). In the case of the adult language, movement to Spec-I' will take place because the f-features will have to be checked and it is at this point that parametric options will play a role. Namely, if L2 learners do not set parameters, English speakers should not allow pro because it is not licensed in their L1. French speakers will allow null subjects if they change the identifier.

Since Rizzi (1994) argues that null subjects in V2 languages such as colloquial German are also null constants, we could propose that the non-native grammar has null constants in the matrix clauses but, how do we explain the null arguments in the embedded clauses?

We could take Hyams's (1994) way out: pro (or any empty category) is always licensed. It is not a parametrized option. But we have not taken this approach because we believe that these properties are related to the V-movement parameter.

In fact, the data show that there seems to be a pro which, in quantitative terms, is not different from the one we find in native speakers production as indicated in Tables VII and VIII.

Table VII
Native Spanish speakers:
production of null subjects in narratives

		Matrix	Subordinate	Total
N#1	pro	.55 (24/43)	.58 (14/24)	.56 (38/67)
	s.pronoun	.11 (5/43)	.04 (1/24)	.08 (6/67)
N#2	pro	.50 (26/52)	.62 (15/24)	.53 (41/76)
	s. pronoun	.17 (9/52)	.04 (1/24)	.13 (10/76)
N#3	pro	.67 (50/74)	.61 (29/47)	.65 (79/121)
	s. pronoun	.14 (11/74)	.17 (8/47)	.15 (19/121)

Table VIII
Native Spanish speakers: production of null subjects and subject pronouns in interviews

		Matrix	Subordinate	Total
NC1	null	.68 (95/138)	.82 (29/35)	.71 (124/173)
	s. pronoun	.12 (17/138)	.08 (3/35)	.11 (20/173)
NC2	null	.67 (87/129)	.85 (23/27)	.70 (110/156)
	s. pronoun	.15 (20/129)	.03 (1/27)	.13 (21/156)
NC3	null	.57 (33/57)	.92 (13/14)	.64 (46/71)
	s. pronoun	.22 (13/57)	.07 (1/14)	.19 (14/71)

But a qualitative analysis shows a different picture:
1. Even though there is no overgeneration of subject pronouns, there is a non-native usage. For instance, many subject pronouns are redundant and, in the case of the French speakers, there are clitic pronouns used as identifiers such as the one in example (24).

(24) *me voy a hablar*

This seems to indicate that the identification system has not been switched yet.
2. Non-native usage of pronominal subjects is the pattern for all speakers: sentences such as those in (25) would not be produced by native speakers.

(25) a. *Y ellos son muy contentos porque ellos sonríen*
And they are very happy because they smile
b. *Ellos bailan porque es un contesto y ellos quieren...*
They dance because is a contest and they want
c. *"¿Por qué crees que son amigos?"*/ Why do you think they are friends?
Porque ellos danzan/ Because they dance

This is what is significant in terms of the differences between native and non-native competence. It is also significant that the patterns found in the case of subject-verb inversion are far from being native like (Liceras 1994, 1995),

which provides more evidence to argue that identification principles and wh-movement rather than licensing requirements guide L2 acquisition.
3. There are also morphological mismatches in the case of all speakers and they occur with null subjects, subject pronouns and nouns, indistinctly. The examples in (26) seem to indicate that they are checking the f-features for identification purposes, that they are creating a new identification system.

(26) a. *Y él... y la dic...* [UB5]
And he...and her say...
b. *yo habl-...yo habla... yo hablo, perdone*
I speak... I speak-... I speak- excuse me
(3rd. person sing) (1st. person sing.)[F# 2]

B) Oriental speakers. If AgrSP is not projected in the L1, as has been proposed for Japanese (Speas 1994)—and assuming that the same applies to Chinese and Korean—the adult non-native grammar of the Oriental speakers may or may not have an AgrSP projection, depending on the level of competence. This will be the case under the assumption that, unlike the [+/-] licensing features, projection of a given category is not a parameter setting mechanism. However, the presence of lexicalized f-features in a given IL may not necessarily evidence that AgrSP has been projected, since those features could be instances of an IL pronominal system (Liceras *et al.* forthcoming). Null topics will serve as identifiers until this identification procedure is replaced by the subject pronouns or the "new" pronominal system (the lexicalized f-features) which is being developed, as shown in (27) and (28).

(27) a. *...pinta, pin-, pintura*
b. *... cantando, cantar, cantan*
c. *...trabajo, trabaje, trabaja*
d. *...voy al...no, vas a la ofisina, va a la oficina*

(28) *ella...gustar el sol*

Evidence that the L1 identification procedure is alive comes from the cases of ambiguity created by the distribution of null subjects in examples such as those in (29).

(29) a. *Alex es un joven, ___ trabaja en la empresa de ropa, ___ no es muy grande y ____ es de su tío. ____Es bastante competente pero ___ no tiene mucho interés en su trabajo.* [J#1]

Alex is a young man, ____works in a clothing store,_____ is not too large and _____belongs to his uncle. _____is rather competent but ____is not too much interested in his work

b. *Cuando la cura rechaza su esposa, ___ se enfadó mucho* [K#1]
(Cuando el cura rechazó a su esposa, él se enfadó mucho)
When the priest rejects his/her/your wife ____got very upset

c. *El gatito le alegre mucho que ____ haga ganado al perro*[K#1]
(Al gatito le alegra mucho que su padre haya ganado al perro)
The little cat is very happy that ____ has won over the dog

It is interesting to point out that we have found only two cases of null objects in the IL of Oriental speakers (none in the case of Indo-European speakers) but we have found many cases of reduplication of object pronouns as in (30), something which does not occur in the IL of Indo-European speakers.

(30) a. *...y cuando él les visita a ellos...* [Ch-2]
and when he them visits them

b. *...sus hijos tenan que abandonarlos a los ancianos a un bosque* [J-1]
their children had to abandon them to the old people in the woods

c. *...no quiso abandonarla a ella en el bosque* [J-1]
3rd. p.s. did not want to abandon her to her in the woods

d. *...Por eso también lo quiere a Alex* [J-2]
that is why also him 3rd. p. sing. loves to Alex

e. *...A ella también lo quiere* [J-2]
to her also him 3rd. p. sing. love

This seems to show that they need the tonic pronouns as identifiers because the clitic system is not explicit enough or they may not have identified it as such.

5. *Conclusion*

We would like to conclude that: a) null subjects in these non-native grammars are neither null constants nor Japanese-like pros; b) the null subjects produced by our Indo-European speakers are instances of pro which is licensed at VP, the default level. This pro moves to Spec-IP to check features but is blind to the parametric feature which would prevent licensing of pro at this level. Identification proceeds via the subject pronouns, as in French, the f-features of the Spanish non-native grammar or both; c) the null subjects produced by our Oriental speakers are also licensed at the VP level and are checked at the Spec-CP level. Identification takes place via null topics, subject pronouns or f-features.

The implication of our proposal is that adult non-native grammars are idiosyncratic because they are not sensitive to features responsible for the parametrization of native grammars. The fact that non-native grammars are not instances of coherent parametric options, explains the presence of subject pronouns but not object pronouns in the IL of the speakers of [+topic-drop] languages. It also explains the non-native usage of subject pronouns as well as the non-native reduplication of object pronouns. These phenomena evidence that it is the identification procedure rather than syntactic licensing what determines the structure of the non-native grammars.

We are aware of the fact that we need to analyze longitudinal data as well as develop highly specific tests to confirm or reject the various hypotheses that have been formulated above. A detailed and refined analysis of the relationship between morphology and production of subject pronouns might also shed further light on the grammatical status of null subjects in non-native grammars.

REFERENCES

Authier, Jean-Marc. 1992. "A Parametric Account of V-governed Arbitrary Null Arguments". *Natural Languages and Linguistic Theory* 10.345-374.

Borer, Hagit. 1984. *Parametric Syntax: Case Studies in Semitic and Romance Languages.* Dodrecht: Foris.

Brown, Roger. 1973. *A First Language. The Early Stages.* Cambridge, Mass.: Harvard University Press.

Chomsky, Noam. 1992. "A Minimalist Program for Lingusitic Theory". *MIT Occasional Papers in Linguistics*. Cambridge, Mass.: MIT.

Haegeman, Liliana. 1990. "Non-overt Subjects in Diary Contexts." *Grammar in Progress. GLOW essays for Henk van Riemsdijk*, ed. by Joan Mascaró & Marina Nespor. Dordrecht: Foris.

Huang, Charles L. 1984. "On the Distribution and Reference of Empty Pronouns". *Linguistic Inquiry* 15.531-574.

Hyams, Nina. 1986. *Language Acquisition and the Theory of Parameters.* Dordrecht: Reidel.

———. 1994. "V2 Null Arguments and COMP Projections". *Language Acquisition Studies in Generative Grammar*, ed. by Teun Hoekstra & Bonnie Schwartz. Amsterdam: John Benjamins.

Koopman, Hilda & Dominique Sportiche. 1991. "The Position of Subjects". *Lingua* 85.211-58.

Lasnik, Howard, & Tim Stowell. 1991. "Weakest Crossover". *Linguistic Inquiry* 22.687-720.

Lebeaux, David. 1988. *Language Acquisition and the Form of the Grammar*. Ph.D. dissertation, University of Massachusetts, Amherst.

Liceras, Juana M. 1994. "La teoría gramatical y los principios que regulan la adquisición del orden de palabras del español". Paper presented at *I-Mesa Redonda de Lingüística Española.* Universidad Autónoma Metropolitana-Iztapalapa. Mexico D. F, March 1994.

———. 1995. "Los niveles de representación gramatical y la fijación de parámetros: el problema de la determinación en la adquisición del español como lengua extranjera". Paper presented at the *Penn State Conference on Acquisition of Spanish as a First or Second Language*, October 1995.

———. 1996. *La adquisición de lenguas segundas y la gramática universal.* Madrid: Síntesis.

———, Lourdes Díaz, Denyse Maxwell and Biana Laguardia. Forthcoming. "A longitudinal study of Spanish non-native grammars: beyond parameters". *The Acquisition of Spanish as First and Second Language*, ed. by Ana Teresa Pérez-Leroux and Wiliam Glass. Sommerville: Cascadilla Press.

Pierce, Amy. 1992. *Language Acquisition and Syntactic Theory.* Dordrecht: Kluwer.

Pollock, Jean-Yves. 1989. "Verb Movement, UG and the Structure of IP". *Linguistic Inquiry* 20.365-424.

Rizzi, Luigi. 1986. "Null Objects in Italian and the Theory of pro". *Linguistic Inquiry* 17.501-557.

———. 1994. "Early Null Subjects and Root Null subjects". *Language Acquisition Studies in Generative Grammar*, ed. by Teun Hoekstra & Bonnie Schwartz. Amsterdam: John Benjamins.

Roberge, Yves. 1990. "Subject Doubling, Free Inversion and Null Arguments". *Canadian Journal of Lingusitics* 31.54-79.

———. 1986. *The Syntactic Recoverability of Null Arguments.* Montreal: McGill-Queen's University Press.

Roeper, Thomas & Bernhard Rohrbacher. 1995. "Null Subjects in Early Child English and the Theory of Economy of Projection". Ms., University of Massachusetts at Amherst.

Speas, Margaret. 1994. "Null Arguments in a Theory of Economy of Projection". *University of Massachusetts Occasional Papers in Linguistics* 17.179-208.

Tsimpli, Ianthi-Maria, and Anne Rousseau. 1991. "Parameter-resetting in L2?". *UCL Working Papers in Linguistics* 3.149-169.

Wang, Qi, Dianne Lillo-Martin, Catherine T. Best, and Andrea Levitt. 1992. "Null Subject versus Null Object: Some Evidence from the Acquisition of Chinese and English." *Language Acquisition* 2.221-254.

Zagona, Karen. 1982. *Government and Proper Government of Verbal Projections.* Ph.D. dissertation, University of Washington, Seattle.

ON THE SPELLING DISTINCTION *B* VS. *U/V* AND THE STATUS OF SPIRANTIZATION IN OLD SPANISH*

FERNANDO MARTÍNEZ-GIL
The Ohio State University

1. *Introduction*

It is reasonably well established by now that variability among languages is not unlimited, but rather constrained by a limited set of universal parameters. The study of general patterns of variability in human language is the domain of linguistic typology. Typological evidence is commonly invoked by historical linguists in deciding matters of language reconstruction (see, for example, Comrie 1993), and it has been occasionally used in the past by scholars attempting to reconstruct either unattested or poorly documented stages in the history of the Romance languages. In fact, for a long time now in historical linguistics, typological considerations have played a central role in the task of reconstructing unattested stages of a language.

The results of this paper highlight the dangers of failing to apply typological criteria in the study of language change. It will be shown that the traditional characterization of a certain sound change in Spanish is typologically implausible, and thus it should be seriously reconsidered. At issue here is the evolution of voiced obstruents in the transition from Proto Hispano-Romance to Old Spanish, and ultimately the phonological evolution of obstruents in the history of Spanish up to the medieval period.

According to the prevalent view among many influential Spanish historical linguists for over three decades now, the Old Spanish consonantal system exhibited the phonemic distinction shown in (1) between the voiced oral stops, derived historically by intervocalic VOI(CING) of Latin voiceless stops /p, t, k/, and their fricative counterparts, derived by intervocalic SPIR(ANTIZATION) of Latin intervocalic voiced stops /b, d, g/ (Martinet 1951-52, 1970, Alarcos Llorach 1974, Lozano 1979, Lloyd 1986).

---

* My special thanks to Dieter Wanner for his input and discussion on several of the issues raised in this paper. All errors are mine.

(1) /b, d, g/ ~ /β, δ, γ/

The evidence produced in support of this claim rests almost exclusively on a renowned observation made by Dámaso Alonso (1949, 1962: 155-ff.) that throughout the Old Spanish period and until the 15th century, the grapheme *b* was consistently used to represent the historical reflex of Latin intervocalic /p/, as illustrated by correspondences such as those in (2a), while *u* or *v* stood for the spirant reflex of both the labiovelar glide /w/ and intervocalic /b/, as reflected in (2b).

(2) a. Lat. *p* (/p/) ↔ OSp. *b* :

Lat.	*OSp.*	
CAPIT	*cabe*	'it fits'
LUPU	*lobo*	'wolf'
APRILE	*abril*	'April'
LE*PORE*	*liebre*	'hare'

b. Lat. *v* (/w/), *b* (/b/) ↔ OSp. *u* or *v* :

Lat.	*OSp.*	
VENIT	*uiene*	'(s)he comes'
CAVALLU	*cauallo*	'horse'
HABERE	*auer*	'to have'
AMABAT	*amaua*	'(s)he loved-imperf'

The striking regularity of this usage led Dámaso Alonso to suspect that it underlied a phonemic distinction holding in intervocalic position between a voiced bilabial stop /b/ (spelled *b*) and its spirant counterpart /β/ (spelled *u*/*v*). For Dámaso Alonso such conjecture must have been fully justified at the time. After all, the alternative scenario of a sudden and ubiquitous agreement among Old Spanish scribes to follow a spelling convention strictly determined by the Latin etyma seems to be out of the question. On the basis of Dámaso Alonso's initial observation, other scholars have gone further and postulate the existence of an analogous phonemic contrast in Old Spanish between voiced stops and spirants for the dental and velar series: /d/~/δ/ and /g/~/γ/ (Martinet 1974: 311-315, Alarcos Llorach 1974: 242-247, Penny 1976: 157, Lozano 1979: 63-71, Lloyd 1987: 232-242). I will refer to this view as the *Stop-Spirant Phonemic Contrast Hypothesis* (the *SSPC Hypothesis*, for short). In presupposing the phonemic opposition in (1), the SSPC hypothesis explicitly embraces the notion that the SPIR of underlying voiced stops, a rule known to have been productive in Western Romance, was lost in Hispano-Romance at some historical stage during the preliterary period, through phonologization of the spirant alternants, and this situation held throughout the Old Spanish period, only for a new SPIR process, almost identical in its relevant details to that of the proto-language, to mysteriously re-emerge and establish itself in the language around the 16th century (Walsh 1991).

A few years before Dámaso Alonsos's initial suggestion of a phonemic contrast /b/~/β/ underlying the medieval *b* ~ *v/u* spelling distinction, Amado Alonso (1949, 1955 [1967]), following the lead of Cuervo (1895), contends that such distinction actually reflected an opposition between a bilabial and a labiodental point of articulation, respectively, a synchronic stage whose historical source would be shared by medieval Galician-Portuguese, and that such opposition had been lost around the 15th or 16th centuries. In spite of Amado Alonso's generous provision of rigorous and detailed arguments for this assessment, only a minority of scholars have espoused his views on the matter (see, for example, Bustos Tovar 1960). Evidently, however, if Amado Alonso was correct, the probability of the putative phonemic subsystem in (1) ever being present in Old Spanish is greatly diminished.

This paper has two primary objectives. The first is to challenge the SSPC Hypothesis by showing that it is strongly at odds with typological considerations. The second is to propose an alternative scenario fully consistent with the historical record as interpreted by Amado Alonso. I will argue that Old Spanish lacked the phonemic contrast between voiced stops and spirants in (1), and that SPIR never ceased to be a productive low-level allophonic rule throughout the history of Spanish, although the phonological conditions governing its application did undergo certain modifications since its emergence in the proto-language.

2. *Some basic historical facts about SPIR*

Let us briefly examine some essential facts related to the emergence of SPIR, and its consequences for the early phonological development of Spanish from the common Latin stock. For convenience, the initial and the final points of the puzzle are presented in (3) and (4) below: the underlying consonant inventories of Latin and Old Spanish, respectively. As is well-known, each simple Latin consonant in (3) had a geminate counterpart.

(3) *Latin underlying consonant system*:

obstruents	p	t	k
	b	d	g
	f	s	(h)
sonorants	m	n	
		l	
		r	
	j		w

(4) *Old Spanish underlying consonant system* (cf. Otero 1971: 105):

obstruents	p	t, t^s	č	k
	b	d, d^z	ǰ	g
	f	s	š	
	v	z	ž	
sonorants	m	n	ñ	
		l	λ	
		r, r̄		
	j			w

It is worth emphasizing again that the point at issue here is whether or not the Old Spanish voiced stops /b, d, g/ in (4) were matched by the corresponding set of spirants /β, δ, γ /, as claimed by the SSPC hypothesis.

SPIR —and in many cases, further deletion (DEL)— of voiced stops is commonly viewed as the first link in a chain of lenition processes that targeted the underlying stops in the Western Romance languages (see, among many others, Jungemann 1955, Weinrich 1958, Bustos Tovar 1960, Alarcos Llorach 1974, Martinet 1952, 1974, Cravens 1984, Harris-Northall 1990, Walsh 1991). The other lenition shifts are, in their relative chronological order, VOI of intervocalic voiceless stops (/p, t, k/ > /b, d, g/), and simplification of geminate consonants. The overall patterns of SPIR and VOI, respectively, are summarized in ($5a-b).

(5) a. *Spirantization of voiced stops*:

b, w	>	β	
d	>	δ	(> ∅)
g	>	γ	

b. *Voicing of voiceless obstruents*:

Stops:			*Fricatives / Affricates*:			
p	>	b	f	>	v/b	
t	>	d	t^s	>	d^z	(t^s < /k/ + /i, e/; /t/ + /j/)
k	>	g	s	>	z	

Interestingly, the processes of SPIR and VOI appear to be closely related in their distributional properties. Thus, both applied after nuclear vowels, as indicated in (6a), and *not* (at least in their initial stages): (i) when preceded by a consonant or a glide; (ii) word-initially after pause; and (iii) when the stops were geminates, as shown schematically in (6b).

(6) a. *SPIR and VOI*:

V_N ____

(V_N = a nuclear vowel)

b. *No SPIR or VOI:*

(i) $\begin{Bmatrix} C \\ G \end{Bmatrix}$ ____

(ii) ## ____

(iii) Geminates

A variety of Latin-Spanish correspondences illustrating SPIR and subsequent DEL of voiced stops are given in (7). Examples are shown in their orthographic form, with the consonants under consideration in boldface for visual clarity.

Phonetic notation is used whenever the conventional spelling may be misleading. The Latin labiovelar glide /w/ has been included with /b/ in (7a), since the former underwent obstruentization to [β], thereby merging with the spirant reflex of /b/ at some stage in Vulgar Latin (see below for further discussion). As illustrated in (7a-c), Del often occurred in intervocalic position.

(7) a. /b, w/ > [β] > ∅:

Lat.	*OSp.*	
TRI**B**UTU	treúdo	'tribute, tax'
SA**B**UCU	saúco	'elder tree'
*SU**B**UMBRA*	*sombra*	'shade, shadow'
*RI**V**U*	*río*	'river'
*BO**V**E*	*buey*	'ox'
*AESTI**V**U*	*estío*	'summer'
*LIXI**V**A*	*lejía*	'bleach'

b. /d/ > [δ] > ∅:

RA**D**ICE	raíz	'root'
TRA**D**UCERE	trauçir, *troçir*	'to translate'
*DISCE**D**ERE*	*deçir*	'to say'
*ME**D**ULLU*	*meollo*	'marrow'
*TAE**D**A*	*tea*	'torch'
*TRA**D**ITORE*	*traidor*	'traitor'
*RANCI**D**U*	*rançio*	'stale'

c. /g/ > [γ] > ∅:

MA**G**ISTRU	maestro	'teacher'
SA**G**ITTA	saeta	'arrow'
*LITI**G**ARE*	*lidiar*	'to fight'
*LE**G**ALE*	*leal*	'loyal'
*MA**G**ICU*	*mego*	'affable'
*LE**G**E*(> **lee*)	*ley*	'law'
*RE**G**INA*	*reína*	'queen'

In some instances, the velar /g/ was also subject to Del when preceded by a vowel and immediately followed by a (tautosyllabic) /r/:

(8)

Lat.	*OSp.*	
AGRU	ero	'field, meadow'
INTEGRU	entero	'whole'
PIGRITIA	*pereza*	'laziness'
QUADRAGINTA	*cuarenta*	'forty'

Although dental spirants underwent spirant Del quite regularly in intervocalic position, /b/, and to a lesser extent also /g/, unexpectedly did not delete in a sizeable number of lexical items, such as those illustrated in (9).

(9)

	Lat.	*OSp.*	
a.	*SEBU*	*sebo*	'fat, grease'
	CAVU	*cavo*	'rabbit hole'
	VIVU	*vivo*	'alive'
	NOVU	*nuevo*	'new'
b.	*JUGU*	*jugo, jogo*	'joke'
	PELAGU	*piélago*	'sea, ocean'
	IRRUGARE	*arrugar*	'to wrinkle'
	PLAGA	*llaga*	'wound'

A good number of forms in Old Spanish exhibited variation between Del, more akin to the Western dialects, and preservation of the voiced spirant, typical of Eastern varieties:

(10)

Lat.	*West. OSp.*	*East. OSp.*	*MSp.*	
a. *NUBES*	*nues*	*nubes, nuves*	*nubes*	'clouds'
TIBI	*tí*	*tibe*	*tí*	'you-dat'
GINGIVA	*enzía*	*enziva*	*encía*	'gum'
PAVORE	*paor*	*pavor*	*pavor*	'fear, terror'
PRIVADU	*priado*	*privado*	*privado*	'private'

Lat.	*West. OSp.*	*East. OSp.*	*MSp.*	
b. *NIDU*	*nío*	*nido*	*nido*	'nest'
CRUDO	*crúo*	*crudo*	*crudo*	'raw, crude'
ALAUDA	*aloa*	*aloda*	*alondra*	'lark'
MEDALIA	*mealla*	*medalla*	*medalla*	'type of coin'
SUDORE	*suor*	*sudor*	*sudor*	'sweat'

	Lat.	West.OSp.	East.OSp.	MSp.	
c.	*NAVI**G**ARE*	*navear*	*nave**g**ar*	*nave**g**ar*	'to sail'
	*FUSTI**G**ARE*	*hostiar*	*hosti**g**ar*	*hosti**g**ar*	'to whip, lash'
	*LI**G**ARE*	*liar*	*li**g**ar*	*liar / li**g**ar*	'to tie, bind'
	*RU**G**A*	*rúa*	*ru**g**a*	*arru**g**a*	'wrinkle'
	*PA**G**U*	*pao*	*pa**g**o*	*pa**g**o*	'(vineyard) estate'

As can be observed in (10) the Old Spanish form with a preserved spirant has survived in Modern Spanish in most instances. Del of voiced stops has traditionally been taken as the safest indication that they had undergone SPIR in a previous stage.

It seems reasonably clear from the historical record that spirant DEL had ceased to be operative in the proto-language prior to the emergence of VOI. This relative chronology is suggested by the fact that Spanish voiced obstruents derived from Latin voiceless ones did not undergo Del under the appropriate conditions, as illustrated by the representative examples in (11), although historically they did undergo SPIR, as they still do in Modern Spanish.

(11)	*Lat.*	*OSp.*	
a.	*LU**P**U*	*lo**b**o*	'wolf'
	*TRI**F**OLIU*	*tré**v**ol*	'clover'
	*RA**PH**ANU*	*rá**b**ano*	'radish'
	*PRA**T**U*	*pra**d**o*	'medow'
	*TRISTI**T**IA*	*triste*$[d^z]$*a*	'sadness'
	*RO**S**A*	*ro*[z]*a*	'rose'
	*ERI**C**IU*	*eri*$[d^z]$*o*	'hedgehog'
	*AMI**C**U*	*ami**g**o*	'friend'

	Lat.	*OSp.*	
b.	*CA**P**RA*	*ca**b**ra*	'goat
	*DU**P**LARE*	*do**b**lar*	'to fold'
	*A**F**RICU*	*á**b**rego*	'south wind'
	*PE**T**RA*	*pie**d**ra*	'stone'
	*SO**C**RU*	*sue**g**ro*	'father-in-law'

Finally, Latin long consonants were degeminated (Deg) at some historical point in Western Romance, as illustrated for Spanish by the correspondences in (12). The Deg process must have taken place *after* voiceless obstruent had already been subject to VOI, since simple voiceless stops derived from geminate ones did not undergo VOI (cf. 12a).[1]

(12)	*Lat.*	*OSp.*	
a.	*CUPPA*	*copa*	'cup'
	SUFFOCARE	*sofocar*	'to suffocate'
	GUTTA	*gota*	'drop'
	OSSU	*hue*[s]*o*	'bone'
	SICCU	*seco*	'dry'
b.	*SUBBULLIRE*	*zabullir*	'to plunge (into water)'
	ADDUCERE	*adozir*	'to adduce'
	**AGGUBBIARE*	*agobiar*	'to overwhelm'

Neither SPIR nor VOI applied when the target obstruent was preceded by a closed syllable. This property can be readily inferred from the fact that Latin voiced stops were never deleted when located after a (necessarily heterosyllabic) consonant, as shown in (13).

(13)	*Lat.*	*OSp.*	
a.	*ARBORE*	*áruor*, *áruol*	'tree'
	ALBA	*alua*	'white, dawn'
	SERVU	*sieruo*	'servant, serf'
	SILVA	*selva*	'(rain)forest'
b.	*TARDE*	*tarde*	'late, evening'
	VIR(I)DE	*verde*	'green'
	CAL(I)DU	*caldo*	'broth'
	QUANDO	*cuando*	'when'
	FUNDU	*hondo*	'deep'
c.	*VIRGA*	*verga*	'rod'
	ALGA	*alga*	'alga'
	LONGU	*luengo*	'long'
	FUNGU	*hongo*	'fungus, mushroom'

In an analogous manner, voiceless stops did not undergo VOI either in postconsonantal position, as can be seen in (14a-b), or after glides, whether pri-

[1] The familiar exception to this generalization is the Latin inflectional morpheme *-TIS*, corresponding to verb forms of the 2nd person plural, whose initial /t/ has undergone both VOI and DEL (cf. *AMATIS* > (OSp.) *amades* >(MSp.) *amáis* 'you-PL love').

mary, as in (14c), or derived by some other sound change, quite generally, by metathesis of a prevocalic glide or by vocalization of a coda consonant, as in (14d).

(14)	*Lat.*	*OSp.*	
a.	*COR**P**U*	*cuer**p**o*	'body'
	*VUL**P**EC(U)LA*	*vul**p**eja*	'vixen'
	*OR**PH**ANU*	*huér**f**ano*	'orphan'
	*POR**T**U*	*puer**t**o*	'port, harbor'
	*AL**T**U*	*al**t**o*	'high, tall'
	*FAL**S**U*	*fal*[s]*o*	'false'
	*SCOR**T**EU*	*escuer*[t^s]*o*	'toad'
	*CAL**C**EA*	*cal*[t^s]*a*	'breeches'
	*POR**C**U*	*puer**c**o*	'pig'
	*CIR**C**A*	*cer**c**a*	'near, close'
	*SUL**C**U*	*sul**c**o, sur**c**o*	'furrow'
b.	*TEM**P**U*	*tiem**p**o*	'time, weather'
	*IM**P**ULSARE*	*em**p**uxar*	'to push'
	*MAN(U)**F**ERIRE*	*man**f**erir*	'to wound'
	*CON**F**UNDERE*	*con**f**onder*	'to confuse'
	*PON**T**E*	*puen**t**e*	'bridge'
	*LAN**C**EA*	*lan*[t^s]*a*	'spear'
	*TRUN**C**U*	*tron**c**o*	'trunk, log'
c.	*PAU**C**U*	*po**c**o*	'little'
	*AU**C**A*	*o**c**a*	'goose'
	*CAU**T**U*	*co**t**o*	'enclosed land'
	*FAU**T**U*	*ho**t**o*	'favor, trust'
	*AU**T**UMNU*	*o**t**oño*	'autumn'
d.	*SA**P**IAT* (>**sa*[j]***pa***)	*se**p**a*	'I know (subj.)'
	CA***PI**AT* (>**ca*[j]***pa***)	*que**p**a*	'I fit (subj.)'
	*CA**P**UIT* (>**ca*[w]***pe***)	co***pe***	'I fitted'
	*SAL**T**U* (>**sa*[w]***to***)	*so**t**o*	'grove'
	*AL**T(E)**RU* (>**a*[w]***tro***)	*o**t**ro*	'(an)other'

3. *Arguments against the SSPC hypothesis*

Let us consider in more detail now the basic tenets of the SSPC hypothesis. The most complete and detailed generative account of this position is given in Lozano (1979), and thus this work will be taken as the main point of reference.[2] According to Lozano, the voiced spirant phonemes in (1) arose largely through restructuring of the Proto Spanish consonant system at the point in which the VOI rule was added to the grammar. It is mainly the lack of plausible motivation for such a restructuring that I will attempt to address in this section. The three major historical stages of the scenario suggested by Lozano (1979: 63-ff.) are given in (15).

(15)		Word-initial and post-consonantal positions:	Intervocalic position:
a.	*Vulgar Latin*:		
	/p, t, k/	[p, t, k]	[p, t, k]
	/b/ (< /b/)	[b]	[b] (or [β])
	/β/ (< /w/)	[β]	[β]
	/d, g/	[d, g]	[d, g]
b.	*Romance I*:		
	/p, t, k/	[p, t, k]	[b, d, g]
	/b/	[b]	[β]
	/β/	[β]	[β]
	/d, g/	[d, g]	[δ, γ]
c.	*Romance II* (***Restructuring***):		
	/p, t, k/ (< /-pp-, -tt-, -kk-/)	[p, t, k]	[b, d, g]
	/b/ (< /-p-/, /-bb-/)	[b]	[b]
	/β/ (< /w/, /-b-/	[β]	[β]
	/d/ (< /-t-/, /-dd-/)	[d]	[d]
	/δ/ (< /-d-/)	—	[δ]
	/g/ (< /-k-/, /-gg-/)	[g]	[g]
	/γ/ (< /-g-/)	—	[γ]

According to Lozano, two major sound changes came about in the Vulgar Latin Stage (15a), and they were critical for the restructuring that took place

---

[2] Similar proposals, although framed in a different theoretical approach, had been put forth in earlier work by Penny (1976).

at the Romance II stage. Initially, SPIR applied optionally to /b/ in intervocalic position. In a subsequent development, the labiovelar glide /w/ shifted into the bilabial spirant /β/. The latter change is thus held responsible for creating the first phonemic distinction between a voiced bilabial stop and its spirant counterpart in the proto-language. Next, at the Romance I stage (15b), the SPIR rule became obligatory, extending its scope to the dental and velar series. Notice, however, that at this stage non-labial stops and spirants still surfaced in complementary distribution, and thus they could still be derived by a SPIR rule. The essence of the SSPC hypothesis derives from the interpretation of the events that took place at the Romance II stage (15c), where post-vocalic voiceless stops have become voiced, and thus they came to contrast with voiced spirants in surface forms.[3] The point of Lozano's restructuring in stage (15c) is to incorporate this surface distinction into underlying representations. As a result, the underlying stop-spirant opposition, initially holding in the labial series, has now been extended to the dental and velar points of articulation, presumably driven by inventory symmetry. The particular synchronic grammars that would generate the output forms at each of the three stages in (15) can be illustrated with the two Proto-Spanish forms grato 'pleasing' (<GRATU) and *grado* 'step' (< *GRADU*), as in (16):

(16) a. *Stage I* (Lozano's Vulgar Latin stage (15a)):[4]

U.R.:	/grato/	/grado/
SPIR:	—	—
Output:	grato	grado

b. *Stage II* (Lozano's Romance I stage (15b)):

U.R.:	/grato/	/grado/
SPIR:	—	graδo
VOI:	grado	—
Output:	grado	grao

[3] Lozano includes DEG in this stage. Technically this process belongs to a later historical period (see Graur 1929, Politzer 1951, Kiss 1972, Barbarino 1981).

[4] Recall in the Vulgar Latin stage (15a), SPIR applied only to /b/, and therefore /d/ in *grado* is not affected by it.

c. *Stage III*. ***Restructuring*** (Lozano's Romance II stage (15c)):

U.R.:	/grado/	/graδo/
Output:	grádo	gráδo

In Lozano's Romance I stage, SPIR is generalized to all underlying voiced stops, and thus it applies to *grado*, as shown in (16b), while VOI would likewise applied to the form *grato*, which now surfaces with a voiced stop. The phonetic contrast that emerged in the Romance I stage become phonemic in the third (Romance II) stage (15c), and as a consequence both SPIR and VOI are dropped from the grammar. Since no other relevant change happened in this stage, the surface forms are identical to the corresponding underlying ones. According to Lozano, a second round of SPIR came about around the 15th century turning into spirants the voiced reflexes of Latin intervocalic voiceless stops, which until then had been realized phonetically as stops.[5] In a final stage the language underwent a second restructuring, which resulted in the complete merger of the Old Spanish stop-spirant phonemic contrast.[6] According to this view, then, the synchronic grammar of Old Spanish never contained a SPIR rule.

Such an analysis, however, raises serious questions. Consider, first, the logic of Lozano's arguments. The underlying stop-spirant /b/~/β/ contrast is assumed exclusively on the basis of the Old Spanish spelling consistency noted earlier. From this premise, Lozano simply concludes that similar contrasts must have also existed in the dental and velar series (/d, g/~/δ, γ /). In favor of this hypothesis, Lozano appeals to the well-known fact that the voiced reflexes of Latin /t, k/ failed to undergo DEL, while the spirant reflexes of Latin /d, g/ were normally subject to this process. However, the argument that the different phonological behavior of both sets in relation to DEL reflects a difference in phonemic status, is actually misconstrued: the voiced reflexes of Latin /t, k/ did not undergo DEL simply because spirant DEL was no longer operative at the point in which VOI was incorporated into the grammar. The documentary evidence supports this explanation: while DEL is amply attested since the 1st cen-

[5] See Walsh (1991) for a similar proposal.

[6] In Lozano's opinion, the most adequate way to characterize the stop-spirant alternations in the present-day grammar of most varieties of Modern Spanish is an archiphonemic analysis (i.e., one in which the value for [continuant] in voiced obstruents is left unspecified in underlying forms), a position which has been almost universally accepted by most generative studies of modern SPIR (see Harris 1984, Mascaró 1984, Hualde 1990, among others).

tury B.C., the first examples of VOI are not found until at least two centuries later (cf. Grandgent 1907: 108-109, 136-137). In addition, a wide variety of historical data surveyed by Amado Alonso (1955 [1967]) indicate that the spelling *u*/*v* word-medially stood for a labiodental [v], and not a bilabial [β], until at least the beginning of the 16th century. In fact, Castilian grammarians of the period contain explicit descriptions of the labiodental [v], such as those of Nebrija in (17a) (end of the 15th century) or Gonzalo Correas in (17b), in whose variety of Spanish the labiodental was apparently still preserved at the beginning of the 17th century.

(17)a. "La *f* con la *v* consonante, puestos los dientes de arriba sobre el beço de baxo, i soplando por las helgaduras dellos: la *f* mas de fuera, la *v* mas adentro un poco."
(Antonio de Nebrija (1492 [1986], fol. 8r.).

b. "[P]ronunziase con los dientes de arriba clavados en el labio de abaxo, levantado el de arriba, abriendo de golpe labio i dientes... tiene esta va mucha vecindad con la be, i por eso muchos las confunden en Castilla la Vieja, i fuera de España."
(Gonzalo Correas 1626 [1954: 73-74]).

Dámaso Alonso cavalierly shoved aside such testimonies alleging, prematurely, as it seems now, that these grammarians were simply attempting to prescribe how the letter *v* should be pronounced, *not* its actual pronunciation. In addition, there is some solid evidence that a voiced labiodental occurred in central and southern Spanish until the middle of the 15th century (Lapesa 1981: 39-40, including fn. 27, 205-206).

As a second objection to Lozano's account, it can be argued that if scribes indeed felt the inexorable need to reflect orthographically the phonemic contrast between a bilabial stop and a bilabial spirant (and understandably so, one may add), it seems puzzling that the same rationale failed to apply in a parallel fashion to the assumed opposition between dentals and velars. In fact, throughout the historical evolution of Spanish I can find no other instance of a putative phonemic opposition so systematically ignored by spelling conventions as the alleged phonemic opposition between dental and velar stops and spirants /d, g/ ~ /δ, γ /, as claimed by proponents of the SSCP hypothesis. It seems highly unlikely that if the dental and velar spirants indeed had phonemic status in Old Spanish, scribes would not had found a way to represent them in writing. In fact, the graphemes *d* and *g* in Old Spanish invariably stood for both the stop and the spirant realizations, irrespective of source or phonological environment. We can only find one reasonable explanation for such practice: that the segments in each pair were allophonic variants of the underlying segment, and hence no compulsion was felt to distinguish orthographically one member of the pair from the other.

A third and most significant problem with the SSPC hypothesis in (1) stems from its typological oddity, both from a substantive and from a formal standpoint. Consider, first, the likelihood of an inventory containing the putative opposition between voiced stops and spirants alleged by the SSPC hypothesis. Among the 317 consonantal inventories that appear in the *UPSID* project surveyed in Maddieson (1984), the largest and most comprehensive record of language inventories done to date, not one single language contains the three-point-of-articulation contrast /b, d, g/ ~ /β, δ, γ / that Lozano and others have attributed to Old Spanish. From this study, only 10 languages (about a 3 per cent)—none of them Indo-European—displays a phonemic contrast solely based on continuance between two voiced bilabials. Among the Indo-European languages, Modern Greek is quite marked in that it exhibits such a distinction between velars; the contrast between dental and labial voiced stops and spirants is typically accompanied by differences in place of articulation: apico-dental /d/ vs. interdental /δ/, and bilabial /b/ vs. labiodental /v/, not unlike Modern English. In short, although many languages are known to exhibit alternations between the two sets in (1) in *surface* forms (Modern Spanish being such a case), their distribution is entirely determined by phonetic environment.

The explanation for the rarity of the contrasts in (1) may well have a perceptual basis. One may speculate that the feature [continuant] alone is not sufficient to establish optimal auditory distinctions between voiced stops and spirants that share a common point of articulation. If this is true, then it is perhaps not surprising that the acoustic saliency of common crosslinguistic stop~fricative distinctions within obstruents, such as those indicated in (18), is commonly enhanced by additional differences in place of articulation and/or stridency in the fricative members (Stevens, Keyser and Kawasaki 1986, Stevens and Keyser 1989).

(18) /p/~/f/, /b/~/v/, /t/~/s/, /d/~/z/, /k/~/x/, etc.

What are we to make, then, of the observed consistency found by Dámaso Alonso in medieval spelling practices? Following the lead of Cuervo (1895) and Amado Alonso (1955 [1967]), I would like to suggest that Old Spanish *b* in intervocalic position was actually used to represent the bilabial spirant [β], while *u/v* stood for the labiodental [v], as summarized in (19).

(19) *Intervocalic distribution of voiced labials in Old Spanish*:

Underlying	*Surface*	*Historical source*	*Spelling*
/b/	[β]	(< Lat. /-p-/)	*b*
/v/	[v]	(< Lat. /v/, /-b-/)	*u* / *v*

The first of the unlikely chain of phonemic events in (15) is specially problematic, since the spirant~stop distribution essentially remained predictable in the proto-language: spirants after vowels and stops in absolute word-initial and post-consonantal positions. Consider, for example, the first restructuring in the Romance II stage in (15c).

A further objection to Lozano's scenario stems from the failure to produce clear motivation in support of the second reanalysis; namely, the loss, a few centuries later, of the stop/spirant opposition, and the concomitant re-emergence of a second round of SPIR, which essentially replicated, in all relevant details, the phonological conditions found in SPIR prior to the presumed restructuring at the Romance II stage. Indeed, such restructuring is suspect because the spirant~stop distribution essentially remained predictable in the proto-language: spirants surfaced after vowels (initially; later, they occurred after any continuant segment), while stops were confined to absolute word-initial and post-consonantal positions.

Lozano does not devote much effort to justify how the putative restructuring in the transition from the Romance I to the Romance II stages in (16b-c) would have come about in the first place. Implicit in her account appears to be the following rationale. Observe that as a consequence of the addition of VOI at the Romance I stage (16b), stops and spirants now contrast intervocallically in phonetic representations. Given the existence of a SPIR rule in this stage, surface forms containing voiced stops are clearly opaque (in the sense of Kiparsky 1971, 1973). The avoidance of such opacity would lead to restructuring (Kiparsky 1971), whereby the surface stop/spirant distinction is absorbed into underlying forms. In other words, children learning the language would have no reason to postulate a SPIR rule intervocalically, since in such an environment both stops and spirants occurred freely. The rule is dropped, and output opacity eliminated. At first glance, the preceding argument appears to be sound, but there is a better alternative. Rule additions, almost without exception, appear to emerge in adult speech (King 1969, Kiparsky 1982). Given the standard assumption that new rules are added to the end of the phonological component, it is reasonable to suppose that VOI and SPIR applied in the grammar of adult proto-language speakers in the counterfeeding order reflected in (16b). As already noted, the presence of both voiced stops and spirant in intervocalic position at this stage would have resulted in surface opacity. Children learning the language had essentially two choices: to restructure the phonemic inventory in the way postulated by Lozano, which we have shown to be implausible, or to keep the SPIR rule and reanalyze as underlying the voiced stops (derived by VOI) occurring in the speech of adults, in which case they would naturally be subject to SPIR.[7] In short, I am suggesting that the VOI rule must have been extremely short-lived, and it presumably did not survive the generation of speakers that had initially implemented it.

Indeed, this second alternative of avoiding opacity in surface forms by submitting to SPIR the emerging intervocalic voiced stops is well-documented in other Romance languages. For example, in the Lugodorese dialect of Sardinian (see Wagner 1941, Blasco Ferrer 1986) voiced stops become spirants in intervocalic position (20a). There is a rule in this variety that voices voiceless stops in identical environments. Interestingly, the latter process yields voiced spirants, not voiced stops, as shown in (20b).

(20)	a. [b]*aca*	'cow'	cf.	*sa* [β]*aca*	'the cow'
	[d]*omu*	'house'	cf.	*sa* [δ]*omu*	'the house'
	[g]*erra*	'war'	cf.	*sa* [γ]*erra*	'the war'
	b. [p]*orcu*	'pig'	cf.	*su* [β]*orcu*	'the pig'
	[t]*erra*	'land'	cf.	*sa* [δ]*erra*	'the land'
	[k]*osa*	'thing'	cf.	*sa* [γ]*osa*	'the thing'

A similar conjunction of VOI and SPIR is known to have occurred in the history of Gallo-Romance (see Steriade 1988, Jacobs and Wetzels 1988). These

[7] A third alternative to the reanalysis problem that appeals to rule reordering is explored in Wireback (1993). Due to space limitations it cannot be discussed here. Wireback's scenario, however, can also be shown to be implausible.

two situations are thus essentially analogous to the scenario just proposed for Proto-Spanish.

A final problem for Lozano's restructuring hypothesis derives from two well-known phonological processes in Old Spanish, and how their interaction was recorded in the Old Spanish orthography. Early Old Spanish underwent an apocope rule that deleted word-final /-e/ when preceded by a single consonant, quite typically, a member of the set /s, d, n, l, r/ (see Lapesa 1971, 1975), as illustrated by the correspondences in (21).

(21)	*Lat.*	*Early OSp.*	*OSp.*	
	MENSE	mese	mes	'month'
	RETE	rede	red	'net'
	PANE	*pane*	*pan*	'bread'
	SOLE	*sole*	*sol*	'sun'
	MARE	*mare*	*mar*	'sea'

Around the 12th century, and presumably due to the influence of cultural and linguistic trends from Gallo-Romance and Catalan, a new and less restrictive type of apocope —commonly known as *extreme apocope*— became established in Old Spanish; the new rule optionally deleted word-final /-e/ (occasionally also /-o/) when preceded either by a single noncoronal consonant or by a consonant cluster of falling sonority (Lapesa 1951, 1975, Catalán 1971, Montgomery 1975, Allen 1976), as shown in (22):

(22)	*Felip / Felipe*	(name)
	com / como	'as'
	siet / siete	'seven'
	dix / dixe (*x* = [š])	'I said'
	noch / noche (*ch* = [č]	'night'
	duc / duque (*c, qu* = [k])	'duke'
	puent / puente	'bridge'
	trist / triste	'sad'

There is evidence that Old Spanish contained a rule that devoiced obstruents word-finally (Pensado Ruiz 1984: 208-ff., Harris-Northall 1991: 47). It is interesting to note that in words subject to apocope, whether extreme or otherwise, the devoicing phenomenon is often —although not systematically— reflected in the spelling, as illustrated in (23) for labials and in (24) for dentals and velars:

(23)	a.	*naf* / *naue* (< *NAVE*)	'ship, boat'
		nuef / *nueve* (< *NOVE*)	'nine'
		nief / *nieue* (< *NEVE*)	'snow'
		bef / *beue* (< *BIBIT*)	'he drinks'
		escrif / *escriue* (< *SCRIBIT*)	'he writes'
	b.	*lop* / *lobo* (< *LUPU*)	'wolf'
		sinap / *sinabe* (< *SINAPI*)	'mustard'

(24)	pit / *pide*	'(s)he asks for'
	humilt / *humilde*	'humble'
	grant / *grande*	'large, great'
	vert / *verde*	'green'
	Diac / *Diago*, *Diego* (*c* = [k])	(name)
	Rodric / *Rodrigo*	(name)

As shown in (23a), the orthographic symbol used to reflect the devoicing the sound represented by *u/v* is the grapheme *f*. Now, since *f* invariably represents the labiodental fricative [f] in Old Spanish, the orthographic reflection of the devoicing process can accounted for straightforwardly and without any additional stipulation if the represented sound is assumed to be the labiodental [v] in the unapocopated forms. If, on the other hand, the graphemes *u/v* reflected a voiced bilabial fricative /β/, as Amado Alonso and his followers have suggested, then devoicing unavoidably involves an additional operation that mutates /β/ from a bilabial to a labiodental place of articulation: /β/ → [f]. Although such shift can be motivated on markedness grounds, this additional complication would be unnecessary if the graphemes in question actually stood for an underlying voiced labiodental. Furthermore, the orthographic symbols for the devoiced nonlabials *d* and *g* in (24), whatever their historical source, are *t* and *c* (the latter also shows the sporadic variants *q*, *k*). Since there is no evidence that the word-final letters *t* and *c* in these items stood for anything other than voiceless stops, we can envisage (synchronic) sample derivations such as those shown in (25), for some representative items from (23-24), where devoicing clearly must apply before (and therefore bleed) SPIR:

(25)	U.R.'s:	/nave/	/lobo/	/pide/	/djago/
	Stress:	náve	lóbo	píde	djágo
	Apocope:	náv	lób	píd	djág
	Devoicing:	náf	lóp	pít	dják
	SPIR:	—	—	—	—
	Output:	náf	lóp	pít	dják

Consider now, for the sake of argument, the hypothetical underlying forms in (26), forming (quasi-)minimal pairs with those in (25). This is precisely the situation that the SSPC hypothesis claims to have existed in Old Spanish, thus predicting that we would have derivations along the lines of (26), yielding surface forms with word-final voiceless spirants. In other words, together with the surface forms in (25), we would expect to find some orthographic testimony in Old Spanish of forms such as those in (26), with a word-final voiceless spirant.

(26)	U.R.'s:	/r̄aβe/	/toβo/	/κιδe/	/sjaγo/
	Apocope:	r̄aβ	toβ	kiδ	sjaγ
	Devoicing:	r̄aφ	toφ	kiθ	sjax
	Output:	r̄aφ	toφ	kiθ	sjax

The fact there is no evidence whatsoever for such forms in the historical record would be difficult to explain in a SSPC analysis, and hence the absence of data such as (26) would have to be attributed to mere accident.

4. *Towards an alternative scenario*

Having established the implausibility of the SSPC Hypothesis, I will now suggest an alternative scenario compatible with the relevant historical data, and with the view taken in this paper that some sort of SPIR rule has remained productive in Spanish throughout its history. I suggest that as in so many other aspects of their historical development, the treatment of voiced labials in Spanish until the 15th century ran almost completely parallel to that of Portuguese. Consider, thus, the fate of the voiced bilabial /b/ in Modern Portuguese (cf. Williams 1938), as illustrated in (27).

(27)		*Lat.*	*Port.*	
	a.	***B**UCCA*	***b**oca*	'mouth'
		***B**ONU*	***b**om*	'good-MASC'
		***B**ASIU*	***b**eijo*	'kiss'
	b.	*LUM**B**U*	*lom**b**o*	'back, loin'
		*PLUM**B**U*	*chum**b**o*	'lead'
		*PALUM**B**A*	pom***b**a*	'dove'
	c.	*FA**B**A*	*fava*	'bean'
		*SCRI**B**ERE*	*escrever*	'to write'
		*CA**B**ALLU*	*cavalo*	'horse'

The data in (27) shows that /b/ stayed as such word-initially (27a) and after nasals (27b), but in intervocalic position it turned into the labiodental /v/ (27c).

A cursory inspection of the Modern French forms in (28) indicates that Gallo-Romance underwent developments which are completely analogous to those of Portuguese in (27) (see Pope 1934, Bourciez 1956, 1967).

(28)	*Lat.*	*Fr.*	
a.	***B**UCCA*	***b**ouche*	'mouth'
	***B**ONU*	***b**on*	'good-MASC'
	***B**ASIARE*	***b**aiser*	'to kiss'
b.	*TUM**B**A*	*tom**b**e*	'tomb, grave'
	*PLUM**B**U*	*plom**b***	'lead'
	*GAM**B**A*	*jam**b**e*	'leg'
c	*HA**B**ERE*	*avoir*	'to have'
	*FA**B**A*	*féve*	'bean'
	*LI**B**RU*	*livre*	'book'

The Latin labiovelar glide /w/ also developed into the labiodental /v/ in most contexts, both in Portuguese (29) and in French (30).[8]

(29)	*Lat*	*Port.*	
a.	*VINU*	*vihno*	'wine'
	VIDUA	*viuva*	'widow'
	VETULU	*velho*	'old'
	Lat.	*Port.*	
b.	OVU	ovo	'egg'
	NOVEM	nove	'nine'
	CAVU	*cavu*	'hollow'
c.	*CORVU*	*corvo*	'crow'
	CALVU	*calvo*	'bald'
	INVIARE	*enviar*	'to send'

---

[8] Note the devoicing of /v/ to [f] in Old French *cerf* in (30c), much as in Old Spanish. Note further that such devocing has been lexicalized in the Modern French item *nef* in (30b).

(30)		*Lat.*	*Fr.*	
	a.	***V**ENTU*	*vent*	‘wind’
		***V**I**V**ERE*	*vivre*	‘to live’
		***V**OCE*	*voix*	‘voice’
	b.	*NA**V**E*	*ne*[f]	‘nave, aisle’
		*LA**V**ARE*	*laver*	‘to wash’
		*NO**V**ELLU*	*nouveau*	‘new’
	c.	*SER**V**IRE*	*servir*	‘serf, servant’
		*CER**V**U* (OFr.)	*cer*[f]	‘stag, deer’
		*MAL**V**A*	*mauve*	‘mauve, purple’
		*CAL**V**A*	*chauve*	‘bold(-headed)’

There are, however, two interesting differences between Hispano- and Gallo-Romance. First, in a typical Hispano-Romance development, /b/ became /v/ are after liquids, as shown by the Portuguese data in (31a), while it is preserved as such in French, as seen in (32a).

(31)		*Lat.*	*Port.*	
	a.	*HER**B**A*	*erva*	‘grass’
		*AR**B**ORE*	*árvore*	‘tree’
		*AL**B**U*	*alvo*	‘white’
		Lat.	*Fr.*	
	b.	*LU**P**U*	*lô**b**o*	‘wolf’
		*A**P**ICULA*	***a**belha*	‘bee’
		*SA**P**ERE*	*sa**b**er*	‘to know’
		*CA**P**ITIA*	*ca**b**eça*	‘head’

(32)		*Lat.*	*Fr.*	
	a.	*HER**B**A*	*her**b**e*	‘grass’
		*AR**B**ORE*	*ar**b**re*	‘tree’
		*AL**B**A*	*au**b**e*	‘dawn’
	b.	*RI**P**A*	*ri**v**e*	‘shore, bank’
		*TRO**P**ARE*	*trou**v**er*	‘to find’
		*SA**P**ERE*	*sa**v**oir*	‘to know’
		*CA**P**ILLOS*	*che**v**eux*	‘hair(s)’

The SPIR rule must have been dropped from the grammar at a very early stage in Portuguese, since in this language Latin intervocalic voiceless stops simply underwent VOI, as shown in (31b), not *also* SPIR, as they did in French (32b).

The general development of voiced labials in Hispano-Romance can be summarized by comparing the Latin-Modern Portuguese phonemic correspondences in (33) (where the dashes indicate word-medial environments):

(33)
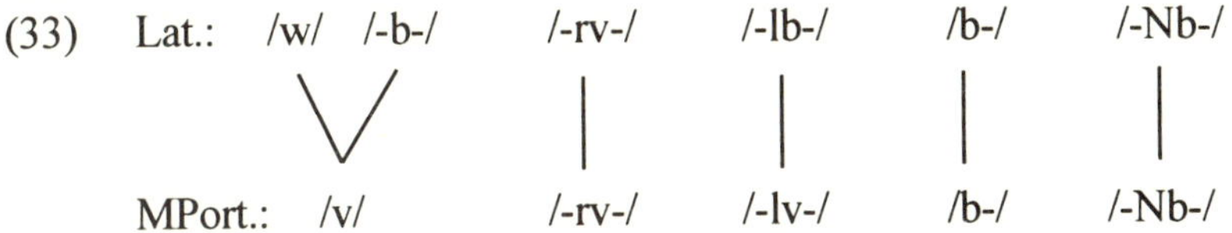

In order to reconstruct in some detail the evolution of voiced labials in Hispano-Romance proposed in this paper, it will be useful to review all the relevant historical rules involved, which I have formalized for convenience in (34) by means of segmental generative statements, listed in a sequence that replicates the assumed chronological order (for convenience, an abbreviation is provided in parenthesis for each of the processes formulated in (34)):[9]

(34) a. *Spirantization of voiced stops* (SPIR) (/b, d, g/ > [β, δ, γ]):

$$\begin{bmatrix} \text{-son} \\ \text{+voice} \\ \text{-long} \end{bmatrix} \quad > \quad [\text{+cont}] \quad / \quad [\text{+syll}] ____$$

b. *Obstruentization of /w/ (OBSTR-W)*:

(i) /w/ > [β]:

$$\begin{bmatrix} \text{-syl} \\ \text{+lab} \\ \text{+voice} \end{bmatrix} \quad > \quad \begin{bmatrix} \text{-son} \\ \text{-back} \\ \text{-rnd} \end{bmatrix}$$

---

[9] The account given in (34) is intended to facilitate comparison with Lozano's account, which is formulated within a linear generative model. The particular theoretical framework is not at issue here, buth rather the sequence of historical events proposed by the SSCP hypothesis.

(ii) [β] > [v]:

c.
$$\begin{bmatrix} \text{-son} \\ \text{+voice} \\ \text{-long} \end{bmatrix} > [\text{+cont}] \ / \ [\text{+cont}] \underline{\qquad}$$

d. *Voicing of voiceless obstruents (*VOI*)* (hence, /p, t, k/ > [b, d, g]):

$$\begin{bmatrix} \text{-son} \\ \text{-long} \end{bmatrix} > [\text{+voice}] \ / \ [\text{+syll}] \underline{\qquad}$$

e. *Degemination of long consonants* (**DEG**):

$$\begin{bmatrix} \text{+cons} \\ \left\langle \begin{matrix} \text{+son} \\ \text{+cor} \end{matrix} \right\rangle \end{bmatrix} > \begin{bmatrix} \text{-long} \\ \langle\text{+high}\rangle \end{bmatrix}$$

f. *Strengthening of /v/* (**STR-v**) (/v/ > [b]):

$$\begin{bmatrix} \text{+lab} \\ \text{+voice} \end{bmatrix} > \begin{bmatrix} \text{+distr} \\ \text{-cont} \end{bmatrix} \left\{ \begin{matrix} \#\# \\ \text{N} \end{matrix} \right\} \underline{\qquad}$$

g. *Bilabial becomes the default place of articulation for voiced labials* (**Def-Bilab**) (i.e., /v/ > /b/):

$$\begin{bmatrix} \text{+lab} \\ \text{+voice} \end{bmatrix} \quad > \quad [\text{+distr}]$$

In an initial (Proto-Romance) stage, SPIR applied after nuclear vowels, as formulated in (34a). The obstruentization of /w/ into the bilabial spirant [β] is captured by (34bi), while (34bii) expresses the subsequent labiodentalization of this spirant in Western Romance. It is natural to suppose that the shift [β] > [v] in (34bii) also affected those [β] derived by SPIR (34a). A phonological restructuring took place then whereby the surface labiodental [v] resulting from either SPIR or /w/-obstruentization was reanalyzed as an underlying /v/. Next, in a typically Hispano-Romance development, /b/ shifted to [v] when located after a liquid (34c) (Menéndez Pidal 1980: 139; cf. (31a) above). This may well have been the first in a sequence of phonetic readjustments that widened the scope of the SPIR rule, whose context changed from "after a syllabic vowel" to "after any continuant", as reflected in (34c). Essentially this is the environment in which SPIR applied throughout the Old Spanish period up to contemporary times. The next relevant historical rule is the VOI of voiceless simple obstruents in Western Romance, stated in (34d), which in our specific case turned /p, t, k/ into /b, d, g/. As stated earlier, VOI induced opacity in surface forms, and this prompted, almost immediately, a reanalysis of intervocalic [b, d, g] (< /p, t, k/) as members of the underlying set /b, d, g/, thus naturally becoming targets of SPIR. In a subsequent stage, long consonants were subject to the Deg rule stated in (34e); the angled brackets are used to reflect the fact that if the geminate was a coronal sonorant, then it also become a palatal. This accounts for the changes /n:/ > /ñ/ and /l:/ > /λ /. I assume that independent principles of markedness account for the absence of palatalization in rhotics. It is reasonable to suppose that Deg of long consonants (34e) was also followed by reanalysis of the simple reflexes as underlying simple consonants. The operation in (34f) reflects the shift from /v/ to /b/ in absolute word-initial and post-nasal positions, a process that came about in Early Old Spanish. The resulting [b] was then presumably reanalyzed as an allophone of /b/. Finally, the merger of /v/ with /b/ took place in two steps.

First, in Early Old Spanish /v/ began to shift to [b] word-initially and also after nasals, as suggested by frequent spelling hesitations such as ***bivir**/vivir* 'to live', *enbiar/enviar* 'to send', etc., found in the earliest documents (Pensado Ruíz 1984: 164-165, 172). The resulting bilabial stops are then reanalyzed as allophones of underlying /b/. This sound change probably compelled the reanalysis /v/ > /b/ (*circa* the 15th century) in a second and final step: the bilabialization of /v/ in all the remaining environments. I have stated this process in (34g) as change in the default value for voiced labials. The historical merger of /v/ with /b/ in Spanish is now complete.

In order to illustrate the preceding remarks, the proposed historical stages and the rules/reanalyses that apply at each stage in the evolution of labials in Hispano-Romance have been summarized in (35). The surface distribution of each set of underlying segments at a given stage is shown for the three complementary environments: **I** = after nasals and after pause word-initially; **II** = after liquids; and **III** = after vowels). Along with the surface distribution in the three given environments in (35) is a brief explanation, when necessary of the relevant event(s) that took place in each period, in line with the account given in (34). The stages comprised in (35) are: Classical Latin (*ClLat.*) (35a), Vulgar Latin (*VLat.*) (35b), Hispano-Romance (*HRom.*) stages I (35c), II (35d), and III (35e), Early Old Spanish (*EOSp.*), Old Spanish (*OSp.*), and Modern Spanish (*MSp.*):

(35) *Surface distribution of labials at several historical stages in Hispano* Romance:

a. *ClLatin:*

	I	**II**	**III**
/w/	[w]	[w]	[w]
/b/	[b]	[b]	[b]
/p/	[p]	[p]	[p]

b. *VLatin*: SPIR (34a) and OBSTR-W (34b):

	I	**II**	**III**
/w/	[β]	[β]	[β]
/b/	[b]	[b]	[β]
/p/	[p]	[p]	[p]

c. *HRom. I*: [β] shifts to [v], which is then analyzed as /v/. In addition, [b] shifts to [v] after liquids in HRom (/Lb/ > [Lv]; *L* = a liquid):

	I	II	III
/v/	[v]	[v]	[v]
/b/	[b]	—	—
/p/	[p]	[p]	[p]

d. *HRom. II*: Emergence of VOI (34d) (/p, t, k/ > [b, d, g]):[10]

	I	II	III
/v/	[v]	[v]	[v]
/b/	[b]	—	—
/p/	[p]	[p]	[β]

The voiced stops derived by VOI are subsequently reanalyzed as members of the underlying set /b, d, g/, and thus are subject to SPIR. Hence, VOI indirectly provided the SPIR rule with a fresh supply of voiced bilabial inputs:

	I	II	III
/v/	[v]	[v]	[v]
/b/	[b]	—	[β]
/p/	[p]	[p]	—

e. *HRom. III*: DEG (34e) creates a new supply of intervocalic voiceless stops, thus filling the gap left by VOI in this position:

	I	II	III
/v/	[v]	[v]	[v]
/b/ (< /-bb-/)	[b]	—	[β]
/p/ (< /-pp-/)	[p]	[p]	[p]

f. *EOSp.*: STR-v (34f) /v/ > [b] word-initially and after nasals (optional at first):

	I	II	III
/v/	[b]	[v]	[v]
/b/	[b]	—	[β]
/p/	[p]	[p]	[p]

---

10 At some historical point during the HRom. I-II stages, the SPIR rule was dropped from the grammar of Proto-Portuguese, but remained in Proto-Spanish.

g. *OSp.*: DEF-BILAB (34g) /v/ > [β] in remaining environments (optional at first), leading to complete merger of /v/ with /b/ (c. the 15th century):

	I	II	III
/v/	[b]	[v] ~ [β]	[v] ~ [β]
/b/	[b]	[β]	[β]
/p/	[p]	[p]	[p]

h. *MSp.* (present-day distribution in standard varieties):

	I	II	III
/b/	[b]	[β]	[β]
/p/	[p]	[p]	[p]

With regards the Hispano-Romance I stage (35c), it is important to note that at this point /v/ contrasts with /b/ word-initially, and after nasals, but not intervocalically within words and after liquids, since all instances of /b/ in the latter environments have shifted to /v/. The immediate consequence of such reanalysis was the creation of a defective distribution of voiced spirants in within words: the SPIR rule still targeted the underlying voiced stops /d, g/, but the bilabial stop /b/ was no longer a target of SPIR, since it had shifted to the labiodental phoneme /v/. However, the VOI rule in the following stage (35d) provided SPIR with a fresh supply of potential targets. In particular, the phonemic shift /p/ > /b/ (spelled *b* in OSp.) in postvocalic position filled in the distributional gap earlier found in the labial series, since at this point /b/ becomes an input to SPIR, as argued earlier.

The series of phonemic mergers/splits undergone by Portuguese and Spanish in its evolution from Hispanic Latin is provided in (36).

(36) *Sequence of phonemic shifts from Latin to Modern Portuguese and Modern Spanish*:

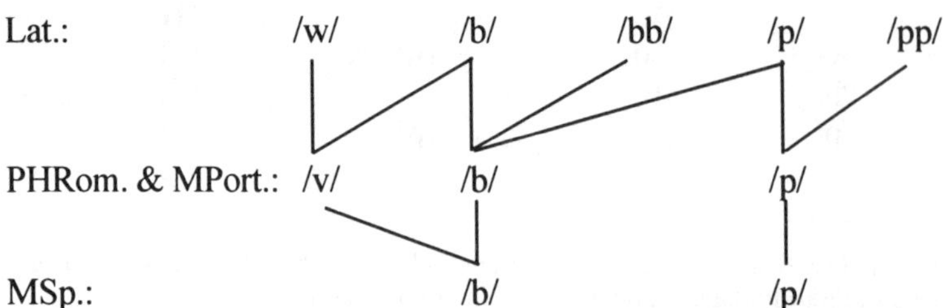

A more detailed schematic rendition of the three Hispano-Romance stages mediating between Vulgar Latin and Modern Portuguese, as proposed in (35)-(36), is presented in (37), which illustrates the surface realization of all Vulgar Latin underlying labials —including geminates— and their historical trajectory into Modern Portuguese.[11]

(37) *Historical stages in the development of labials from Latin to Modern Portuguese*:

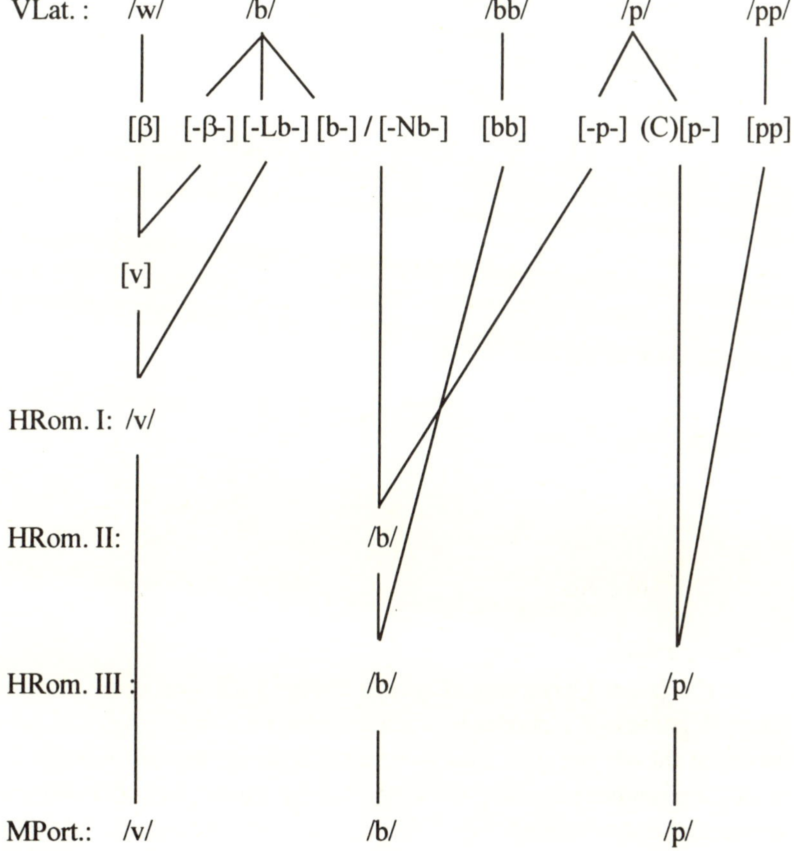

[11] In (37), '-C-' = an intervocalic consonant; 'C-' = word-initial after a pause; *L* = a liquid; *N* = a nasal).

Recall that in our account, Spanish followed the same course as Portuguese in all relevant aspects, up to the Hispano-Romance III stage in (37). We pick up Spanish at this stage in (38), showing how word-initial and post-nasal /v/ became a bilabial stop in the Early Old Spanish period, and later, around the 14th or 15th century, intervocalically and after liquids, yielding what is in essence the standard Modern Spanish distribution of stops and spirants.

(38) *Historical stages in the development of labials from HRom. III to Modern Spanish*:

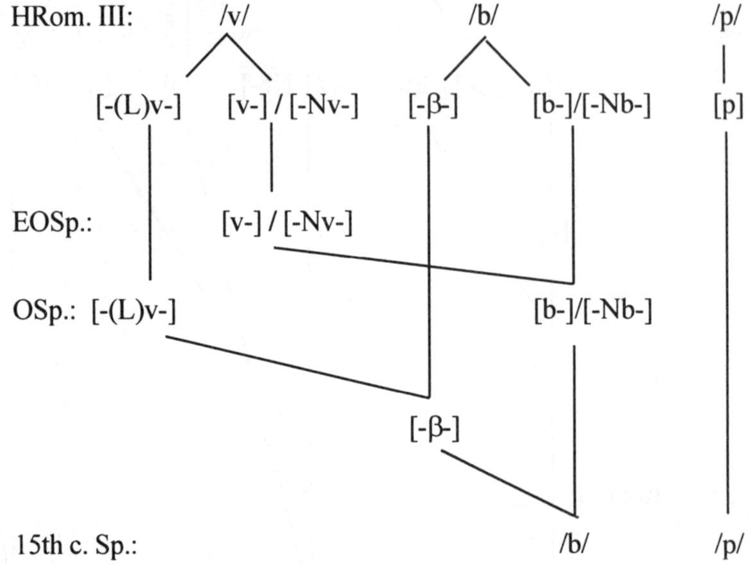

5. *Conclusion*

In this paper I have argued against the the widely accepted view that Old Spanish possessed a phonemic contrast between voiced stops and spirants. It has been shown that such a position raises makes a number of implicit claims which are neither plausible nor supported by the available documentary evidence. Several arguments of a different nature have been offered that call the traditional assumption into question. I have proposed an alternative scenario fully consistent with the historical record in which Spir never ceased to be a productive synchronic rule of Spanish throughout its history, even though we have also seen that the phonological environments conditioning its operation did undergo some changes, becoming more inclusive, reflecting a well-known mechanism of phonological change: *rule generalization* (King 1969, Kiparsky 1982). Thus, SPIR originally occurred after syllabic vowels only, but in Old Spanish its context had presumably been extended to after any continuant segment. Against the generally accepted thesis of Dámaso Alonso (1962) and subsequent work, I have suggested an account that fits better with Amado Alonso's (1949, 1955 [1967]) proposal that Old Spanish still maintained a labiodental reflex of Latin /b, w/. It is reasonable to infer that such reflex is directly inherited from Proto Western-Romance, since it is also found in French and Portuguese, although it was probably lost at an early stage in the eastern Iberian Romance languages such as Aragonese and Catalan (see Badía Margarit 1951). Dámaso Alonso (1962) was certainly justified in his rejection of Amado Alonso's suggestion that the 15th century bilabialization of /v/ had extended from the Basque Country and surrounding areas southward to Castilian and westward to Galician, becoming established in these regions in less than a century. To the extend that this sound change in effect spread from a focal point, as Dámaso Alonso contends, its diffusion may have taken a much longer period than Amado Alonso originally believed. However, Amado Alonso was probably correct in most other respects; the weight of the arguments put forth in this paper vindicates his view that a phonemic contrast between voiced stops and spirants was never part of the phonology of Old Spanish.

REFERENCES

Alarcos Llorach, Emilio. 1974. *Fonología española* (4th ed.) Madrid: Gredos.

Allen, J. H. D. 1976. "Apocope in Old Spanish". *Estudios ofrecidos a Emilio Alarcos Llorach*, 15-30. Oviedo: Universidad de Oviedo.

Alonso, Amado. 1949. "Examen de las noticias de Nebrija sobre la antigua pronunciación española". *Nueva Revista de Filología Hispánica* 3.65-70.

———. 1967. *De la pronunciación medieval a la moderna en español*, volumen I, Madrid: Gredos.

———. 1962. *La fragmentación fonética peninsular*. Madrid: CSIC.

Badía Margarit, Antonio. 1951. *Gramática histórica catalana*. Barcelona: Noguer.

Barbarino, J. L. 1981. *Latin and Romance Intervocalic Stops: A Quantitative and Comparative Study*. Madrid: Porrúa.

Blasco Ferrer, 1986. *La lingua sarda contemporanea.* Cagliari: Edizione della Torre.

Bourciez, Edouard. 1956. *Eléments de linguistique romane.* Paris: Klincksieck.

———. 1967. *Phonétique française: étude historique.* Paris: Klincksieck.

Bustos Tovar, Eugenio. 1960. *Estudios sobre asimilación y disimilación en el iberorrománico.* Madrid: Revista de Filología Española, Anejo 70.

Catalán, Diego. "En torno a la estructura silábica del español de ayer y del español de mañana". *Sprache und Geschichte, Festschrift für Harry Maier zum 65 Geburstag.* München: Wilhelm Fink Verlag, 77-110. (Reprinted in Catalan 1989).

———. 1989. *El español. Orígenes de su diversidad,* Madrid: Paraninfo.

Comrie, Bernard. 1993. "Typology and Language Reconstruction". *Historical Linguistics: Problems and Perspectives,* ed. by Charles Jones, 74-97. New York: Longman.

Correas, Gonzalo. 1626 [1954]. *Arte de la lengua española castellana.* Ediciones de E. Alarcos García. Madrid: CSIC.

Cravens, Thomas D. 1984. *The Phonological Unity of Intervocalic Stop Weakening in Romance.* Doctoral dissertation, University of Illinois at Urbana-Champaign.

Cuervo, Rufino J. 1895. "Disquisiciones sobre antigua ortografía y pronunciación castellanas". *Revue Hispanique* 2.1-69.

Grandgent, Charles H. 1907. *An Introduction to Vulgar Latin.* Boston: Heath and Co.

Graur, A. 1929. *Les consonnes géminées.* Paris: Champion.

Harris, James. W. 1984. "La espirantización en castellano y la representación fonológica autosegmental". *Working Papers in Linguistics* 1, Universitat Autònoma de Barcelona, 149-167.

Harris-Northall, Ray. 1990. *Weakening Processes in the History of Spanish Consonants.* London: Routledge.

Hualde, José I. 1991. *Basque Phonology.* New York: Routledge.

Jacobs, Haike, and Leo Wetzels. 1988. "Early French Lenition: A Formal Account of an Integrated Sound Change". *Features, Segmental Structures and Harmony Processes* ed. by Harry van der Hulst & Norval Smith, 105-129. Dordrecht: Foris.

Jungemann, Fredrik H. 1955. *Las teorías del sustrato y los dialectos hispano-romances y gascones.* Madrid: Gredos.

King, Robert D. 1969. *Historical Linguistics and Generative Grammar.* Englewood Cliffs, New Jersey: Prentice-Hall.

Kiparsky, Paul. 1971. "Historical Linguistics". *A Survey of Linguistics Science* ed. by W. Dingwall Park, 576-649. Maryland: University of Maryland Press [Reprinted in Kiparsky 1982].

———. 1973. "Phonological Representations". *Three Dimensions of Linguistic Theory* ed. by Osamu Fujimura, 1-136. Tokio: Taikusha

———. 1982. *Explanation in Phonology*. Dordrecht: Foris.

Kiss, Sandor. 1971. *Les transformations de la structure syllabique en latin tardif.* Debrecen: Kossuth Lajos Tudományegyetem.

Lapesa, Rafael. 1951. "La apócope de la vocal en castellano antiguo: Intento de explicación histórica". *Estudios dedicados a Menéndez Pidal*, vol. II, 185-226. Madrid: Consejo Superior de Investigaciones Científicas [Reprinted in Lapesa 1985, 167-197].

———.1975. "De nuevo sobre la apócope vocálica en castellano medieval". *Nueva Revista de Filología Hispánica* 24.13-23 [Reprinted in Lapesa 1985, 198-208].

———. 1981. *Historia de la lengua española* (9th ed.). Madrid: Gredos.

———. 1985. *Estudios de historia lingüística española*. Madrid: Paraninfo.

Lloyd, Paul M. 1987. *From Latin to Spanish*. Philadelphia: Memoirs of the American Philosophical Society, vol. 173.

Lozano, Carmen. 1979. *Stop and Spirant Alternations: Fortition and Spirantization Processes in Spanish Phonology*. Bloomington, Indiana: Indiana University Linguistics Club.

Maddieson, Ian. 1984. *Patterns of Sounds*. New York: Cambridge University Press.

Martinet, André. 1951-1952. "The Unvoicing of Spanish Sibilants". *Romance Philology* 5.133-156.

———. 1952. "Celtic Lenition and Western Romance Consonants". *Language* 28.192-217.

———. 1974. *La economía de los cambios fonéticos*. Madrid: Gredos.

Mascaró, Joan. 1984. "Continuant Spreading in Basque, Catalan, and Spanish". *Language Sound Structure* ed. by Mark Aronoff & Richard T. Oehrle, 287-298. Cambridge, Mass.: MIT Press.

Menéndez Pidal, Ramón. 1980. *Manual de gramática histórica española* (16th ed.) Madrid: Espasa Calpe.

Montgomery, Thomas. 1975. "La apócope en español antiguo y la 'i' final latina". *Studia Hispanica in Honorem R. Lapesa*, vol. III. Madrid: Gredos, 351-362.

Nebrija, Antonio de. 1492 [1986]. *Gramática de la Lengua Castellana.* (Text established on the "princeps" edition of 1492 by G. P. Galindo Romeo and L. Ortiz Muñoz). Madrid: Ediciones de la Junta del Centenario.

Otero, Carlos P. 1971. *Evolución y revolución en romance*, vol. 1. Barcelona: Seix Barral.

Penny, Ralph. 1976. "The Convergence of *B*, *V* and *-P-* in the Peninsula: A Reappraisal". *Medieval Studies Presented to Rita Hamilton* ed. by A. D. Deyermond, 149-159. London: Tamesis.

Pensado Ruiz, Carmen. 1984. *Cronología relativa del castellano*. Salamanca: Ediciones Universidad de Salamanca.

Pope, M. K. 1934. *From Latin to Modern French with Special Consideration of Anglo-Norman*. Manchester, England: University of Manchester Press.

Politzer, Robert L. 1951. "On the Chronology of the Simplification of Geminates in Northern France". *Modern Language Notes* 1951, 527-531.

Steriade, Donca. 1988. "Gemination and the Proto-Romance Syllable Shift". *Advances in Romance Linguistics* ed. by David Birdsong & Jean-Pierre Montreuil, 371-409. Foris: Dordrecht.

Stevens, Kenneth, Samuel J. Keyser, and H. Kawasaki. 1986. "Towards a Phonological and Phonetic Theory of Redundant Features". *Invariance and Variability in Speech Processes* ed. by J. Perkell & D. Platt, 426-449. Hillsdale, New Jersey: Lawrence Earlbaum.

———, and Samuel J. Keyser. 1989. "Primary Features and their Enhancement in Consonants". *Language* 65.81-106.

Wagner, Max L. 1941. *Historische Lautlehre des Sardischen*. Halle: Max Niemeyer Verlag.

Walsh, Thomas. 1991. "The Demise of Lenition as a Productive Phonological Process in Hispano-Romance". *Linguistic Studies in Medieval Spanish* ed. by Thomas Cravens & Ray Harris-Northall, 149-163. Madison, Wisconsin: Hispanic Seminary of Medieval Studies.

Weinrich, Harold. 1958. *Phonologische Studien zur romanischen Sprachgeschichte* (*Forschungen zur romanische Philologie, Heft 6*). Münster-Westfalen: Aschendorffsche Verlag.

Wireback, Kenneth J. 1993. *The Role of Phonological Structure in Sound Change: from Latin to Spanish and Portuguese*. Unpublished doctoral dissertation, Pennsylvania State University.

Williams, Edwin. 1968. *From Latin to Portuguese: Historical Phonology and Morphology of the Portuguese Language*. Philadelphia: University of Pennsylvania Press.

PPs WITHOUT Ps IN SPOKEN RIOPLATENSE SPANISH[1]

FRANCISCO OCAMPO
University of Minnesota

Introduction

In data from casual conversations among Rioplatense speakers it is possible to find examples of prepositional phrases where the preposition is lacking, as in examples (1) to (4):

(1) *si quieren* ***las papas*** *les ponen jengibre, quedan ricas* 2a3[2]
if you wish the potatoes to them you put ginger they remain tasty
'you may add ginger to the potatoes if you wish, they come out tasty'

(2) *Lo que pasa es que* ***los micros*** *se amontona mucho la gente* 22a17
it what happens es that the buses cl[3] crowd together a lot the people
'what happens is that people are crowded together in the buses'

(3) M: *tengo miedo que se caiga por eso lo puse acá, nena*
I have fear that cl it falls down for this it I put here, girl
'I am afraid it would fall down, this is why I put it here, girl'

E: *a:h claro lo ponemos* ***una bolsita*** *querés decir* 16a34[4]
oh clear it we put a little bag you want to say
'oh yes, you mean we put it in a little bag'

---

[1] I would like to thank the participants of the LSRL XXVI, for their comments. Special thanks to Mario Saltarelli for his insightful suggestions. The final responsibility, of course, is mine.

[2] The numbers and letters indicate the location of the example in the corpus.

[3] Clitic

[4] The conventions used in the transcription are as follows. Three periods between square brakets '[...]' indicate that data is omitted, any portion inside square brakets [aeropuerto] has been added to the data for aclaratory purposes. A hiatus of any kind in the speech flow is marked by '-'. A pause is indicated by parentheses '()'. Underlined words indicate that they are perceived as salient (strong primary stress, or high pitch, or uttered with louder voice, etc.). Lengthening is indicated by colons ':' after a vowel or a consonant. The portions relevant for the analysis are shown **in bold characters**.

(4) *se ríen acá* ***lo del elefante****, pero allá las cosas que*
cl they laugh here the thing of the elephant, but there the things that
hacen 17a15
they do
'here people laugh because of the elephant, but over there the things [politicians] do [are unbelievable].'

Notice the lack of preposition in (1) *[a] las papas*, in (2) *[en] los micros*, in (3) *[en] una bolsita*, and in (4) *[por] lo del elefante*. These deletions occur only in casual speech. Most Rioplatense speakers would judge these sentences ungrammatical, if presented to them in isolation and in written form. Besides, speakers are not aware that they produce these forms quite frequently. This raises the general issue of grammaticality judgements (Schütze 1996).

These deletions are manifestations of a more general phenomenon of deletion in rapid casual speech, as shown in the following examples:

(5) *bueno* ***el caso que*** *ella se va sola a la iglesia los domingos* 1b7
well the case that she cl goes alone to the church the Sundays
'well, the thing is that on Sundays she is able to go to church by herself'

(6) *hay propuestas este: en Francia* ***para todo el mundo*** *dé trabajos*
there are proposals er in France for all the world give works
acerca de esto
about of this
'there are proposals in France so that everybody present papers about this' 11b8

(7) *pero no hay nadie de los que* ***tenga edad nuestra*** *que recuerde*
but no there is nobody of the that has age our that remembers
el treinta
the thirty
'but there is nobody who is our age who remembers the thirties' 17a10

In (5) the verb *ser* suffers deletion: *el caso [es] que*, in (6) the relative *que*: *para [que] todo el mundo*, and in (7) the article *la*: *tenga [la] edad nuestra*.

Lambrecht 1994:193 points out for English a phenomenon comparable to the one exemplified in (1) to (4):

(8) The typical family today, the husband and the wife both work (Lambrecht)

For Spanish, Klein-Andrew (Forthcoming:2) discusses the absence of the preposition in the case of personal pronouns: in (9) the speaker utilizes the pronoun *yo* instead of the standard form *a mí*.

(9) *y yo me entró una tos que me ahogaba del humo*
and I me it entered a cough that me it was choking from the smoke
'and me, a cough took over me that just about choked me, from the smoke'
(Klein-Andreu)

Hypothesis

These deletions, cannot be dismissed as performance errors, an opinion also shared by Klein-Andrew (forthcoming); they occur with a certain frequency and in particular contexts. This deletion may have a theoretical significance. Spanish is among the languages that make a grammatical distinction between noun phrases serving as core arguments and those having oblique roles. Core arguments are generally unmarked, while obliques are marked by prepositions. This difference is attributed to the fact that for core arguments such relationship between the noun phrase and the verb is reflected in the semantics of the verb, while for obliques, the relationship with the verb is indicated by a preposition (Thompson forthcoming). Also, the preposition not only relates noun phrases to verbs, but also relates noun phrases to noun phrases.

The deletion of the preposition in casual speech, as seen in examples (1) to (4), gives rise to the question of how the hearer is able to establish the relationship between the noun phrase and the verb, or between two noun phrases in the absence of the preposition. There are three factors which are instrumental for the hearer to establish this relation: (i) syntactic: the presence of a parallel structure, (ii) conversational, and (iii) processes of grammaticalization. Sometimes more than one factor is simultaneously at play. First I will describe the contexts where the preposition is missing, and then I will refer to each of these three factors.

The data for this work consists of a corpus of 20 hours of recorded informal conversations encompassing a total of 30 middle class speakers from La Plata, Argentina.

Contexts

There is a phonetic context that correlates with the absence of the preposition *a*, as seen in (10):

(10) *llamaron* [...] *para decir que la llevaran* ***algún lado*** 26b18
they called for to say that her they take some place
'they called [...] in order to say that they took her some place'

The preposition *a* may be deleted in the data when either the previous or the following word, or both, end with the sound [a].

The second context where a preposition is frequently omitted is before a relative pronoun, as seen in (11):

(11) *y a mí me pasó una vez con otro también ahí*
and to me to me it happened one time with other also there
'and this happened to me once with another one also there'

en la escuela ***que*** *fui a votar* 17a7
in the school that I went to vote
'in the school where I went to vote'

Here the preposition *en* is missing in *[en] que*. (Notice that the speaker could have utilized the relative *donde* to avoid the preposition). The deletion of the preposition before a relative pronoun is spread in Rioplatense Spanish. In this particular context sociolinguistic factors might be at work. This deletion of the preposition could be seen as the generalization of an ultracorrection process avoiding the *dequeísmo*, the excessive use of the combination *de que*, which is regarded as uneducated speech.

The third context where the preposition may be suppressed is when the constituent appears in initial position, as shown in examples (12) to (15):

(12) *se fueron al sur ()* ***ellos*** *les gusta mucho pescar trucha* 22b2
cl they went to the south they to them they like a lot to fish trout
'they went to the south () they like to fish trout a lot'

(13) (The ongoing topic is the fact that when the speaker was a teenager and went out on a date she was allowed by her mother to return late on the condition that the date would escort her home. Here the speaker refers to the different attitude of her mother-in-law)

bueno, ***eso*** *se enteraba la madre de él y yo era una loca* 17b30
well that cl find out the mother of him and I was a prostitute
'well, if his mother found that out she would consider me a prostitute'

(14) (This is a fragment of an oral narrative about a robbery in a bus)
y: el tipo, bueno, una vez que despluma a medio mundo, los hace
and the guy well one time that he robs to half world them cl makes
'and: the guy, well, once he robs everybody he makes them descend.'

bajar. Pero () qué te cuento que se queda con tres chicas, elige
descend but what you cl I tell that cl he stays with three girls he chooses
'But I tell you that he stays with three girls, he chooses'

a tres chicas, que se tienen que quedar en el micro - con el chofer,
to three girls who cl have that remain in the bus with the driver
'three girls who have to remain in the bus - with the driver,'

y ***el chofer*** *le dice que siga dando vueltas* 11b20
and the driver to him cl he tells that he continue giving tours
'and the driver, he tells him to drive around'

(15) *Exquisitos son con salsa de soya. Son perfectos.* ***Salsa de soya*** *y*
exquisite they are with sauce of soy they are perfect sauce of soy and
'They are exquisit with soy sauce. They are prefect. With soy sauce and'

una gotita de aceite son perfectos. 1a20
a little drop of oil they are perfect
'a little drop of oil they are perfect.'

In (12) the preposition *a* is deleted in *[a] ellos*. In this example the referent of the noun phrase without preposition is the topic of the sentence and is anaphorically linked with the rest of the construction by the means of the clitic *les*. In (13) the preposition *de* is omitted in *[de] eso*. Here, the referent of the noun phrase is also the topic of the construction but is not anaphorically linked. In (14) the preposition *a* is missing in *[a] el chofer*. The referent of the noun phrase is not the topic of the sentence, and is anaphorically linked with the construction by the means of the clitic *le*. In (15) the preposition deleted is *con* in *[con] salsa de soya*. Here, the referent of the noun phrase is not a topic and is not anaphorically linked.

Among non topical constructions in initial position I found in the data examples similar to the ones discussed by Klein-Andrew (forthcoming):

(16) *ellos los van a llevar a ustedes. [al aeropuerto]*
they to you go to take to you to the airport
***Nosotros** la despedida es acá*
us the farewell is here
'they will take you [to the airport]. The farewell for us will be here.' 13a5

The standard form would be *[para] nosotros*. Klein-Andrew hypothesizes that these constructions in first position indicate that their referent is the center of attention of the utterance.

Prepositions are also deleted in non-initial position, as shown in examples (17) and (18):

(17) (The topic of the conversation are antique irons heated by coals)
porque la costumbre acá ***la gente*** *fue he visto las vidrieras,*
because the habit here the people it was I have seen the show windows
'because the habit of the people was, I have seen the show windows,'

era pintarlas de blanco 16a9
it was to paint them of white
'it was to paint them [the antique irons] in white'

(18) *mirá hay* ***una región*** *un mito que es así* 22a1
look there is a region a mith that is like this
'look, there is a myth like this in a region'

In (17) the preposition *de* which relates the noun *costumbre* to the noun phrase *la gente* is missing. In (18) the preposition deleted is *en* which indicates the relationship between the verb *hay* and the noun phrase *la región*.

On Table1 the tokens and percentages of constructions with deleted prepositions are listed, classified by the four contexts previously discussed.

Table 1

Contexts	**Tokens**	**Percent**
Phonetic	21	10
P + Rel	78	38
Initial	69	33
Non-Initial	40	19
Total	208	100

The establishment of the relationship

I will adress now the issue of how the relationship between the noun phrase and the verb, or between noun phrases, can be established by the hearer. As stated before, there are three factors which enable the hearer, in the absence of the preposition, to establish a relationship between the noun phrase and the other constituents: syntactic, conversational, and grammaticalization. This makes it possible to infer a message. I will first address the syntactic factor. It consists of the presence of a competing structure which leaves open the possibility of ambiguity. This can be seen in example (15):

(15) *Exquisitos son con salsa de soya. Son perfectos.* ***Salsa de soya*** *y*
exquisite they are with sauce of soy they are perfect sauce of soy and
'They are exquisit with soy sauce. They are perfect. With soy sauce and'

una gotita de aceite son perfectos. 1a20
a little drop of oil they are perfect
'a little drop of oil they are perfect.'

There is a structure that can compete for interpretation, shown in (19):

(19) *[Salsa de soya y una gotita de aceite] y [son perfectos].*
sauce of soy and a little drop of oil and they are perfect
'soy sauce and a litlle drop of oil, and they are perfect'

The hearer can interpret the utterance as the two coordinated structures: *salsa de soya y una gotita de aceite* and *son perfectos* in which the noun phrase in question is no longer syntactically dependent on the verb.

A competing structure is also available in the case of noun phrases in first position whose referents are topics, as in (20):

(20) *la mayoría tienen () todas hijas mujeres () y: y:* ***la mujer tampoco la***
the majority have all daughters women and and the wife neither her
'the majority have daughters only a:nd a:nd they can't stand their women either.'

soportan*. Ninguno soporta, ni a la mujer ni a las hijas*
they stand nobody stands neither to the wife nor to the daughters
mujeres 22b4
women
'None of them can stand neither the wife nor the daughters.'

In (20) the hearer can reinterpret the noun phrase la mujer as left dislocated, therefore outside of the sentence, and anaphorically linked by means of the clitic *la*.

A related issue is if the anaphoric linkage plays any role in the deletion of the preposition. It could be argued that as the syntactic relation is expressed by the clitic, the preposition becomes redundant. Table 2 shows that out of the 69 constructions that appear in first position, 32 of them, that is 46%, have linked topics. These results seem to support the hypothesis.

Table 2

Constructions that appear in first position

	tokens	percent
linked topic	32	46
unlinked topic	13	19
linked non-topic	2	3
unlinked non-topic	22	32
total	69	100

On the other hand, if we oppose the categories topical versus non-topical, and linked versus unlinked (Table 3), we see that 65% (45 out of a total of 69) of all constructions that appear in first position are topic, while approximately 50% (34 out of a total of 69) of all constructions are linked. It is possible then to conclude that the preposition is more likely to be deleted in a topical construction than a non-topical one while, on the other hand, the linkage factor is irrelevant in the prediction of deletion.

Table 3

Topicality vs. Linkage

	tokens	percent
topic	45	65
non-topic	24	35
total	69	100
linked	34	49
unlinked	35	51
total	69	100

The second factor that enables the hearer to establish a relationship between the noun phrase and the rest of the sentence is conversational. The participants of oral exchanges have at their disposition contextual information, linguistic and extralinguistic, which can be used to compensate for the absence of the preposition, as in (21):

(21) *y - los - que: tienen esos terre::nos, que han hecho la propaganda,*
and those who have those lots that have done the publicity
'and - those - who have these lots, they have advertised them,'

se están vendiendo, de dos pesos que valían esos terrenos,
cl are selling from two pesos that were worth these lots
'they are being sold, they had a value of two pesos'

*ahora los están vendiendo:: **dólares**.*
now them cl are selling dollars
'now they are being sold in dollars'

Here the preposition *en* is omitted in non-initial position. Nevertheless the hearer can ascertain the relationship between the referent of the noun phrase *dólares* and the verb *vender* by taking into consideration contextual information.

The third factor is that hearers are able to establish the relationship between a noun phrase and a verb as a result of processes of grammaticalization (Heine, Claudi & Hünnemayer 1991). In this process the meaning of the preposition turns more and more abstract becoming at the end purely relational. It is in this last stage where the preposition can be deleted. For example, the preposition *en* in Spanish has a concrete locative meaning, as in (22):

(22) *Franco estuvo en el hospital* 26a25
was in the hospital
'Franco was in the hospital'

On the other hand, in (23) *en* has a temporal meaning:

(23) *en el ratito que ella está* 26b6
in the little while that she is
'in the little time that she stays'

Claudi et al (1991:49) describe these two stages in terms of a space-to-time metaphor that follows their postulated chain of increasing abstraction. It is in this more abstract temporal stage where the deletion of *en* can be claimed to be related to grammaticalization. In (24), for example, the hearer does not need the preposition, the meaning of the verb is enough to establish the relationship between the verb and the noun phrase.

(24) *Alfonsín termina* ***el sesentainueve*** 17a23
finishes the sixty-nine
'Alfonsín [the president] leaves office on sixty-nine.'

This is also the case of the so called *preposición régimen* in Spanish whose extremely abstract meaning makes it a candidate for deletion. In (25) we see the absence of the preposition *de* which is placed by grammatical convention after the verb *acordarse*:

(25) *¿Ustedes se acuerdan* ***los brasileños*** *cuando vinieron acá a la Argentina?*
you cl remember the brazilian when they came here to the
'Do you remember the brazilians when they came here to Argentina?'
15b10

In cases like (25) it is possible to postulate that the relationship between the verb and the noun phrase is no longer expressed by the preposition, but reflected by the verb. Therefore, these noun phrases are no longer obliques but arguments of the verb.

I have described first the four contexts in which prepositions are deleted. Then I have postulated three factors that enable the hearer to ascertain the relationship between the referent of the noun phrase and the verb. It is possible that these three factors: a competing structure, the context, and processes of grammaticalization, override the perception of ungrammaticality. These factors do not necessarily operate alone. There are many cases in the data where there is more than one factor at play. Also notice that it is this kind of variation —where a grammaticality judgement is revised—which sets the conditions for a possible language change. Notice, however, that this conceivable language change is likely to be of limited scope: it will envolve individual verbs but will not encompass the general loss of the preposition in Spanish. Although there is a process of erosion of the existing prepositions, the mechanism of grammaticalization is also creating new ones out of nouns, adverbs, or adjectives.

REFERENCES

Heine, Bernd, Ulrike Claudi, and Friederike Hünnemayer. 1991. *Grammaticalization. A conceptual Framework.* Chicago: The University of Chicago Press.

Klein-Andrew, Flora. Forthcoming. "Conversational Focus". *Advances in Sign-based Linguistics* ed. by Ellen Contini-Morava & Barbara Sussman Goldberg. Berlin & New York: Mouton de Gruyter.

Lambrecht, Knud. 1994. *Information Structure and Sentence Form.* Cambridge: CUP.

Schütze, Carson T. 1996. *The Empirical Base of Linguistics. Grammaticality Judgements and Linguistic Methodology.* Chicago: The University of Chicago Press.

Thompson, Sandra. Forthcoming. "Discourse Motivations for the Core-oblique Distinction as a Language Universal". *Functionalism in Linguistics* ed. by Akio Kamio. Berlin & New York: Mouton de Gruyter.

THE INVERSION CONSTRUCTION IN INTERROGATIVES IN SPANISH AND CATALAN

FRANCISCO ORDÓÑEZ
Graduate Center, CUNY

1. *Introduction*

In Spanish and Catalan, as illustrated in examples (1a) and (2a), there is an obligatory subject-verb inversion in interrogatives.

(1) a. *A quién visitó Juan?* (Sp)
Who visited Juan
b. **A quién Juan visitó?*
Who Juan visited

(2) a. *Qui veu en Joan?* (Cat)
who sees Joan
b. **Qui en Joan veu?*
who Joan sees

Some linguists (e.g. Torrego, 1984) have taken this inversion to be the output of the movement of the verb to a position to the left of the subject. Accepting this account, Rizzi (1991) explains the obligatoriness of the movement in terms of the wh-criterion,[1] a well-formedness principle at LF that requires a Spec-head configuration between a wh-word and a head with wh-features:

(3) Wh-criterion. (from Rizzi 1991)
a. A wh-operator must be in a Spec-head configuration with an x [+wh]
b. A X [+wh] must be in a Spec-head configuration with a wh-operator.

Rizzi postulates that the carrier of the wh-feature in (1a) and (2a) is the verbal inflection, which has moved to C overtly in order to enter into a Spec head agreement with the Word. Such a configuration is not obtained in (1b) and (2b) since the subject in Spec IP is placed between the wh-word and the inflectional head.

---

[1] Rizzi discusses mainly English, Italian, and French. However, his proposal is perfectly valid for Spanish and Catalan.

Nevertheless, Overt V-to-C is problematic on several levels.[2] Theoretically, it is incompatible with Kayne's (1994) antisymmetry proposal, particularly in its consequences for the position of clitics, and it leads to the erroneous conclusion that postverbal subjects could occupy the position of Spec of IP. In addition, it leads to a nonuniform account of inversion phenomena. Finally, crosslinguistically, this approach assumes a similarity between the Catalan and Spanish inversion phenomena and the V2 and Sub-Aux inversion of Germanic. This parallelism, I will show, cannot account for differences in the distribution of clitics and the possible placements of subjects after the auxiliaries in questions.

The alternative proposed here relies on the basic idea that V-to-C takes place at LF in these two languages, and that this movement is blocked by the intervening effect of pre-verbal subjects, which I take to be in a topic position.

1.1 *Antisymmetry and the landing site of clitics*

Kayne (1994) in the *Antisymmetry of syntax* concludes that pro-clitics in Romance cannot be adjoined to the same inflectional projection as the verb in sentences such as (4) and (5):

(4) *Juan le escribió* (Sp.)
Juan to-him wrote

(5) *En Joan li dóna el llibre* (Cat.)
Joan to-him gives the book.

The argument is presented in (6):

(6)

a. incompatible with LCA

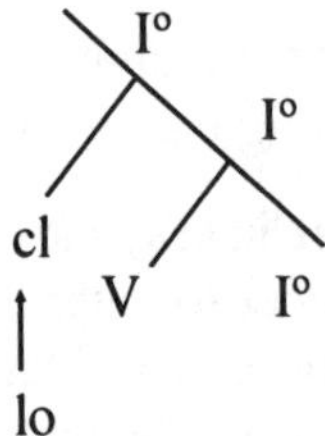

b. compatible with LCA

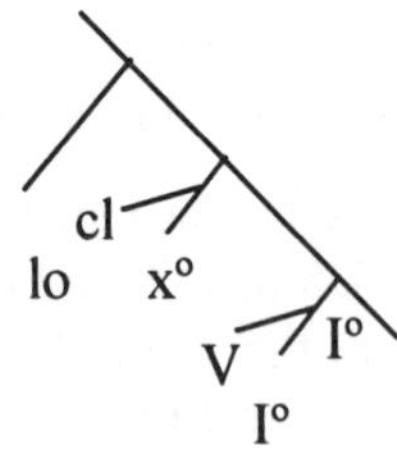

[2] Suñer (1994) is the first to deny the existence of overt V-to-C in Spanish. I will not repeat her compelling arguments in this paper.

The Linear Correspondence Axiom (LCA) (Kayne, 1994) bars multiple adjunction to the same head as shown in (6a) in which the pro-clitic is adjoined to the same head as the verb. Therefore, pro-clitics must be adjoined to an inflectional projection above the landing position of the verb, as represented in (6b).[3]

In this respect, Kayne's approach coincides with Sportiche's (1992) and Uriagereka's (1995), which also take pro-clitics to be adjoined to functional projections above the ones to which verbs are adjoined in finite declaratives.[4]

Since right adjunctions are also banned in the antisymmetry approach, there are two possible resolutions when the verb has to move to a position above the clitics, such as C. One, the verb could move directly over the position of the clitics as illustrated in (7a),[5] or it could move left adjoining to the clitic itself, and move along with it to C, as shown in (7b).[6] In either case, the order obtained is always verb-clitic.

(7)

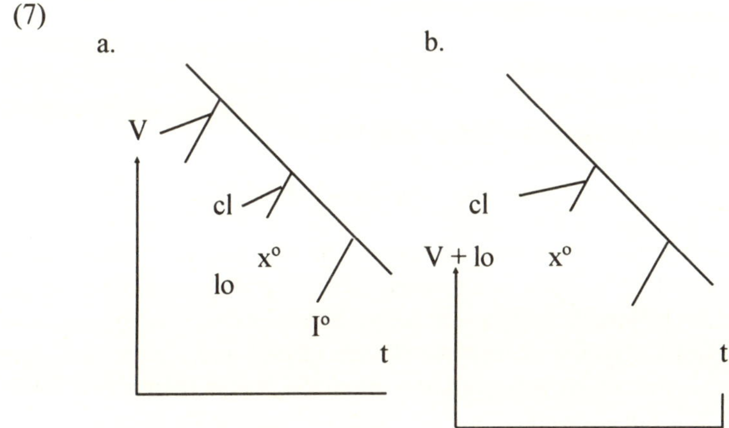

---

[3] Another possibility compatible with the LCA is that the clitic adjoins itself to the verb, which is already adjoined to the inflectional projection. However, this possibility is unlikely given that pronominal elements are excluded from appearing within words. (See Kayne, 1994, p. 42).

[4] Sportiche (1992) takes clitics to be in functional projections, or place holders. Uriagereka (1995) takes clitics to be adjoined to a functional projection that he calls Focus phrase.

[5] This possibility is entertained by Terzi (to appear). The movement of the verb over the place holder would not constitute a violation of the HMC under the shortest movement approach proposed by Ferguson and Groat (1995).

[6] This would be a case of incorporation as proposed by Cinque and Benincà (1993).

From this perspective, the postulation of movement of the verb to C in interrogatives in Romance would predict the V-Cl order. However, the contrasts in (8) and (9) for Spanish and Catalan show that the prediction is not borne out. The sequence V-Cl for interrogatives is ungrammatical.

(8) a. **¿Qué escribió le?*
What wrote-to her/him
b. *¿Qué le escribió?*

(9) a. **Què dónes li?*
what give-for her/him
b. *Què li dónes?*

In this respect, Spanish and Catalan clearly differ from the cases of the V-2 in Germanic. The V-2 phenomenon has been analyzed as involving the movement of the verb to C. In clear contrast to the Spanish or Catalan examples, the Germanic object clitics necessarily follow the verb in second position as shown in the contrasts in (10a) and (10b):

(10) a. *Gestern hat sich der Hans ein Buch gekauft.*
(from Kayne 1995, pg. 43)
Yesterday has cl the Hans a book bought.
'Yesterday Hans has bouught a book for himself'
b. **Gestern sich hat der Hans ein Buch gekauft*

Finally, Kayne's account leads naturally to the idea that verbs have moved further in the order V-cl than in the order Cl V. This allows a simple characterization of the difference between imperatives/infinitives versus finite verbs in Spanish and Catalan. For instance Rivero (1994) and Rivero and Terzi (1995) propose that verbs in imperatives move to C to get their illocucionary force. Thus, it is not surprising that V-Cl order obtains in these cases:

(11) a. *dóna-li* (Cat)
give it to him/her
b. **li dóna*

(12) a. *cómpralo* (Sp)
buy it.
**lo compra*

Similarly, Kayne (1991) proposes that infinitives in Italian (and by extension Spanish and Catalan) move to a projection higher than the one where the clitics are adjoined.[7]

(13) a. *Comprarlo* (Sp)
To buy it
b. * *Lo comprar*

(14) a. *donar-li* (Cat)
To give to him
b. **li donar*

This differentiation between infinitives and imperatives on the one hand, and normal finite verbs on the other is problematic for the overt V to C analysis in interrogatives. This approach leads to the conclusion that the clitic and verb have moved together as a unit in interrogatives. Thus, it inevitably leaves the contrasts between V-Cl and Cl-V entirely unmotivated in terms of verb movement. Unlike, an antisymmetry based account, it cannot elucidate why the properties of the verb (e.g. tense) play a crucial role in motivating one order or the other in the same language. For example, it might be expected that the verb should allow the Cl-V in imperatives in some Romance languages. However, such a possibility is barred in Romance languages with a specific imperative morphology as pointed out by Rooryck (1992).

In conclusion, the idea that pro-clitics and verbs are not adjoined to the same inflectional projection together with the general ban on right adjunctions, is incompatible with the existence of V-to-C in interrogatives in Spanish and Catalan. An analysis that denies V-to-C in finite interrogatives in Romance accounts straightforwardly for the difference between Germanic V-2 and Romance interrogatives. In particular it shows why clitics have to follow the verb in the Germanic but not in the Romance cases. Finally, it also gives a simple characterization of the distribution of the clitics in the different tenses in terms of verb movement.

1.2 *The position of the post-verbal subjects in interrogatives*

Another problematic issue for the overt V-to-C approach is encountered in the position of subjects in interrogatives. Spanish and Catalan are pro-drop

---

[7] Kayne's (1991) proposal would need to be modified since it involved adjunction of the clitic to a maximal projection.

languages and, in principle, subjects could either be in Spec of IP as in (15) or appear in a lower Spec position coindexed with an expletive *pro* in Spec of IP as in the Catalan example (16).

(15) $[_{IP}$El cotxe $[_{I}$ arriba]] (Cat)
The car arrives

(16) $[_{IP}$pro$_i$ arriba $[_{VP}$el cotxe$_i$]](Cat)

Given the hypothesis that postulates overt V-to-C, there are two possible analyses of the position of post-verbal subjects in interrogatives. Either they occupy the Spec of IP position or they simply occupy the lower Spec of VP position.

(17) [CP Wh- V $[_{IP}$ **SUB** $[_{VP}$ **SUB**]]]

As I will show, there are important reasons to doubt that subjects occupy Spec of IP in interrogatives. If this conclusion is correct, that removes one of the most compelling reasons for the movement of the verb to a higher C, namely the nonvacuous movement of the verb over Spec of IP position.

1.2.1 *Auxiliaries and Vpp*. On Rizzi's account, an auxiliary, in moving to C, leaves the Vpp in some projection internal to the IP. This leads to the prediction that subjects in Spec of IP might be placed between the auxiliary and the Vpp. However, examples (18)-(20) show that this prediction is not borne out.

(18) a. **Qui va la Magda veure?* (Cat)
who aux- Magda see
'who did Magda see'

b. *Qui va veure la Magda?*
Who aux-see Magda

(19) a. **Qui havia la Magda vist?* (Cat)
who had Magda seen

b. *Qui havia vist la Magda?*
Who had seen Magda

(20) a. **A quién había la madre de Juan visto?*(Sp)
Who had John's mother seen?

b. *A quién había visto la madre de Juan?*(Sp)
who had seen John's mother

In this respect, there is a clear cross-linguistic difference between Spanish and Catalan on the one hand and English and German on the other. In the Germanic languages, the subject is necessarily placed between the auxiliary and the Vpp, as in (21) and (22):

(21) a. Who has John's mother seen?
b. *Who has seen John's mother?

(22) a. *Was hat dein Bruder gekauft?*
What has your brother bought?
b. **Was hat gekauft dein Bruder?*
What has bought your brother

In order to explain this parametric contrast, maintaining the V-to-C approach, one might conclude, that contrary to German and English, the auxiliary and Vpp do not form a breakable unit in Romance because the Vpp incorporates to the auxiliary. However, there is good reason to be doubtful about such an alternative. For instance, Suñer (1988) has shown that an incorporation approach would be implausible for Spanish, given the fact that certain tenses in some dialects allow the insertion of material between the auxiliary and the Vpp.[8] On the other hand, Rizzi (1991) mentions that the auxiliary-vpp sequence is breakable in Italian with adverbials. Nevertheless, the subject cannot intervene between the auxiliary and the Vpp.

---

[8] In my dialect the aux-vpp unit is breakable with infinitives and with certain subjunctive tenses. Observe that even in these two cases the complementizer is filled by *de* in (i) and by *si* in (ii). Therefore, it is unlikely that the auxiliary is in C.

(i) *De haberlo yo sabido, no te habría dicho nada.*
of having-it I known, I wouldn't have told you anything.
'Had I known, I would not have told you anything.'

(ii) *?Si le hubiese yo hecho caso, no tendría ningún problema.*
If I to him/her had paid attention I would not have problems.

The length of the intervening subject is also an important factor that limits the possibility of breaking the verb and auxiliary. There is a clear contrast between the above examples and the following. In this respect the construction differs clearly from the English Subj-Aux inversion.

(iii) **De haberlo la chica que visitaste el otro dia sabido, no tendrías problemas ahora mismo.*
Of having the girl that you visited the other day known, you would had no problems.

(iv) **Si le hubiese la chica que visitaste el otro dia hecho caso...*

Finally, its is important to notice that some of the examples Suñer (1988) mentions, in which a tense Aux Vpp can be broken, come from the Caracas dialect. This variety belongs to the Caribbean dialect area which also allows the insertion of the subject between the verb and the Wh-word. (Thanks to E. Herburger, a native speaker of this dialect for the relevant information). An analysis of the properties of these constructions goes beyond the scope of this paper.

(23) a. **Che cosa ha il direttore detto?* (From Rizzi 1991)
What has the director said
b. *Che cosa ha detto il direttore?*
What has said the director

In conclusion, if Aux moves to C with compound tenses the subject cannot be in Spec of IP as would be expected given the English and German examples.

1.2.2 *Catalan and the position of subjects*. More evidence against the idea that the subject occupies the Spec of IP in interrogatives is given by Catalan in examples of a verb with one DP object and with modals. The overt movement to C approach predicts that subjects in Spec of IP should precede any other object complement in a lower inflectional projection in Catalan. However, the contrasts given in (24) show that the subject must necessarily follow the object.[9]

(24) a. * *A qui donarà la Magda el llibre?* V S O
whom will give Magda the book.
'Who will Magda give the book to?'
b. *A qui donarà el llibre la Magda?* V O S
whom will give the book Magda.

The same problem is attested with more complex verbal structures involving modals. If the modal had moved to C, the subject should appear in Spec of IP between the modal in C, and the infinitive that appears in the embedded clause. However, the contrast in (25) and (26) show that these sequences are ungrammatical.

(25) a. **A qui vol la teva germana [donar aquest llibre]?* Modal-SU-INF
to who wants your sister give this book?
'Who does your sister want to give this book to?'
b. *A qui vol [donar aquest llibre] la teva germana ?* Modal-INF-SU
to who wants give this book your sister

(26) a. **A qui pot la teva germana [demanar aquest llibre]?* Modal-SU-INF
to who can your sister ask this book
'Who can your sister borrow this book from?'

---

[9] The same argument applies for Italian. Spanish differs in this respect since the order V S O is available.

b. *A qui pot [demanar aquest llibre] la teva germana ?* Modal-INF-SU
who can ask this book your sister

1.2.3 *Floating quantifiers.* Floating quantifiers are licensed in both these languages as shown in (27)-(29)

(27) *Aquellos turistas vienen todos de Francia* (Sp)
these tourists come all from France.

(28) *Mis vecinos recibieron ambos una carta de recomendación* (Sp)
my neighbors received both a letter of recommendation

(29) *Aquests turistes vénen tots de França* (Cat)
these tourists come all from France

Sportiche (1988) analyzed these cases of floating quantifiers as instances where the NP subject and the floating quantifier originate as a syntactic unit in Spec of VP. In a later stage of the derivation the subject moves to some inflectional projection leaving the floating quantifier stranded behind as represented in (30):

(30) $[_{IP}$ *Aquests turistes*$_i$ $[_{I}$ *vénen* $[_{VP}$ *tots* t_i *de França*]]](Cat)
these tourists come all from France

If the verb had moved to C in interrogatives, the FQ might still be stranded with the subject in Spec of IP. However, the sequence V-Sub-FQ is ungrammatical:[10]

(31) * $[_{CP}$ *D'on vénen* $[_{IP}$ *aquests turistes* $[_{VP}$ *tots* t]]] ?(Cat)
from where come those tourists all
'Where do all those tourists come from?'

(32) * $[_{CP}$ *¿De dónde vienen* $[_{IP}$ *estos turistas* $[_{VP}$ *todos*]]]? (Sp)
from where come those tourist all
'Where do all those tourists come from?'

(33) * $[_{CP}$ *¿Qué recibieron* $[_{IP}$*tus vecinos* $[_{VP}$ *ambos*]]]? (Sp)
what received your neighbors both
'What did your both neighbors receive?'

---

[10] The argument against V-to-C based on the distribution of FQ is equally valid if FQs are treated as predicative adverbials.

To finish, all these constraints on the placement of subjects point to the conclusion that subjects cannot appear in Spec of IP in interrogatives in Spanish and Catalan. If V-to-C existed in these languages, it would always have to take place vacuously.

In order explain why subjects cannot appear in Spec of IP, Rizzi (1991) following Rizzi and Roberts (1989), postulates that V-to-C in interrogatives destroys the Spec-head configuration necessary for case assignment to the subject in Spec of IP. Consequently, nominative case is alternatively assigned by tense to the right in sentences like (1a) and (2a).

This solution is problematic in various respects. First of all, we are forced to conclude that expletive or argumental, pro, which by hypothesis is in Spec of IP, does not receive case in interrogatives. On the other hand, this idea clashes with the derivational approach advocated in the minimalist program (Chomsky 1995). From this latter perspective, once a configuration for case is obtained at a certain stage of the derivation, it cannot be undone in later steps.

Finally, this solution is too strong given the existence of Aux-to-Comp constructions. Rizzi (1982) postulated that these constructions involve movement of the Aux-to-C. The auxiliary in C would assign case to the subject in Spec of IP. This at least implies that it is possible for the verb in C to assign nominative case in certain instances.

(34) [*Avendo* [*Mario* t [*accettato di aiutarci.*]]]
Having Mario accepted to help us

1.3 V-to-C *and the* "free inversion" *construction*

Spanish and Catalan allow subjects to appear post-verbally in declarative sentences in what it is called "free inversion":

(35) *Van venir* *alguns estudiants* (Cat)
came some students.

(36) *Vinieron* *varios estudiantes* (Sp)
came some students

The obvious question is whether there should be a common analysis of this type of inversion and the one resulting from interrogatives. The answer must be affirmative since both constructions show exactly the same constraints.

For instance, subjects are not allowed between the auxiliary and the Vpp as shown in examples (37).

<u>Aux-SU-V versus Aux-V-SU</u>

(37) a. * *La había* *la madre de Juan* *visto.* (Sp) Aux-SU-V
cl- had Juan's mother seen.
'Juan's mother had seen her.'
b. *La había visto* *la madre de Juan.* Aux-V-SU
cl- had seen Juan's mother

Also, the subject cannot appear between the object and the verb in the Catalan example (38):

<u>Catalan V S O versus V O S</u>

(38) a. * *Em donarà* *la Magda* *el llibre.* V S O
cl-to me will give Magda the book.
'Magda will give the book to me.'
b. *Em donarà* *el llibre* *la Magda.* V O S
cl-to me will give the book Magda.

Additionally, the subject cannot appear between the infinitive and the modal verb in (39):

<u>Modal-SU-INF versus Modal-INF-SU</u>

(39) a. **Vol* *la teva germana* *demanar aquest llibre.* Modal-SU-INF
wants your sister to order this book
'Your sister wants to oder this book.'
b. *Vol* *demanar* *aquest llibre* *la teva germana.* Modal-INF-SU
wants to order this book your sister.

Finally the sequence V S FQ is not allowed either.

(40) a. **Vénen* *de França* *aquests turistes* *tots.* (Cat) V-SU—FQ
come from France these tourists all
'All these tourists come from France.'

However, the possibility of extending the overt V-to-C to the free inversion construction is problematic in two respects: From a theoretical point of view, it is not clear what the trigger for V-to-C movement could be since there is no obvious criterion to be satisfied. Even more importantly, the free inversion construction can appear in embedded sentences with a filled overt complementizer as in (41):

(41) *M'han dit* **que** ***vindran*** ***alguns estudiants*** (Cat)
to me have told that will come some students.
'They told me that some students will come'

The impossibility of extending the overt V-to-C analysis for the cases of free inversion poses problems to this approach overall. On the one hand, it is clearly unsatisfactory to have two analyses for constructions that are otherwise alike, one in which V-to-C applies vacuously, as in the interrogative construction, and one in which V-to-C does not apply at all, as in the free inversion construction. On the other hand, it shows that the explanation of the constraints on subjects appearing in Spec of IP in the interrogatives is insufficient; the explanation could not be extended to the free inversion construction. There must be a common account for the contrasts. This account evidently cannot rely on overt V-to-C.

In conclusion, the overt V-to-C approach encounters serious problems when it is extended to the so called free inversion construction since that construction can appear in embedded sentences with a filled complementizer. It leads to a duplication of analysis for constructions that otherwise have the same properties. It is evident that a uniform account will have to deny the V-to-C approach to interrogatives altogether.

2. *The obligatoriness of inversion in Interrogatives in Spanish and Catalan*

Once the overt V-to-C approach is eliminated, the explanation for the ungrammaticality in (1b) and (2b) clearly needs to be approached in terms of what blocks pre-verbal subjects from appearing in interrogative contexts:

(1b) **A quién Juan visitó?*
Who Juan visited

(2b) **Qui en Joan veu?*
who Joan sees

There are various possible ways to account for this prohibition.

2.1 *A -Minimality*

Suñer (1994) explores the possibility that the ungrammaticality of (1b) and (2b) could be due to the fact that subjects in Spec of IP block the movement of a wh-word. She proposes a specific principle of argumental agreement, which expresses the idea that an argumental wh-word in Spec of CP maintains a long distance agreement relation with the inflection of the verb. Such an argumental agreement relationship cannot be interrupted by any other argumental DP in between the highest verb in I and the wh-word. Therefore, the ungrammaticality of (1b) and (2b) is accounted for because the subject in Spec of IP counts as an argumental element, which blocks such a relationship.

(42) Argumental Agreement Licensing (From Suñer 1994)

a. Argumental wh-phrases must be licensed through symmetric Arg-agreement between α (=SpecC) and β (=c)
b. β arg agrees with γ (=V) only if βand γ are arg-marked and no other Arg-marked element is closer to γ .

Sentences with post-verbal subjects as (43) do not have the same effect since the element in Spec of IP is a non argumental *pro*, which by (44) does not count as a possible blocking element:

(43) *A quién* $[_{IP}$ pro$_{expl}$ *visitó Juan*] ?
Who Juan visited

As in the case V-to-C, however, this solution encounters problems when the status of argumental *pro* is considered in sentences like (43). If argumental *pro* occupies Spec of IP as in (45a), it should have the same blocking effect of a lexical argument DP and a sentence like (44) should be ungrammatical. Alternatively, the analysis to be adopted would involve a non argumental *pro* in Spec of IP co-indexed to an argumental *pro* in Spec of VP as in (45b). However, such an alternative cannot be adequate either since argumental *pro* in Spec of VP would fail to be identified by Agr S , which is too far away.

(44) *A quién visitó?*
Who visited-3p.s?
'Who did he visit'

(45) a. *A quién* pro$_{+arg}$ *visitó*
b. *A quién* pro$_{-arg}$ *visitó* $[_{VP}$pro$_{+arg}]$

Moreover, this approach turns also to be problematic from a cross-linguistic point of view. It is not clear why subjects in Spec of IP in English or German do not have the same blocking effects given the grammaticality of run-of-the-mill English sentences like (46).

(46) What did he buy

2.2 *A-bar minimality*

The elimination of V-to-C, the different behaviors of lexical subjects and pro, and also the difference of Spanish and Catalan with respect to English and German lead to the conclusion that preverbal lexical subjects in Spanish and Catalan must have a different distribution from pro and from DP subjects in English and German. The question then is what that distribution is. One hypothesis is that pre-verbal lexical subjects in Spanish and Catalan are dislocated to a more peripheral position. This notion is not new to this study. It has been proposed for Spanish by Contreras (1991), Zubizarreta (1994), Uribe Etxebarria (1995) Ordóñez and Treviño (1995); for Rumanian by Dobrovie-Sorin (1991) ; and for Catalan by Solà (1992) and Rigau (1988). The idea will be implemented following recent proposals by Baker (1996) on the polisynthesis parameter for non-configurational languages.

Under Baker's proposal *pro* apprears in Spec of IP, while DPs appear displaced to a more peripheral position. Following the antisymmetry proposal and the ban on multiple adjunction, I will assume that preverbal lexical DPs are in the Spec of a topic projection.

(47)

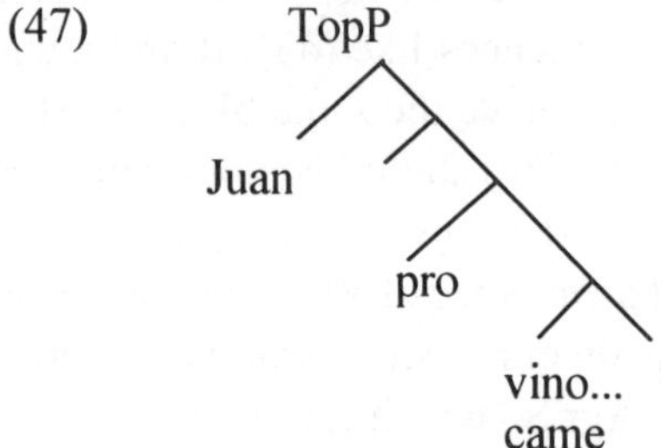

Since *pro* and lexical subjects occupy different positions, the fact that *pro* does not have any intervention effects on the extraction of the wh-word is less surprising. Also, the contrast between Spanish and Catalan with respect to German and English becomes understandable if pre-verbal subjects in English are not topicalized, but occupy a Spec of IP position like *pro.*

The idea that subjects occupy a more external position in Spanish than in English could be corroborated from the behavior of complementizer-less dependent clauses in both languages. It is well-known that complementizers can be dropped in English clauses like (48). Certain dialects of Spanish also allow this complementizer deletion (see Torrego 1982). The important fact to notice is that, contrary to English, pre-verbal subjects are not allowed in complementizerless dependent clauses as shown in (49b).

(48) Jane regrets Melissa is not home.

(49) a. *Lamento* *no esté contenta Carmen.* (Sp) (from Torrego 1982)
I regret is not happy Carmen
'I regret Carmen is not happy'
b. **Lamento* *Carmen no esté contenta* (Sp) (from Torrego1982)
I regret Carmen is not happy

It is tempting to think that the ungrammaticality of (50a) in Spanish is parallel to the ungrammaticality of a sentence of English with a peripheral adjunct as in (50b).

(50) a. **Lamento* $[_{Top\,P}$ *Carmen*$_i$ [IP pro $_i$ *no esté contenta*]]*
b. Jane regrets $[_{Top\,P}$ yesterday $[_{IP}$ Melissa went to his house]]

By the analysis given before, the adjunct yesterday in English and the preverbal subject in Spanish would occupy more peripheral positions, which could not be licensed in this type of construction. Thus, preverbal subjects in English correspond to *pro* in Spanish as lexical subjects in Spanish correspond to adjuncts in English.

If subjects in Spanish and Catalan are in an A' position, it would be possible to understand the ungrammaticality of (1b) and (2b) in terms of A' minimality. Unfortunately, this position is problematic. From this perspective, topics in an A' position would block the movement of the wh-word to Spec of CP. Nevertheless, Torrego (1984) has shown that the extraction of a wh-word over a pre-verbal subject is available in embedded declaratives where long distance wh-movement has taken place as in (51a). The same possibility seems to be available with other nonsubject topics in embedded declaratives such as in (52a). If a subject in topic position were blocking the extraction of wh-element, there should not be any contrast between (a) and (b) in the two groups of sentences:

(51) a. *Qué pensabas* *que* [$_{Top P}$ *la revista* [$_{IP}$ *había publicado*]] (Sp)
What you thought that the magazine had published
'What did you think that the magazine had published?'
b. **Qué* [$_{Top P}$ *la revista* [$_{IP}$ *había publicado*]]? (Sp)
What the magazine had published
'What did the magazine publish?'

(52) a. *Qué imaginabas* *que* [$_{Top}$ *a ti* [$_{IP}$*te iban a regalar?*]](Sp)
What you thought that to you they were going to give?
'What did you think that they were going to give to you?'
b. **Qué* [$_{Top P}$ *a ti* [$_{IP}$ *te iban a regalar*]]? (Sp)
What for you they were going to give.
'What were they going to give to you?'

Thus, it is promising to think that lexical subjects are in a topic position in Spanish and Catalan. This explanation would account for why lexical subjects, but not *pro,* have a blocking effect in interrogatives. However, the simple idea that topics would create an A' minimality effect in interrogatives seems to be too strong given the facts from long distance extraction out of embedded declaratives.

2.3 V-to-C *at* LF

The contrast between (51) and (52) is also indicative of one other syntactic effect: The blocking of the lexical DP subject only occurs in the sentence where the wh-word lands. Therefore, the principle that explains the contrast in (1) and (2) must be very local. I will maintain, with Rizzi (1991), that this local principle is agreement, as stated in the Wh-criterion. However, I will adopt the idea that this Wh-agreement is satisfied by the movement of the verb at LF as has already been proposed by Sportiche (N.D.) for the cases of complex inversion of French.[11] Thus, the agreement relation is obtained before Spell Out in the English example (53), while it is obtained at LF in the Spanish/Catalan counterpart (54):

(53) [$_{CP}$ What did [$_{IP}$ he I [$_{VP}$ buy t]]]? (wh-criterion before Spell Out)

(54) [$_{CP}$ *A quién* C° [$_{IP}$ pro [*I' visitó*]]]]? (Sp) [wh-criterion at LF)

[11] Wind (1993) has a similar proposal in terms of percolation of features of in the Complex Inversion in French

In English topics or adjuncts block overt head movement of the auxiliary *do* to C as in (55).

(55) * [$_{CP}$What did [$_{TopP}$yesterday TOP° [IP Peter buy?

Given the ban on multiple adjunctions, these adjuncts are in the Spec of a topic projection. Thus, movement of the auxiliary over that topic head produces an HMC violation. The reason for that violation could be due to the fact that topic head is not suitable landing site for the auxiliary head which is specified with a Wh-feature.

Spanish and Catalan subjects are also in that topic position. The counterpart of the previous English example is the Spanish and Catalan examples (1b) and (2b), represented in (56). In similar fashion, the movement of the verb at LF in Spanish and Catalan would be blocked by the topic head introduced by the lexical pre-verbal subject:

(56)* [$_{CP}$*A quién* C [TopP*Juan* Top^0 [$_{IP}$pro *visitó*]]]? (Al LF)

Thus, this analysis gives an understanding of why pre-verbal lexical subjects, but not *pro,* are blockers for the relation between the wh-word and the verb. Since there is an agreement relationship between the highest verb and the wh-word, embedded topics as a lower constitiuent are irrelevant .

3. *Conclusion*

It has been shown that movement of the verb in Spanish and Catalan in overt syntax conflicts in important ways with antisymmetry theory and its implications for the landing sites of clitics. The difference betwen Catalan and Spanish with respect to the Germanic languages examined here in this respect can only be understood if the former languages lack overt V-to-C. It has also been shown that post-verbal subjects in interrogatives are not in Spec of IP. These post-verbal subjects in interrogatives behave like post-verbal subjects in the so-called free inversion construction. It has been pointed out that the overt V-to-C approach is unable to give a uniform account of both constructions.

Once overt V-to-C is eliminated, however, a puzzle appears: Why do empty subjects in Spanish and Catalan not have the same blocking effects as overt subjects?. Similarly, why do DP subjects in English, contrary to Catalan and Spanish, allow such extraction? The answer appears to be that lexical subjects in Catalan and Spanish must occupy a topic position. Finally, to explain why there is obligatory inversion in interrogatives, I adopt the idea that V-to-C applies at LF. Subjects in topic position block the V-to-C at LF.

Appendix

Finally, some remarks need to be made about the fact that certain wh-words do not trigger obligatory inversion in Spanish. Some authors (Torrego, 1984) and (Suñer, 1994) have proposed that non argumental wh-words do not require inversion, while argumental wh-words do.

I think that the distinctions in the obligatority of the inversion do not cut across the argumental-non argumental distinction so much as the one between complex and non complex wh-elements as proposed in Ordóñez and Treviño (1995):

(57) a. * *Cuándo* *tus hermanas* *se fueron?*
When your sisters left
b. *En qué momento* *tus hermanas* *se fueron?*
In which moment your sisters left

(58) a. **Cómo* *tu hermana* *se cayó* *de la cama?*
How your sister fell from bed?
b. *De qué manera* *tu hermana* *se cayó de la cama?*
In which way your sister fell from bed.

(59) a. **Dónde* *tus amigos* *se divorciaron?*
Where your friends got divorce.
b. *En qué lugar* *tus amigos* *se divorciaron?*
In which place your friends got divorced.

The same problem cuts across argumental wh-questions. Speakers find an improvement of complex wh-word over non complex ones:[12]

(60) a. **A quién* *tu hermana* *visitó?*
Who your sister visited
b. *A cuál de estas chicas* *tu hermana (la) había visitado en Sicilia?*
Which of the girls your sister had visited in Sicily

---

[12] Calabrese (1982) reports a similar phenomenon in Italian, as illustrated in (i)

(i) *Qualle delle ragazze che abbiamo incontrato, Mario ha conosciuto in Sicilia?*
(From Calabrese 1985)
Which of the girls that we just saw, Mario has already met in Sicily?

c. *A cuál de las chicas que vinieron tu hermana (la) había visitado?*
Which of the girls that came your sister had visited

Observe that in English overt V-to-C in questions is triggered no matter how complex the wh-element is as in the contrast in (61). This constitutes another argument against a uniform treatment of Spanish/Catalan Inversion construction and the the V-2/Aux-NP inversion of Germanic.

(61) a. Which of the girls that we had met has Mario fallen in love with?
b. *Which of the girls that we had met Mario has fallen in love with?

I would like to adopt the idea that complex wh-word in the preceding examples in Spanish are not in Spec CP but are "left dislocated." Therefore, since there is no Wh-criterion to be satisfied it becomes less surprising that pre-verbal subjects can intervene between the complex wh-word and the verb. As pointed out by Rizzi (1995), complex negative quantifiers in Italian can also be left dislocated contrary to simple ones as shown in the following contrast:

(62) a. *Nessuno di questi ragazzi lo conosco veramente bene* (From Rizzi 1995)
No one of these boys cl- I know very well.
b. **Nessuno l'ho visto.*
No one cl-have seen

In Rizzi's view, the reasons for this contrast have to do with the possibility of the quantifier in the Spec of the complex DP to move at LF and bind a variable inside that DP as in (63). Even if the whole DP is left dislocated, the quantifier in its Spec can still form the operator-variable configuration needed.

(63) *Nessuno [ec di questi ragazzi] TOP lo conosco veramente bene.*

The similarity between these cases requires a uniform treatment. In other words, if the behavior of simple versus complex negative quantifiers is the same as that of simple versus complex question words, these contrasts are likely to have the same explanation. I would like then to suggest that the complex wh-constituents are left dislocated and that the quantifier part is moved at LF in order to obtain the needed quantificational interpretation. They, thus, function in a similar fashion to the negative cases.[13]

---

[13] An important question that arises is the fact that resumptive clitics do not seem to be required in the examples with complex quantifiers even if they are left dislocated. The same applies for

(64) *A Cuál [ec de las chicas]* TOP *tu hermana la había visitado antes?*
Which of these girls your sister has seen before.

In conclusion, the complexity of the wh-words seems to be an important factor that determines the possibility of inversion in Spanish. Following Rizzi (1995), I have proposed an alternative where complex wh-words are left dislocated.

REFERENCES

Baker, Mark. 1996. *The Polysynthesis Parameter*. New York: Oxford University Press.

Benincà, Paola & Guglielmo Cinque. 1993. "Su alcune differenze fra enclisi e proclisi". *Omaggio a Gianfranco Folena*, 2313-2336. Editoriale Programma, Padova.

Calabrese, Andrea. 1982. "Alcune ipotesi sulla struttura informazionale della frase in italiano e sul rapporto con la struttura fonologica". *Rivista di Grammatica Generativa* 3-38.

Cinque, Guglielmo. 1990. *A'-Dependencies*. Cambridge, Mass.: MIT Press.

Chomsky, Noam. 1995. *The Minimalist Program*. Cambridge, Mass.: MIT Press.

Contreras, Heles. 1991. "On the Position of Subjects". *Perspectives on phrase structure: Heads and Licensing, Syntax and Semantics*, ed. by Susan Rothstein, 61-79. San Diego: Academic Press.

Dovrobie-Sorin, Carmen. 1991. "The Syntax of Romanian: Comparative Studies in Romance". Ms., CNRS, Paris.

Fergusson Scott & E. Groat. 1995. "Defining Shortest Move". Ms., Harvard University.

Kayne, Richard. 1991. "Romance Clitics, Verb movement, and PRO". *Linguistic Inquiry* 22.647-686.

______. 1994. *The Antisymmetry of Syntax*. Cambridge, Mass.: MIT Press.

---

complex negative quantifiers at least in Spanish:

(i) *A ninguno de estos chicos tú conoces realmente.*

It is still conceivable that these quantifiers in the Spec of the left-dislocated DP are capable of licensing the variable internal to the IP and therefore accounting for the non presence of the clitic. It has been noticed by Cinque (1991) that certain quantifiers can be left-dislocated and nevertheless license a variable.

(ii) *Qualcosa farò.* (Cinque 1991)

Ordóñez, Francisco & Esthela Treviño. 1995. "The Preverbal Slot in Spanish". Paper presented at the *XXV Linguistic Symposium on Romance Languages*. Seattle: University of Washington.
Rigau, Gemma. 1988. "Strong Pronouns". *Linguistic Inquiry* 19.503-511.
Rivero, María Luisa. 1994. "Clause Structure and V-movement in the Language of the Balkans". *Natural Language and Linguistic Theory* 31.301-332.
——— & Arhonto Terzi. 1995. "Imperatives, V-Movement and Logical Mood". *The Journal of Linguistics* 31.301-332.
Rizzi, Luigi. 1982. *Issues in Italian Syntax* Dordrecht: Foris.
———. 1990. *Relativized Minimality*. Cambridge, Mass.: .MIT Press.
———. 1991. "Residual Verb Second and the Wh-Criterion". *Technical Reports* 2. University of Geneva.
———. 1995. "The fine Structure of the Left Periphery". Ms., University of Geneva.
——— & Ian Roberts. 1989. "Complex Inversion in French". *Probus* 1.1-30.
Rooryck, Johan. 1992. "Romance Enclitic Ordering and Universal Grammar". *The Linguistic Review* 9.219-250.
Solà, Jaume. 1992. *Agreement and Subjects*. Ph.D. dissertation, Universitat Autònoma de Barcelona.
Sportiche, Dominique. 1988. "A Theory of Floating Quantifiers and Its Corollaries for Constituent Structure". *Linguistic Inquiry* 19.203-238.
———. 1992. "Clitics, Voice and Spec/Head Licensing." *GLOW Newsletter* 28.46-47.
Sportiche, Dominique. ND. "Subject Clitics in French and Romance: Complex Inversion and Clitic Doubling". Ms., UCLA.
Suñer, Margarita. 1988. "Haber + Past Participle". *Linguistic Inquiry* 18.683-690.
———. 1994. "V-movement and the Licensing of Argumental Wh-phrases in Spanish". *Natural Language and Linguistic Theory* 12.335-372.
Terzi, Arhonto. To appear. "The Linear Correspondence Axiom, the Adjunction Sites of Clitics". *Configurations*, ed. by Anna Maria Di Sciullo. Cornell: Casadilla Press.
Torrego, Esther. 1982. "More Effects of Successive Cyclic Movement". *Linguistic Inquiry* 13.561-565.
———. 1984. "On Inversion in Spanish and Some of Its Effects". *Linguistic Inquiry* 15.103-129.
Uriagereka, Juan. 1995. "Aspects of the Syntax of Clitic Placement in Western Romance". *Linguistic Inquiry* 26.79-124.
Uribe Etxebarria, Myriam. 1995. "On the Structure of Spec IP and Its Relevance for Scope Asymmetries in Spanish and Englsih". *Contemporary Re-*

search in Romance Linguistics, ed. by John Amastae, 355-367. Amsterdam: John Benjamins.

Wind de, J.M. 1993. "Against V-to-C in French Complex Inversion". *Issues and Theory in Romance Linguistics: Selected Papers from the Linguistic Symposium on Romance Languages XXIII*, ed. by Michael Mazzola. Washington D.C.: Georgetown University Press.

Zubizarreta, María Luisa. 1994. "El orden de palabras en español y el caso nominativo". *Gramática del Español*, ed. by Violeta Demonte, 21-51. México, D.F.: El Colegio de México.

SCALAR EFFECTS IN ITALIAN METAPHONY

SYLVIA ZETTERSTRAND
Harvard University

1. *Introduction*

Scalar processes of vowel raising and lowering have been the focus of recent attention.[1] The sound change known as metaphony[2] may be said to fall under this heading, in that the input vowels are variably approximated to the height of the conditioning segments (*i* and *u*), without this always resulting in total height assimilation.

This paper considers metaphonic data from Italian in the light of three current models of vowel height: the Dependency and Complementarity Model (Goad 1991, 1993), the Hierarchical Model (Clements 1991, 1995, 1996) and the Incremental Constriction Model (Parkinson 1995). Each of these models has largely evolved in response to the Articulatory Model (Sagey 1986, Halle 1995). The goal of this paper is to examine how the facts of Italian metaphony would be described within the four competing feature geometries advocated by these models, and to determine whether indeed one of the models is better suited than the others for this purpose.

The paper is organized as follows. Section 2 illustrates the range of metaphonic alternations to be considered. Following Maiden (1991), it discusses the requirements that an explanatory account of metaphony must meet. Section 3 presents Calabrese's 1988, 1996 analysis of Italian metaphony within the framework of the Articulatory Model. Sections 4, 5, and 6 discuss the analysis of the data within the three other models. Section 7 contains some concluding remarks and pending issues.

2. *Metaphonic alternations*

According to Maiden (1991:112), the most common outputs of Italian metaphony are the following:

---

[1] See for instance Kirchner 1995, Clements 1996 and Flemming 1996.

[2] The assimilatory raising of mid and low stressed vowels in the environment of a following (usually suffixal) unstressed high vowel.

(1) *e*→ i
o→ u
ɛ→ *y*ɛ, ye, *e*
ɔ→ wɔ,wo, *o*
a →ɛ, ye

There is a striking asymmetry in this pattern of metaphonic raisings. Whereas the high-mid vowels are always assimilated to the height of the conditioning segments *i u*, the assimilation of all lower vowels is only partial. In fact, the lower the input vowel, the farthest its metaphonic output is from *i u* in terms of height. Maiden (1991:124) refers to this progressively lesser susceptibility of lower vowels to metaphony as the *height hierarchy* or the *implicational hierarchy*.

The historical evidence suggests that at an initial stage metaphony targeted only the high-mid vowels, and that it was later extended to the low-mid vowels, and finally to the low vowel (albeit metaphony of *a* is relatively rare). The diphthongs *ye wo* are presumably later developments of *y*ɛ and wɔ, in which the nuclear vowel has undergone further raising. The outputs wɛ and we, which are also found in some dialects as the outputs of ɔ metaphony, are the result of an independent rule, in which the vowel has been dissimilated for the feature [back]. The most widespread output of metaphony of *a* is ɛ. A separate rule is responsible for changing the feature [back]. The diphthong ye might be due to a later sound change as well.[3]

Regardless of the order in which the raisings might have occurred historically, the fact is that synchronically there is a regular pattern of alternations that appears in many of the nominal and verbal paradigms, even after primitive suffixal *-i* and *-u* were removed. The following data from the dialects of Servigliano, Northern Salentino and Castro dei Volsci illustrate this pattern of metaphonic alternations:[4]

---

[3] For reasons of brevity, this paper will only consider the most widespread outputs of Italian metaphony. That is: *e o*→ i u ; ɛɔ→ *e o* ; ɛɔ→ yɛ *w*ɔ ; *a*→ ɛ. Hypermetaphonic outputs will also be considered when relevant.

[4] Some of the forms in the tables represent intermediate stages in the derivations. In some dialects, final vowels have been reduced to schwa on the surface, thus obscuring the original phonetic conditioning of metaphony.

(2)

Servigliano

Fem Sg	Masc Sg	Gloss
pésa	*písu*	'heavy'
lónga	*lúngu*	'long'
modέsta	modéstu	'modest'
mɔ́rta	mórtu	'dead'

Northern Salentino

Singular	Plural	Gloss
mése	mísi	'month'
krótʃ*e*	*krútʃi*	'cross'
pέte	*pyέti*	'foot'
kɔ́re	*kwέri*	'heart'

Castro dei Vosci

Fem Pl	MascPl	Gloss
sékke	síkki	'dry'
spóse	*spúsi*	'spouse'
vέkkye	*vyékkye*	'old'
nɔ́ve	nwóvi	'new'
áwte	*έwti*	'high'

As expected, all three dialects have the *e o* ~ *i u* alternation. In Servigliano, ε *and* ɔ alternate with *e* and *o*; whereas in Northern Salentino and Castro dei Volsci, they alternate with the diphthongs *y*ε, wε and ye wo, respectively. Castro dei Volsci also exemplifies the rarer alternation between the low vowel *a* and ε. An analysis in which the metaphonic allomorphy is accounted for by listing the surface alternants, would make it appear that the pattern of alternations summarized in (1) is totally accidental (Calabrese 1996:13).

An explanatory account of the data presented in (2) should be able to (Maiden 1991):[5]

[5] Maiden (1991:138) proposes an analysis of metaphony within the framework of Dependency Phonology, that will not be considered in this paper. See Calabrese 1996 for some comments on this approach.

(3)

a. Describe the variety of outputs from a primitive metaphonic configuration
b. Explain why only the highest input vowels are fully assimilated, while all other vowels are only partially assimilated
c. Account for the height hierarchy: metaphony of a presupposes metaphony of ɛ, and metaphony of ɛ *and* ɔ presupposes metaphony of *e o*

I will use these three criteria to evaluate the adequacy of the analyses of Italian metaphony within the competing frameworks for the description of vowel height.

3. *The Articulatory Model*

The Articulatory Model uses three binary features to specify vocalic height: [high], [low] and [ATR]. In the feature geometry, [high] and [low] are Dorsal dependents, while [ATR] is a Tongue Root dependent:[6]

(4)

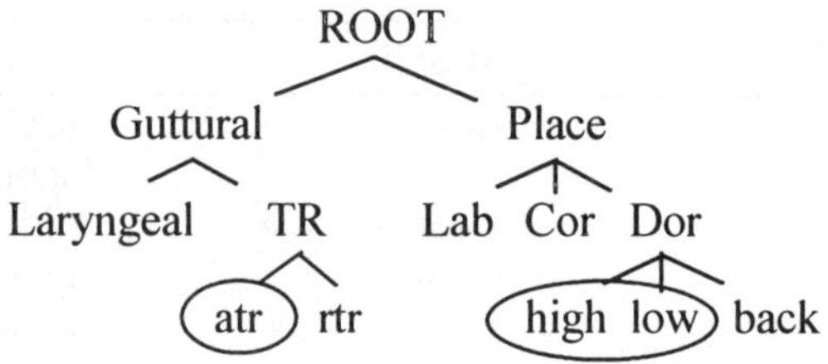

The best analysis of Italian metaphony within this framework is that of Calabrese 1988, 1996. The idea is that Universal Grammar contains a series of filters (or feature co-occurrence constraints) indicating that certain feature combinations are impossible or phonologically complex, for acoustic or articulatory reasons. In (5), I have listed the filters that are relevant for vowel height in order of decreasing complexity. The second feature mentioned in each filter is considered to be marked with respect to the first feature:

(5)

*[+high, +low]
*[+low, +ATR]
*[+high, -ATR]
*[-high, +ATR]

---

[6] Throughout this paper, only relevant portions of the feature geometries are given.

The other important component of Calabrese's analysis is that there are three repair strategies or simplification procedures, whose function is to convert a disallowed feature configuration into a less complex feature combination. These repair strategies are listed schematically in (6):

(6)

Delinking:	$[\alpha F_1, \underline{\beta F_2}] \rightarrow [\alpha F_1, -\beta F_2]$
Negation:	$[\alpha F_1, \underline{\beta F_2}] \rightarrow -[\alpha F_1, \beta F_2] \rightarrow [-\alpha F_1, -\beta F_2]$
Fission:	$[\alpha F_1, \underline{\beta F_2}] \rightarrow [\alpha F_1, -\beta F_2] \rightarrow [-\alpha F_1, \beta F_2]$

In delinking, the marked feature value is delinked and a convention (the last resort convention) inserts the opposite (and thus compatible) value. In negation, the values of both incompatible features are changed into their opposites. Finally, in fission, the two incompatible features are linearized; producing two successive feature bundles, each containing only one of the incompatible features.

In the Articulatory Model, the Italian vowel system would be specified as:

(7)

	i u	*e o*	ɛ ɔ	a
low	–	–	–	+
high	+	–	–	–
ATR	+	+	–	–

Metaphony can then be stated as a single rule: spread [+high] from i and *u*. The disallowed configurations that arise as a result of this rule would be repaired by one the three repair strategies. Thus, the spreading of [+high] to *e o* directly produces *i u*. When ɛ ɔ are targeted by the rule, the filter *[+high, -ATR] is violated. Repair by negation produces the outputs *e o*, as in Servigliano; repair by fission yields the diphthongs of Northern Salentino and Castro dei Volsci. When the low vowel *a* is the target, the filter *[+high, +low] is violated. Applying negation we obtain the vowel ɛ of Castro dei Volsci . These results are summarized below:

(8)

e o → i u
ɛ ɔ → *[+high, -ATR]→ (negation) [-high, +ATR] e o
ɛ ɔ → *[+high, -ATR]→ (fission) [+high, +ATR][-high, -ATR] *y*ɛ *w*ɔ
a → *[+high, +low] → (negation) [-high, -low] ɛ

The filters and simplification procedures, on which this analysis crucially relies, are not ad hoc devices introduced to describe metaphony. They form part of a broader framework that accounts for the notion of phonological markedness (Calabrese 1995). However, a by-product of this approach is an account of Italian metaphony that meets all three requirements listed in (3):

(9)

a. The primitive metaphonic configuration is the feature [+high], and the diversity in the outputs is the result of implementing different repair strategies
b. The vowels *e o* are the only ones that are fully assimilated, because spreading of [+high] automatically produces ***i u***
c. The height hierarchy is explained in terms of the number of filter violations that result when [+high] is spread: *a* is hardly ever raised because the two filters *[+high, +low] and *[+high, -ATR] are violated; ɛ ɔ are more likely to be raised, because only the filter *[+high, -ATR] is violated; *e o* are always raised for the reason stated in (b), no filter is ever violated

4. ***The Dependency and Complementarity Model***

Goad's 1991, 1993 model of vowel height utilizes three monovalent features: [open], [low] and [ATR]. These features are exclusively dominated by a Vocalic node, departing from the articulator-based geometry discussed in section 3:

(10)

ROOT
Laryngeal Supralaryngeal
Place VO
Lab Cor Dor Phar open
rnd front rtr low/atr

In Goads model, the node Vocalic has an acoustic interpretation; it dominates features that affect the frequency of the first formant. The feature [open] corresponds to the Articulatory Models feature [-high]; thus, high vowels are represented with a bare Vocalic node.

Another distinguishing characteristic of this model, is that negative and positive co-occurrence constraints are encoded directly in the feature geometry in terms of structural relations between nodes/features. A *complementarity* relation, indicated by a slash, expresses a negative co-occurrence restriction. Thus, the representation above expresses that the features [low] and [ATR] are mutually exclusive in the same segment (phonologically [+low, +ATR] vowels are excluded altogether). A *dependency* or dominance relationship expresses that the presence of the subordinate feature or node logically implies the presence of the superordinate feature or node. The features [open] and [low] are said to be in such a relationship ([+low] vowels are necessarily [-high]). Crucially, the same is not true for [open] and [ATR]. [ATR] does not imply [open], otherwise it would be impossible to represent languages where high vowels contrast for [ATR].

A further claim of this model is that the feature [ATR] will only be selected by a language if contrasts among the vowels can not be captured with the feature [low] alone (Goad 1993:201). Given this theoretical framework, the Italian vowel system would have to be represented as a three-height system:

(11)

iu	eo	ɛ ɔ a
VO	VO	VO
	|	|
	[open]	[open]
		|
		[low]

The raisings *e o* → *i u* and ɛ ɔ → *e o* can be easily described if metaphony is stated as: delink a terminal Vocalic feature. The feature [open] would be delinked in the first case, and [low] in the second case. By formulating metaphony in this way, we can explain why only the highest input vowels are raised to *i u*. This is the only possible outcome if terminal [open] is delinked from the representation of *e o*. Requirement (3b) is satisfied. However, there are other problems with this approach.

Firstly, it is impossible to state a rule that will simultaneously raise *e o* to *i u*, and derive diphthongs from ɛ ɔ. Secondly, if ɛ ɔ *a* do indeed have the same height, it is hard to explain why *a* seems to behave differently from ɛ *and* ɔ; namely, it is rarely affected by metaphony, and when it is, it is usually changed to ɛ. Thus, this model fails to give a unitary account of all the outputs of metaphony. It is also unable to explain the height hierarchy.

The failure of this model to satisfy criteria (3a) and (3c) stems from two assumptions: that there is no feature corresponding to the Articulatory Model's feature [+high]; and that ɛ ɔ and *a* have the same phonological height. The first assumption makes it impossible to isolate a metaphonic feature, nor to appeal to any sort of repair mechanism. It is also contrary to the widely held view that assimilation be expressed as feature spreading, as has been already noted by Parkinson (1995:9).

The second claim forces one to characterize the distinct behavior of ɛ ɔ, in most dialects, as opposed to *a*, by unnecessarily complicating the structural description of the rule: metaphony targets vowels that are Dorsal [front] and Dorsal, Labial (as opposed to the vowel *a*'s bare Dorsal node). In the dialects where *a* is affected by metaphony, the change of *a* to ɛ would have to be described by a separate rule, suggesting that it is unrelated to the shifts in height undergone by the other non-high vowels.

The Dependency and Complementarity Model's analysis of metaphony would not fare any better, if one were to allow the use of both [low] and [ATR] in characterizing the vowel inventory. This would result in the representation:

(12)

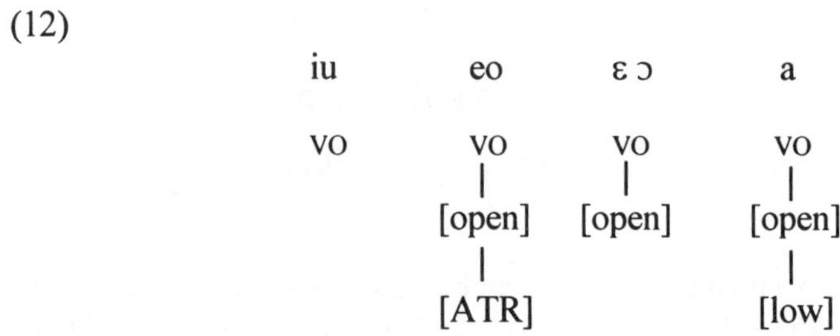

With this representation, all the objections made earlier still hold. Furthermore, it is no longer possible to describe the raisings *e o* → *i u* and ɛ ɔ→ *e o* as a single process. The first change would involve the deletion of structure, while the second involves the addition of structure. This representation also makes several incorrect predictions.

Recall that in this model there is no feature corresponding to [+high], so that high assimilation is not feature spreading *per se*. It falls under the scope of what Trubetzkoy calls *assimilative neutralization, in* which: 'the opposition members loose their opposition mark in the vicinity of those phonemes that do not have the particular opposition mark' (Goad 1993:177). If the absence of height features in *i u* can cause other vowels to loose their height features, then the model wrongly predicts that ε ɔ → *e o* (vowel lowering) should be a possible outcome of metaphony. The optimal outcome of metaphony of the mid series should be ε ɔ → *i u*, because only a single height feature has been delinked. The raising *e o* → *i u* should be just as natural as *a* → i u, given that the same formal operation is involved: the delinking of two height features. All of these predictions are contrary to the observed height hierarchy.

The first, and more likely, analysis of metaphony within the Dependency and Complementarity framework in (11) did not satisfy criteria (3a) and (3c); and the second analysis in (12) failed to satisfy all three criteria. I conclude, therefore, that this framework is not appropriate for the description of Italian metaphony.

5. ***The Hierarchical Model***

The central claim of the Hierarchical Model is that vowel height is a uniform phonetic and phonological dimension. Vocalic height is viewed as an abstract space, which may be repeatedly subdivided into registers, thus deriving the number of vowel heights required by a language. Registers are designated by the binary feature [$open_i$]The set of features [open 1]...[$open_n$] derived via the register splitting process, is exclusively dominated by the Aperture node:

(13)

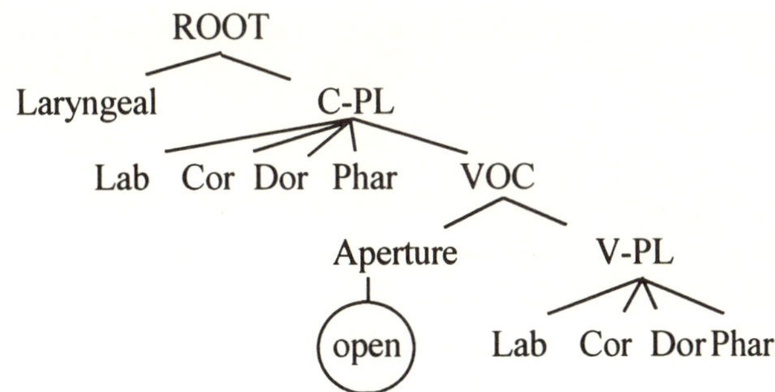

If one assumes that the first three vocalic registers correspond to the Articulatory Model's features [low], [high] and [ATR] (Clements 1991, 1996), such that:[7]

(14)
[αlow] ↔ [αopen 1]
[αhigh] ↔ [-αopen 2]
[αATR] ↔ [-αopen 3]

Then the Italian vowel system would be specified as:

(15)

	i u	*e o*	ɛ ɔ	*a*
open 1	–	–	–	+
open 2	–	+	+	+
open 3	–	–	+	+

The Hierarchical Model is ideally suited to describe the stepwise raisings e o → *i u,* ɛ ɔ → *e o, a*→ ɛ. Metaphony could be stated as: spread [-open] from [-open 2] vowels (constrained by Structure Preservation). Because all [$open_n$] features are subdivisions of a primitive feature [open] the rule would be interpreted as applying to any of three ranks of [open] features: [-open 2] spreads in the first case, [-open 3] in the second case, and [-open 1] in the third case. However, the non-structure preserving outputs, that is, the diphthongs, can not be derived in this way.

It would seem that the only way in which this model could describe all the outputs, in order to satisfy requirement (3a), would be by incorporating the notions of filters and repair. This would amount to translating Calabreses analysis into this framework. This can be achieved in a straightforward way, given the feature equivalencies above. The following two filters would be required:

(16)
*[+open 1, -open 2]
*[-open 2, +open 3]

[7] The equivalencies in (14) do not imply that the Hierarchical Model and the Articulatory Model are notational variants of each other. The two model differ in substantial ways.

Metaphony could be stated as: spread [-open 2] and repair disallowed configurations. The spreading of [-open 2] from *i u* would result in:

(17)

e o→ i u

ɛ ɔ→ *[-open 2, +open 3]→ (negation) [+open 2, -open 3] e o

ɛ ɔ→ *[–open 2, +open 3]→(fission) [-open 2, -open 3] [+open 2, +open 3] *yɛ wɔ*

a → *[+open 1, -open 2]→ (negation) [-open 1, +open 2] ɛ

By expanding the Hierarchical Model in the manner shown above, one can indeed account for requirements (3a), (3b) and (3c); however, note that the filters in this model would be more abstract in nature, in that they are not independently motivated. It is not clear why one particular subdivision of the articulatory space should be preferred over others. A filter like *[+high, +low] can never be violated for physiological reasons, yet the corresponding filter *[+open 1, -open 2] is strictly theory internal. In addition, for reasons that go beyond the scope of this paper, supplementing the Hierarchical Model with filters and repair strategies, as required for an adequate account of metaphony, is not as straight-forward as it might initially appear.[8]

6. *The Incremental Constriction Model*

The final model to be considered incorporates Clements' and Hume's proposal that vowels and consonants share the same set of articulator nodes, but it differs substantially as to the structure beneath a vowels Aperture node. In the Incremental Constriction Model, vowels are characterized by multiple occurrences of the privative feature [closed]. As in the Hierarchical Model, the number of features is determined by the number of height contrasts in a language. Crucially, only terminal [closed] features may spread or delink:

[8] One of the reasons for this is that in the Hierarchical Model the traditional feature ATR is not always encoded on the same tier. It may be represented on tier 3 and thereafter. The model also allows for height distinctions that can not be expressed in terms of [high], [low] and [ATR] (Sesotho dialects). These, amongst other reasons, makes it much harder to constrain hierarchical representations by using filters or by any other means. See Zetterstrand 1996 for further details.

(18)

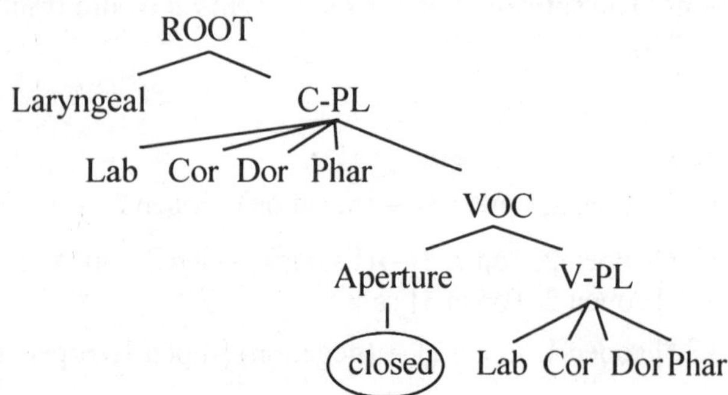

In this model, Italian vowels would be represented as:

(19)

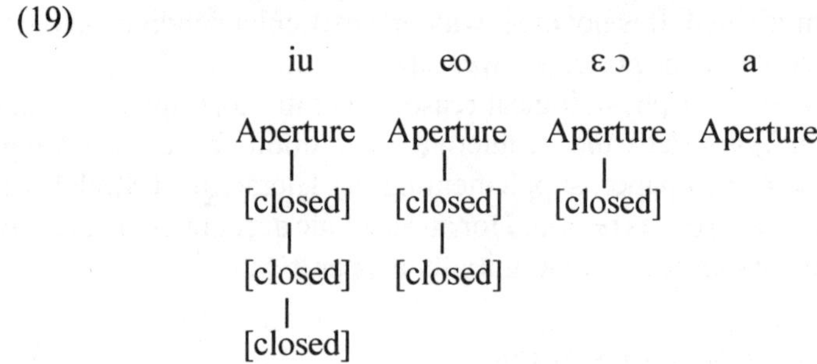

As in the Hierarchical Model, it is trivial to describe one-step raising. Metaphony would be stated as: spread [closed] from *i u*. Once again, the problem is how to derive diphthongs from ɛ ɔ as part of the same process. Requirement (3a) is not satisfied. Nor can one account for the height hierarchy, requirement (3c). If metaphony is a process whereby *i* and *u* spread the feature [closed], why should this feature be less likely to spread to ɛ ɔ, and even less likely to spread to *a*?

A possible way of accounting for the low vowels lesser susceptibility to metaphony would bc to take place of articulation features into consideration. For instance, one could suggests that there is a filter *[Pharyngeal, [closed]]. Raising of *a* to ɛ would result from the delinking of pharyngeal in response to a violation of that filter (a separate rule provides Coronal). However, this still would not allow us to derive the diphthongs, nor to explain why ɛ ɔ (as opposed to *e o*) are less likely to be raised, because no filter is violated by spreading [closed] to ɛ ɔ.

Another alternative is to claim that ɛ ɔ also have a Pharyngeal component, and that there is tendency for vowels that are specified as Pharyngeal not to acquire additional [closed] features. But even under this interpretation of the filter, it is hard to motivate the appearance of a diphthong. What would be the reason for adding yet another [closed] feature to create a glide?

Note that the Incremental Constriction Model does satisfy requirement (3b). If only the terminal [closed] feature can spread, total height assimilation is only possible when *e o* are targets of the rule. In the case of all other input vowels, partial height assimilation results. However, the hypothesis that spreading be limited to terminal features, is problematic when one broadens the data that falls under the heading metaphony.

In particular, when we consider the phenomenon that has been labeled hypermetaphony (Maiden 1991). These are cases in which *i u* have triggered raising beyond the expected degree, such as:

(20)

ɛ ɔ → *i u*
a → *e*
a → *i*

Theses outputs are considered 'deviant', but nevertheless there ought to be a way of deriving them. The only way in which the Incremental Constriction Model could derive these outputs would be by allowing spreading of more than one [closed] feature as a marked option. Metaphony would have to be formulated as a rule that spreads [closed] from i u. This would normally be interpreted as spreading of terminal [closed]. The markedness of the hypermetaphonic outputs would be expressed by the fact that the marked option of spreading non-terminal [closed] features (and of all other [closed] features beneath them) has been selected. Thus, the raising *a* → i would be considered more marked than *a* → e, because in the first case two non-terminal features have been spread, as opposed to one non-terminal feature in the second case.

7. *Concluding remarks*

After having examined Italian metaphony within the scope of the four models under consideration, I conclude that Calabrese's analysis, which is based on the Articulatory Model's feature geometry, provides the best account of all the facts. This is the only analysis that satisfies all three requirements set forth in section 2: (a) It describes all outputs as a single process (b) It explains why only *e o* are fully assimilated (c) It accounts for the height hierarchy.

The Dependency and Complementarity Model's analyses proved to be the least adequate. The first analysis only satisfied (b). The second analysis failed to satisfy all three requirements, and it was found to make wrong predictions. The Incremental Constriction Model is unable to satisfy (a). In particular, it can not derive the diphthongs. It is also unclear whether it can account for the height hierarchy. It was also observed that hypermetaphonic outputs can only be derived in this model by relaxing the requirement that only terminal height features spread.

A central insight of Calabrese's analysis is that the various metaphonic outputs of the non-high vowels reflect a tension between 'high' conditioners and 'low' inputs (Maiden 1991:134). The feature geometries of the Dependency and Complementarity Model and the Incremental Constriction Models make it impossible to express this tension. Therefore, both models are unable to give a unitary account of all the metaphonic changes.

On the other hand, the Hierarchical Model (expanded with filters) can express this tension in terms of feature incompatibility; and by supplementing it with repair strategies based on those filters, it can satisfy (a), (b) and (c). The objections that were raised against this model are independent of metaphony: the filters are harder to state and lack independent motivation.

Although Calabrese's analysis has been shown to be better suited for the description of metaphony, there are still pending issues. One of them is the status of *negation* within the broader theory. Negation is a very powerful formal operation that changes the values of two features simultaneously.[9] It is rarely (if ever) attested outside of vowel systems .[10] Another issue regards whether some sort of ranking should be imposed on the repair strategies. For instance, consider the hypermetaphonic raisings *a*→ *e* and *a*→ *i.* These changes

---

[9] See Calabrese (1995:389) for a list of all the attested cases of negation in vowel systems.

[10] Vaux (personal communication) reports a case of negation involving laryngeal features.

can be described by invoking two repair strategies, in response to the violation of two filters. Thus:

(21)

a →*[+high, +low]→ (delinking) [+high, -low] →*[+high, -ATR] (negation) [-high, +ATR] e

a →*[+high, +low]→ (delinking) [+high, -low] →*[+high, -ATR] (delinking) [+high, +ATR] i

This suggests that both outputs are equally marked, although according to the height hierarchy *i* should be more marked than *e,* because it is farthest away from the input vowel *a.* The solution to both these issues requires further investigation.

REFERENCES

Calabrese, Andrea. 1988. *Towards a Theory of Phonological Alphabets.* Ph.D. dissertation, MIT.

———. 1995. "AC constraint-based Theory of Phonological Markedness and Simplification Procedures". *Linguistic Inquiry* 26.373-463.

———. 1996. "Metaphony Revisited". Ms., Harvard University.

Clements, George N. 1991. "Vowel Height Assimilation in Bantu Languages". *Berkeley Linguistic Society Proceedings of the Special Session on African Language Structures* 17.25-64.

———. 1996. "Stepwise Vowel Height Assimilation". *Handout of Presentation at the Cortona Phonology Meeting*, April 12-14, 1996.

Clements, George N., & Elizabeth Hume. 1995. "The Internal Organization of Segments". *Handbook of Phonological Theory*, ed. by John Goldsmith, 245-306. Cambridge, Mass.: Blackwell.

Flemming, Edward. 1996. "Evidence for Constraints on Contrast: The Dispersion Theory of Contrast". Ms., UCLA.

Goad, Heather. 1991. "Dependency and Complementarity in Vowel Geometry". *The Linguistic Review* 8:185-208.

———. 1993. *On the Configuration of Height Features.* Ph.D. dissertation, USC.

Halle, Morris. 1995. "Feature Geometry and Feature Spreading". *Linguistic Inquiry* 26:1:1-46.

Kirchner, Robert. 1995. "Going the Distance: Synchronic Chain Shifts". Ms., UCLA.

Maiden, Martin. 1991. *Interactive Morphophonology: Metaphony in Italy.* Padstow, Cornwall. T. J. Press.

Parkinson, Frederick. 1995. "A Formal Account of Romance Metaphony". Paper presented at the *Montreal-Toronto-Ottawa Workshop on Phonology*.

Sagey, Elizabeth. 1986. *The Representation of Features and Relations in Non-linear Phonology*. Ph.D. dissertation, MIT.

Zetterstrand, Sylvia. In preparation. *The Phonological Representation of Vowel Height*. Ph.D. dissertation, Harvard University.

INDEX OF AUTHORS*

* Page numbers in italics refer to individual contributions and cover self-references.

INDEX OF TERMS & CONCEPTS

INDEX OF LANGUAGES & LANGUAGE FAMILIES

The *Current Issues in Linguistics Theory* series (edited by E. F. Konrad Koerner, University of Ottawa) is a theory-oriented series which welcomes contributions from scholars who have significant proposals to make towards the advancement of our understanding of language, its structure, functioning and development.

Current Issues in Linguistics Theory (CILT) has been established in order to provide a forum for the presentation and discussion of linguistic opinions of scholars who do not necessarily accept the prevailing mode of thought in linguistic science. It offers an alternative outlet for meaningful contributions to the current linguistic debate, and furnishes the diversity of opinion which a healthy discipline must have. In this series the following volumes have been published thus far or are scheduled for publication:

1. KOERNER, Konrad (ed.): *The Transformational-Generative Paradigm and Modern Linguistic Theory.* 1975.
2. WEIDERT, Alfons: *Componential Analysis of Lushai Phonology.* 1975.
3. MAHER, J. Peter: *Papers on Language Theory and History I: Creation and Tradition in Language. Foreword by Raimo Anttila.* 1979.
4. HOPPER, Paul J. (ed.): *Studies in Descriptive and Historical Linguistics. Festschrift for Winfred P. Lehmann.* 1977.
5. ITKONEN, Esa: *Grammatical Theory and Metascience: A critical investigation into the methodological and philosophical foundations of 'autonomous' linguistics.* 1978.
6. ANTTILA, Raimo: *Historical and Comparative Linguistics.* 1989.
7. MEISEL, Jürgen M. & Martin D. PAM (eds): *Linear Order and Generative Theory.* 1979.
8. WILBUR, Terence H.: *Prolegomena to a Grammar of Basque.* 1979.
9. HOLLIEN, Harry & Patricia (eds): *Current Issues in the Phonetic Sciences. Proceedings of the IPS-77 Congress, Miami Beach, Florida, 17-19 December 1977.* 1979.
10. PRIDEAUX, Gary D. (ed.): *Perspectives in Experimental Linguistics. Papers from the University of Alberta Conference on Experimental Linguistics, Edmonton, 13-14 Oct. 1978.* 1979.
11. BROGYANYI, Bela (ed.): *Studies in Diachronic, Synchronic, and Typological Linguistics: Festschrift for Oswald Szemérenyi on the Occasion of his 65th Birthday.* 1979.
12. FISIAK, Jacek (ed.): *Theoretical Issues in Contrastive Linguistics.* 1981. Out of print
13. MAHER, J. Peter, Allan R. BOMHARD & Konrad KOERNER (eds): *Papers from the Third International Conference on Historical Linguistics, Hamburg, August 22-26 1977.* 1982.
14. TRAUGOTT, Elizabeth C., Rebecca LaBRUM & Susan SHEPHERD (eds): *Papers from the Fourth International Conference on Historical Linguistics, Stanford, March 26-30 1979.* 1980.
15. ANDERSON, John (ed.): *Language Form and Linguistic Variation. Papers dedicated to Angus McIntosh.* 1982.
16. ARBEITMAN, Yoël L. & Allan R. BOMHARD (eds): *Bono Homini Donum: Essays in Historical Linguistics, in Memory of J.Alexander Kerns.* 1981.
17. LIEB, Hans-Heinrich: *Integrational Linguistics. 6 volumes. Vol. II-VI n.y.p.* 1984/93.
18. IZZO, Herbert J. (ed.): *Italic and Romance. Linguistic Studies in Honor of Ernst Pulgram.* 1980.
19. RAMAT, Paolo et al. (eds): *Linguistic Reconstruction and Indo-European Syntax. Proceedings of the Colloquium of the 'Indogermanischhe Gesellschaft'. University of Pavia, 6-7 September 1979.* 1980.
20. NORRICK, Neal R.: *Semiotic Principles in Semantic Theory.* 1981.
21. AHLQVIST, Anders (ed.): *Papers from the Fifth International Conference on Historical Linguistics, Galway, April 6-10 1981.* 1982.
22. UNTERMANN, Jürgen & Bela BROGYANYI (eds): *Das Germanische und die Rekonstruktion der Indogermanischen Grundsprache. Akten des Freiburger Kolloquiums der Indogermanischen Gesellschaft, Freiburg, 26-27 Februar 1981.* 1984.

23. DANIELSEN, Niels: *Papers in Theoretical Linguistics. Edited by Per Baerentzen.* 1992.
24. LEHMANN, Winfred P. & Yakov MALKIEL (eds): *Perspectives on Historical Linguistics. Papers from a conference held at the meeting of the Language Theory Division, Modern Language Assn., San Francisco, 27-30 December 1979.* 1982.
25. ANDERSEN, Paul Kent: *Word Order Typology and Comparative Constructions.* 1983.
26. BALDI, Philip (ed.): *Papers from the XIIth Linguistic Symposium on Romance Languages, Univ. Park, April 1-3, 1982.* 1984.
27. BOMHARD, Alan R.: *Toward Proto-Nostratic. A New Approach to the Comparison of Proto-Indo-European and Proto-Afroasiatic. Foreword by Paul J. Hopper.* 1984.
28. BYNON, James (ed.): *Current Progress in Afro-Asiatic Linguistics: Papers of the Third International Hamito-Semitic Congress, London, 1978.* 1984.
29. PAPROTTÉ, Wolf & René DIRVEN (eds): *The Ubiquity of Metaphor: Metaphor in language and thought.* 1985 (publ. 1986).
30. HALL, Robert A. Jr.: *Proto-Romance Morphology. = Comparative Romance Grammar, vol. III.* 1984.
31. GUILLAUME, Gustave: *Foundations for a Science of Language.*
32. COPELAND, James E. (ed.): *New Directions in Linguistics and Semiotics.* Co-edition with Rice University Press who hold exclusive rights for US and Canada. 1984.
33. VERSTEEGH, Kees: *Pidginization and Creolization. The Case of Arabic.* 1984.
34. FISIAK, Jacek (ed.): *Papers from the VIth International Conference on Historical Linguistics, Poznan, 22-26 August. 1983.* 1985.
35. COLLINGE, N.E.: *The Laws of Indo-European.* 1985.
36. KING, Larry D. & Catherine A. MALEY (eds): *Selected papers from the XIIIth Linguistic Symposium on Romance Languages, Chapel Hill, N.C., 24-26 March 1983.* 1985.
37. GRIFFEN, T.D.: *Aspects of Dynamic Phonology.* 1985.
38. BROGYANYI, Bela & Thomas KRÖMMELBEIN (eds): *Germanic Dialects:Linguistic and Philological Investigations.* 1986.
39. BENSON, James D., Michael J. CUMMINGS, & William S. GREAVES (eds): *Linguistics in a Systemic Perspective.* 1988.
40. FRIES, Peter Howard (ed.) in collaboration with Nancy M. Fries: *Toward an Understanding of Language: Charles C. Fries in Perspective.* 1985.
41. EATON, Roger, et al. (eds): *Papers from the 4th International Conference on English Historical Linguistics, April 10-13, 1985.* 1985.
42. MAKKAI, Adam & Alan K. MELBY (eds): *Linguistics and Philosophy. Festschrift for Rulon S. Wells.* 1985 (publ. 1986).
43. AKAMATSU, Tsutomu: *The Theory of Neutralization and the Archiphoneme in Functional Phonology.* 1988.
44. JUNGRAITHMAYR, Herrmann & Walter W. MUELLER (eds): *Proceedings of the Fourth International Hamito-Semitic Congress.* 1987.
45. KOOPMAN, W.F., F.C. Van der LEEK , O. FISCHER & R. EATON (eds): *Explanation and Linguistic Change.* 1986
46. PRIDEAUX, Gary D. & William J. BAKER: *Strategies and Structures: The processing of relative clauses.* 1987.
47. LEHMANN, Winfred P. (ed.): *Language Typology 1985. Papers from the Linguistic Typology Symposium, Moscow, 9-13 Dec. 1985.* 1986.
48. RAMAT, Anna G., Onofrio CARRUBA and Giuliano BERNINI (eds): *Papers from the 7th International Conference on Historical Linguistics.* 1987.
49. WAUGH, Linda R. and Stephen RUDY (eds): *New Vistas in Grammar: Invariance and Variation. Proceedings of the Second International Roman Jakobson Conference, New York University, Nov.5-8, 1985.* 1991.
50. RUDZKA-OSTYN, Brygida (ed.): *Topics in Cognitive Linguistics.* 1988.

51. CHATTERJEE, Ranjit: *Aspect and Meaning in Slavic and Indic. With a foreword by Paul Friedrich.* 1989.
52. FASOLD, Ralph W. & Deborah SCHIFFRIN (eds): *Language Change and Variation.* 1989.
53. SANKOFF, David: *Diversity and Diachrony.* 1986.
54. WEIDERT, Alfons: *Tibeto-Burman Tonology. A comparative analysis.* 1987
55. HALL, Robert A. Jr.: *Linguistics and Pseudo-Linguistics.* 1987.
56. HOCKETT, Charles F.: *Refurbishing our Foundations. Elementary linguistics from an advanced point of view.* 1987.
57. BUBENIK, Vít: *Hellenistic and Roman Greece as a Sociolinguistic Area.* 1989.
58. ARBEITMAN, Yoël. L. (ed.): *Fucus: A Semitic/Afrasian Gathering in Remembrance of Albert Ehrman.* 1988.
59. VAN VOORST, Jan: *Event Structure.* 1988.
60. KIRSCHNER, Carl & Janet DECESARIS (eds): *Studies in Romance Linguistics. Selected Proceedings from the XVII Linguistic Symposium on Romance Languages.* 1989.
61. CORRIGAN, Roberta L., Fred ECKMAN & Michael NOONAN (eds): *Linguistic Categorization. Proceedings of an International Symposium in Milwaukee, Wisconsin, April 10-11, 1987.* 1989.
62. FRAJZYNGIER, Zygmunt (ed.): *Current Progress in Chadic Linguistics. Proceedings of the International Symposium on Chadic Linguistics, Boulder, Colorado, 1-2 May 1987.* 1989.
63. EID, Mushira (ed.): *Perspectives on Arabic Linguistics I. Papers from the First Annual Symposium on Arabic Linguistics.* 1990.
64. BROGYANYI, Bela (ed.): *Prehistory, History and Historiography of Language, Speech, and Linguistic Theory. Papers in honor of Oswald Szemérenyi I.* 1992.
65. ADAMSON, Sylvia, Vivien A. LAW, Nigel VINCENT and Susan WRIGHT (eds): *Papers from the 5th International Conference on English Historical Linguistics.* 1990.
66. ANDERSEN, Henning and Konrad KOERNER (eds): *Historical Linguistics 1987.Papers from the 8th International Conference on Historical Linguistics,Lille, August 30-Sept., 1987.* 1990.
67. LEHMANN, Winfred P. (ed.): *Language Typology 1987. Systematic Balance in Language. Papers from the Linguistic Typology Symposium, Berkeley, 1-3 Dec 1987.* 1990.
68. BALL, Martin, James FIFE, Erich POPPE &Jenny ROWLAND (eds): *Celtic Linguistics/ Ieithyddiaeth Geltaidd. Readings in the Brythonic Languages. Festschrift for T. Arwyn Watkins.* 1990.
69. WANNER, Dieter and Douglas A. KIBBEE (eds): *New Analyses in Romance Linguistics. Selected papers from the Linguistic Symposium on Romance Languages XVIIII, Urbana-Champaign, April 7-9, 1988.* 1991.
70. JENSEN, John T.: *Morphology. Word structure in generative grammar.* 1990.
71. O'GRADY, William: *Categories and Case. The sentence structure of Korean.* 1991.
72. EID, Mushira and John MCCARTHY (eds): *Perspectives on Arabic Linguistics II. Papers from the Second Annual Symposium on Arabic Linguistics.* 1990.
73. STAMENOV, Maxim (ed.): *Current Advances in Semantic Theory.* 1991.
74. LAEUFER, Christiane and Terrell A. MORGAN (eds): *Theoretical Analyses in Romance Linguistics.* 1991.
75. DROSTE, Flip G. and John E. JOSEPH (eds): *Linguistic Theory and Grammatical Description. Nine Current Approaches.* 1991.
76. WICKENS, Mark A.: *Grammatical Number in English Nouns. An empirical and theoretical account.* 1992.
77. BOLTZ, William G. and Michael C. SHAPIRO (eds): *Studies in the Historical Phonology of Asian Languages.* 1991.

78. KAC, Michael: *Grammars and Grammaticality.* 1992.
79. ANTONSEN, Elmer H. and Hans Henrich HOCK (eds): *STAEF-CRAEFT: Studies in Germanic Linguistics. Select papers from the First and Second Symposium on Germanic Linguistics, University of Chicago, 24 April 1985, and Univ. of Illinois at Urbana-Champaign, 3-4 Oct. 1986.* 1991.
80. COMRIE, Bernard and Mushira EID (eds): *Perspectives on Arabic Linguistics III. Papers from the Third Annual Symposium on Arabic Linguistics.* 1991.
81. LEHMANN, Winfred P. and H.J. HEWITT (eds): *Language Typology 1988. Typological Models in the Service of Reconstruction.* 1991.
82. VAN VALIN, Robert D. (ed.): *Advances in Role and Reference Grammar.* 1992.
83. FIFE, James and Erich POPPE (eds): *Studies in Brythonic Word Order.* 1991.
84. DAVIS, Garry W. and Gregory K. IVERSON (eds): *Explanation in Historical Linguistics.* 1992.
85. BROSELOW, Ellen, Mushira EID and John McCARTHY (eds): *Perspectives on Arabic Linguistics IV. Papers from the Annual Symposium on Arabic Linguistics.* 1992.
86. KESS, Joseph F.: *Psycholinguistics. Psychology, linguistics, and the study of natural language.* 1992.
87. BROGYANYI, Bela and Reiner LIPP (eds): *Historical Philology: Greek, Latin, and Romance. Papers in honor of Oswald Szemerényi II.* 1992.
88. SHIELDS, Kenneth: *A History of Indo-European Verb Morphology.* 1992.
89. BURRIDGE, Kate: *Syntactic Change in Germanic. A study of some aspects of language change in Germanic with particular reference to Middle Dutch.* 1992.
90. KING, Larry D.: *The Semantic Structure of Spanish. Meaning and grammatical form.* 1992.
91. HIRSCHBÜHLER, Paul and Konrad KOERNER (eds): *Romance Languages and Modern Linguistic Theory. Selected papers from the XX Linguistic Symposium on Romance Languages,University of Ottawa, April 10-14, 1990.* 1992.
92. POYATOS, Fernando: *Paralanguage: A linguistic and interdisciplinary approach to interactive speech and sounds.* 1992.
93. LIPPI-GREEN, Rosina (ed.): *Recent Developments in Germanic Linguistics.* 1992.
94. HAGÈGE, Claude: *The Language Builder. An essay on the human signature in linguistic morphogenesis.* 1992.
95. MILLER, D. Gary: *Complex Verb Formation.* 1992.
96. LIEB, Hans-Heinrich (ed.): *Prospects for a New Structuralism.* 1992.
97. BROGYANYI, Bela & Reiner LIPP (eds): *Comparative-Historical Linguistics: Indo-European and Finno-Ugric. Papers in honor of Oswald Szemerényi III.* 1992.
98. EID, Mushira & Gregory K. IVERSON: *Principles and Prediction: The analysis of natural language.* 1993.
99. JENSEN, John T.: *English Phonology.* 1993.
100. MUFWENE, Salikoko S. and Lioba MOSHI (eds): *Topics in African Linguistics. Papers from the XXI Annual Conference on African Linguistics, University of Georgia, April 1990.* 1993.
101. EID, Mushira & Clive HOLES (eds): *Perspectives on Arabic Linguistics V. Papers from the Fifth Annual Symposium on Arabic Linguistics.* 1993.
102. DAVIS, Philip W. (ed.): *Alternative Linguistics. Descriptive and theoretical Modes.* 1995.
103. ASHBY, William J., Marianne MITHUN, Giorgio PERISSINOTTO and Eduardo RAPOSO: *Linguistic Perspectives on Romance Languages. Selected papers from the XXI Linguistic Symposium on Romance Languages, Santa Barbara, February 21-24, 1991.* 1993.
104. KURZOVÁ, Helena: *From Indo-European to Latin. The evolution of a morphosyntactic type.* 1993.

105. HUALDE, José Ignacio and Jon ORTIZ DE URBANA (eds): *Generative Studies in Basque Linguistics.* 1993.
106. AERTSEN, Henk and Robert J. JEFFERS (eds): *Historical Linguistics 1989. Papers from the 9th International Conference on Historical Linguistics, New Brunswick, 14-18 August 1989.* 1993.
107. MARLE, Jaap van (ed.): *Historical Linguistics 1991. Papers from the 10th International Conference on Historical Linguistics, Amsterdam, August 12-16, 1991.* 1993.
108. LIEB, Hans-Heinrich: *Linguistic Variables. Towards a unified theory of linguistic variation.* 1993.
109. PAGLIUCA, William (ed.): *Perspectives on Grammaticalization.* 1994.
110. SIMONE, Raffaele (ed.): *Iconicity in Language.* 1995.
111. TOBIN, Yishai: *Invariance, Markedness and Distinctive Feature Analysis. A contrastive study of sign systems in English and Hebrew.* 1994.
112. CULIOLI, Antoine: *Cognition and Representation in Linguistic Theory. Translated, edited and introduced by Michel Liddle.* 1995.
113. FERNÁNDEZ, Francisco, Miguel FUSTER and Juan Jose CALVO (eds): *English Historical Linguistics 1992. Papers from the 7th International Conference on English Historical Linguistics, Valencia, 22-26 September 1992.*1994.
114. EGLI, U., P. PAUSE, Chr. SCHWARZE, A. von STECHOW, G. WIENOLD (eds): *Lexical Knowledge in the Organisation of Language.* 1995.
115. EID, Mushira, Vincente CANTARINO and Keith WALTERS (eds): *Perspectives on Arabic Linguistics. Vol. VI. Papers from the Sixth Annual Symposium on Arabic Linguistics.* 1994.
116. MILLER, D. Gary: *Ancient Scripts and Phonological Knowledge.* 1994.
117. PHILIPPAKI-WARBURTON, I., K. NICOLAIDIS and M. SIFIANOU (eds): *Themes in Greek Linguistics. Papers from the first International Conference on Greek Linguistics, Reading, September 1993.* 1994.
118. HASAN, Ruqaiya and Peter H. FRIES (eds): *On Subject and Theme. A discourse functional perspective.* 1995.
119. LIPPI-GREEN, Rosina: *Language Ideology and Language Change in Early Modern German. A sociolinguistic study of the consonantal system of Nuremberg.* 1994.
120. STONHAM, John T. : *Combinatorial Morphology.* 1994.
121. HASAN, Ruqaiya, Carmel CLORAN and David BUTT (eds): *Functional Descriptions. Theorie in practice.* 1996.
122. SMITH, John Charles and Martin MAIDEN (eds): *Linguistic Theory and the Romance Languages.* 1995.
123. AMASTAE, Jon, Grant GOODALL, Mario MONTALBETTI and Marianne PHINNEY: *Contemporary Research in Romance Linguistics. Papers from the XXII Linguistic Symposium on Romance Languages, El Paso//Juárez, February 22-24, 1994.* 1995.
124. ANDERSEN, Henning: *Historical Linguistics 1993. Selected papers from the 11th International Conference on Historical Linguistics, Los Angeles, 16-20 August 1993.* 1995.
125. SINGH, Rajendra (ed.): *Towards a Critical Sociolinguistics.* 1996.
126. MATRAS, Yaron (ed.): *Romani in Contact. The history, structure and sociology of a language.* 1995.
127. GUY, Gregory R., Crawford FEAGIN, Deborah SCHIFFRIN and John BAUGH (eds): *Towards a Social Science of Language. Papers in honor of William Labov. Volume 1: Variation and change in language and society.* 1996.
128. GUY, Gregory R., Crawford FEAGIN, Deborah SCHIFFRIN and John BAUGH (eds): *Towards a Social Science of Language. Papers in honor of William Labov. Volume 2: Social interaction and discourse structures.* 1997.
129. LEVIN, Saul: *Semitic and Indo-European: The Principal Etymologies. With observations on Afro-Asiatic.* 1995.

130. EID, Mushira (ed.) *Perspectives on Arabic Linguistics. Vol. VII. Papers from the Seventh Annual Symposium on Arabic Linguistics.* 1995.
131. HUALDE, Jose Ignacio, Joseba A. LAKARRA and R.L. Trask (eds): *Towards a History of the Basque Language.* 1995.
132. HERSCHENSOHN, Julia: *Case Suspension and Binary Complement Structure in French.* 1996.
133. ZAGONA, Karen (ed.): *Grammatical Theory and Romance Languages. Selected papers from the 25th Linguistic Symposium on Romance Languages (LSRL XXV) Seattle, 2-4 March 1995.* 1996.
134. EID, Mushira (ed.): *Perspectives on Arabic Linguistics Vol. VIII. Papers from the Eighth Annual Symposium on Arabic Linguistics.* 1996.
135. BRITTON Derek (ed.): *Papers from the 8th International Conference on English Historical Linguistics.* 1996.
136. MITKOV, Ruslan and Nicolas NICOLOV (eds): *Recent Advances in Natural Language Processing.* 1997.
137. LIPPI-GREEN, Rosina and Joseph C. SALMONS (eds): *Germanic Linguistics. Syntactic and diachronic.* 1996.
138. SACKMANN, Robin (ed.): *Theoretical Linguistics and Grammatical Description.* 1996.
139. BLACK, James R. and Virginia MOTAPANYANE (eds): *Microparametric Syntax and Dialect Variation.* 1996.
140. BLACK, James R. and Virginia MOTAPANYANE (eds): *Clitics, Pronouns and Movement.* 1997.
141. EID, Mushira and Dilworth PARKINSON (eds): *Perspectives on Arabic Linguistics Vol. IX. Papers from the Ninth Annual Symposium on Arabic Linguistics, Georgetown University, Washington D.C., 1995.* 1996.
142. JOSEPH, Brian D. and Joseph C. SALMONS (eds): *Nostratic. Sifting the Evidence.* n.y.p.
143. ATHANASIADOU, Angeliki and René DIRVEN (eds): *On Conditionals Again.* 1997.
144. SINGH, Rajendra (ed): *Trubetzkoy's Orphan. Proceedings of the Montréal Roundtable "Morphophonology: contemporary responses (Montréal, October 1994).* 1996.
145. HEWSON, John and Vit BUBENIK: *Tense and Aspect in Indo-European Languages. Theory, typology, diachrony.* 1997.
146. HINSKENS, Frans, Roeland VAN HOUT and W. Leo WETZELS (eds): *Variation, Change, and Phonological Theory.* 1997.
147. HEWSON, John: *The Cognitive System of the French Verb.* 1997.
148. WOLF, George and Nigel LOVE (eds): *Linguistics Inside Out. Roy Harris and his critics.* 1997.
149. HALL, T. Alan: *The Phonology of Coronals.* 1997.
150. VERSPOOR, Marjolijn, Kee Dong LEE and Eve SWEETSER (eds): *Lexical and Syntactical Constructions and the Construction of Meaning. Proceedings of the Bi-annual ICLA meeting in Albuquerque, July 1995.* 1997.
151. LIEBERT, Wolf-Andreas, Gisela REDEKER and Linda WAUGH (eds): *Discourse and Perspectives in Cognitive Linguistics.* 1997.
152. HIRAGA, Masako, Chris SINHA and Sherman WILCOX (eds): *Cultural, Psychological and Typological Issues in Cognitive Linguistics.* n.y.p.
153. EID, Mushira and Robert R. RATCLIFFE (eds): *Perspectives on Arabic Linguistics Vol. X. Papers from the Tenth Annual Symposium on Arabic Linguistics, Salt Lake City, 1996.* 1997.
154. SIMON-VANDENBERGEN, Anne-Marie, Kristin DAVIDSE and Dirk NOËL (eds): *Reconnecting Language. Morphology and Syntax in Functional Perspectives.* 1997.

155. FORGET, Danielle, Paul HIRSCHBÜHLER, France MARTINEAU and María-Luisa RIVERO (eds): *Negation and Polarity. Syntax and semantics. Selected papers from the Colloquium Negation: Syntax and Semantics. Ottawa, 11-13 May 1995.* 1997.
156. MATRAS, Yaron, Peter BAKKER and Hristo KYUCHUKOV (eds): *The Typology and Dialectology of Romani.* 1997.
157. LEMA, José and Esthela TREVIÑO (eds): *Theoretical Analyses on Romance Languages. Selected papers from the 26th Linguistic Symposium on Romance Languages (LSRL XXVI), Mexico City, 28-30 March, 1996.* 1998.
158. SÁNCHEZ MACARRO, Antonia and Ronald CARTER (eds): *Linguistic Choice across Genres. Variation in spoken and written English.* 1998.
159. JOSEPH, Brian D., Geoffrey C. HORROCKS and Irene PHILIPPAKI-WARBURTON (eds): *Themes in Greek Linguistics II.* 1998.
160. SCHWEGLER, Arnold, Bernard TRANEL and Myriam URIBE-ETXEBARRIA (eds): *Romance Linguistics: Theoretical Perspectives. Selected papers from the 27th Linguistic Symposium on Romance Languages (LSRL XXVII), Irvine, 20-22 February, 1997.* 1998.
161. SMITH, John Charles and Delia BENTLEY (eds): *Historical Linguistics 1995. Volume 1: Romance and general linguistics.* n.y.p.
162. HOGG, Richard M. and Linda van BERGEN (eds): *Historical Linguistics 1995. Volume 2: Germanic linguistics.Selected papers from the 12th International Conference on Historical Linguistics, Manchester, August 1995.* n.y.p.